Companion
Dictionary
of the Bible

Companion Dictionary of the Bible

Publishing House
St. Louis

Copyright © 1985 by Concordia Publishing House,
3558 South Jefferson Avenue, St. Louis, MO 63118.
Manufactured in the United States of America.

Library of Congress Catalog Data
Main entry under title:

Companion dictionary of the Bible.

    1. Bible—Dictionaries.   I. Concordia Publishing House.
BS440.0595 1985   220.3   84-15633
ISBN 0-570-03947-9

---

1   2   3   4   5   6   7   8   9   10   PP   94   93   92   91   90   89   88   87   86   85

Preface

The *Companion Dictionary of the Bible* has been produced for home Bible students who are looking for a convenient, easy-to-read Bible dictionary that provides simple and clear explanations of the words and proper names commonly used in the Bible along with definitions of key terms in the thought and life of the church. While based on the popular *Concordia Bible Dictionary* by Erwin L. Lueker, which was published in 1963, this new volume omits technical and obscure details and concentrates on providing the basic Scriptural and historical information in which the average Bible student is interested.

It differs from many on the market in a number of ways. Rather than being comprehensive, entries have been limited to those people, places, terms, objects, and events in the Bible that are of a more significant nature for general Bible study. While this means fewer entries, it also results in a limited use of phrases and abbreviations. Hence, entries in this book are generally easier to read and comprehend. Choice of words and the grammatical structure of sentences has also been deliberately kept simple to encourage easy usage and readability.

Pronunciation helps follow a simplified, easy-to-use spelling system rather than the more complicated phonetic or diacritical system, which many people are unable to decipher. A guide to pronunciation follows this preface. The meaning of proper names is given after the pronunciation when such meaning has been established by Bible scholars as certain or probable.

Several entries are revised summaries based on material included in A. W. Klinck's *Home Life in Bible Times*. When this is the case, it is indicated at the end of the entry. The *Concordia Self-Study Commentary*, published in 1979, was also consulted in the preparation of the dates, audiences, and outlines of the Biblical books.

It is our hope that the *Companion Dictionary of the Bible* will become a faithful tool and companion for lay Bible students of all ages who desire to study and better appreciate the treasures of God's Word.

THE PUBLISHER

Guide to Pronunciation

To show you one acceptable way to pronounce the difficult words and proper names in the Bible, pronunciations are given in parentheses after these entries, spelled the way they sound in English. This pronunciation system is roughly phonetic, that is, a given sound in spoken English is generally represented by the same letter or group of letters. Stressed syllables are indicated by the capitalization of that syllable's letters. Thus Aaron is shown as AIR-uhn, Adam as AD-uhm, and so forth.

a vowels

a	as in add, mask
ah	as in father
air	as in fare
ay	as in late
uh	as in account, sofa

i vowels

i	as in till
i/uh	as in charity

e vowels

e	as in end
ee	as in eve, here
i	as in evade
u	as in maker

o vowels

o	as in old, obey, dog
ah	as in odd
aw	as in lord
oo	as in food
u	as in connect, foot

u vowels

u	as in burn, but
yoo	as in cube, unite
uh	as in circus

AARON (AIR-uhn, of uncertain meaning). Moses' assistant, the first high priest (Exodus 4:14-17; 7). Aaron was born in Egypt. His family was from the tribe of Levi, the descendants of one of the 12 sons of Jacob (Exodus 6:19-20). Miriam was his older sister, and Moses was his younger brother (Numbers 26:59).

Aaron was praised because he spoke well in public (Exodus 4:14). At God's command Aaron spoke to the people for Moses because Moses did not believe himself to be a good public speaker.

During a battle in the wilderness between the Children of Israel and the Amalekites, Aaron helped Hur hold up Moses' hands (Exodus 17:12). While Moses was on Mount Sinai receiving the Ten Commandments, the people became impatient; so Aaron made the golden calf (Exodus 32). Aaron and Miriam criticized Moses because of the foreign woman he had married (Numbers 12:1).

Moses anointed Aaron and Aaron's sons to the priesthood (Numbers 3:1-3). The Lord confirmed Aaron as His high priest when the rod with Aaron's name on it blossomed (Numbers 17). Because Aaron and Moses doubted God at Meribah, they were not allowed to enter the Promised Land (Numbers 20:12-13). Aaron's son Eleazar followed him as high priest. Aaron died at 123 years of age and was buried on Mount Hor (Numbers 20:22-29).

AARONITES (AIR-uhn-ights). All the priests who descended from Aaron, the first priest.

AARON'S ROD. By making the rod with Aaron's name on it blossom, God proved Aaron's authority. This rod was placed before the ark of the covenant (Numbers 17; Hebrews 9:4).

ABASE. To humble or make low. The proud and wicked are to be abased (Job 40:11). God abases the proud (Job 22:29).

ABBA (AB-ah, the Aramaic word for father). A word taken from children's language to express filial address to God (Mark 14:36; Romans 8:15). *Ab* or *abi* are also used to form proper names, for example, Abraham.

ABEDNEGO (ah-BED-ne-go, servant of Nego). The Babylonian name given to Azariah, one of Daniel's friends (Daniel 1:7). Abednego was thrown into the fiery furnace for not worshiping the golden idol set up by King Nebuchadnezzar (Daniel 3).

ABEL, I (AY-buhl, perhaps meaning son or vapor). The second son of Adam and Eve. Abel was a keeper of sheep. When God was pleased with Abel's sacrifice, Abel's brother, Cain, became jealous and murdered him (Genesis 4:1-8). In the New Testament Abel is described as a righteous man because, by faith, he offered God a more acceptable sacrifice than Cain (Hebrews 11:4).

ABEL, II (AY-buhl, meadow). A prefix for the names of towns and places (Genesis 50:11; Judges 7:22).

ABHORRENCE (ab-HAWR-uhns). Aversion or loathing; shrinking or withdrawing from someone or something that is disgusting. Believers abhor wicked, unholy things and sins (Deuteronomy 7:26; Psalm 119:163). The wicked abhor both God's law and the person who speaks God's truth (Leviticus 26:43; Amos 5:10). God abhors those who worship false gods and break His law (Leviticus 26:30).

ABIATHAR (ah-BIGH-ah-thahr, father of abundance). The son of the high priest Ahimelech. When Saul put Abiathar's father and 84 other priests to death, Abiathar escaped and fled to David's camp for protection (1 Samuel 22:20-23). He became David's counselor and with Zadok brought the ark of the covenant to Jerusalem (1 Chronicles 15:11-14; 27:33). Toward the close of David's reign Abiathar joined with Joab in supporting David's son Adonijah as the next king. Solomon became the new king, however, and expelled Abiathar from office (1 Kings 1:7, 19, 25, 41-42; 2:26-27).

ABIJAH (ah-BIGH-jah, the Lord is father). 1. A descendant of Aaron's son Eleazor. When David organized the priests into 24 divisions, the eighth division was named after Abijah (1 Chronicles 24:10; Nehemiah 12:17). Zechariah, the father of John the Baptizer, belonged to this division (Luke 1:5).

2. The second son of Samuel. Because Abijah was a wicked judge, the elders asked for a king (1 Samuel 8:2-4).

3. The son of Jeroboam I (1 Kings 14:1-18).

4. The son of Rehoboam and Maacah. Abijah was also known as Abijam. After his father died, Abijah became the next king of Judah. In an effort to regain the 10 northern tribes, he made war on Jeroboam I. Abijah reigned three years, following in the wicked ways of his father, and then he died (1 Kings 15:1-8; 2 Chronicles 12:16; 13).

5. The wife of Ahaz and mother of Hezekiah (2 Chronicles 29:1).

ABIMELECH (ah-BIM-uh-lek, the father is Melech or king). 1. The king of Gerar who made a covenant with Abraham (Genesis 20; 21:22-34).

2. The king of Gerar who made a covenant with Isaac (Genesis 26:1-33). He may have been the same person as the king who made the covenant with Abraham.

3. Gideon's son by his concubine (Judges 8:31).

4. The son of Abiathar and grandson of Ahimelech the priest. Abimelech, who is sometimes referred to as Ahimelech, was a priest during David's reign (1 Chronicles 18:16).

5. The name given to the Philistine king (probably King Achish) in the title of Psalm 34 (1 Samuel 21:10; Psalm 34). It is thought that Abimelech was the throne name or title of Philistine kings.

ABNER (AB-nur, father is light). The son of Ner and commander of his cousin Saul's army (1 Samuel 14:50-51; 17:55; 26:5-14). When Saul died, Abner brought Ishbosheth, Saul's son, to Mahanaim and made him king over Israel (2 Samuel 2:8-9). Then Abner and his men met David's army in combat at the pool of Gibeon and were defeated (2 Samuel 2:12-17). Later Abner quarreled with Ishbosheth and left his camp to join with David. Although David received him in peace, David's commander, Joab, and Joab's brother Abishai murdered Abner because he had killed their brother in the battle at Gibeon (2 Samuel 3:6-30). David mourned for Abner and described him as a prince and great man (2 Samuel 3:31-39).

ABOMINATION (ah-bahm-i-NAY-shuhn). That which is disgusting, loathsome, detestable, particularly in a religious context. The term is applied to animals the Israelites were not allowed to eat, pagan practices, and idolatry (Leviticus 7:18, 21; Deuteronomy 29:17; 1 Kings 11:5; Hosea 9:10).

ABOMINATION OF DESOLATION. This is mentioned in Daniel 9:27, 11:31, and 12:11 and may refer to the time when Antiochus Epiphanes desecrated the sanctuary by putting an idol to Zeus on the altar where sacrifices were offered. Ultimately Daniel's prophecy concerning the Abomination of Desolation finds its fulfillment in Messianic times.

Christ also referred to the Abomination of Desolation. (Matthew 24:15-16; Mark 13:14). In doing so, He may have been thinking about the statue of Caligula in the temple. In a figurative sense, this term is applied to the neglect of the Gospel in the church.

ABRAHAM (AY-brah-ham, father of a multitude). The son of Terah and founder of the Hebrew nation. Abraham's name, before God changed it, was Abram. Abram and his family descended from Shem and lived in Ur of the Chaldees. Abram had two brothers, Nahor and Haran. After Haran died, Terah, Abram, Abram's wife, Sarai, and Haran's son, Lot, left Ur for Canaan. But when they arrived in Haran, a city in Mesopotamia, they settled there instead. When Terah was 205 years old, he died in Haran (Genesis 11).

After Terah's death the Lord told Abram to leave his country, his family, and his father's house for a land the Lord would show him. He also promised to make Abram a great nation and bless him and all the families of the earth in him. So Abram, now 75 years old, left Haran with Sarai, Lot, and all their possessions and began the journey to Canaan. In Canaan Abram pitched his tent by Shechem's holy place, the oak of Moreh. The Lord appeared to him there and promised to give the land to Abram's descendants. Then Abram built an altar to the Lord both there and, a little later, east of Bethel. When a famine came to the land, Abram went to Egypt. In order to be well received by Pharaoh, Abraham told Sarai to say she was only his sister. Not realizing she was also Abraham's wife, Pharoah decided to marry Sarai because her beauty pleased him. When plagues fell on his household, however, Pharaoh found out that Abram had deceived him. He told Abram to take his family and many possessions and leave (Genesis 12).

Abram and his family returned with Lot to the altar near Bethel. Because of bickering and fighting between their herdsmen, Abram and Lot decided to part ways. Lot, given his choice of the land, chose the Jordan plain and pitched his tent as far as Sodom. The Lord repeated his promise to bless Abram, who moved to the oak of Mamre at Hebron (Genesis 13).

When four kings defeated five other kings in the territory where Lot lived and took Lot captive, Abram chased after the enemies, recovered the goods they had stolen, and rescued Lot. After this Abram received a blessing from Melchizedek, the priest and king of Salem (Genesis 14).

Then God made a covenant with Abram, sealing His promise to make of Abram a great nation by giving him and his descendants the land of Canaan (Genesis 15). But when Sarai did not become pregnant, she thought she could not have children of her own, so she gave her maid, Hagar, to Abram. He and Hagar had a son whom they named Ishmael (Genesis 16). Then God changed Abram's name to Abraham and promised that His everlasting covenant would be fulfilled in Isaac. He made circumcision the sign of the covenant (Genesis 17). God also changed Sarai's name to Sarah.

One day while Abraham was sitting at the door to his tent by the oak of Mamre, the Lord appeared to him and told him that Sarah would bear him a son within the year. When Sarah heard this, she laughed because she thought she was too old to have a baby. The Lord rebuked her for laughing and told her nothing was too difficult for Him (Genesis 18). When Abraham was 100 years old, Isaac was born. Soon after that Hagar and Ishmael were cast out (Genesis 21).

Then the Lord tested Abraham's faith in His promise by commanding him to sacrifice his son Isaac. At the last minute the angel of the Lord stopped Abraham from doing this. He told Abraham not to harm Isaac and provided a ram instead (Genesis 22).

Since Abraham did not want Isaac to marry a Canaanite woman, he sent his servant back to his homeland to get a wife for Isaac. The servant returned with Rebekah, Abraham's great-niece. She became Isaac's wife (Genesis 24). When Abraham was 175 years old, he died and was buried in the cave of Machpelah (Genesis 25).

God called Abraham, who is later described as the friend of God, from a family that served idols (Joshua 24:2). God took the first step in making the covenant with Abraham, a covenant in which He bound Himself to give without receiving anything in return. Circumcision is a sign of His covenant (Romans 4:11).

By faith Abraham was just, as God wanted him to be, and thus became the father of all believers (Romans 4; Galatians 3). This faith showed itself in works (James

2:21). In Christ, Abraham's seed, all nations of the earth are blessed (Galatians 3:16). Believers are the spiritual sons and heirs of Abraham (Romans 4:13-14; Galatians 3:29).

ABRAHAM'S BOSOM. A term for everlasting life (Luke 16:22).

ABRAM (AY-bruhm, exalted father). See *Abraham*.

ABSALOM (AB-sah-luhm, father is peace). The handsome son of David and Maacah (2 Samuel 3:3). When Amnon, his half-brother, raped Absalom's sister, Absalom killed him. Then Absalom fled to Geshur, where he stayed for three years (2 Samuel 13—14).

Four years after his return to Jerusalem, Absalom made plans to seize the throne from his father, David. To this end, he gathered people around him who were unhappy with David's rule. Ahithophel advised Absalom to attack David before the king had time to regroup his followers, but Hushai cautioned Absalom to wait. He told Absalom that he would need a big army to defeat David's able warriors (2 Samuel 17).

The two armies met in the forest of Ephraim, where Absalom's men were defeated by David's. When Absalom was fleeing, his hair became tangled in an oak branch. While he was hanging from the tree, Joab killed him with three spears. When David heard that Absalom was dead, he grieved for his son (2 Samuel 18).

ABSTINENCE (AB-stuh-nuhns). The act of abstaining from, or not partaking, of something. There are various examples of abstinence in the Old Testament. The Israelites were to abstain from eating fat and blood, certain kinds of meats, parts of the offering sacred to the altar, and meats consecrated to idols (Exodus 34:15; Leviticus 3:9-17; 11). Abstinence also was commanded under some special circumstances (Judges 13:14; Numbers 6:3; Jeremiah 35:6; Luke 1:15).

In matters that are neither commanded nor forbidden the New Testament does not command abstinence. It allows one freedom to decide for oneself as long as the decision is made in love and does not go against one's conscience (Acts 15; Romans 14:1-3; 1 Corinthians 8). The New Testament opposes sects which live by the Law (Colossians 2:16; 1 Timothy 4:3-4).

ABYSS (ah-BIS). When the New Testament speaks of "abyss," it is referring to Satan's domain, hell. It is the source of all evil (Luke 8:31; Romans 10:7; Revelation 9:1-11; 11:7; 17:8; 20:1, 3).

ACHAN, ACHAR (AY-kan, AY-kahr, trouble). A descendant of Judah who went against God's command and stole spoils of war at Jericho. For this act Achan was stoned to death in the Valley of Achor (Joshua 7; 22:20).

ACHOR (AY-kawr, trouble). The valley south of Jericho where Achan was stoned to death (Joshua 7:24-26; 15:7; Isaiah 65:10; Hosea 2:15). Today this valley is identified with el-Buqei'a, which is about 10 miles south of Jericho.

ACQUITTAL. Forgiveness (Romans 5:18).

ACTS, BOOK OF. The fifth book of the New Testament. According to tradition, Luke, the beloved physician, wrote both the gospel named for him and the Book of Acts. Acts traces the growth of the early Christian church and credits this growth to the work of the Holy Spirit. Primarily, it describes the mission activity first of Peter and then of Paul.

Date: A.D. 65 to 70?

Audience: Gentiles

Outline: 1. The church in Jerusalem (1:1—8:3). 2. The Word of the Lord becomes a light to the Gen-

tiles: the church in Judea and Samaria and regions beyond this (8:4—12:24). 3. The church extended to Jews and Gentiles in the West (12:25—28:31). See also *Paul; Peter.*

ADAM (AD-uhm, human being; man). The first human being. God created Adam in His own image. He placed him in the Garden of Eden and gave him dominion over animals and all other creatures. God made Eve from one of Adam's ribs so that Adam would have a helpmate. God told Adam and Eve to have children and rule over the earth. When Adam and Eve broke God's commandment by eating the fruit of the tree in the middle of the garden, God drove them out of Eden. Adam died when he was 930 years old (Genesis 1—5).

Paul says that the first man, Adam, is the source of sin and death and the second man, Christ, is the source of life and righteousness (Romans 5:12-21; 1 Corinthians 15:22, 45; Ephesians 4:22-24; Colossians 3:9-10).

ADAMANT (AD-ah-mant). A hard metal or mineral, perhaps a diamond (Jeremiah 17:1). It is a symbol of hardness (Zechariah 7:12).

ADIAPHORA (ad-i-AF-o-rah). A term the church uses to refer to matters that are neither commanded nor forbidden by Scripture. In these matters individuals have freedom to make their own decisions or choices as long as they act in love and do not go against their consciences (Romans 14:3; 1 Corinthians 6:12; 8; 10:23; Colossians 2:16-17). The New Testament places Levitical observances and some human decrees in this class (Matthew 23:8-10; Luke 22:26; 1 Peter 2:8). See also *liberty.*

ADONAI (AD-o-nigh, my lord). The Hebrews spoke this word whenever they saw the consonants YHWH, which spell *Yahweh*, the word for Lord. When *Adonai* and *Yahweh* are combined, they form the word *Jehovah*.

ADONIJAH (ad-o-NIGH-jah, Lord is my lord). The fourth son of David. Encouraged and supported by Joab and Abiathar, Adonijah proclaimed himself king. David, however, appointed Solomon as the new king. Solomon first pardoned Adonijah but later had him executed (1 Kings 1—2; 1 Chronicles 23:1; 28:5).

ADOPTION. The act of choosing a child or older person and making him or her a member of one's family (Exodus 2:10; Esther 2:7). Paul says believers are adopted children of God. They have become members of God's family, the true Israel (the church), by the work of the Holy Spirit, who brought them to faith in Christ (Romans 8:14-17; 9; Galatians 3:26-28). That Christians have the Holy Spirit in their hearts witnesses to the fact that they are children and heirs of God (Galatians 4:6-7).

ADULTERY. In the Old Testament adultery refers to sexual intercourse between a man and another man's wife (Deuteronomy 22:22-24). Under the law of Moses the two people who had committed adultery were punished by death (Leviticus 20:10; John 8:5). Symbolically, adultery expressed the sins of God's people Israel when they backslid from Him (Jeremiah 3:9; Ezekiel 23:36-49).

Jesus interprets the Sixth Commandment as forbidding all kinds of sexual indecency in both deed and thought (Exodus 20:14; Matthew 5:28). The New Testament lists adultery among the sins of the flesh (Galatians 5:19).

ADVENT OF CHRIST. This term refers to Christ's coming in three ways. 1. The coming of Christ in the flesh—as the Baby born in Bethlehem, the one who lived on earth,

who died, and who rose again (Zechariah 9:9; Matthew 21:4).

2. The spiritual coming of Christ in the hearts of people through faith and His presence in the church (John 14:18, 23).

3. Christ's return for judgment at the end times (Matthew 24:30). See also *Parousia*.

ADVERSARY (AD-vur-ser-ee). 1. A political or personal enemy (Judges 2:3).

2. An enemy of God and His people. The devil especially is an adversary of God and His people (1 Timothy 5:14; 1 Peter 5:8).

ADVOCATE (AD-vo-kayt). Someone who pleads the cause of another (1 John 2:1). Often this word refers to the Holy Spirit and is translated as comforter or counselor (John 14:16).

AENEAS (i-NEE-uhs). A paralyzed man at Lydda who was healed by Peter (Acts 9:32-35).

AGABUS (AG-ah-buhs). A prophet who came to the church at Antioch while Paul and Barnabas were there and prophesied worldwide famine. Later Agabus warned Paul that he would be arrested in Jerusalem (Acts 11:28; 21:10-11).

AGAPE (Ah-GAH-pay). See *love; love feast*.

AGED. Old age was regarded as a token of God's favor, and old people were respected for their wisdom (Job 5:26; 15:10; 32:4; Zechariah 8:4). Young people were commanded to honor them (Leviticus 19:32).

AGORA (AG-o-rah). The name for the market place and forum in Athens, Ephesus, and other cities (Acts 17:7).

AGRAPHA (AG-rah-fah, unwritten). Sayings ascribed to Jesus that are not recorded in the gospels (John 21:25; Acts 20:35).

AGRICULTURE. After the conquest of Canaan, Joshua allotted the conquered territory to 9 1/2 tribes. The tribes of Reuben and Gad and half the tribe of Manasseh had already received their allotment under Moses (Joshua 13—14; Numbers 32). Joshua also gave each household a small section of land to be its inheritance forever. These family plots were improved over the years by the generations that followed. The people removed boulders, cultivated the ground carefully, and built terraces (Isaiah 5:1-2).

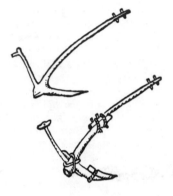

After the first rainfall, the ground was cultivated. This was done either by hand with a shovel and mattock or else by a plow drawn by a donkey, cow, or ox. Sometimes a heavy, forked branch of a tree was used as a plow. At other times branches were bound and pegged together so that one long end became the tongue, a shorter end became the plowshare (which might be shod with stone or iron), and a third end became the handle by which the plow was steered.

After the plow had torn up the ground, large lumps were broken up with a mattock and then raked fine with a harrow, a bundle of brushwood, or a wooden platform shod with stones or iron spikes.

The farmer sowed the grain by hand, taking it from a basket or from folds in his garment. After sowing the ground, he harrowed it again or drove his animals back and forth over the ground to trample in the seed.

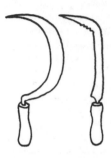

Ripe grain was cut with a sickle. Some early sickles were made from the lower jawbone of donkeys or cows. Other people at this time used more modern-looking sickels of bronze or iron set in wooden handles. These instruments eventually replaced the more primitive ones.

After the reaper cut the grain, he raked it up and tied it into bunches with its own straw. Fallen or missed grain was left for poor gleaners (Ruth 2:2-3). The grain was transported from the field to the threshing floor on a rack fixed to a cart or bound to the back of a donkey. Sometimes this rack was carried on a litterlike frame by two women.

The threshing floor was a roughly circular plot of clay or a limestone rock carefully patched and leveled. Workers opened the bundles of grain and spread them about a foot deep over this area. Then unmuzzled cows, calves, sheep, and donkeys trampled the grain out of the straw (Deuteronomy 25:4). A primitive threshing sled or wooden flails were also used. Grain was winnowed by tossing the straw and grain into the air with a wooden shovel or fork. Then it was cleansed with a sieve. After this the grain was washed, dried, and stored in insect-proof jars.

In Scripture the processes of agriculture are often applied to the spiritual realm (Matthew 3:12; 9:37-38; 13:18, 39; John 4:35; Galatians 6:7). (Klinck)

AHAB (AY-hab, father's brother). After his father, Omri, died, Ahab became the seventh king of Israel (1 Kings 16:29). He ruled for 22 years and was more evil in God's eyes than all the kings who had gone before him. Ahab married Jezebel, a princess from Tyre who worshiped the pagan idols Baal and Astarte. Ahab began to worship these gods with his wife. He built an altar to Baal and killed the prophets of the Lord. On Mount Carmel the prophet Elijah demonstrated to Ahab and all the people that Baal and his prophets were false.

Later Ahab had his eye on Naboth's vineyard and sulked when Naboth refused to sell it to him. So Jezebel arranged to have Naboth killed. Then Ahab claimed the vineyard as his own. Because of this wicked act, God sent Elijah to tell Ahab that dogs would lick Ahab's blood in the same place where Naboth had been killed (1 Kings 21:1-19). This prophecy came true when Ahab died in battle from an arrow wound and his chariot was taken to the pool of Samaria, where dogs licked the blood off it (1 Kings 22:33-38). Some items connected with Ahab have been recovered from excavation sites.

AHASUERUS (ah-haz-yoo-EE-ruhs). 1. The father of Darius the Mede (Daniel 9:1).

2. The Persian king who married Esther (Esther 1:2, 19; 2:16-17). The Hebrew name in the Book of Esther corresponds to the Aramaic and Babylonian spelling of Xerxes, who reigned from 486 to 465 B.C. For this reason it is believed that Ahasuerus and Xerxes were the same man.

AHAZ (AY-haz, possessor). 1. The idolatrous son of Jotham. When his father died, Ahaz became the 12th king of Judah. During his reign Judah became a vassal of Assyria. Ahaz turned his back on God and built altars to worship false gods. When he died, he was buried in Jerusalem (2 Chronicles 28:22-27). Isaiah, Hosea, and Micah prophesied during the reign of Ahaz.

2. The son of Micah and great-great-grandson of King Saul (1 Chronicles 8:35-36; 9:42).

AHAZIAH (ay-ha-ZIGH-ah, Lord has grasped). 1. The son of Ahab and Jezebel. When his father died, Ahaziah became the eighth king of Israel. He was wicked and worshiped the idol Baal-zebub. When Ahaziah became sick, Elijah delivered a message to him from God. Elijah told Ahaziah that he was going to die since he did not worship the true God (1 Kings 22; 2 Kings 1; 2 Chronicles 20).

2. The son of Jehoram and sixth king of Judah. He was also known as Jehoahaz and Azariah (2 Chronicles 21:17; 25:23). His rule was wicked in the eyes of the Lord (2 Kings 8:25—9:28; 2 Chronicles 22).

AHIJAH (a-HI-ja, brother of the Lord). 1. The son of Ahitub and great-grandson of Eli, the priest. Ahijah was the high priest at Gibeah (1 Samuel 14:3, 18).

2. A scribe or secretary of King Solomon (1 Kings 4:3).

3. A prophet at Shiloh. He told Jeroboam that the Kingdom of Israel was going to split at Solomon's death and that Jeroboam would rule over the 10 northern tribes (1 Kings 11:29-39). Later when Jeroboam's

son became sick, Jeroboam sent his wife to the prophet. Ahijah told her that the child would die because of Jeroboam's wickedness (1 Kings 14:6-16). A record of events in the "prophecy of Ahijah the Shilonite" is referred to in 2 Chronicles 9:29.

AHIMELECH (ah-HIM-uh-lek, brother of Melek). 1. A priest at Nob who helped David by giving him holy bread and a sword. When Saul heard this, he ordered his soldiers to kill Ahimelech and the priests with him (1 Samuel 21:1-9; 22:9-19).
2. See *Abimelech 4.*

AHITHOPHEL (ah-HITH-o-fel, brother is folly). One of David's counselors. Although Ahithophel's counsel was wise, he was untrustworthy. When Absalom decided to overthrow his father and become the new king, Ahithophel joined forces with Absalom, advising him how to go about the task. However, when Absalom took Hushai's advice instead, Ahithophel went home and hanged himself (2 Samuel 15:12, 31; 16:23; 17:1-23; 1 Chronicles 27:33).

AI (AY-igh, ruin). A city about 1 1/2 miles from Bethel. In the conquest of Palestine, Joshua and the Israelites attacked Ai twice, the second time successfully. Ai is mentioned numerous times in Scripture (Genesis 12:8; 13:3; Joshua 7; 8; 9:3; 10:1-2; 12:9; Ezra 2:28; Nehemiah 7:32; Jeremiah 49:3).

AIJALON (AY-jah-lahn, deer field). A town in Dan (Joshua 19:42; 21:24; Judges 1:35; 1 Samuel 14:31; 1 Chronicles 6:69; 8:13; 2 Chronicles 11:10; 28:18). During a battle Joshua told the sun to stand still in Gibeon and the moon in the Valley of Aijalon (Joshua 10:12).

ALABASTER. Carbonate of lime, a white or cream-colored mineral that is easy to carve. It resembles marble and was popular for making per-

fume vases (Song of Solomon 5:15; Matthew 26:7; Mark 14:3; Luke 7:37).

ALEXANDER (al-eg-ZAN-dur). 1. Alexander the Great, king of Macedonia. He was born in Macedonia (now Greece) in 356 B.C. and died in Babylon (now Iraq) in 323 B.C. One of the greatest generals of all times, Alexander was responsible for the spread of Greek culture in Asia and Egypt.
2. The son of Simon of Cyrene (Mark 15:21).
3. A person who tried to quiet the riot of the silversmiths at Ephesus (Acts 19:33).
4. The coppersmith who did Paul "great harm" (2 Timothy 4:14). He may be the same Alexander whom Paul speaks against in 1 Timothy 1:20.

ALEXANDRIA (al-eg-ZAN-dri-ah). The Egyptian city founded by Alexander the Great in 332 B.C. It was a center for Greek culture and was noted for its libraries, architecture, and commerce. Because many Greek-speaking Jews lived in Alexandria, a translation of the Hebrew text of the Bible into Greek was undertaken. This text, known as the Septuagint, was begun in the third century B.C. and completed in 50 B.C. Later Alexandria became a Christian center noted for its scholarship and textual criticism (Acts 6:9; 27:6; 28:11).

ALLEGIANCE (uh-lee-JUHNS). The act of being loyal to kings and to God (1 Chronicles 12:29; Isaiah 19:18).

ALLEGORY. A figure of speech where that which is seen or heard represents something similar to it. The word *allegory* is used only once in the Bible (Galatians 4:24), but as a figure of speech it is used frequently, for example, "vine" in John 15. Some Bible translations, such as the Revised Standard Version (RSV), also use the word *allegory* more frequently (Ezekiel 17:2; 20:49; 24:3; Revelation 11:8).

ALMS (AHMZ). Gifts, freely given, to the needy. In the Old Testament alms-giving was a duty that God commanded His people to perform (Deuteronomy 15:11; Leviticus 19:9). Later it became an important religious duty (Psalm 19:17; 112:9). Christ and the apostles encouraged the giving of alms (Matthew 25:35-36; Mark 9:41; Acts 6:1-6; Romans 15:25-27; 1 Corinthians 16:1-4; 2 Corinthians 9:7-9). Containers for receiving alms stood in the temple (Mark 12:41).

ALPHA (AL-pha). The first letter of the Greek alphabet. When alpha is used with omega (the last letter of the alphabet), it means the beginning and the end (Revelation 1:8, 11; 21:6; 22:13. See also Isaiah 41:4; 44:6).

ALPHABET. Letters used in writing and printing. Picture writing known as pictograms have been found in Palestine from the fourth millennium B.C., and heiroglyphics from the end of the third millennium. The Serabic alphabet, for example, that which was found at Sarabit al-Khadim in the Sinai Peninsula, dates from between 1850 and 1500 B.C. It is an early example of Semitic writing. The King James Version of the Bible records the letters of the Hebrew alphabet in Psalm 119. The alphabet found on the Moabite stone closely resembles Old Testament Hebrew. See also *writing*.

ALPHAEUS (al-FEE-uhs). 1. The father of James (the Less) and Joses (Matthew 10:3; Mark 3:18).

2. The father of Matthew the tax collector (Matthew 9:9; Mark 2:14).

ALTAR (high). An elevation made usually of earth or stone, although other materials were sometimes used (Exodus 20:24-26). According to an ancient Old Testament principle, an altar was erected wherever the Lord showed Himself (Genesis 8:20; 12:7; 26:25; 35:1). The tabernacle had two altars. The first was the altar of burnt offering (Exodus 27:1-2). All sacrifices were offered at this altar. These sacrifices were to remind Israel that it had access to God only through atonement. The second altar was the altar of incense (Exodus 30:1-10). It symbolized adoration.

AMALEKITES (AM-ah-lek-ights). An ancient group of nomads who descended from Esau (Genesis 36:12). They were called first of the nations (Numbers 24:20) and lived south of Canaan in the Sinai Peninsula, penetrating north into the Arabah. Traditionally they were enemies of Israel (Psalm 83:7). The Amalekites were defeated by Gideon, Saul, and David (Judges 7; 1 Samuel 15; 30:18).

AMASA (AM-ah-sah, burden). David's nephew and Joab's cousin (2 Samuel 17:25; 1 Chronicles 2:17). Although Amasa was the captain of the rebel forces under Absalom, David forgave him and made him the commander-in-chief of his army in place of Joab (2 Samuel 19:13). Later, Joab, pretending to greet Amasa with a kiss, struck him with a sword and killed him (2 Samuel 20:4-13).

AMAZIAH (am-a-ZIGH-ah, Lord is mighty). The son of Joash and ninth king of Judah. Amaziah became king after his father was murdered. Once he was firmly in power, Amaziah had his father's murderers put to death. He led an army against the Edomites, defeated them, and captured their capital. Later, he fought against Jehoash, king of Israel, but was defeated and taken prisoner. Some years later, Amaziah was murdered at Lachish (2 Kings 12:21; 14—15; 2 Chronicles 24:27;

25—26).
AMBASSADOR. An envoy or messenger of great power (Isaiah 18:2; Ezekiel 17:15). Paul called himself an ambassador of Christ (2 Corinthians 5:20; Ephesians 6:20; Philemon 9).
AMEN (AY-MEN, true). 1. Amen is a name for Jesus. It emphasizes that He is the Truth (Revelation 3:14). 2. The word *Amen* is spoken when one wants to express "so be it." It indicates confirmation or agreement (Numbers 5:22; Deuteronomy 27:15-26; Matthew 6:13; 1 Corinthians 14:16). God's promises are described as Amen (2 Corinthians 1:20).
AMMONITES (AM-un-ights). The people who lived east of the Dead Sea and the Jordan River. Their capital city was Rabbah-Ammon (Deuteronomy 3:11), which is modern day Amman. Saul defeated the Ammonites in battle, and David took their capital (1 Samuel 11; 2 Samuel 12:26-31). The Ammonites worshiped idols and were fierce enemies of Israel (Deuteronomy 23:3-6; Judges 3:13; 1 Samuel 11:1-11; Nehemiah 4:3-9; Jeremiah 49:1-6; Ezekiel 25:1-7; Amos 1:13).
AMON, I (A-mun, skilled workman). The 15th king of Judah. He was the son and successor of King Manasseh and the father of King Josiah. Amon worshiped idols. He was murdered by his servants (2 Kings 21:19-26; 2 Chronicles 33:21-25).
AMON, II (A-mun). The ancient Egyptian city of Thebes. It was a center for the worship of the sun-god Amon (Jeremiah 46:25; Nahum 3:8).
AMORITES (AM-o-rights). A powerful nation in Canaan that occupied both sides of the Jordan River (Genesis 10:16; 14:7; Numbers 21:26-31; Joshua 5:1; 13:15-21). When Samuel judged Israel, Israel had peace with the Amorites (1 Samuel

7:14). Solomon made the Amorites his bond servants (1 Kings 9:20, 21).
AMOS (AY-mus, burden). A shepherd of Tekoa who became a prophet to Israel during the reigns of Uzziah and Jeroboam II. His prophecy is recorded in the Book of Amos.
AMOS, BOOK OF. The third book of the Minor Prophets as they appear in the Old Testament. It was written by the prophet Amos and emphasizes the judgment of God.
Date: Mid-8th century B.C.
Audience: Israelites
Outline: 1. God's judgment on all nations (1—2). 2. Oracles on the guilt and doom of Israel (3—6). 3. Five visions of judgment (7—9:6). 4. Word of promise and hope (9:7-15).
AMOZ (AY-mahz, strong). Isaiah's father (Isaiah 1:1).
AMPLIAS, AMPLIATUS (AM-pli-uhs, am-pli-AY-tuhs, enlarger). Paul's friend at Rome to whom he sent a greeting (Romans 16:8).

AMULETS (AM-yuh-lets). Charms people wore to protect themselves against sickness, accident, sorcery, and evil spirits (Isaiah 3:20).
ANALOGY OF FAITH. A term that means there is agreement or harmony among Scriptural teachings. According to this rule the interpretation of each Bible passage should

harmonize, not conflict, with the sum total of Scriptural teachings (Romans 12:6).

ANANIAS (an-ah-NIGH-uhs, the Lord has covered). 1. A member of the church in Jerusalem. Ananias died suddenly after he and his wife tried to deceive and cheat the church (Acts 5:1-6).

2. The disciple at Damascus who was sent to restore Paul's sight (Acts 9:10-20; 22:12).

3. A high priest before whom Paul was tried (Acts 23:1-5; 24:1).

ANATHEMA (ah-NATH-i-mah). In the Old Testament anathema is a vow by which persons or things were devoted to God. Nonliving things devoted to God were given to the priests (Numbers 18:12-14); living things were killed (Leviticus 27:28-29). Later, anathema removed a person from the group (Ezra 10:8). In the New Testament anathema is a solemn curse that implies separation (Romans 9:3; 1 Corinthians 12:3).

ANATHEMA MARANATHA (ah-NATH-i-mah mar-ah-NATH-ah). This is a term that means accursed person (1 Corinthians 16:22).

ANATHOTH (AN-ah-thahth, answers). A levitical city in Benjamin, noted as the birthplace of Jeremiah (Joshua 21:18; Jeremiah 1:1; 11:21-23; 29-27). Today it is identified with 'Anata.

ANCESTOR (Joshua 19:47; Judges 18:29; Hebrews 7:10). See also *father 1.*

ANCIENT OF DAYS. A name Daniel applies to the Lord to inspire awe and reverence for Him and to convey His majesty (7:9-22).

ANDREW (AN-droo, manly). The brother of Simon Peter (Matthew 4:18; Mark 1:16-18). Andrew came from Bethsaida and was a fisherman by trade (John 1:44). He was a disciple of John the Baptizer but was directed by John to Jesus as the Lamb of God (John 1:35-42). Convinced that Jesus was the Messiah, Andrew brought his brother Peter to Jesus (John 1:41-42).

Later Andrew became a permanent disciple of Jesus and was appointed an apostle (Matthew 4:18-19; 10:2; Mark 1:16-17; 3:18; Luke 6:14; Acts 1:13). Once when Jesus asked how He could feed a great number of people, Andrew called Jesus' attention to a boy with five loaves and two fish (John 6:8). With Philip, Andrew told Jesus about some Greek people who wished to see Him (John 12:20-22). Andrew was also one of the disciples who asked Jesus about the destruction of the temple (Mark 13:3-4). According to tradition Andrew was crucified on November 30 in Achaia on a cross shaped like an *X.*

ANGELS (messengers). 1. Unseen, spiritual, holy, heavenly beings who continually do God's bidding (Psalm 89:5, 7; 104:4; Matthew 4:6; 22:30; Hebrews 1:14; 2:7). Angels protect and serve those who fear God (Genesis 28:12; 48:16; 2 Kings 6:17; Psalm 34:7; Isaiah 63:9). They differ in rank and dignity (Daniel 10:13, 21; Luke 1:19, 26; Romans 8:38; Ephesians 1:21).

2. An angel of the Lord may refer to an angel who carries out God's will (1 Kings 19:5, 7). Frequently, however, when the "angel of the Lord" is mentioned in the Bible, it refers to a distinct person and yet a being who is of the essence of the Lord, who reveals God, and who has the Lord's name and presence (Genesis 16:10, 13; 18:2-4, 13-14, 33; 32:30; Exodus 23:21; 32:14). For these reasons the angel of the Lord is often identified with the Second Person of the Trinity, the preincarnate Son of God.

3. Evil angels are fallen spirits (2 Peter 2:4). See also *demons; Satan.*

4. The ''angels of the seven churches'' are representatives of the churches mentioned in the Book of Revelation. John may be referring to the pastors of those churches (Revelation 1:20; 2:1, 8, 12, 18; 3:1, 7, 14).

5. John the Baptizer is called a messenger (or angel) who was sent to prepare the way for Christ (Matthew 11:10; Mark 1:2; Luke 7:27).

ANGER. See *wrath.*

ANKLET. An ornamental metallic or glass ring that was worn around the ankle (Isaiah 3:18).

ANNA (AN-ah, grace). The prophetess who thanked God when she saw the infant Jesus in the temple (Luke 2:36-38).

ANNAS (AN-uhs, merciful). The high priest at Jerusalem from A.D. 7 until approximately A.D. 15 (Luke 3:2). He was appointed by Quirinius and deposed by Valerius Gratus. Annas was the father-in-law of Caiaphas, the high priest before whom Jesus was tried (John 18:13). Five of Annas's sons were also high priests. During the time when they and Caiaphas held office, Annas was also regarded virtually as high priest, perhaps because he was the head of the family and therefore the most influential member (John 18:13; Acts 4:6).

ANOINT. To apply oil to a person or thing. A common custom among Egyptians, Hebrews, Greeks, and Romans, anointing was done for several reasons. 1. Sometimes it was simply a part of grooming. After washing or bathing, people anointed themselves (Ruth 3:3). Anointing was also an expression of joy (Psalm 23:5; 45:7).

2. Hosts anointed their guests as an act of courtesy or respect (Luke 7:46).

3. Anointing was also done as an act of consecration and at a person's induction to the office of priest or

king (Genesis 28:18; Exodus 30:23-26; 40:15; 1 Samuel 9:16).

4. The sick were anointed as an act of healing (James 5:14).

5. Christ was anointed with the Holy Ghost (Luke 4:18; Acts 4:27; 10:38; Psalm 45:7; Isaiah 61:1).

ANT. The ant is held up as an example of diligence and wisdom (Proverbs 6:6-8; 30:24, 25).

ANTELOPE. This is one of the animals God's people were allowed to eat because it was ceremonially fit for food (Deuteronomy 14:5; Isaiah 51:20).

ANTICHRIST (AN-ti-krighst, against Christ). One who is both an enemy of Christ and a usurper of His rights and names. In the New Testament John alone uses the word *antichrist* (1 John 2:18, 22; 4:3; 2 John 7). The other passages in Scriptures that speak about an antichrist were applied early in the history of the church to the Antichrist (Daniel 7–8; 22:31-35; 2 Thessalonians 2:3-12; Revelation 10; 13; 17—18).

ANTILEGOMENA (an-ti-lee-GAHM-i-nah, spoken against, questioned). Those books of the New Testament that were not received as canonical by the church everywhere until the latter part of the fourth century are called antilegomena. They include James, Jude, 2 and 3 John, 2 Peter, Hebrews, and Revelation.

ANTIOCH (AN-ti-ahk, from Antiochus, Syrian king). 1. A city in Syria on the south bank of the Orontes. It was founded around 300 B.C. by Seleucus Nicator. In 64 B.C. Pompey made Antioch the seat of the legate of Syria and a free city. Both Barnabas and Paul worked in Antioch, and it was in Antioch that the followers of Jesus were first called Christians (Acts 11:19-26; 13:1-3; 14:26; 15; 18:22; Galatians 2:11). Today Antioch is called Antakya and is located in Turkey.

2. A city in Pisidia, Asia Minor, which was also founded by Seleucus Nicator (Acts 13:14-52; 14:21).

ANTIOCHUS (an-TIGH-o-kus, opponent). 1. Antiochus III, called the Great, was the king of Syria from 223 to 187 B.C. He was the sixth ruler of the Seleucid dynasty (Daniel 11:14-19).

2. Antiochus IV, whose given name was Epiphanes, was the son of Antiochus III. He was the eighth ruler of the Seleucid dynasty, reigning from 175 to 164 B.C. He was both an intolerant and energetic ruler.

3. Antiochus V, whose name was Eupator, was the son of Epiphanes. He ruled only two years, from 164 to 163 B.C., before he was slain.

ANTIPAS (AN-ti-pas, like father). 1. A Christian who suffered martyrdom at Pergamos (Revelation 2:13). According to tradition he was a bishop who was burned in a brazen bull under Domitian.

2. Herod Antipas, the son of Herod the Great.

ANTIPATER (an-TIP-ah-tur, like father). The father of Herod the Great.

ANTIPATRIS (an-TIP-ah-tris). A city Herod the Great built between Caesarea and Jerusalem. Herod named the city after his father. Paul was a prisoner there (Acts 23:31).

ANTITYPE. A perfect thing that is represented or prefigured by a type (1 Peter 3:21). For example, Christ is the antitype of the paschal lamb (type).

ANTONIA (an-TO-ni-ah). A fortress on the northwest side of the temple. It was rebuilt by Herod the Great and named by him in honor of Mark Antony. Roman soldiers who watched over the temple area were housed there (Acts 21:31-40; 22—23).

APOCALYPSE (ah-PAHK-ah-lips, uncover). Another name for the Book of Revelation.

APOCALYPTIC LITERATURE. There are two types of apocalyptic literature: canonical and uncanonical. The first includes Daniel and Revelation. These books reveal events of the last time, judgment, and the hereafter.

The uncanonical apocalyptic literature appeared during the period of late Judaism and early Christianity. It includes Enoch, Baruch, the Apocalypse of Peter, the Ascension of Isaiah, the Assumption of Moses, the Book of Jubilees, and the Shepherd of Hermas.

APOCRYPHA (ah-PAHK-ri-fah, hidden). A term the church fathers used for writings that were difficult to understand or obscure and for books whose authorship was unknown. Gradually the term came to be used for those books which were outside the canon. During the time of the Reformation the uncanonical books which appeared in the Vulgate (the Latin translation of the Bible by Jerome), but did not appear in the Hebrew Old Testament, were classed as apocryphal. They included 1 and 2 Esdras, Additions to Esther, Song of the Three Children, History of Susanna, Bel and the Dragon, Prayer of Manasses, Judith, 1 and 2 Maccabees, Ecclesiasticus (Sirach), and Wisdom of Solomon.

APOLLOS (ah-PAHL-us, belonging to Apollo). A well-educated Jewish man from Alexandria. John baptized him, and Aquila and Priscilla instructed him more accurately in the Christian faith (Acts 18:24-28). After this Apollos became an eloquent preacher and a friend of Paul (1 Corinthians 1:12; 3:4-22; 4:6; 16:12; Titus 3:13).

APOSTASY (ah-PAHS-tah-see). Forsaking the Lord or departing from the faith (Jeremiah 2:19; 5:6; Hebrews 6:6). The Scriptures contain many warnings against apostasy (Hebrews 6:1-8; 10:26-29; 2 Peter 2:15-21). An apostate, one who forsakes the Lord, should not be confused with an errorist or a heretic. (The latter, unlike an apostate, still professes faith even though he or she rejects a particular teaching or teachings of the church.)

APOSTLE (one sent forth). 1. In one sense the New Testament uses the word *apostle* as the official name for Jesus' 12 disciples: Simon Peter, Andrew, John, Philip, James Bartholomew (perhaps another name for Nathanael), Thomas, Matthew (Levi), Simon Zelotes, Jude (Thaddeus), James the Less, and Judas Iscariot. Judas Iscariot's place was taken by Matthias (Acts 1:15-26). And, later, on his way to Damascus, Paul also was called to be an apostle (Acts 9; 1 Corinthians 1:1; 2 Corinthians 10—12).

The apostles were acquainted personally with Jesus (Acts 1:21-22). They established the Christian church (Mark 16:20; Acts), and through their written and spoken testimony, they laid the foundation of the church (Ephesians 2:20).

2. In a general sense, the New Testament uses the word *apostle* to refer to anyone commissioned to preach the Gospel (Romans 10:13-15; 2 Corinthians 8:23; Philippians 2:25).

3. Christ is referred to as an apostle (Hebrews 3:1).

APOTHECARY (ah-PAHTH-i-keree, to perfume). A person who mixed ointments (Exodus 30:25, 35; Nehemiah 3:8). Bezaleel made anointing oil for the holy place (Exodus 31:11; 37:29). The people who made perfumes also prepared burial spices and, according to excavation finds, medicinal herbs (2 Chronicles 16:14).

APPEAL. In ancient Israel appeals were made to the head of the tribe. At Moses' time, Moses himself first handled all appeals. But when this became too burdensome for him, he appointed judges for this purpose (Exodus 18:13, 26). Later supreme decisions were made at the sanctuaries (Deuteronomy 17:8-11).

Both judges and kings handled appeals (Judges 4:5; 2 Samuel 15:3). Jehoshaphat established courts and delegated his authority of appeal to judges (2 Chronicles 19:8). These courts were reestablished by Ezra (Ezra 7:25). After the Sanhedrin was instituted, it became the highest court of appeal for the Jews. Roman citizens could appeal to the emperor (Acts 25:11-12).

AQUILA (AK-wi-lah, eagle). A Jewish man who was born in Pontus. He was a tentmaker by trade (Acts 18:1-3). With his wife, Priscilla, Aquila was a prominent co-worker of Paul (Acts 18:18-19, 26; Romans 16:3; 1 Corinthians 16:19; 2 Timothy 4:19).

ARABAH (AR-ah-bah, desert). The name of the valley between the Dead Sea and the Gulf of Aqaba (Deuteronomy 1:1, 7; 11:30; Joshua 3:16; 1 Samuel 23:24; 2 Samuel 2:29; 2 Kings 14:25; Jeremiah 39:4; Ezekiel 47:8).

ARABIA (ah-RAY-bi-ah, desert). Originally, the northern part of the peninsula between the Red Sea and the Persian Gulf (Isaiah 21:13; Jeremiah 25:24) but later the entire peninsula (Nehemiah 2:19; 6:1; Acts 2:11; Galatians 1:17; 4:25).

ARAM (AY-ram). 1. A son of Shem (Genesis 10:22, 23; 1 Chronicles 1:17).

2. The area where the Aramaean people (Syrians) lived. It extended from the Lebanon Mountains to beyond the Euphrates River and from the Taurus Mountains to south of Damascus. Several divisions of the

Aramaean people are mentioned in the Old Testament.

ARAMAIC (ar-ah-MAY-ik). A Semitic language in Aram which spread to all of southwest Asia. It was incorrectly called Chaldee on the basis of Daniel 2:4—7:28. Aramaic inscriptions from as early as 850 B.C. still exist today. Parts of the Old Testament are in Aramaic (Daniel 2:4—7:28; Ezra 4:8—6:18; 7:12-26; Jeremiah 10:11). Jesus also spoke Aramaic.

ARARAT (AR-ah-rat). A name for Armenia and its mountain range, especially its two peaks, which are 14,000 and 10,000 feet high (Genesis 8:4; Jeremiah 51:27). Armenia is a mountainous country north of Assyria, extending from the Black Sea to the Caspian Sea and from the Caucasus Mountains to the Taurus Mountains.

ARCHAEOLOGY (ahr-kee-AHL-o-jee). A study of the material remains of the past. Biblical archaeology is concerned with Palestine and the ancient countries with which the Hebrews and early Christians came into contact.

Modern archaeology is usually traced to Napoleon's expedition to Egypt in 1798. About 100 scholars went with him on this trip to study the Egyptian monuments. Another man, C. J. Rich of the East India Company in Bagdad, made the first excavations in Mesopotamia, and in 1838 and 1852, Edward Robinson of Union Theological Seminary made observations in Palestine.

From these beginnings Biblical archaeology developed. Although earlier excavations (1800—1890) were mainly concerned with finding objects of interest, the scientific aspects of archaeology soon developed (1890—1915). The results of Biblical archaeology often are used in Bible dictionaries.

ARCHANGEL (ARK-AYN-juhl). Chief angel (1 Thessalonians 4:16; Jude 9). See also *angels 1*.

ARCHELAUS. See *Herod 2*.

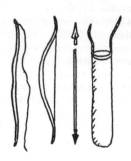

ARCHERY. The art or practice of shooting with a bow and arrow, the weapons used in ancient times. Some famous archers were the Philistines, the Benjaminites, the Medes, and the Elamites (1 Samuel 31:3; 1 Chronicles 8:40; Isaiah 13:18; Jeremiah 49:35). The word *arrow* is used figuratively for deep trouble, danger, power, and a wicked tongue (Job 6:4; Psalm 91:5; 127:4; Jeremiah 9:8). *Bow* is also used figuratively (Psalm 78:56-57). A quiver is a case for carrying arrows (Genesis 27:3).

ARCHITECTURE (AHR-kuh-tek-chur). The art or science of building. Hebrew architecture, in the proper sense of the word, came into being around the time of the kings. David built a house trimmed with cedar, and Solomon built palaces and a harem (2 Samuel 7:2; 1 Kings 7). The palaces of later kings were more showy, often decorated with ivory (Amos 3:15). The temple, city gates, pillars, and the like offered further opportunity for architectural development and achievement.

Jesus' disciples admired the splendor of Jerusalem under Herod (Mark 13:1). For examples of early architecture, see *homes*.

ARCHIVES. A place for storing official papers (Ezra 5:17; 6:1).

AREOPAGITE (ar-i-AHP-ah-jight). A member of the court that met at the Areopagus or Mars' Hill in Athens (Acts 17:34).

AREOPAGUS (ar-i-AHP-ah-guhs). Hill of Ares or Mars, the Greek god of war. The Areopagus was also a council during Paul's day (Acts 17:19-34). Its chief concern was with education and religion.

ARIEL (AIR-i-el, lion of God). 1. A leader whom Ezra sent to obtain ministers for the house of God (Ezra 8:16).
2. A poetic name for Jerusalem (Isaiah 29:1-10).

ARIELS. Although sometimes translated as lionlike men or sons of Ariel, the meaning of this word is unknown (2 Samuel 23:20; 1 Chronicles 11:22).

ARIMATHAEA, ARIMATHEA (ar-i-mah-THEE-ah, height). The home of the Joseph who buried Jesus in his own new tomb (Matthew 27:57; Luke 23:51).

ARIOCH (AR-i-ahk, servant of moon-god). The captain of Nebuchadnezzar's guard (Daniel 2:14).

ARISTOBULUS (ah-ris-to-BYOO-luhs, best counselor). A Christian at Rome. Paul sent greetings to his household (Romans 16:10).

ARK (chest). The name given to three vessels in the Bible. 1. The floating home God commanded Noah to make in order to save himself, his family, and certain animals from the Flood. The ark was made of gopherwood and was about 450 feet long, 75 feet wide, and 45 feet high (Genesis 6—8).
2. The basket into which baby Moses was placed (Exodus 2:3-10).
3. The ark of the covenant, a chest about 3 3/4 feet long and 2 1/4 feet wide. It was made of acacia wood and lined and covered with gold. The solid gold lid of this chest

was called the mercy seat. It had two cherubs on it, one on each end. Poles passed through two golden rings at the bottom of the ark so that the ark could be carried (Exodus 25:10-22). The ark held manna, the stone tablets of the Law, Aaron's rod, and the book of the Law (Exodus 16:33; 25:21; 31:18; Numbers 17:10; Deuteronomy 31:26; Hebrews 9:4).

The ark went before Israel in its wilderness journeys "to seek out a resting place for them" (Numbers 10:33). Priests carried it into the Jordan, where it halted the waters of the river so that the people could cross over on dry land into Palestine (Joshua 3:11-17). In the days of Eli and Samuel, the ark was kept in the temple at Shiloh (1 Samuel 3:3).

Once the Israelites carried the ark into battle for good luck, but the Philistines defeated them and captured the ark (1 Samuel 4). Convinced by ill fortune, however, that the ark was too dangerous to keep, the Philistines soon returned the ark to the Israelites at Beth-Shemesh (1 Samuel 6:12-20). When 70 of the men there died because they had looked into the ark, the people at Beth-Shemesh asked the people of Kiriath-jearim to come and take it (1 Samuel 7:1-2).

David brought the ark to Jerusalem (2 Samuel 6:12-23). Later it was placed into the Holy of Holies in Solomon's temple (1 Kings 8:1-9).

The ark is also called the ark of testimony and the ark of God (Exodus 25:16, 22; 1 Samuel 3:3).

ARMAGEDDON (ahr-mah-GED-on, hill of Megiddo). The name the New Testament gives to the final battlefield for the forces of good and evil (Revelation 16:16).

Also written Har-Magedon, the name may be derived from the hill on the southern rim of Esdraelon where many battles were fought. It was on this plain that Barak defeated the Canaanites and Gideon defeated the Midianites (Judges 5:19; 7). Both Ahaziah and Josiah were killed there (2 Kings 9:27; 23:29).

ARMENIA (ahr-MEE-ni-ah). See *Ararat.*

ARMLET, BRACELET. A piece of jewelry usually worn on the upper arm.

ARMOR, ARMS. Weapons used in battle. The offensive weapons, or arms, of the Hebrews included swords, javelins, spears, bows and arrows, slings, engines, darts, hammers, battle axes, maces or mauls, and battering rams (1 Samuel 13:19; 17:6; 2 Samuel 2:23; 2 Kings 3:25; 2 Chronicles 26:15; Job 41:26; Jeremiah 51:20; Ezekiel 4:2).

The defensive weapons, or armor, that the Hebrews used included coats of mail, greaves and war boots, helmets, bucklers, shields, girdles, and breastplates (1 Samuel 17:5-6, 38; 1 Chronicles 5:18; 12:24; Isaiah 5:27; 9:5; 59:17).

ARMOR-BEARER. Someone who carried an officer's armor, guarded him, and helped him in whatever way he could. Abimelech, Jonathan, and Saul each had an armor-bearer (Judges 9:54; 1 Samuel 14:7; 31:4)

ARMORY. A place where weapons were kept (Nehemiah 3:19; Song of Solomon 4:4; Isaiah 39:2; Jeremiah 50:25).

ARMY. In order for the Children of Israel to defend themselves against hostile attacks, they organized themselves into armies. In the wilderness they marched according to tribes. All males, except for the Levites, could be called into the army at the age of 20 (Numbers 1—2). In time of war the number of fighting men were gathered for war by inspectors (Deuteronomy 20:1-9; 2 Kings 25:19). Army divisions were subdivided into companies of thousands and hundreds under their respective captains and still further into families (Numbers 2:34; 31:14). The kings also had bodyguards (1 Samuel 13:2).

The first standing army in Israel was organized during the reign of Saul (2 Chronicles 25:6). A captain of the host or commander was in charge of this army (1 Samuel 14:50). The army first consisted of infantry or foot soldiers (1 Samuel 4:10), but in time horsemen and chariots were added (2 Samuel 8:4; 1 Kings 10:26, 28-29).

The Roman army consisted of legions which were divided into cohorts (Acts 10:1; 21:31). Cohorts were further divided into three maniples, and each maniple into two centuries (Matthew 8:5; 27:54).

ARNON (AHR-nahn). The river flowing east of the Jordan into the Dead Sea. The Arnon formed a natural boundary, first between the Amorites and Moabites (Numbers 21:13; Judges 11:18) and later between Israel and the Moabites (Deuteronomy 2:24; Joshua 12:1).

AROD (AY-rahd). A son of Gad and the forefather of the Arodites (Numbers 26:17). He is referred to as Arodi in Genesis 46:16.

AROER (ah-RO-ur, naked). 1. A Reubenite town on the Arnon (Deuteronomy 2:36). During Jehu's time King Hazael of Syria took Aroer from Israel, but later it fell back to Moab (2 Kings 10:33; Jeremiah 48:19-20). Today it is called 'Ara'ir.

2. A town 12 miles southeast of Beersheba in the southern part of Judah (1 Samuel 30:26-28).

ARPACHSHAD (ahr-PAK-shad). The son of Shem and an ancestor of Abraham (Genesis 11:10-13).

ARPAD, ARPHAD (AHR-pad, AHR-fad). A city in the northern part of Syria near Hamath (Jeremiah 49:23).

ARROWS. See *archery*.

ARSENAL. See *armory*.

ARTAXERXES (ahr-tugh-ZURK-seez). 1. The Persian king who stopped the rebuilding of the temple (Ezra 4:7, 23-24). His name was probably Smerdis.

2. Longimanus, the Persian king who reigned from 465 to 425 B.C. He sent Ezra to Jerusalem and was also a friend to Nehemiah (Ezra 7; Nehemiah 2:1-8).

ARTEMIS

ARTEMIS (AHR-ti-mis). The Greek goddess of the moon, woods, and fields corresponding to the Roman Diana. She was a hunter and a symbol of chastity. The Artemis worshiped in Ephesus was a combination of Artemis and Ashtoreth (Acts 19:24-28).

ARUBBOTH, ARUBOTH (ah-RUB-uth, Ah-ROO-both). A district assigned to Benhesed to provide food for Solomon's court (1 Kings 4:10).

ARUMAH (ah-ROO-mah, height). A place near Shechem where Abimelech lived (Judges 9:41).

ASA (ay-SAH, physician). The son of Abijah and the third king of Judah. Asa was the first of the five kings of Judah who did "what was good and right in the eyes of the Lord" (2 Chronicles 14:2). Asa began his reign with 10 years of peace, during which time he made many religious reforms (2 Chronicles 14:1, 3-5; 15:1-17).

Then Zerah, the Ethiopian, waged war upon Judah, but with the Lord's help Asa and his armies defeated them (2 Chronicles 14:9-15). Later in his reign Asa purchased the help of Ben-hadad of Damascus against Baasha of Israel (1 Kings 15:16-22; 2 Chronicles 16:1-10). In his later years Asa was not as true to the Lord as he had been in his earlier years. He died in the 41st year of his reign.

ASAHEL (AS-ah-hel, God had made). 1. The nephew of David and a brother of Joab. Asahel was killed by Abner (2 Samuel 2:18-23).

2. A Levite and teacher of the Law under Jehoshaphat (2 Chronicles 17:8).

3. An overseer of the temple in Hezekiah's reign (2 Chronicles 31:13).

ASAIAH (ah-SAY-yah, Lord had made). An officer who was sent by

Josiah to ask Huldah, the prophetess, about the Law (2 Kings 22:12, 14; 2 Chronicles 34:20).

ASAPH (AY-saf, collector). 1. A Levite, the son of Berechiah. Asaph sounded the cymbals before the ark when it was brought to the city of David (1 Chronicles 15:16-19). He was then given the permanent job of sounding the cymbals for religious functions (1 Chronicles 16:4-5, 7).

Asaph's family, with him at the head, was one of the families in charge of music and song (1 Chronicles 25:1-9). Like the other chief singers, Asaph was called a seer (2 Chronicles 29:30; Nehemiah 12:46). Psalms 50 and 73 to 83 are called Psalms of Asaph.

2. The father of Joah, Hezekiah's recorder (2 Kings 18:18; Isaiah 36:3, 22).

3. A keeper of the royal forest in Palestine under Artaxerxes Longimanus, king of Persia (Nehemiah 2:8).

ASCENSION. Forty days after His resurrection Christ finally parted from His disciples and returned to His Father in heaven. The ascension marks the end of Christ's bodily ministry on earth (Mark 16:19; Acts 1:1-12; Ephesians 4:8-10; 1 Peter 3:22).

ASCENTS, SONG OF. The title given to Psalms 120 to 134. Some scholars think these psalms were named this because they may have been sung on the 15 steps that led from the court of women to the court of men. Others think that the word *degrees*, or *ascents*, refers to the way the poetic thought of the music advanced.

ASENATH (AS-i-nath, devotee of Neith, Egyptian goddess). The daughter of Potiphera, priest of On. Pharoah gave her to Joseph to be his wife (Genesis 41:45, 50). They had two children, Manasseh and Ephraim (Genesis 46:20).

ASH. Probably a Syrian fir (Isaiah 44:14).

ASHAN (AY-shuhn, smoke). A town assigned to the tribe of Judah that was later transferred to Simeon (Joshua 15:42; 19:7; 1 Chronicles 4:32). It was made a city of refuge and given to the Levites (1 Chronicles 6:59).

ASHARELAH (ash-ah-REE-lah). A son of Asaph. Asharelah was in charge of temple music (1 Chronicles 25:2).

ASHBEL (ASH-bel, man of lord). The second son of Benjamin (1 Chronicles 8:1).

ASHDOD (ASH-dahd). One of the five chief cities of the Philistines. It was situated between Gaza and Joppa and was the center of worship for the god Dagon (Joshua 13:3; 1 Samuel 5). Although assigned to Judah, it was never taken by that tribe (Joshua 15:46-47). When the Philistines captured the ark at Ebenezer, they carried it to Ashdod but soon returned it (1 Samuel 5—6). Uzziah, king of Judah, broke down the wall of Ashdod, and a number of years later it was captured by Sargon II of Assyria (2 Chronicles 26:6; Isaiah 20:1). In 630 B.C. Ashdod was partially destroyed by Psammetichus of Egypt. In New Testament times it was called Azotus (Acts 8:40)

ASHDODITES, ASHDOTHITES (ASH-dahd-ights, Ash-DAHTH-ights). The people who lived in Ashdod (Joshua 13:3; Nehemiah 4:7).

ASHER (ASH-ur, happiness). 1. The eighth son of Jacob (Genesis 30:12-13; 35:26).

2. The territory along the seashore north of Carmel that was given to the tribe that descended from Asher (Joshua 19:24-31).

3. See *Hazor*.

ASHERAH (ah-SHER-rah). A Canaanite goddess of sex and war. She was the wife or sister of El. The word *Asherah* means goddess or wooden image (Deuteronomy 16:21; 1 Kings 15:13; 16:33).

ASHERIM (ah-SHER-rim). The plural form of Asherah.

ASHERITES (ASH-ur-ights). The people from the tribe of Asher (Judges 1:32).

ASHEROTH (ah-SHER-rahth). The feminine plural form of Asherah.

ASHES. People in Bible times sat in or sprinkled themselves with ashes to show humiliation, grief, or penitence (2 Samuel 13:19; Esther 4:3; Job 2:8; Jeremiah 6:26; Matthew 11:21). When people felt depressed, they demonstrated this by eating ashes (Psalm 102:9). Because of the ageless custom of burning captured cities, the expression "to reduce to ashes" implied complete destruction (Ezekiel 28:18; 2 Peter 2:6). The ashes of a red heifer were used for cleansing the unclean (Numbers 19:17-22).

ASHKELON (ASH-kuh-lahn, migration). One of the five chief cities of the Philistines. It was located about 12 miles north of Gaza. During the time of the judges, the tribe of Judah captured Ashkelon, but the Philistines soon got it back (Judges 1:8; 14:19; 1 Samuel 6:17). Ashkelon's destruction is foretold in both Zephaniah 2:4 and Zechariah 9:5. In A.D. 1270 the Bibars destroyed it.

ASHKENAZ (ASH-kuh-naz). Noah's great-grandson (Genesis 10:3). His descendants lived near Ararat.

ASHPENAZ (ASH-pi-naz). The chief of the eunuchs in Babylon during Nebuchadnezzar's time. Ashpenaz gave Daniel and his friends their new names (Daniel 1:3, 7).

ASHTORETH (ASH-to-reth). A Canaanite goddess who was worshiped particularly at Sidon (1 Kings 11:5,

33; 2 Kings 23:13). During the time of the judges the people of Israel periodically stopped worshiping the Lord and served Ashtoreth instead (Judges 2:13; 10:6). Toward the end of his reign Solomon built altars in Israel for the worship of Ashtoreth (1 Kings 11:5; 2 Kings 23:13).

Ashtoreth has been equated with Ishtar of the Babylonians, Astarte of the Greeks and Romans, and Venus. The plural form of her name is Ashtaroth. Her male partner was Baal.

ASIA (AY-zhah). When the New Testament speaks of Asia, it may be referring to either Asia Minor (Acts 19:26), Proconsular Asia (Acts 20:4; 1 Corinthians 16:19), or more restricted areas (Acts 2:9).

ASP. A poisonous snake (Deuteronomy 32:33; Isaiah 11:8; Romans 3:13). See also *serpent.*

ASRIEL (AS-ri-el, vow of God). A descendant of Manasseh and founder of a family (Numbers 26:31).

ASSHUR (AHS-shoor). The second-named son of Shem (Genesis 10:22). The people who descended from Asshur settled in Assyria. See also *Assyria.*

ASSHURIM (uh-SHOO-rim). A tribe that descended from Abraham (Genesis 25:3).

ASSOS (AS-ahs). A seaport of Mysia in Asia Minor (Acts 20:13-14).

ASSYRIA (uh-SIR-i-ah). The country that dominated the Biblical world from the 9th to the 7th century B.C. At its height Assyria encompassed the land between the Black Sea, the Caspian Sea, the Persian Gulf, and the Mediterranean Sea (including Egypt). Its capital city was Nineveh. Semitic in origin, it appears that the people of Assyria were originally colonists from Babylonia (Genesis 10:11). They wrote with ideograms and syllabic signs. Chief among their gods were Asshur, Anu, Bel, and Ea.

The kings of Assyria often invaded Israel (2 Kings 15:19; 29; 16:7-9; 2 Chronicles 28:20). In 721 B.C. the Assyrians finally carried the Israelites into captivity (2 Kings 17:6; 18:11).

In 612 B.C. Nineveh fell to the Medes, and after the battle of Carchemish in 605 B.C., the Assyrians as a nation ceased to exist.

ASTROLOGERS (as-TRAHL-o-jurs). People who tried to predict the future by studying the stars (Daniel 2:27; 4:7; 5:7, 11).

ATHALIAH (ath-ah-LIGH-ah, affected of the Lord). The wicked daughter of Ahab and Jezebel. Under Athaliah's influence, her husband, King Jehoram, introduced Baal worship to Judah. Later when her son King Ahaziah was killed, Athaliah seized the throne and reigned for six years. While trying to stop a rebellion, she was killed by her guard (2 Kings 11; 2 Chronicles 22—24).

ATHARIM (ATH-ah-rim). The route the Israelites followed when approaching Canaan (Numbers 21:l).

ATHENS (ATH-enz, city of Athena). In ancient times Athens was the capital of Attica; today it is the capital of Greece. Located near the Gulf of Aegina, Athens grew up around the 512-foot-high rocky hill known as the Acropolis. It was connected to the harbor Piraeus by five-mile-long walls. Athens was a center for both learning and civilization. During his second missionary journey Paul visited the city and spoke to a group of people on the Areopagus (Acts 17:19-22).

ATONEMENT (ah-TON-muhnt). "At-one-ment." Atonement is the removal of the separation that exists between God and people because of sin. It is accomplished by the life and death of Jesus in humanity's place (Romans 5:11).

ATONEMENT, DAY OF. A Hebrew festival held on the 10th day of the seventh month. It was observed with fasting, humiliation, and sacrifice for sin (Exodus 30:16; Leviticus 16; 23:27-32).

ATTAI (AT-ay-igh, ready). A son of Rehoboam and Maacah (2 Chronicles 11:10).

ATTALIA (At-ah-LIGH-ah). A seaport on the coast of Pamphylia (Acts 14:25).

AUGURY. Using signs or omens to predict the future. This practice was forbidden (2 Kings 21:6; 2 Chronicles 33:6). See also *enchantment; magic.*

AUGUSTUS (aw-GUS-tuhs, venerable). The title of Gaius Julius Caesar Octavianus, the first Roman Emperor. He reigned from 27 B.C. to A.D. 14. Christ was born during his rule (Luke 2:1).

AVENGER OF BLOOD. When a person was murdered, it was the duty of the person's nearest relative to pursue the murderer and obtain satisfaction for the relative's death, generally by killing the murderer (Deuteronomy 19:6). The person who made satisfaction for a relative's death in this way was known as the avenger of blood.

AVIM, AVIMS, AVITES, AVVIM (AY-vim, AY-vims, AY-vights, AV-im). 1. Aborigines who lived in

Gaza before the time of Moses (Deuteronomy 2:23).

2. A town probably named after the Avites (Joshua 18:23).

AVVA (Av-ah). A city of the Assyrian Empire. People from Avva helped colonize Samaria (2 Kings 17:24).

AZARIAH (az-ah-RIGH-ah, help by the Lord). 1. The prophet who met King Asa on his return from victory over Zerah. Asa followed Azariah's advice by putting away idolatry and restoring the altar of God. A national reformation followed (2 Chronicles 15:1-8).

2. A son of Obed and another of Joash's captains. He also helped restore the throne to Joash (2 Chronicles 23:1).

3. A son of Jeroham and one of Joash's captains. He helped place Joash on the throne (2 Chronicles 23:1).

4. The son and successor of Amaziah. Azariah was the 10th king of Judah (2 Kings 14:21; 15:1-7; 1 Chronicles 3:12). He is also referred to as Uzziah.

5. The Hebrew name of Abednego, one of Daniel's friends (Daniel 1:7; 2:17). Azariah was thrown into the fiery furnace for not worshiping the golden idol set up by King Nebuchadnezzar (Daniel 3).

AZAZEL (ah-ZAH-zel). The word occurs only in Leviticus 16, where its meaning is unknown. Several meanings for it have been suggested, however. 1. A solitary place. 2. A scapegoat, or goat that was allowed to run away. 3. A devil or demon of the wilderness. 4. Dismissal or removal.

AZGAD (AZ-gad, strong of fortune). The head of a family of Israelites, a large number of whom returned from Babylon with Zerubbabel (Ezra 2:12; 8:12; Nehemiah 7:17).

AZMAVETH (az-MAY-veth, death is strong). 1. One of David's warriors (2 Samuel 23:31). His sons joined David's army at Ziklag (1 Chronicles 12:3).

2. David's treasurer (1 Chronicles 27:25). Perhaps the same as *1*.

3. A village of Judah or Benjamin situated between Geba and Anathoth (Ezra 2:24; Nehemiah 12:29).

AZOTUS (ah-ZO-tuhs). See *Ashdod*.

AZUBAH (ah-ZYOO-bah, forsaken). King Jehoshaphat's mother (1 Kings 22:42; 2 Chronicles 20:31).

AZUR (AY-zur). See *Azzur*.

AZZUR (AZ-ur, helpful). The father of Hananiah, the false prophet (Jeremiah 28:1).

B

BAAL (BAY-uhl, lord, possessor). 1. A common name for god among the Phoenicians. It was also a name used for the master of the house and a person who owned land or cattle (Exodus 21:28; 22:7; Job 31:39).

2. The storm-god of the Phoenicians and Canaanites. Baal gave increase to families, crops, fields, and flocks. He was worshiped on high places with self-torture and human sacrifices (Jeremiah 19:5). Often he was associated with the goddess Ashtoreth (Judges 2:13; 6:30; 1 Kings 16:32-33).

Early in their history, the Hebrews were attracted to Baal worship (Numbers 22:41; Deuteronomy 4:16; Judges 2:13; 6:28-32). Altars to Baal were built in Palestine. Jezebel in Israel and Athaliah in Judah championed Baal worship (1 Kings 16:31-32; 18:17-40; 2 Kings 11:18; 2 Chronicles 17:3; 21:6; 22:2). Numerous times the altars and images of Baal were torn down and destroyed, and the people of Israel returned to the Lord; yet Baal worship persisted in Judah and Israel (2 Kings 21:3; 23:4-5; 2 Chronicles 28:2; Jeremiah 19:4-5; Hosea 2:8).

3. Often Baal is combined with other words or syllables in the names of people and places, for example, Baal-Hazor.

BAAL-BERITH (BAY-uhl-BEE-rith, Baal of the covenant). God worshiped at Shechem (Judges 8:33; 9:4).

BAAL-HAZOR (BAY-uhl-HAY-zawr, Baal of a village). A place near Ephraim, where Absalom had a sheep farm. It is here that he had his half-brother Amnon murdered (2 Samuel 13:23).

BAALI (BAY-ahl-igh, my master). The name Israel gave to God (Hosea 2:16).

BAALIM (BAY-uhl-im). The plural of Baal (Judges 2:11).

BAALIS (BAY-ah-lis). A king of the Ammonites (Jeremiah 40:14).

BAAL-PERAZIM (BAY-uhl-pi-RAY-zim, Baal of openings). A place where David defeated the Philistines (2 Samuel 5:20; 1 Chronicles 14:11).

BAAL-ZEBUB (BAY-uhl-ZEE-bub, Baal of flies). The name by which Baal was worshiped in Ekron (2 Kings 1:2-6). See also *Beelzebub, Beelzebul.*

BAAL-ZEPHON (BAY-uhl-ZEE-fahn). A place near which the Israelites camped before crossing the Red Sea (Exodus 14:2, 9; Numbers 33:7).

BAANAH (BAY-ah-nah, son of affliction). An officer in the army of Ish-bosheth, Saul's son. Baanah and his brother killed Ish-bosheth (2 Samuel 4:2-12).

BAASHA (BAY-ah-shah). The son of Ahijah of the tribe of Issachar. Baasha became the third king of Israel while Asa was king of Judah. Baasha began a long war with Asa. He built Ramah to block the flow of traffic in and out of Judah (1 Kings 15:16-17). Baasha ruled Israel for 24 years (1 Kings 15:27-34; 16:7).

BABEL (BAY-buhl, gate of God). 1. A city in the Plain of Shinar (Genesis 10:10; 11:9).

2. The Tower of Babel was a brick structure built on the Plain of Shinar. As a result of this building project, God confused people's language and scattered the people over

the face of the earth (Genesis 11:4-9).

BABYLON (BAB-i-lahn, Greek form of Babel). An ancient city-state on the Plain of Shinar. It is first mentioned in Genesis 10:8-10. Babylon began its rise to power in the 19th century B.C. The great Hammurabi became its ruler in the 18th century B.C. But it did not reach the height of its power until Nebuchadnezzar II, who reigned from 605 to 562 B.C. Then in 539 B.C., Babylon was conquered by Cyrus of Persia.

Babylon was noted for its temple of Bel (or Marduk) and the Ishtar Gate, as well as for its ziggurats, hanging gardens, bridges, palace, and overall strength and splendor. The prophets often spoke about it (Isaiah 13—14; 21; 46—47; Jeremiah 50—51). In the New Testament *Babylon* is used figuratively for that which opposes God both within and without the church (1 Peter 5:13; Revelation 14:8; 16:19; 17:5; 18:2, 10, 21).

BABYLONIA (Bab-i-LO-ni-ah). A region of West Asia, the capital of which was Babylon. Babylonia was also called Shinar (Genesis 10:10; 11:2; Isaiah 11:11) and the land of the Chaldeans (Jeremiah 24:5; Ezekiel 12:13).

BACA (BA-kah, weeping or balsam tree). An unidentified valley in Palestine that was named for its balsam trees, which produced a tearlike gum. Some people identify Baca with Rephaim because of the balsam trees there (2 Samuel 5:22-24). It is usually interpreted figuratively, however, to describe any vale of tears (Psalm 84:6).

BACKBITE. To speak evil of someone (Proverbs 25:23 Psalm 15:3).

BAG. Used for carrying weights, stones, and money (Deuteronomy 25:13; 1 Samuel 17:40; 2 Kings 5:23). Judas's "bag" was proba-

bly a chest (John 12:6; 13:29).

BAKEMEATS. Baked foods (Genesis 40:17).

BAKER. Some people in Israel earned their living by baking (1 Samuel 8:13; Jeremiah 37:21). Often rulers had their own bakers (Genesis 40; 1 Samuel 8:13).

BALAAM (BAY-lahm). The son of Beor, probably a Midianite (Deuteronomy 23:4; Numbers 31:8). Balaam was the diviner hired by King Balak of Moab to curse Israel. God, however, used Balaam to bless Israel instead (Numbers 22—24).

Before leaving the king of Moab, Balaam told him that the Lord would surely curse the Israelites if Balak could get them to worship false gods (Numbers 31:15-16; Revelation 2:14). Balak did this. To avenge themselves, the Israelites warred against the Midianites, killing their kings and Balaam (Numbers 31:8).

BALAK (BAY-lak, destroyer). The king of Moab. He hired Balaam to curse Israel (Numbers 22—24; Joshua 24:9; Judges 11:25; Revelation 2:14).

BALANCE. An instrument for weighing (Leviticus 19:36; Ezekiel 45:10; Amos 8:5). In a figurative sense the word *balance* is used for measuring the worth or trouble of people (Job 6:2; Psalm 62:9; Daniel 5:27). It is also a symbol of fair dealing (Job 31:6; Proverbs 11:1).

BALDNESS. Natural baldness is not mentioned often in the Bible. Sometimes it was connected with leprosy or misery (Leviticus 13:40-43; Isaiah 3:24).

Shaving the head was a sign of mourning (Jeremiah 16:6; Ezekiel 7:18). The Israelites were forbidden from doing this because they were a holy people (Deuteronomy 14:1-2). However, it was sometimes a punishment used for captives (Deuteronomy 21:12). When a Nazirite shaved his head, it marked the end of his vow (Numbers 6:9, 18). "Baldhead" was a term of ridicule (2 Kings 2:23).

BALM OF GILEAD. The resin or gum of trees that at one time grew in Gilead (Genesis 37:25; Jeremiah 8:22; 46:11). This balm or ointment was used to heal wounds (Jeremiah 51:8). It made up part of the export trade of Palestine (Genesis 37:25; Ezekiel 27:17).

BALSAM TREE. An unidentified plant in Palestine (2 Samuel 5:22-24; 1 Chronicles 14:14-15).

BAMAH (BAH-mah, high place). A place where idols were worshiped (Ezekiel 20:29).

BAMOTH. (BAY-mahth, heights). A camp of the Israelites located in the land of the Moabites (Numbers 21:19-20).

BAND. The 10th part of a Roman legion, a cohort or battalion (Matthew 27:27; Acts 10:l; 27:l). See also *army*.

BAPTISM (bap-tiz'm). When the word *baptism* appears in the Old Testament, it often means to dip, bathe, or wash (Exodus 30:17-21; 2 Kings 5:14; Psalm 68:23). The Jews baptized proselytes; ceremonial washings were also common (Mark 7:3-4; Hebrews 9:10).

John's Baptism was connected with repentance so that those baptized might be spiritually prepared to recognize and receive the Messiah. It worked the forgiveness of sins (Matthew 3; Mark 1:4-8) but was distinguished from the Baptism Jesus instituted (Luke 3:16; John 1:26; Acts 1:5; 11:16; 19:4-6).

The baptism Jesus received from John was unique since Jesus was without sin and therefore had no reason to repent. It signified His public entrance into His work of saving the world from sin (Matthew 3:13-15; Mark 10:38; Luke 12:50).

In Christian Baptism an individual participates in the death and resurrection of Christ (Romans 6:3-11; Colossians 2:12) and is made a member of Christ (1 Corinthians 1:13; Galatians 3:27; Ephesians 4:5). Baptism works the forgiveness of sins; it delivers one from spiritual death and the devil; and it gives eternal salvation to all who believe in Christ (Acts 2:38; 22:16; Galatians 5:16; 1 Peter 3:21). Baptism also makes an individual a member of the body of Christ, the church (1 Corinthians 12:13; Galatians 3:27-28; Ephesians 5:26). The blessings of Baptism are received by faith (Romans 6:11).

Christian Baptism must include the application of water in the name of the Triune God, Father, Son, and Holy Spirit. The way the water is applied to the individual, however, can vary (John 3:23; Acts 2:38; 8:12, 36; 10:47-48; 16:15, 33). The New Testament makes no distinction between adult and infant baptism.

BARABBAS (bah-RAB-bas, son of Abba). The prisoner that the mob in Jerusalem asked Pilate to free instead of Jesus (Matthew 27:16-26; Mark 15:7-15; Luke 23:18-25; John 18:40).

BARACHEL (BAR-ah-kel, blessed of God). The father of Job's friend Elihu (Job 32:2, 6).

BARAK (BAIR-uhk, lightning). The Israelite whom Deborah, the prophetess and judge, summoned to lead an army against Sisera, commander-in-chief of the king of Canaan. Under Barak's leadership the Israelites defeated the Canaanites and killed Sisera (Judges 4; 5:1, 12; Hebrews 11:32).

BARBARIAN (rude). At first, anyone who did not speak Greek was called a barbarian. The name was used to imply vulgarity and lack of culture. Later, barbarians were those people outside the Greek-Roman culture. When the New Testament talks about barbarians, no slur is intended (Acts 28:4; Romans 1:14; 1 Corinthians 14:11; Colossians 3:11).

BAREFOOT. To go barefoot was a sign of distress or of reverence for a holy place (Exodus 3:5; 2 Samuel 15:30; Isaiah 20:2-4).

BAR-JESUS. A Jewish magician and false prophet in the court of Sergius Paulus. When Bar-Jesus tried to hinder the conversion of Sergius Paulus by interfering with Paul's work, he was struck blind for awhile (Acts 13:6-12).

BAR-JONA (bahr-JO-nah, son of Jonah or son of John). The apostle Peter's last name (Matthew 16:17).

BARLEY. A cereal grain grown in Palestine and neighboring areas (Leviticus 27:16; Ruth 1:22). The Hebrews called it the hairy, bristling thing. It was made into cakes or loaves and was often eaten by the poor (Judges 7:13; 2 Kings 4:42; John 6:9).

BARNABAS (BAHR-nah-buhs, son of exhortation). A Levite from Cyprus whose last name was Joses (Acts 4:36-37). Barnabas was Paul's friend and co-worker (Acts 9:27). He helped Paul at Tarsus and went with him on his first missionary journey and to the council at Jerusalem (Acts 11—15). Because of a disagreement he had with Paul

over John Mark, Barnabas separated from Paul before the second missionary journey (Acts 15:36-41).

In his epistles Paul speaks highly of Barnabas (1 Corinthians 9:6; Galatians 2:1, 9, 13; Colossians 4:10).

BARSABAS, BARSABBAS (BAR-sah-buhs, BAR-sab-uhs, son of Sabas). 1. The last name of Joseph, one of the men nominated by the apostles to take the place of Judas Iscariot (Acts 1:23).

2. The last name of Judas, a member of the church at Jerusalem. He was sent on their behalf to Antioch with Silas, Paul, and Barnabas (Acts 15:22). Judas and Joseph Barsabbas may have been brothers.

BARTHOLOMEW (bahr-THAL-o-myoo, son of Tolmai). One of the 12 apostles (Matthew 10:3; Mark 3:18; Luke 6:14; Acts 1:13). Bartholomew may have been the last name of Nathanael (John 1:45).

BARTIMAEUS (bahr-ti-MEE-uhs, son of Timaeus). A blind beggar at Jericho (Mark 10:46-52).

BARUCH (BAIR-uhk, blessed). 1. Jeremiah's friend, scribe, and fellow prisoner (Jeremiah 32:12; 36:4-32; 43:3-6). Two apocryphal books are attributed to Baruch.

2. One of Nehemiah's co-workers. He helped in rebuilding the wall of Jerusalem (Nehemiah 3:20; 10:6).

BASEMATH (BAS-i-math, fragrance). 1. A Hittite wife of Esau (Genesis 26:34). She is referred to as Adah in Genesis 36:2.

2. Ishmael's daughter. She was Esau's last wife (Genesis 36:3-4, 13, 17). In Genesis 28:9 she is referred to as Mahaloth.

3. One of Solomon's daughters (1 Kings 4:15).

BAT. This animal is classed among the fowls in the Old Testament and is considered unclean (Leviticus 11:19; Deuteronomy 14:18).

BATH. See *measures 3c.*

BATHE. Bathing and cleanliness were practiced by the Hebrew people from earliest times (Ruth 3:3; 2 Samuel 12:20; Song of Solomon 5:3, 12). They associated bathing with cleanliness before God. It held a chief place in their rituals (Exodus 19:10; Leviticus 13—16; 17:15-16).

BATH-SHEBA (bath-SHEE-bah, daughter of oak). The wife of Uriah, the Hittite, an officer in David's army (2 Samuel 11:3-4). After David had arranged Uriah's death on the battlefield, Bathsheba became David's wife (2 Samuel 11:6-27). Four sons, including Solomon, were born to David and Bathsheba (2 Samuel 5:14; 1 Chronicles 3:5).

BDELLIUM (DEL-i-uhm). The name the Greeks gave to a fragrant gum resin. The Old Testament lists it with precious stones (Genesis 2:12; Numbers 11:7).

BEARD. A badge of manly dignity. Tearing, cutting or neglecting one's beard was a sign of mental abnormality, affliction, or mourning (1 Samuel 21:13; 2 Samuel 19:24; Jeremiah 41:4-5). When greeting another person, it was customary to take hold of his beard (2 Samuel 20:9). Men also swore oaths by their beards (Matthew 5:36). Lepers were not allowed to have beards (Leviticus 4:9). The Egyptians shaved their beards (Genesis 41:14). Shaving the corners of the beard, a practice followed by some nationalities but forbidden to the Israelites, was probably part of a heathen religious act (Leviticus 19:27; Jeremiah 9:26).

BEAST. 1. A mammal, not man, distinguished from birds and other land animals (Genesis 1:29-30).

2. Wild animals (Isaiah 13:21; Mark 1:13).

3. Animals, including birds and reptiles (Ecclesiastes 3:18; Acts 28:5).

4. A destructive power that is an enemy of God's kingdom and people (Daniel 7; Revelation 12:3; 13:1-10; 17:3-18). See also *Leviathan.*

5. In Revelation 13:2-18, a beast identified with the Antichrist fights Christians and persuades people to worship the first beast.

BEATITUDES (bee-AT-uh-toods). Declarations of blessedness (Matthew 5:3-11; Luke 6:20-22). Isolated beatitudes appear throughout the New Testament (for example, Matthew 11:6; 13:16; Luke 7:23; John 20:29; James 1:12; 1 Peter 3:14; Revelation 1:3; 14:13). See also *blessing.*

BECHER (BEE-kur, young camel). The second son of Benjamin (Genesis 46:21).

BED. Poor people and travelers often slept on the ground or a mat (Genesis 28:11; Matthew 9:6). Early bedsteads were made of wood, iron, and even ivory (Deuteronomy 3:11; 2 Kings 1:4, 6; Amos 6:4). They had a mattress, pillow, and covering (1 Samuel 19:13; Isaiah 28:20). At times, beds had ornamental trimmings and canopies (Esther 1:6; Amos 6:4). See also *homes; litter.*

BEE. Many Bible passages speak of bees (Exodus 3:8; Deuteronomy 1:44; 1 Kings 14:3; Ezekiel 27:17). These insects are plentiful in Palestine, where they nest in rocks, woods, and the remains of dead animals (Judges 14:8; 1 Samuel 14:25; Psalm 81:16).

BEELZEBUB, BEELZEBUL (bee-EL-zee-bub, bee-EL-zee-bul). The prince of the demons (Matthew 10:25; 12:24; Mark 3:22; Luke 11:15, 18-19). Jesus identified him with Satan (Luke 11:18). See also *Baal-zebub.*

BEER (BEE-ur, well). 1. A place where Israel set up camp (Numbers 21:16-18).

2. A place to which Jotham fled (Judges 9:21).

BEER-LAHAI-ROI (BEE-uhr-lah-high-roy, well of living one who sees me). The well where the Lord appeared to Sarah's handmaid, Hagar, and where Isaac lived for awhile (Genesis 16:6-14; 24:62; 25:11).

BEER-SHEBA (BEE-uhr-SHEE-bah, well of oath, or of seven). A town in southern Judah. The expression "from Dan to Beer-sheba" is used to designate the northern and southern extremities of Israel (2 Samuel 3:10). Abraham made a covenant with Abimelech, and Isaac's servants dug a well there (Genesis 21:31; 26:33).

BEHEMOTH (bi-HEE-mahth). The Hebrew word for hippopotamus (Job 40:15-24).

BEKA, BEKAH (BEE-kah). A half shekel (Exodus 38:26).

BEL (BAHL, lord). Marduk, the patron god of Babylon. The Hebrews called him Merodach (Isaiah 46:1; Jeremiah 50:2).

BELIAL (BEE-li-uhl). In the Old Testament the word *Belial* is not a proper noun but one that means worthlessness, wickedness, or restlessness (Deuteronomy 13:13; Judges 19:22; 1 Samuel 2:12). Belial is personified in 2 Corinthians 6:15.

BELL. Bells of gold were attached to the priests' robes (Exodus 28:33-35; 39:25). People also wore bells on their ankles and put them on horses (Isaiah 3:16-18; Zechariah 14:20).

BELLOWS. A device made of skins and used for blowing the fire of a furnace (Jeremiah 6:29).

BELSHAZZAR (bel-SHAZ-ur, Bel protect king). The son of Nabonidus, the grandson of Nebuchadnezzar, and the last ruler of the Neo-Babylonian Empire (Daniel 5).

BELTESHAZZAR (bel-ti-SHAZ-ur, protected by Bel). The name Ne-

buchadnezzar gave to Daniel (Daniel 1:7).

BENAIAH (bi-NAY-yah, son of the Lord) The son of Jehoiada, the priest (1 Chronicles 27:5). Benaiah was known for his brave deeds (2 Samuel 23:20-21; 1 Chronicles 11:22-23). He was captain of David's bodyguard and, later, commander-in-chief of Solomon's army (2 Samuel 8:18; 1 Kings 2:34-46).

BEN-AMMI (ben-AM-ee, son of my kindred). Lot's son. He is the ancestor of the Ammonites (Genesis 19:38).

BENE-JAAKAN (BEE-ni-JAY-ah-kuhn, sons of Jaakan). A place in the wilderness where the Israelites camped (Numbers 33:31-32).

BEN-HADAD (ben-HAY-dad, son of Hadad). The name of two or three Syrian rulers. 1. Ben-hadad I was king of Damascus at the same time as Asa ruled Judah. Ben-hadad helped Asa oppose Baasah, king of Israel (1 Kings 15:18-21; 2 Chronicles 16:1-6).

2. Another king named Ben-hadad defeated King Ahab of Israel (1 Kings 20:1-34). Then in the days of Jehoram he again attacked Israel (2 Kings 6:24—7:20; 8:28). He was killed by Hazael, who took over his throne (2 Kings 8:7-15). Some people identify him with Ben-hadad I.

3. Ben-hadad II, son of Hazael. When Jehoahaz ruled Israel, first Hazael and then his son Ben-hadad II attacked the 10 tribes (2 Kings 13:3-13). On three different occasions, however, Josiah was able to defeat Ben-hadad II and recover the cities of Israel (2 Kings 13:22-25).

BENJAMIN (BEN-jah-muhn, son of right hand). 1. The youngest son of Jacob and Rachel. Just before she died, Rachel named him Benoni (son of my sorrow), but Jacob renamed him Benjamin (Genesis 35:16-20). Jacob loved Benjamin very much (Genesis 42).

2. The tribe that descended from Benjamin (Genesis 49:27). When Joshua divided the land among the 12 tribes, the tribe of Benjamin received territory between Judah and Ephraim (Joshua 18:11-28). Saul, the first king of Israel, and Paul, the apostle, were Benjaminites (1 Samuel 9:1-2; Philippians 3:5).

BENJAMIN, GATE OF. A gate in Jerusalem (Jeremiah 20:2).

BEN-ONI (ben-O-nigh, son of my sorrow). See *Benjamin 1.*

BEOR (BEE-awr, torch). Balaam's father (Numbers 22:5; 2 Peter 2:15).

BERA (BEE-rah). The king of Sodom in the days of Abraham (Genesis 14:2).

BERACAH, BERACHAH (BER-ah-kah, blessing). 1. A Benjaminite who helped David at Ziklag when David was fleeing from Saul (1 Chronicles 12:3).

2. A valley in Judah near Tekoa. Jehoshaphat celebrated his victory over the Ammonites and Moabites there (2 Chronicles 20:26).

BEREA, BEROEA (bi-REE-ah). A city in Macedonia (Acts 17:10-14; 20:4). On his second missionary journey Paul started a church there.

BERNICE (BUR-NEE-si, bringing victory). The oldest daughter of Herod Agrippa. She and her brother Agrippa listened to Paul's defense at Caesarea (Acts 25:23; 26:30).

BERYL (BER-il). One of the precious stones in the high priest's breastpiece (Exodus 28:20; 39:13).

BETHANY (BETH-ah-ni, house of affliction). A village on the Mount of Olives about two miles from Jerusalem (Matthew 21:17; Luke 19:29). Bethany was the home of Mary, Martha, and Lazarus (John 11:1). Today it is el 'Azariyeh.

BETH-AVEN (beth-AY-ven, house of nothingness). 1. A town east of Bethel, near Ai (Joshua 7:2).

2. Bethel (Hosea 4:15).

BETH-CAR (BETH-kahr, house of the lamb). A place to which the Israelites pursued the Philistines (1 Samuel 7:11).

BETHEL (BETH-uhl, house of God). A town about 12 miles north of Jerusalem (Genesis 28:19). Abraham camped near it (Genesis 12:8). Originally it was called Luz by the Canaanites, but after his vision Jacob renamed it Bethel and built an altar there (Genesis 28:11-19).

In the division of territories Bethel was assigned to Benjamin (Joshua 18:13). Later the tribe of Ephraim captured it (Judges 1:22-26). The ark was brought to Bethel from Shiloh (Judges 20:1, 27). When Jeroboam was king, he set up a golden calf in Bethel and made it a center of idolatry (1 Kings 13:1-32). The children of Bethel mocked Elisha (2 Kings 2:23-24). Its ruins are called Beitin.

BETHESDA (bi-THEZ-dah, probably means house of twin outpourings). A spring-fed pool at Jerusalem that has five porches (John 5:2). In 1888 such a pool, probably Bethesda, was found near St. Anne's Church.

BETHLEHEM (BETH-li-uhm, house of bread). A town six miles south of Jerusalem. Originally it was called Ephrath or Ephrathah, but after the conquest of Canaan, it was renamed Bethlehem-judah to distinguish it from Bethlehem of Zebulun (Judges 17:7). In Micah 5:2 it is referred to as Bethlehem Ephrathah. Bethlehem was the burial place of Rachel, the home of Ruth, and the birthplace of David and Jesus (Genesis 35:19; Ruth 1:19; 1 Samuel 17:12; Matthew 2:1-2).

2. A town in Zebulun (Joshua 19:15).

BETH-PEOR (beth-PEE-awr, house of Peor). A place in Moab where Israel camped while fighting Sihon and Og (Deuteronomy 3:29; 4:46; Joshua 13:20). Moses was buried in the valley opposite Beth-Peor (Deuteronomy 34:6).

BETH-PHAGE (BETH-fah-jee, house of figs). A village near Bethany not far from the descent of the Mount of Olives (Matthew 21:1; Mark 11:1).

BETHSAIDA (beth-SAY-i-dah, house of fishing). 1. A city on the Sea of Galilee, probably near Capernaum (John 1:44, 12:21). Bethsaida was the home of Peter, Andrew, and Philip. Along with Chorazin and Capernaum, Bethsaida was rebuked by Jesus for not receiving His teachings (Matthew 11:21; Luke 10:13).

2. Another Bethsaida on the east side of the Sea of Galilee. On one occasion Jesus fed 5,000 people there (Luke 9:10-17). Another time He restored sight to a blind man (Mark 8:22-26).

BETH-SHAN, BETH-SHEAN, BETH-SAN (beth-SHAN, beth-SHEE-uhn, beth-SAN, house of security, or house of Shahan). A fortress city strategically located in the Valley of Jezreel. Dating to the early part of the third millenium B.C., Beth-shan was under Egyptian rule for three centuries. Under Joshua, Beth-shan was allotted to the tribe of Manasseh. The tribe found the city too formidable to conquer, however, because of the Philistines who held the city with their chariots of iron (Joshua 17:11-16). After Saul died on Mount Gilboa, the Philistines hung his body on the wall of Beth-shan, put his armor in the temple of Ashtoreth, and placed his head in the temple of Dagon (1 Samuel 31:10-13; 1 Chronicles 10:10).

BETH-SHEMESH (beth-SHEE-mesh, house of sun). A city in northern Judah set aside for priests (Joshua 15:10; 21:16). There Je-

hoash, king of Israel, defeated Amaziah of Judah and took him prisoner (2 Kings 14:11, 13). While Ahaz was king, Beth-shemesh was occupied by the Philistines (2 Chronicles 28:18). During one battle the Philistines captured the ark of the covenant, but a plague convinced them to return it. They put the ark on a cart pulled by cattle and headed it towards Beth-shemesh (1 Samuel 6:1-21).

BETHUEL (bi-THYOO-uhl, house of God). The nephew of Abraham and father of Laban and Rebecca (Genesis 22:20-24; 24:29).

BETROTHAL (bi-TROTH-uhl). See *marriage.*

BIBLE (book). The name given to the collection of 39 Old Testament and 27 New Testament books. See also *canon.*

BIDKAR (BID-kahr). Jehu's captain (2 Kings 9:25).

BIER. A stretcher used to carry the bodies of those who had died to their graves (2 Samuel 3:31; 2 Chronicles 16:14; Luke 7:14).

BILDAD (BIL-dad, Bel has loved). A Shuhite who was one of Job's three friends (Job 2:11). Bildad made three speeches (Job 8; 18; 25).

BILGAH (BIL-gah, cheerful). The head of the 15th division of priests during David's time (1 Chronicles 24:14).

BILHAH (BIL-hah). Rachel's handmaid and Jacob's concubine. Bilhah was the mother of two of Jacob's sons, Dan and Naphtali (Genesis 29:29).

BINDING AND LOOSING. See *key.*

BIRD. The Bible mentions a number of birds, classifying them as clean and unclean (Leviticus 11:13-19; Deuteronomy 14:11-19). It particularly describes the characteristics of the eagle, hawk, and ostrich (Job 39.13-30; Matthew 6:26). People in Bible times ate bird's eggs (Isaiah

10:14; Luke 11:12).

BISHLAM (BISH-lam). A Persian officer who complained to Artaxerxes about the rebuilding of Jerusalem (Ezekiel 4:7).

BISHOP. 1. According to Septuagint usage a bishop was a person who supervised matters in religion, the state, or the army (Numbers 4:16; Judges 9:28; 2 Kings 12:11; 2 Chronicles 34:12, 17).

2. The New Testament uses the word *bishop* as another title for a presbyter or elder (Titus 1:5, 7; 1 Timothy 3:1; 4:14; 5:17, 19). Anyone who ruled, supervised, or cared for the church was called a bishop (Acts 20:17, 28; Romans 12:8; 1 Peter 5:2).

BITHYNIA (bi-THIN-i-ah). A country in northwest Asia Minor whose capital was Nicaea. Although Paul and his companions wanted to bring the Gospel to Bithynia, they did not, because the Holy Spirit was leading them to Europe instead (Acts 16:6-10). Nevertheless, there were Christians in Bithynia in the first century. Peter greets them in his letter (1 Peter 1:1).

BITTER, BITTERNESS. 1. The opposite of sweet (Exodus 15:23).

2. Sorrow, trouble (Exodus 1:14; Job 7:11).

3. Inner displeasure (Ephesians 4:31).

4. Evil (2 Samuel 2:26).

5. Hostile wickedness (Acts 8:23).

6. Wickedness that corrupts (Hebrews 12:15).

BITTER HERBS. Plants such as lettuce, endive, horseradish, and water cress. The Israelites ate bitter herbs in the Passover feast to remind themselves of their slavery in Egypt (Exodus 12:8; Numbers 9:11).

BITUMEN (bi-TYOO-muhn, slime). A mineral pitch or asphalt used for sealing together wood, bricks, and the like (Genesis 11:3; 14:10; Exodus 2:3). Bitumen pits were located along the Euphrates and Dead Sea.

BLASPHEMY (BLAS-fi-mee). Speaking evil of God (Psalm 74:10; Revelation 16:9). Blasphemy was punished by stoning (Leviticus 24:16). False charges of blasphemy were brought against Naboth, Stephen, and Jesus (1 Kings 21:10-13; Matthew 26:65-66; Acts 6:11).

BLASPHEMY AGAINST THE HOLY SPIRIT. See *sin, unpardonable*.

BLEMISH. Any spot or deformity (Leviticus 21:18-20; 22:20-24).

BLESSING. Something that makes one happy. 1. God blesses (Genesis 12:1-3; 2 Samuel 6:11).

2. Godly people can give blessings by asking God to bestow His favor on an object or person (Genesis 12:2; 27:28-29; Numbers 23—24).

3. God's blessing can also be a direct application of His grace through the Word (Genesis 48:17-19; Numbers 6:22-27; Matthew 19:13).

4. Well-known blessings include the Mizpah, the Aaronic blessing, and the apostolic blessing (Genesis 31:49; Numbers 6:11-17; 2 Corinthians 13:14).

BLINDNESS. Since blindness was common in Bible times, blind beggars are often mentioned in the Scriptures (Matthew 9:27; 12:22). Some ancient tribes blinded the people they captured (Judges 16:21; 1 Samuel 11:2). God told the Israelites to be kind to blind people (Leviticus 19:14; Deuteronomy 27:18).

BLOOD. Because blood contains the essence of human and animal life and is necessary for that life, the two were often thought of as the same thing (Genesis 9:4; Leviticus 17:11, 14; Deuteronomy 12:23). The Israelites were forbidden to eat blood or the flesh of animals from which the blood had not been carefully removed (Genesis 9:4; Acts 15:20, 29).

Under Mosaic law the blood of animals was used in all offerings for sin, for "without the shedding of blood there is no forgiveness of sins" (Hebrews 9:22). These Old Testament offerings pointed forward to Christ's supreme sacrifice on Calvary that took away the sins of the world. The expression "the blood of Christ" refers to His atoning death (1 Corinthians 10:16; Ephesians 2:13; 1 Peter 1:2, 19).

BLOODGUILT. The guilt of murder (Exodus 22:2-3; 1 Samuel 25:26, 33; Hosea 12:14).

BLOT. To destroy or abolish. To blot out sin is to fully remove it (Isaiah 44:22). To blot people out of God's book is to cut them off from fellowship with God and His people and to give them over to eternal death (Exodus 32:32; Psalm 69:28).

BOANERGES (bo-ah-NUE-jeez, sons of thunder). A name Christ gave to James and John (Mark 3:17).

BOATS. Biblical references to boats within Palestine are not numerous because the Hebrew people were, for the most part, farmers not seagoers. There were small fishing and passenger boats on the Sea of Galilee, however, and perhaps small boats or ferry boats on the Jordan River (2 Samuel 19:18; Matthew 4:21; 9:1; Mark 1:19; John 6:17).

Solomon built a fleet of ships at Ezion-geber on the Red Sea (1 Kings 9:26). His fleet sailed the Mediterranean with the Phoenician navy of King Hiram (1 Kings 10:22; 2 Chronicles 9:21). Later Jehoshaphat and Ahaziah also built ships at Ezion-geber (2 Chronicles 20:35-37).

The Bible frequently refers to the ships of other nations (Proverbs 31:14; Psalm 107:23). Luke's account of Paul's voyage to Rome is a good picture of the adventures at sea during New Testament times (Acts 27—28).

BOAZ (BO-az). 1. A wealthy Bethlehemite who was a relative of Elimelech, Ruth's father-in-law. Boaz married Ruth. They had a son, Obed, who became David's grandfather. Obed was an ancestor of Jesus (Ruth; Matthew 1:5).

2. The left pillar in the porch of Solomon's temple (1 Kings 7:21; 2 Chronicles 3:17; Jeremiah 52:21).

BOIL. An inflamed open sore (Exodus 9:8-11). Boils were a common symptom of leprosy (Leviticus 13:18-20). Hezekiah and Job suffered from boils (2 Kings 20:7; Job 2:7).

BONE. Often used figuratively to show a close relationship (Genesis 2:23; Judges 9:2; 2 Samuel 19:12).

BOOK. See *writing*.

BOOTH. A temporary hut or shelter, usually made of tree branches (Genesis 33:17; Leviticus 23:34; Job 27:18; Isaiah 1:8). See also *homes*.

BOOTY. Spoils of war. It consisted of everything of value in a conquered town. At the conquest of Canaan the Israelites were told to kill all living things and destroy all idols and the places where idols were worshiped (Numbers 33:52). Often the army took the spoils and divided them among themselves, the rest of the people, and the Levites (Numbers 31:26-47). David made a law that the troops who guarded the baggage should share in the spoils of war equally with those who did the fighting (1 Samuel 30:21-25).

BOTTLE. Containers made of skin or earthenware (Jeremiah 19:10-11; Matthew 9:17).

BOTTOMLESS PIT. See *abyss.*

BOW. See *archery.*

BOWING. A combination of bending the knee and moving the head forword. Bowing was a respectful way to greet someone (Genesis 23:7; 1 Kings 1:53).

BOX. A flask or jar for holding oil or perfume (2 Kings 9:1, 3; Mark 14:3).

BOZRAH (BOZ-rah). A city in Edom (1 Chronicles 1:43-44). Both Amos and Jeremiah predicted its destruction (Amos 1:12; Jeremiah 49:13, 22). Today it is called Buseirah.

BRAMBLE. See *thorns and thistles.*

BRANCH. A title applied to the Messiah as David's offspring (Jeremiah 23:5; 33:15; Zechariah 3:8; 6:12). A branch is also a symbol of prosperity (Genesis 49:22).

BRAZEN SERPENT. When the children of Israel complained in the wilderness against God and Moses, God sent fiery serpents against them. Many of the people died. Then God told Moses to make a serpent of bronze (or copper) and set it on a pole. Whenever a person who had been bitten by a snake looked at this bronze serpent, he or she lived (Numbers 21:5-9). This bronze serpent was a type of Christ (John 3:14).

BRAZIER. See *hearth 1; homes.*

BREASTPIECE, BREASTPLATE.
1. A sacred article of dress worn by the high priest (Exodus 28; 29:5).
2. Armor designed to protect the body in battle (1 Kings 22:34; Isaiah 59:17; Revelation 9:9).

BREECHES. See *dress.*

BRIMSTONE. Sulphur (Genesis 19:24). Often used figuratively for destruction and punishment (Job 18:15; Psalm 11:6; Isaiah 34:9; Revelation 21:8).

BROOK. A small stream that usually flows only during the rainy season (Deuteronomy 2:13). The Kishon and Kidron were brooks (1 Kings 18:40; 2 Samuel 15:23).

BROOM. A bush with many, almost leafless branches and pinkish white flowers (1 Kings 19:4-5; Job 30:4; Psalm 120:4).

BROTHER. 1. A male who has the same parents or the same mother or father as oneself (Genesis 27:6; 38:1; Judges 8:19).
2. A male relative, such as a nephew or cousin (Genesis 14:16; Matthew 12:46).
3. Someone from the same tribe (Numbers 8:26; Nehemiah 3:1).
4. Someone from the same country (Judges 14:3; Matthew 5:47).
5. A friend or companion (Job 6:15; Nehemiah 5:10).
6. Someone who is greatly loved (2 Samuel 1:26).
7. A peer (Matthew 23:8).
8. All men (Genesis 9:5; Matthew 5:22; 18:35).

BROTHERS OF THE LORD. James, Joses, Simon, and Judas are referred to as the Lord's brothers (Matthew 13:55). Sisters of Jesus are also mentioned in Matthew 13:56. There are differences of opinion as to whether these are full brothers and sisters, cousins, or children of Joseph by a former marriage.

BUCKLER. See *armor, arms.*

BULL, BULLOCK. A male ox or cow (Psalm 22:12; Ezekiel 4:15). A bullock is a young bull (Isaiah 65:25). A wild bull or wild ox refers to an antelope (Deuteronomy 14:5; Isaiah 51:20).

Oxen were used for plowing, threshing, pulling wagons, and bearing burdens (Numbers 7:3; Deuteronomy 22:10; 25:4; 1 Chronicles 12:40). People also ate them and sacrificed them (Deuteronomy 14:4; 1 Kings 1:9).

BULRUSH. A marsh plant, such as the papyrus, or a swamp plant, such as the reed or rush (Exodus 2:3; Isaiah 18:2; 19:15).

BURIAL. The people of Israel nearly always buried their dead, usually within 24 hours. When a person died, his or her body was washed, wrapped in a cloth or closely bound in bands, and, if the person had been wealthy, annointed with spices and perfumes (Jeremiah 34:5; Matthew 27:59; John 11:44; 12:7; Acts 9:37). Then it was carried on a bier to the grave (2 Samuel 3:31; Luke 7:14). Although holes in the ground were sometimes used as places of burial, often the grave was a cave or hole cut out of rock (Genesis 25:9-10; Matthew 27:60).

When a person died, friends expressed their grief by loudly weeping and wailing (Mark 5:38). Often professional mourners were hired (Jeremiah 9:17).

BURNT OFFERING. See *sacrifice.*

BUSHEL. See *measures 2h.*

BUTLER. An officer who was in charge of wines and drinking vessels in a royal household (Genesis 40; 41:9). Butlers were sometimes called cupbearers (1 Kings 10:5; 2 Chronicles 9:4). Nehemiah was the cupbearer of King Artaxerxes (Nehemiah 1:11).

BYPATH, BYWAY. Paths off the main roads. Byways were traveled to escape danger (Judges 5:6). Figuratively, bypaths describe departure from the way of God (Jeremiah 18:15).

CAESAR (SEE-zur). A title given to all the Roman emperors after Julius Caesar (Matthew 22:17; John 19:15; Acts 17:7). The New Testament mentions by name the caesars Augustus, Tiberius, and Claudius (Luke 2:1; 3:2; Acts 11:28). Nero is also referred to in Acts 25:8. He was the caesar under whom Peter and Paul were martyred.

CAESAREA (Ses-ah-REE-ah, for Caesar). A city built during the period between 25 to 13 B.C. by Herod the Great. Caesarea, located about 23 miles south of Mount Carmel, was the Roman capital of Palestine. It was the home of Cornelius, in whose house Peter preached to the Gentiles (Acts 10:1, 24; 11:11). Philip also stopped in Caesarea at the end of his preaching tour (Acts 8:40).

Paul visited Caesarea a number of times (Acts 9:30; 18:22; 21:8, 16). The Roman commander at Jerusalem also sent Paul to Caesarea to be heard by Felix. From there Paul was sent to Rome (Acts 23:23, 33; 25). Today Caesarea is known as Kaisariyeh.

CAESAREA PHILIPPI (Ses-ah-REE-ah fi-LIP-igh). A city at the foot of Mount Hermon. Philip the Tetrarch, Herod's son, enlarged the city and called it Caesarea Philippi to distinquish it from the other Caesarea. Peter made his well-known confession, ''You are the Christ, the Son of the living God,'' in Caesarea Philippi (Matthew 16:13-20).

CAIAPHAS (KAY-yah-fahs). The son-in-law of Annas. Caiaphas was the high priest during the time of Jesus' public ministry and crucifixion (Matthew 26:3, 57; Luke 3:2). After Jesus raised Lazarus from the dead, Caiaphas advocated putting Jesus to death. Caiaphas was afraid that the people would believe in Jesus and that this would lead to the destruction of their holy place and nation by the Romans (John 11:45-50). So he and the chief priest planned Jesus' death (Matthew 26:3-5). After Jesus' arrest, He was brought before Caiaphas. Caiaphas said Jesus was guilty of blasphemy and sent Him to the Roman governor Pilate with the recommendation that Jesus be put to death (Matthew 26:57; John 18:28).

Caiaphas also took part in the trial of Peter and John (Acts 4:6-22).

CAIN (KAYN, acquisition, spear). The oldest son of Adam and Eve. He made his living by farming. Cain killed his brother Abel (Genesis 4). See also *Abel, I.*

CALEB (KAY-luhb, dog). The son of Jephunneh and 1 of the 12 spies whom Moses sent into Canaan (Numbers 32:12). When the spies returned, only Caleb and Joshua encouraged the people to take the land (Numbers 13:6—14:9). Because of his faithfulness, Caleb was allowed to enter the Holy Land. When the land was distributed, Caleb received Hebron (Joshua 14).

CALENDAR. See *time.*

CALF. A young bull or cow. The Hebrews considered a "fatted calf" to be the best possible food (Genesis 18:7; 1 Samuel 28:24; Luke 15:23).

While Moses was receiving the tablets of the Law on Mount Sinai, Aaron made an image of a calf out of gold and set it up in the wilderness for the people to worship (Exodus 32:4).

Jeroboam also set up two golden calves, one at Bethel and one at Dan (1 Kings 12:28-29). At first these images were viewed as symbols of God, but soon they came to be worshiped as common idols. Calf worship was denounced (Hosea 8; 10; 13).

CALVARY (KAL-vah-ree). A place outside the city gate of Jerusalem where Christ was crucified and near where He was buried (Matthew 28:11; John 19:17-18; 41; Hebrews 13:11-13).

The word *Calvary* is the Latin rendering of the Greek word for skull. The Hebrew word for skull, *Golgotha*, is also used to refer to this place (Matthew 27:33; Mark 15:22; John 19:17). Its name may be due to the shape of the hill or to the number of executions carried out there.

CAMEL. In Bible times one-humped Arabian camels or dromedaries were valued animals. Some were used as pace animals and were frequently found in caravans, carrying heavy loads of goods across the hot, sandy land (2 Kings 8:9). Others were bred for riding, often traveling 60 to 75 miles per day (Isaiah 66:20).

Camels were considered a source of wealth (Judges 7:12; 2 Chronicles 14:15; Isaiah 30:6). Abraham had camels among his livestock (Genesis 12:16). Job had 3,000 camels before he lost everything and 6,000 after God restored his fortune (Job 1:3; 42:12).

Because camels were unclean, the Israelites were not allowed to eat them (Leviticus 11:4). They did make clothing, however, from the camels' hair (2 Kings 1:8; Zechariah 13:4; Matthew 3:4).

CAMP, ENCAMPMENT (place of pitching a tent). The place where an army or other body of transient people set up their tents (Exodus 14:9;

1 Samuel 4:1, 5; 2 Kings 7:7). Camps were erected both for short periods of time and as temporary dwellings.

When the Israelites were in the wilderness, they kept clean and orderly camps. They patterned their camps after a square, with an equal number of tribes on each side and the tabernacle and Levites in the center (Numbers 1:47—2:34; 3:14-39).

CANA (KAY-nah). A town in Galilee near Nazareth (John 2:1-11; 4:46; 21:2).

CANAAN (KAY-nuhn). 1. One of Ham's sons (Genesis 10:6). His descendants occupied Canaan and took their name from that country (Genesis 10:15-19).

2. Canaan, one of the old names for Palestine, was the country between the Jordan and Mediterranean (Exodus 6:4; Numbers 34:3-12). After the people of Israel captured the land, it was referred to as the Holy Land (Zechariah 2:12).

CANAANITE (KAY-nahn-ight). 1. A person who lived in Canaan (Genesis 10:18-20; Numbers 13:29; Joshua 11:3). The Canaanites were talented people who early developed arts and sciences. Their language included Phoenician and Ugaritic. Their religion, however, was immoral, centering around wargods and fertility goddesses. They worshiped such well-known deities as El, Baal, Astarte, and Asherah.

2. Simon the Canaanite, one of the 12 apostles. Although he is referred to by this name in Matthew 10:4, he is usually known as Simon the Zealot.

CANDACE. A queen of Ethiopia mentioned in Acts 8:27.

CANON. The collection of books of the Bible accepted by the church as genuine and inspired. By New Testament times the 39 books of the Old Testament were already recognized as canonical (Romans 3:2). Although a few of the 27 New Testament books were questioned for awhile, they gradually found their way into the canon.

CAPERNAUM (kah-PUR-nay-uhm, town of Nahum). A city on the northwest coast of the Sea of Galilee (Matthew 4:13; John 6:24). Capernaum had its own customs station and synagog (Matthew 9:9; Luke 7:5). It was the headquarters of Jesus and the apostles and the scene of many miracles (Matthew 9:1; Mark 2:1).

CAPPADOCIA (Kap-ah-DO-shi-ah). A province in the eastern part of Asia Minor. People from Cappadocia were present when the Holy Spirit descended upon the disciples at the Feast of Pentecost (Acts 2:9). Later Peter wrote a letter to the exiles of the Dispersion that included those who lived in Cappadocia (1 Peter 1:1).

CAPTAIN. As a military title, *captain* was applied broadly to any officer who held a leadership position, from a commander-in-chief to a commander of the body guard (Genesis 21:22; 37:36). The captain of the temple was not a military officer but a priest who was in charge of the temple guard (Acts 4:1). Christ is called the Captain of our salvation (Hebrews 2:10).

CAPTIVITY. In the Old Testament the term *captivity* mainly refers to the subjection of God's people to their enemies, especially in a foreign land. Over a period of years the 10 tribes of the Northern Kingdom (Israel) were taken prisoner by the Assyrian kings Tiglath-pileser, Shalmaneser, Sargon II, and Esarhaddon (2 Kings 15:29; 17:3, 5; 1 Chronicles 5:26). The Southern Kingdom (Judah) was taken captive in stages by King Nebuchadnezzar of Babylon (2 Kings 18:13; 24:14; 25:11; 2 Chronicles 36:20). The prophets Ezra and Nehemiah describe the return of God's captive people to their homeland.

In the New Testament unbelievers are described as captives of the devil and his kingdom (Galatians 4:3, 8). But Jesus announced that He came to set people free from the devil and sin (Luke 4:18). By His death and resurrection Jesus captured sin, death, and the devil (Ephesians 4:8).

CARAVAN (KAR-ah-van). A group of traveling merchants, pilgrims, or others who joined together for a mutual purpose or for protection. These people often used camels, donkeys, and horses to carry their goods (Genesis 37:25). They followed regular routes, such as the famous one leading from Damascus across the Esdraelon to the Mediterranean Sea (Judges 8:11; Job 6:18-19).

CARBUNCLE (KAHR-bung-k'l). A precious gem in the high priest's breastpiece (Exodus 28:17; Ezekiel 28:13; Isaiah 54:12).

CARCHEMISH (KAHR-kuh-mish). A Hittite city on the west bank of the Euphrates River (2 Chronicles 35:20; Isaiah 10:9). In 605 B.C., Nebuchadnezzar of Babylon defeated Egypt in a battle at Carchemish.

CARMEL (KAHR-mel, garden). 1. A mountainous range of hills in the territory of Asher in Palestine. It averages 1,500 feet in height and runs 12 to 15 miles in length. This range forms the southwest boundary of the Plain of Esdraelon, and on its northwestern end, it juts into the Mediterranean Sea (Joshua 19:26; 2 Kings 2:25; Jeremiah 50:19). Elijah defeated 850 heathen prophets on Mount Carmel (1 Kings 18).

2. A town in Judah about seven miles southeast of Hebron (Joshua 15:55). It was the home of Nabal, the first husband of David's wife Abigail (1 Samuel 25:2-44).

CARPENTER. A general term for a builder who worked in wood, stone, and metal (2 Samuel 5:11; 2 Chronicles 24:12; Isaiah 44:13). Joseph, Mary's husband, was a carpenter (Matthew 13:55; Mark 6:3). See also *trade*.

CART. A two-wheeled vehicle for carrying people or freight. Carts were pulled usually by oxen (1 Samuel 6:7-16; Amos 2:13).

CASSIA. (KASH-i-ah). An aromatic wood used in anointing oil. It probably tasted like cinnamon (Exodus 30:24; Ezekiel 27:19).

CASTLE. 1. A fortified building or stronghold (Nehemiah 7:2).

2. The tower of Antonia in Jerusalem (Acts 21:37; 22:24).

CATTLE. A term broadly used in the Old Testament to include large or small domestic animals, such as horned cattle, horses, donkeys, camels, sheep, and goats (Genesis 1:24-25; Exodus 12:29; Numbers 20:19; Psalm 50:10; Job 1:3).

CAVE. A hollow place or cavern in the side of a hill or cliff. Caves are often found in areas of limestone, of which Palestine has a great deal. The people in Bible times used caves as dwellings, as places of refuge, and for burials (Genesis 19:30; 23:1-20; 49:29; Judges 6:2; 1 Samuel 14:11; Matthew 27:60). See also *homes*.

CEDAR. Most often the cedar referred to in Scriptures is the tall tree found in Lebanon. The wood of this tree was prized for its use in palaces, temples, idols, and ship masts (2 Samuel 5:11; 1 Kings 5:5-6; Isaiah 44:14-15; Ezekiel 27:5).

CENCHREA, CENCHREAE (Sen-KREE-ah, SEN-kri-ee). A harbor of Corinth visited by Paul (Acts 18:18). Phoebe was a deaconess or servant of the Christian church there (Romans 16:1).

CENSER. A container for burning incense. Censers for the tabernacle were made of copper; those for the temple were made of gold (Leviticus 16:12; Numbers 16:39; 2 Chronicles 4:22)

CENSUS. A numbering and registration of people. The Old Testament records several censuses (Exodus 38:26; Numbers 1:2-3; 26:51; 1 Chronicles 21:1-6; 27:24; 1 Kings 5:15; 2 Chronicles 2:17-18; Ezekiel 2:64). The New Testament mentions the Roman census in Luke 2:1 and Acts 5:37.

CENTURION (sen-TYOO-ri-ahn, hundred). A Roman officer in command of 100 soldiers (Mark 15:39; Luke 7:1-10; Acts 10:1).

CEPHAS (SEE-fuhs, rock). The Aramaic name Jesus gave to Peter (John 1:42; 1 Corinthians 1:12).

CHAFF (CHAF). The leftover part of winnowed grain (Job 21:18; Zeph-aniah 2:2); also straw or dry grass (Isaiah 5:24; Jeremiah 23:28). Figuratively, the word *chaff* often refers to something that has no value or is bad (Matthew 3:12).

CHALDEA (kal-DEE-ah). Originally the southern part of Babylonia on the Persian Gulf; later, nearly all of Babylonia (Genesis 10:10; 11:31; Job 1:17; Isaiah 48:20; Jeremiah 50:10).

CHALDEANS, CHALDEES (kal-DEE-ahnz, kal-DEEZ). People who came from or lived in Chaldea. Their roots can be traced beyond 1,000 B.C. In the 8th century B.C., Chaldean kings conquered and ruled Babylon and began to extend their rule over the then-known world (2 Kings 24:2; 25; Isaiah 13:19-22; Jeremiah 21:4-14; Daniel 1:4). Chaldeans were noted astronomers (Daniel 2:2; 4:7). See also *Babylonia.*

CHALKSTONE. Limestone rock used to make mortar (Isaiah 27:9). See also *lime.*

CHAMBERLAIN (CHAYM-burlin). An important officer, good at keeping secrets, who served a ruler (2 Kings 23:11; Esther 1:10; Acts 12:20). The chamberlain looked after the private chambers or rooms of the ruler's palace.

CHARIOT. A two-wheeled vehicle for travel and war (Genesis 41:43; 46:29; 2 Kings 5:9; Acts 8:28). Israel's enemies used chariots (Exodus 14:7; Joshua 11:4; Judges 4:3; 1 Samuel 13:5). Beginning with the time of David, Israel also used them (2 Samuel 8:4; 1 Kings 9:19; Isaiah 31:1).

CHARMER. See *magic.*

CHASTISEMENT (CHAS-tiz-muhnt). Discipline or action for instruction and correction (Deuteronomy 8:5; Proverbs 13:24; 19:18; 1 Corinthians 11:32; Ephesians 6:4). Chastisement is not punishment for sin.

CHEBAR (KEE-bahr). A river of Chaldea on whose banks Ezekiel had visions (Ezekiel 1:1, 3).

CHEDORLAOMER (ked-or-la-O-mer, servant of god Lagamar). The king of Elam against whom Abraham fought (Genesis 14).

CHEMOSH (KEE-mahsh, subduer). The god of Moab who was worshiped with child sacrifices (Numbers 21:29; 2 Kings 3:27). To please one of his foreign wives, Solomon built a place to worship Chemosh (1 Kings 11:7). Later King Josiah destroyed this place of idol worship (2 Kings 23:13).

CHERETHIMS, CHERETHITES (KER-i-themz, KER-i-thights). A Philistine tribe that lived in southwest Canaan (1 Samuel 30:14; Ezekiel 25:16). Some of the Cherethims were members of David's bodyguard (2 Samuel 8:18; 15:18).

CHERITH (KEE-rith). A brook east of the Jordan where Elijah hid during the first part of the famine he had predicted (1 Kings 17:3, 5).

CHERUB (CHER-uhb). The plural form of this word is cherubim (CHER-ah-bim). The Bible pictures cherubim as winged, heavenly beings with the faces of men and the bodies of lions. Ezekiel describes them as four-winged and four-faced (Ezekiel 1:5-12; 10:1-22).

When God drove Adam and Eve out of Paradise, He put cherubim at the entrance of Eden to guard it (Genesis 3:24). To adorn the ark of the covenant, craftsmen made two golden cherubim and placed them on top of it (Exodus 25:18-22; 37:7-9; Hebrews 9:5). Cherubim were also embroidered on the curtain and veil of the tabernacle (Exodus 26:1, 31). Solomon placed two cherubim in the Holy of Holies in the temple (1 Kings 6:23-28; 8:7).

The Bible pictures the Lord as living between cherubim and as riding on them (Numbers 7:89; 2 Samuel 22:11; Psalm 18:10; 80:1).

CHIEF PRIEST. See *priest.*

CHILEAB (KIL-i-ab). A son of King David and Abigail (2 Samuel 3:3).

CHILION (KIL-i-on, pining). A son of Elimelech and Naomi (Ruth 1:2).

CHINNERETH, CHINNEROTH (KIN-i-reth, KIN-i-rahth, harp). 1. A fortified city of Naphtali on the northwest shore of the Sea of Galilee (Joshua 19:35).

2. The region around the city of Chinnereth. It is often identified with the Plain of Gennesaret (1 Kings 15:20; Matthew 14:34).

3. An old name for the Sea of Galilee (Numbers 34:11; Joshua 11:2). See also *Galilee, Sea of.*

CHLOE (KLO-ee, green grass). A Christian woman who was well known to the Christians at Corinth (1 Corinthians 1:11).

CHRIST (KRIGHST). See *Jesus Christ; Messiah.*

CHRISTIAN (KRIS-chuhn). A follower of Christ. The disciples were first called Christians at Antioch, Syria (Acts 11:26; 26:28; 1 Peter 4:16).

CHRONICLES, FIRST AND SECOND BOOK OF (KRAHN-i-k'lz). Two historical books in the Old Testament. Bible scholars generally believe they were written by one person (perhaps Ezra) and originally formed one book. The books speak of the history of the priests from the death of Saul to the end of the captivity.

Date: 450 to 400 B.C.

Audience: Israelites

Outline: 1. History of Israel's ancestors: geneology from Adam to David (1:1—9:34). 2. History of David (9:35—29:30). 3. History of Solomon, the builder of the temple (2 Chronicles 1:1—9:31). 4. Division of the kingdom (10:1—11:4). 5. Davidic rulers in Judah (11:5—36:23).

CHRONOLOGY (kro-NAHL-o-jee). The science of dating Biblical events. To arrive at these dates, scholars use statements in the Bible, for instance, Luke 3:1-2, as well as historical events and dates. The chronology of a man named Ussher is one well-known system of dating Biblical events. Many scholars do not agree with all of his dates, however.

Dates often given for key events are approximately 2100 to 1800 B.C. for the time of the Patriarchs, 1441 (or sometimes 1290) B.C. for the Exodus, 1000 to 587 B.C. for the period of the kings, around 740 to 600 B.C. for the captivity of Israel, 587 to 400 B.C. for the captivity of Judah, and 6 to 5 B.C. for the birth of Christ. See also *time*.

CHURCH. The church is the collected gathering of God's people. In the Old Testament the word used for church means assembly or congregation (Deuteronomy 23:2; Psalm 149:1; Ezra 10:8). The New Testament speaks of the church both as the Christians gathered in a specific place and as all Christians everywhere of all time (Matthew 16:18; Acts 5:11; 8:1; 1 Corinthians 10:32).

The church draws its life and nourishment from the Gospel in the Word and Sacrament. It passes on its life by preaching and sharing the sacraments (Matthew 28:19, 20; Acts 20:28; 1 Corinthians 4:17; 2 Corinthians 8:18).

According to the New Testament the church belongs to God in Christ (Acts 20:28; 1 Corinthians 1:2; Galatians 1:22; 1 Thessalonians 2:14). It is described as the fellowship of God's people, the bride of Christ, the body of Christ, and a building of which Jesus Christ is the chief Cornerstone (Romans 12:5; Ephesians 2:20-22; 4:4; 5:25-33; 1 Peter 2:9). See also *fellowship*.

CIRCUMCISION (sur-kuhm-SIZH-uhn, cutting around). Removal of the foreskin of the penis. God instituted the rite of circumcision upon Abraham and his descendants (Genesis 17:10). It showed that He would be their God and that they were to belong to Him, worshiping and obeying only Him. While in the wilderness, Moses made circumcision a legal institution (Leviticus 12:3; John 7:22-23). The Hebrew people looked down upon those who were not circumcised (Judges 14:3; 15:18; 1 Samuel 14:6). Some other nations, such as the Egyptians, also practiced circumcision.

Christians in the New Testament era refused to force Gentiles to submit to circumcision (Acts 15:5; Galatians 5:2).

To circumcise one's heart means to purify it so that it will be able and willing to love God (Deuteronomy 10:16; 30:6).

CISTERN. A hole dug in the earth or rock to hold rainwater or water from a spring (Proverbs 5:15; Ecclesiastes 12:6; Isaiah 36:16; Jeremiah 2:13). Empty cisterns were sometimes used as prisons (Genesis 37:22-24).

CITIZEN, CITIZENSHIP. 1. An inhabitant of a city or country (Judges 9:2-20; Luke 15:15).

2. A Roman citizen had special rights, including the right to appeal to the emperor. The rights of Roman citizenship belonged to those who were born Roman citizens, who purchased citizenship, or who received citizenship through special service or favor (Acts 16:37-39; 22:25-29; 23:27).

3. Christians are citizens of heaven, together with the saints (Ephesians 2:19; Philippians 3:20).

CITY OF GOD. See *Jerusalem*.

CITY OF REFUGE. See *refuge, cities of*.

CLAUDIUS (KLAW-di-uhs). The Roman emperor from A.D. 41 to 54. Claudius took over after Caligula. He banished all the Jews from Rome (Acts 18:2).

CLAUDIUS LYSIAS (KLAW-di-uhs LIS-i-uhs). See *Lysias, Claudius.*

CLEOPAS (KLEE-o-pas, of renowned father). One of the two disciples to whom Christ appeared on the way to Emmaus (Luke 24:18).

CLOPAS (KLO-pahs). Another name for Alphaeus. He was the husband of one of the Marys who stood beside the cross (John 19:25).

CLOUD. Most of the time when the Bible refers to clouds, it is speaking figuratively. Clouds show God's power and wisdom (Psalm 135:7; Proverbs 8:28; Nahum 1:3). Sometimes they stand for a great number or for great trouble or danger (Isaiah 44:22; 60:8; Ezekiel 30:3; Hebrews 12:1). Clouds are also a sign of God's presence (Isaiah 19:1).

COAT. See *dress.*

COCK. A male chicken. Cockcrowing is mentioned in Matthew 26:34, Mark 13:35, and Luke 22:34. It refers to the time between 12 and 3 a.m.

COFFER. A box fastened to the cart on which the Philistines returned the ark (1 Samuel 6:8, 11, 15).

COHORT. See *army; band.*

COL-HOZEH (kahl-HO-ze, all-seeing). Baruch's father.

COLLEGE. A suburb of Jerusalem (2 Kings 22:14; 2 Chronicles 34:22).

COLONY. A settlement of Roman citizens in a conquered territory. Often the colonists were retired Roman soldiers who settled in places where they could keep the enemies of the empire in check.

COLOSSAE, COLOSSE (ko-LAHS-ee). An old city of Phrygia. Paul began a church at Colossae on his third missionary trip.

COLOSSIANS, LETTER OF PAUL TO (ko-LAHSH-ahnz). Paul wrote this letter to the church at Colossae probably while he was a prisoner at Rome for the first time. (Some scholars think Paul may have been jailed in Caesarea or Ephesus when he wrote this letter rather than in Rome.)

In his letter, Paul warned the Colossians against false teachers who taught such things as angel worship and severe self-denial. These people were making Christianity a religion based on the Law and said that Jesus was only a lesser God.

    Date: A.D. 52 to 56 or 59 to 61

    Audience: Christians at Colossae

    Outline: 1. Introduction, greetings, thanksgiving, and prayer (1:1-14). 2. The completeness and all-sufficiency of Christ and the Gospel (1:15—2:23). 3. Life in Christ (3:1-4:16). 4. Personal matters and conclusion (4:7-18).

COMMANDMENTS. See *Decalog.*

COMMONWEALTH. See *citizen, citizenship.*

COMMUNION. See *fellowship; Lord's Supper.*

COMPASSION. See *mercy.*

CONANIAH (kahn-ah-NIGH-ah, Lord has established). A Levite who was in charge of the offerings and tithes during King Hezekiah's reign (2 Chronicles 31:12-13).

CONCUBINE (KAHNG-kyoo-bighn). A lesser wife who was often taken from among the purchased slaves or captives (Genesis 16:1; Judges 8:31). Although her status was lower, her rights were protected by the law (Exodus 21:7-9; Deuteronomy 21:10-14).

CONDUIT. A channel cut in the rock or made underground for the purpose of moving water from one place to another (2 Kings 18:17; 20:20; Isaiah 7:3; 36:2).

CONFESS. To acknowledge publicly or make known as one's own. One confesses Christ by acknowledging one's faith in Him and His Gospel and by obeying Him (Matthew 10:32; Luke 12:8). One confesses one's sins by admitting them, either publicly or privately, to God or another person (Psalm 32:5; James 5:16; 1 John 1:9).

2. To acknowledge, praise, and thank God (Isaiah 48:1; Daniel 9:4).

3. To declare openly one's faith (Hebrews 3:1; 4:14).

CONGREGATION. The Hebrew people viewed as one holy, religious group (Numbers 16:3). Sometimes the word *congregation* refers to an assembly of all the people (Exodus 12:6; 35:1); sometimes it refers to the people even when they are not assembled (Exodus 12:3; Leviticus 4:13). The leader of the congregation often represented it (Joshua 23:12; Judges 21:10-20). See also *church*.

CONSCIENCE (KAHN-shuhns). A sense of right and wrong with an inner urge to do right and a guilty feeling if one goes against one's own standard of right and wrong (Acts 23:1; 1 Timothy 1:5; 1 Peter 3:16). A "weak" conscience has a faulty norm (1 Corinthians 8:10-13).

CONSECRATE (KAHN-si-kraht). To set someone or something aside for God. Levites were set apart for the priesthood (Exodus 13:2). Precious metals, persons, nations, fields, and cattle were consecrated to God (Exodus 19:6; Leviticus 27:28; Numbers 6:2-13; Joshua 6:19; 2 Chronicles 29:33).

All Christians are consecrated or set aside for God (1 Peter 2:9). There are also special consecrations. For example, Barnabas and Paul were set aside for the work of the ministry (Acts 13:2). See also *ordination*.

CONTRITION (kun-TRISH-uhn). A sure knowledge of one's sin, grief because of it, and fear of God's punishment (Psalm 51:17; Isaiah 57:15; Luke 15:18; Acts 2:37). Contrition comes before forgiveness (Psalm 34:18; Isaiah 66:2).

CONVERSION (kun-VUR-shuhn). An act of God's grace by which a sinful person is turned around and brought into Christ's kingdom (Colossians 1:13). Conversion is accomplished by the Holy Spirit, who brings the person to faith in Christ through the Word (Psalm 51:13; Isaiah 55; John 3:16; Acts 3:19; 11:21; 26:18; Romans 1:16; 2 Corinthians 3:16; 1 Peter 2:25).

CONVOCATION. A meeting of the people that was called for the purpose of worshiping God (Leviticus 23:2-8; Numbers 28:18-25).

CORAL. The Hebrews highly valued coral, ranking it with precious stones (Job 28:18; Lamentations 4:7).

CORBAN (KAWR-ban). An offering or sacrifice to God (Leviticus 1:2-3; 2:1; 3:1; Numbers 7:12-17). In Mark 7:11, corban refers to money or service dedicated to God.

CORD. Cord was made of flax, animal hides, date tree fibers, or camel hair. It was used for holding together tents, binding prisoners, scourging, and making ship ropes (Exodus 35:18; Judges 15:13; John 2:15; Acts 27:32).

CORINTH (KAHR-inth). A wealthy, worldy Greek city on the isthmus connecting Peloponnesus and the mainland. Corinth was destroyed by the Romans in 146 B.C. and rebuilt by Caesar in 46 B.C. Paul began a church there (Acts 18:1; 20:2-3).

CORINTHIANS, FIRST LETTER OF PAUL TO (KO-RIN-thi-ahnz). While he was in Ephesus on his third missionary journey, Paul wrote this letter to correct the abuses in the church at Corinth and to strengthen the faith of the people there.

Date: A.D. 55 (spring)
Audience: Christians at Corinth
Outline: 1. Paul's ministry and splits within the church (1:1—4:21). 2. Moral problems (5:1—6:20). 3. Marriage (7:1-40). 4. The eating of meat offered to idols (8:1—11:1). 5. Disorders in the worship life of the church (11:2—14:40). 6. The resurrection of the dead (15:1-58). 7. Practical and personal matters (16:1-24).

CORINTHIANS, SECOND LETTER OF PAUL TO (KO-RIN-thiahnz). While in Macedonia on his third missionary journey, Paul wrote this letter to the Corinthians to praise them for their repentance and to speak well of the ministry.
Date: A.D. 55 (fall)
Audience: Christians at Corinth
Outline: 1. Joy over repentance and praise for the ministry (1—7). 2. Collection for the saints in Jerusalem (8—9). 3. Paul's coming visit to Corinth (10—13).

CORNELIUS (kawr-NEEL-yuhs, of a horn). A Roman centurion and the first Gentile convert (Acts 10).

CORNERSTONE. The foundation stone laid at the corner of a building as its starting point (Job 38:6; Isaiah 28:16). Christ is the Cornerstone or Head Stone of the church (Matthew 21:42; Ephesians 2:20; 1 Peter 2:5-7).

COS (KAHS). An island in the Aegean Sea mentioned in connection with Paul's third missionary journey (Acts 21:1).

COULTER (KOL-tur). A plowshare (1 Samuel 13:19-21).

COUNCIL. 1. A group of people gathered for discussion and decision-making (Genesis 49:6; Acts 25:12).
2. The Sanhedrin and lesser courts (Matthew 26:59; Acts 5:34; Mark 13:9). See also *appeal; Sanhedrin.*

COURT, COURTYARD. The enclosed yard of a house, palace, or prison (2 Samuel 17:18; Jeremiah 32:2), or the outer area of the tabernacle and temple (Exodus 27:9; 1 Kings 6:36). See also *homes.*

COVENANT (KUHV-i-nahnt). A mutual agreement between two or more tribes, nations, or individuals to do or refrain from doing something. People called upon God to witness the pacts they made with others (Genesis 21:17; 31:50; Joshua 9:6; 1 Samuel 20:8).

The covenants God made with Noah and Abraham were pledges of His grace (Genesis 9:9-16; 15:7-21). In the covenant God made with Israel, He promised to continue being their God and to care for them. They in turn promised to be His people and keep His commandments (Exodus 24). The prophets spoke of a new covenant that would center in a person (Isaiah 42:6; 49:8; Jeremiah 31:31-34).

In the New Testament covenant one is placed into a right relationship to God through the work of Christ (Hebrews 7:22; 8:6-13; 2 Corinthians 3:6-18). The New Covenant stresses the forgiveness of sins accomplished through the shedding of Christ's blood (Matthew 26:28; Romans 11:26-27). This leads to a new, holy life (Galatians 5:22-26; Hebrews 8—10). See also *Baptism; circumcision; Lord's Supper; Passover.*

CRACKNEL (KRAK-n'l) A type of hard biscuit with holes (1 Kings 14:3).

CREATION. An act of God by which He calls something into being (Genesis 1—2). God is the one who does the creating (subject); the object of His creation is an entirely new thing. God creates by His Word (John 1:3; Ephesians 3:9; Hebrews 1:2).

CRETE, CRETAN, (KREE-tahns). Crete is an island in the Mediterranean Sea about 165 miles long and 6 to 35 miles wide. Paul began a church there (Acts 27:7-13; Titus 1:5-14). It also is called Caphtor.

The people of Crete were referred to as Cretans. They were known for being good sailors and skillful archers. According to Paul they were also untruthful (Titus 1:12). Some Cretans were present in Jerusalem on the Day of Pentecost (Acts 2:11).

CRISPUS(KRIS-puhs, curled). A ruler of the synagog at Corinth who was brought to the Christian faith by Paul (Acts 18:8; 1 Corinthians 1:14).

CROCUS. See *rose*.

CROSS. The cross commonly was found in four forms: (1) The simple upright beam; (2) St. Anthony's cross, which was in the form of the letter *T*; (3) St Andrew's cross, which was in the shape of an *X*; and (4) the Latin cross, with the crossbeam near the upper part of the upright beam ( ). The Greek cross ( ) and the double and triple crosses were additional forms. The cross upon which Christ died may have been of the Latin type (Matthew 27:32-35).

The word *cross* is often used figuratively for the Gospel, for Christ's sufferings, and for that which is suffered as, and as a result of being, a disciple (Matthew 16:24; Galatians 6:14; Ephesians 2:16).

CRUCIFIXION (kroo-sah-FIK-shuhn). A method of killing a person by putting the person on a cross. Crucifixion was practiced by the Egyptians, the Persians, the Greeks, the Romans, and other old civilizations (Genesis 40:19; Ezekiel 6:11). Jesus was crucified by the Romans (Matthew 27; Mark 15; Luke 23; John 19).

CRUSE (KROOZ). A small jar, jug, or shallow saucer used for holding oil or water (1 Kings 17:12; 1 Samuel 26:11; 2 Kings 2:20).

CUBIT (KYOO-bit). See *measures 1d*.

CUP. A small drinking vessel made from a horn or of clay or metal (Genesis 44:2; 1 Samuel 16:13; Matthew 26:27). Figuratively, the word *cup* is used to express one's lot in life (Psalm 11:6; Matthew 26:39; Mark 10:38). See also *homes*.

CUPBEARER. See *butler*.

CURDS. See *food*.

CURSE (KURS). The opposite of bless. On the human level, to curse means to wish evil, harm, or suffering on someone (Genesis 9:25; 49:7); on the divine level, it implies judgment.

God cursed the serpent and the earth after Adam and Eve's fall into sin (Genesis 3:14, 17). God's curse was also spoken on various sins (Deuteronomy 27:15-26). Under the Mosaic law a person who cursed his or her parents was put to death (Leviticus 20:9). Christians are told to bless, not curse, those who curse them (Matthew 5:11; Luke 6:28; Romans 12:14).

CUSH (KUSH). 1. A son of Ham and grandson of Noah. Cush was the father of Nimrod (Genesis 10:8; 1 Chronicles 1:10).

2. The territory in the region of the Tigris and Euphrates Rivers (Genesis 2:13).

CUSHITE (KUSH-ight). A person from Ethiopia (Numbers 12:1).

CUTH, CUTHAH (KUTH, KYOO-thah). A city of Babylonia whose people worshiped Nergal. Sargon, king of Assyria, brought people from Cuth to colonize the area of Samaria that he had sacked in 721 B.C. (2 Kings 17:24, 30).

CYPRESS. A tall fir tree (1 Kings 5:8; Isaiah 14:8).

CYPRUS (SIGH-pruhs). An island about 148 miles long and 50 miles wide in the Mediterranean Sea off the coast of Syria. It was famous for its copper.

Cyprus was the home of many Jewish people. Barnabas came from Cyprus, and Stephen preached there (Acts 4:36; 11:19-20). Paul, Barnabas, and Mark visited there on the first missionary journey (Acts 13:4; 15:39).

CYRENE (sigh-REE-ni). The capital city of Cyrenaica (Tripoli) in northern Africa. It was colonized by Greeks (Matthew 27:32; Mark 15:21; Acts 2:10).

CYRUS (SIGH-ruhs). The founder of the Persian Empire. In 539 B.C. he captured Babylon. Cyrus was a humane king. He issued a decree allowing the captive Hebrews to go back to their native land and rebuild their temple (2 Chronicles 36:22-23; Ezra 1:1-14; Isaiah 44:28). Cyrus died in battle in 530 B.C. See also *Daniel; Ezra.*

DAGON (DA-gahn, may mean grain or fish). A pagan god with the body of a fish and the head and hands of a man. He was the god of natural powers, especially of grain. The Canaanites in Mesopotamia worshiped Dagon, and he was the national god of the Philistines. Temples were built to him at Ashdod and Gaza and in Israel (Judges 16:21-30; 1 Samuel 5:1-7; 1 Chronicles 10:10). Samson destroyed a temple to Dagon at Gaza (Judges 16:30).

DAMASCUS (Dah-MAS-kuhs). An old Syrian city situated on a plateau watered by the Abana and Pharpar Rivers (Genesis 14:15; 2 Kings 5:12). The plateau is about 2,300 feet above sea level and is at the eastern foot of the Anti-Lebanon Mountains. Damascus played an important part in Biblical history. Both David and Jeroboam II captured it (2 Samuel 8:6; 2 Kings 14:28). The rulers of Damascus who played a prominent role in the history of Israel and Judah were Rezon (1 Kings 11:23-25), Ben-hadad (1 Kings 15:19-20; 22:15-37; 2 Kings 8:15; 2 Chronicles 16:3), Hazael (2 Kings 8:15; 13:22-25), and Rezin (2 Kings 16:5, 7-8). Paul was converted to Christianity near Damascus (Acts 9:1-18).

DAMNATION. Those who do not believe in Christ will be separated from God eternally and will receive awful punishment (Matthew 23:33; Mark 16:16; 2 Thessalonians 1:9). This punishment is described as fire, outer darkness, and imprisonment (Matthew 5:26; 8:12; Mark 9:44).

DAN (DAN, judge). 1. The fifth son of Jacob by Bilhah (Genesis 30:5-6).

2. The tribe that descended from Dan and the territory allotted to it in Canaan (Numbers 1:12, 38-39; Judges 1:34-35).

3. A city, formerly named Laish, that was in the extreme north of Palestine. Members of the tribe of Dan captured and renamed it (Joshua 19:47; Judges 18).

DAN TO BEER-SHEBA. An expression used to refer to the length of Palestine (Judges 20:1; 1 Chronicles 21:2). Dan was in the extreme north of Palestine, and Beer-Sheba was in the south.

DANCE. When people wanted to express joy or celebrate victory, they often danced (Judges 11:34; Job 21:11; Luke 15:25). Dancing as part of a religious ceremony or as an act of worship was common among the Hebrews (Psalm 149:3). The women were usually the onces who danced, but occasionally men did as well (Exodus 15:20; Judges 21:21, 23). David, for instance, danced before the ark (2 Samuel 6:14-23). Dancing was also used for bad purposes (Exodus 32:19; Mark 6:22).

DANIEL (DAN-yuhl, God is my judge). A prophet who was born into a princely family of Judah around the time of Josiah's reformation. In 605 B.C., when Daniel was just a young man, King Nebuchadnezzar's soldiers took him captive to Babylon (Daniel 1:1, 3). Nebuchadnezzar's chief servant gave Daniel the Babylonian name

Belteshazzar and trained him in the wisdom of the Chaldeans (Daniel 1:4-5). Even though he was in a foreign land, Daniel continued to have faith in the Lord.

God blessed Daniel with great learning and the ability to interpret dreams (Daniel 1:17). Because of these abilities, Daniel held a high, powerful position in the Babylonian court under Kings Nebuchadnezzar, Belshazzar, Darius, and Cyrus. Throughout his life, Daniel showed concern for his people.

DANIEL, BOOK OF. A prophetic book that is listed among the Writings in the Hebrew Scriptures. It is placed where it is because the author, Daniel, even though he had the gift of prophecy, was a not a prophet by vocation but a government official.

The book is written in both Hebrew and Aramaic. Because it is apocalyptic in character, it is full of symbolic and picture language. For this reason Bible scholars have interpreted it in a number of ways.

The title "Son of Man," which Jesus often used of Himself, is found in Daniel 7:13-14. The New Testament refers to the Book of Daniel in a number of places (Matthew 24:15; Luke 1:19, 26; Hebrews 11:33, 34).

Date: About 547 B.C.

Audience: People of Judah (in captivity)

Outline: 1. Daniel, adviser and official of kings of Babylon (1—6). 2. Daniel, the seer of the Messianic kingdom (7—12).

DARIC (DAR-ik). A Persian gold coin that had the picture of a king with a bow and javelin on one side and a square figure on the other side (1 Chronicles 29:7; Ezra 2:69; 8:27; Nehemiah 7:70-72).

DARIUS (Dah-REE-uhs). A common name for the Medo-Persian rulers.

1. Darius the Mede. He was the son of Ahasuerus and the governor of Babylon under Cyrus (Daniel 5:31; 9:1). He is mentioned often in the Book of Daniel (6:1, 6, 9, 25, 28; 11:1).

Darius was tricked into writing a law that required everyone in the land to worship only him for 30 days. When Daniel broke this law by worshiping the Lord, he was thrown into a lions' den (Daniel 6:4-24).

2. Darius Hystaspes. He ruled from 521 to 486 B.C. and was the fourth and greatest king of the Persian Empire. He renewed the edict of Cyrus that allowed the Hebrews to return to their native land, and he helped them in rebuilding their temple (Ezra 4:5, 24; 5:5-7; Zechariah 1:1, 7; 7:1).

3. Darius the Persian. The last king of Persia, he reigned from 336 to 300 B.C. He was defeated by Alexander the Great (Nehemiah 12:22).

DAVID (DAY-vid, beloved). The second king of Israel. He was from the tribe of Judah and was the youngest son of Jesse of Bethlehem (1 Samuel 16:1-13; 1 Chronicles 2:13-15). After God rejected Saul as king, He sent the prophet Samuel to Bethlehem to anoint David as the next king (1 Samuel 16:13).

When Saul became troubled by evil spirits and bad moods, his servants told him to find a lyre player to soothe him. So Saul sent for David because he had heard that David had great musical gifts. David came and played the harp for Saul (1 Samuel 16:14-23). Later David killed Goliath, the Philistine warrior, when everyone else was afraid to fight him (1 Samuel 17).

David was loved by Jonathan, Saul's son, but feared and envied by Saul (1 Samuel 18). When Saul tried to take David's life, David fled to Gath, where he pretended to be mad (1 Samuel 18:1-3; 19—21; Psalm 34 title). Living in a cave, David gathered 400 men around him who were unhappy with Saul's rule (1 Samuel 22). Among them was Abiathar, the priest. With this group of men David protected the Israelites from the Philistines and bands of robbers. In return for this, the Israelites gave David and his men food (1 Samuel 23—25).

Informed of David's activities, Saul led his men in pursuit of David (1 Samuel 26). Eventually David left Judah and lived in Ziklag. Some time later the Philistines went to war with Saul. When David heard that Jonathan had been killed and that Saul had killed himself, he was sad (1 Samuel 27—30).

Then the tribe of Judah, to which David belonged, elected him king (2 Samuel 2—4). Ish-bosheth, Saul's son, was made king of the rest of the tribes. When Ish-bosheth was killed two years later, David was elected king over all of the tribes (2 Samuel 5). David set to work to unite the tribes into one kingdom. He took Jerusalem from the Jebusites and made it his capital. Then he defeated the Philistines (2 Samuel 5:17-25; 21:15-22; 1 Chronicles 14:8-17). After this he brought the ark to Jerusalem, organized worship, and planned a beautiful temple (2 Samuel 6—7; 1 Chronicles 13; 15—17; 22:7-10).

To ensure the safety of the nation of Israel and to keep it from being polluted by the idolatry of the surrounding countries, David waged war on and subdued the Moabites, Aramaens, Ammonites, Edomites, and Amalekites (2 Samuel 8; 10; 12:26-31).

David was a great king and a man of devout faith in God. Yet he was also a sinful human being. He committed a great sin when he had Bathsheba's husband, Uriah, killed so that he could marry Bathsheba himself (2 Samuel 11:1—12:23; 24; 1 Chronicles 21; Psalm 51). David also had many family problems (2 Samuel 12—19; 1 Kings 1).

David reigned 40 years (2 Samuel 2:11; 5:4-5; 1 Chronicles 29:27). Before he died, he said that Solomon should be the next king (1 Kings 1—2).

David is referred to as the sweet psalmist of Israel (2 Samuel 23:1). Over 73 psalms are said to have been written by him. He was a man after God's own heart and ancestor of Jesus (1 Samuel 13:14; Matthew 22:41-45; Acts 13:36).

DAVID, CITY OF. 1. A part of Jerusalem that David captured. He called it the City of David and made it his capital. It stood on the ridge south of the temple area (2 Samuel 5:6-9).

2. Bethlehem, the birthplace or home of David (Luke 2:4).

DAY. See *time.*

DAY OF ATONEMENT. See *Atonement, Day of.*

DAY OF THE LORD. 1. In the Old Testament the Day of the Lord refers to a day of victory for the kingdom of God, the day upon which evil is defeated. It is that day when God reveals Himself as the Lord, judges evil, and completes His work of redemption among people (Isaiah 1:12; 13:6, 9; Ezekiel 13:5; Zephaniah 1:14).

2. In the New Testament the Day of the Lord refers to the day when Christ comes in the glory of the Father, the day of judgment. To those who do not trust in Christ, that day will be a day of terror (Matthew 10:15; Romans 2:5-6; 2 Peter 3:7, 12); to believers, it will be a day of great joy (Matthew 16:27; 24:30; John 6:39; 2 Corinthians 1:14; Philippians 1:6, 10). See also *Parousia.*

DAY'S JOURNEY. See *measures 1h.*

DEACON (DEE-k'n, minister or servant). Someone who serves (Luke 22:25-27; Mark 10:45; Acts 6:1-2). In the early church deacons were chosen to relieve the apostles of caring for the physical needs of widows and other poor people (Acts 6:1-6). At times Paul uses the word of himself and his ministry (Romans 15:25; Colossians 1:7, 23, 25). Qualifications for the office of deacon are given in Philippians 1:1 and 1 Timothy 3.

DEACONESS (DEE-k'n-es). A female helper in the church (Romans 16:1).

DEAD. 1. A lifeless body (Genesis 23). See also *burial; death.*

2. People who do not have faith in Christ are spiritually dead (Ephesians 2:1).

3. Believers are dead to the Law (Colossians 2:20).

4. Faith that produces no works is dead (James 2:17).

DEAD SEA. See *Salt Sea.*

DEATH. When life ceases. The Bible describes death as separation from the body or departure (Ecclesiastes 12:7; 2 Corinthians 5:1-5; 2 Timothy 4:6). Death is a result of sin (Genesis 2:17; Romans 5:12-14). Because all human beings are sinful, all will die (Hebrews 9:27). For those who believe in Christ, death is the beginning of eternal bliss (2 Corinthians 5:1; Philippians 1:23; 2 Timothy 4:6-8; James 1:12).

DEBORAH (DEB-o-rah, bee). 1. Rebekah's nurse (Genesis 24:59; 35:8).

2. A prophetess and judge of the Israelites who urged Barak to fight Sisera (Judges 4:4-14). After the battle Deborah wrote a song of triumph for the victory (Judges 5).

DEBT. That which is owed to another person. Within certain limits people who were unable to pay their debts could have their property, family, and even their own persons seized as payment (Leviticus 25:25-41; Deuteronomy 15:1-15; 24:6-13).

DECALOG (DEK-ah-log). The Ten Commandments, which God wrote on tables of stone and gave to Moses on Mount Sinai (Exodus 20; 31:18; 32:15-19; Deuteronomy 10:1-5). The Ten Commandments form the basis of God's law. In the Old Testament they are also referred to as the words (Exodus 20:1; 34:28; Deuteronomy 4:13; 5:22).

In the New Testament they are called commandments (Matthew 19:17; Ephesians 6:2). Jesus' interpretation of the commandments is found in Matthew 5:17-48; 19:16-22; Mark 2:24-27; Luke 6:1-10; and 13:10-16. Perfect love is the fulfillment of the commandments (Matthew 22:35-40).

DEDICATION. The act of devoting something to a holy use. For example, the people dedicated the tabernacle, the altar, and the temple, as well as other things to God (Exodus 40; Numbers 7; Deuteronomy 20:5; 2 Chronicles 24:7; Ezra 6:16-17).

The Feast of Dedication, an annual festival of the Jewish people, was the occasion when they remembered the cleansing of the temple (John 10:22).

DEEP. 1. The sea or its deepest part (Genesis 7:11); Job 38:30).

2. See *abyss.*

DEGREES, SONG OF. See *Ascents, Song of.*

DELILAH (De-LIGH-lah, coquette). A Philistine woman from Sorek whom Samson loved. The Philistines bribed Delilah to discover the secret of Samson's strength (Judges 16:4-20).

DEMAS (DEE-mas). One of Paul's co-workers. Demas left Paul and went to Thessalonica (Philemon 24; Colossians 4:14; 2 Timothy 4:10).

DEMETRIUS (De-MEE-tri-uhs, belonging to Demeter). A silversmith at Ephesus (Acts 19:23-30).

DEMONS. Evil spirits who are against God and His work. Jesus called them unclean spirits (Mark 5:8). They form a hierarchy under Satan and take possession of persons in peculiar ways (Matthew 8:16; Mark 1:32; Luke 8:36).

DENARIUS (de-NAIR-i-uhs). A silver coin that looked like a dime. In New Testament times it was equal to a day's wage for people who worked on the land (Matthew 18:28; Mark 6:37; Luke 7:41; John 6:7).

DEUTERONOMY (dyoo-tur-ON-o-mi). The fifth book of the Pentateuch. It is named "Words" in the Hebrew Scriptures because of its opening sentence: "These are the words that Moses spoke to all Israel . . . " (1:1).

The book contains Moses' three farewell addresses and a renewal of Israel's covenant with God. Mosaic authorship is claimed in Deuteronomy 31:9, 24, 26.

Date: 15th to 13th century B.C.

Audience: Israelites

Outline: 1. Covenant history and terms reviewed; its laws set forth and adapted (1—26). 2. The future in view of covenant faithfulness: covenant validity, alternatives, and terms set forth (31—34).

DEVIL. See *demons; Satan.*

DEW. A heavy dew was considered a great blessing. It refreshed the earth and helped make it fertile (Genesis 27:28; Judges 6:37-40). The absence of dew was looked upon as an evil (2 Samuel 1:21; 1 Kings 17:1). Dew was considered a symbol of silent blessing (Deuteronomy 32:2; Psalm 110:3).

DIADEM. A headdress worn by men, women, high priests, and kings (Job 29:14; Isaiah 3:23; 28:5; Ezekiel 21:26). The diadems of olden times were often made of silk and covered

DIAL   DOCTRINE

with gems.

DIAL. See *time.*

DIANA. See *Artemis.*

DIDYMUS (DID-i-muhs, twin). The last name of the disciple Thomas (John 11:16; 20:24; 21:2).

DINAH (DIGH-nah, judged). Jacob and Leah's daughter. Shechem, the prince, raped her (Genesis 30:21; 34).

DIONYSIUS (digh-o-NISH-uhs, devotee of Dionysus). A member of the Areopagus, the supreme court at Athens. Dionysius was converted by Paul (Acts 17:34).

DISCERNING OF SPIRITS. The ability some Christians have that enables them to decide whether others speak by God's Spirit or by false spirits. This ability is given to them by the Holy Spirit (1 Corinthians 12:10).

DISCIPLE (learner). A pupil. The prophets, Jesus, John the Baptizer, and the Pharisees all had followers or disciples (Isaiah 8:16; Matthew 5:1; 9:14; 22:16). The word is used especially of the 12 disciples (Matthew 10:1; 11:1; 20:17). See also *apostle.*

DISCIPLINE. See *chastisement; education.*

DISEASE. The physical diseases and ailments mentioned in the Bible were generally the same as the ones existing today. They include fever (Matthew 8:14), boils (Job 2:7), gangrene (2 Timothy 2:17), dropsy (Luke 14:2), hemorrhoids or ulcers (Deuteronomy 28:27; 1 Samuel 5:6), dysentery (Acts 28:8), itch (Deuteronomy 28:27), scab (Deuteronomy 28:27), scurvy (Leviticus 21:20), leprosy (Exodus 4:6), insanity (1 Samuel 21:15), plague (Exodus 9:3), palsy (Matthew 9:2), worms (Acts 12:23), fractures (Leviticus 21:19), bruises (Isaiah 1:6), lameness (Luke 14:21), impotence (John 5:3), illness (John 5:5), inflammation (Leviticus 13:28), discharge (Leviticus 15:2), sores (Isaiah 1:6), and wounds (Luke 10:34).

Doctors are rarely mentioned in the Old Testament (Genesis 50:2; Job 13:4). By New Testament times, however, medicine was a regular profession (Matthew 9:12; Luke 4:23; Colossians 4:14). Figuratively, sin is described as a great disease (Isaiah 1).

DISPERSION. The body of Israelites scattered about in lands other than their own. Through Moses, God warned the people that they would be scattered in other lands if they departed from the Mosaic law (Deuteronomy 4:27; 28:64-68). These prophecies were largely fulfilled in the Assyrian and Babylonian captivities. Some scattering also took place due to smaller captivities or to migration and traveling.

In New Testament times groups of Jewish people could be found in nearly all parts of the civilized world (Jeremiah 25:34; John 7:35; James 1:1; 1 Peter 1:1).

DIVINATION (div-uh-NAY-shuhn). The practice of foretelling future events or discovering hidden knowledge (1 Samuel 6:2; Ezekiel 21:21; Daniel 2:2). Divination was often practiced by heathen nations, but it was forbidden to Israel (Leviticus 19:26; Deuteronomy 18:10; Isaiah 19:3; Acts 16:16). Rods, arrows, cups, a liver, dreams, and oracles were among the means used for divination (Genesis 44:5; Deuteronomy 13:3; Isaiah 41:21-24; Ezekiel 21:21; Hosea 4:12).

DOCTOR. When the word *doctor* is used in the Bible, it usually refers to teacher (Luke 2:46; 5:17). See also *disease.*

DOCTRINE. Something that is taught; instruction or teaching (Deuteronomy 32:2; Proverbs 4:2; Matthew 15:9; 1 Timothy 4:13; 2 Timothy 3:10).

59

DOG. An unclean animal that ran wild in the streets and was generally despised (Exodus 11:7; 22:31; 2 Samuel 3:8; Matthew 7:6). Sometimes dogs were looked upon more favorably (Luke 16:21). To call someone a dog was an insult. Enemies, lustful people, those who did not appreciate holy things, teachers of false doctrine, Gentiles, and wicked people are referred to as dogs (Deuteronomy 23:18; Psalm 22:16; Matthew 5:26; 7:6; Philippians 3:2; Revelation 22:15).

DOOR. Biblical writers often use the word *door* figuratively. Christ says that He is the Door or the Way to be saved (John 10:9). The word *door* is also used to picture the entrance or way into a sinner's heart, the way to God's grace, and the entrance into heaven (Luke 13:25; Revelation 3:20; 4:1). The picture of God opening a door is a way of saying that He provides the opportunity to preach the Gospel (Acts 14:27; Colossians 4:3). See also *homes.*

DOORPOST. The framework around the doorway. Following an Egyptian custom, the Israelites often wrote important matters on their doorposts (Deuteronomy 6:9).

DORCAS (DAWR-kuhs, gazelle). The Greek name for Tabitha, a Christian woman who lived at Joppa and was well known for her deeds of love. Peter raised her from the dead (Acts 9:36-42).

DOTHAIM, DOTHAN (DO-thay-im, DO-thuhn, two wells). A place near Shechem and Samaria where Joseph was sold to the Ishmaelite traders and where Elisha had a vision (Genesis 37:17-28; 2 Kings 6:13-23).

DOVE. A gentle, timid bird that nests in holes in the sides of cliffs (Song of Solomon 1:15; Jeremiah 48:28; Ezekiel 7:16; Hosea 11:11).

At Jesus' baptism the Holy Spirit appeared in the form of a dove (Matthew 3:16). Poor people often sacrificed turtledoves (Leviticus 12:6-8; Luke 2:24).

DOXOLOGY (doks-AHL-o-jee). Words or songs of praise to God (Psalm 96:6; Luke 2:14; Romans 11:36; Ephesians 3:21; 2 Timothy 1:17).

DRAGON. 1. A sea monster (Psalm 74:13; Isaiah 27:1).

2. A mythical monster used to picture Satan (Revelation 12:3).

3. Egypt (Ezekiel 29:2).

DRAM. See *daric.*

DREAM. Thoughts and ideas one has while sleeping. There are a number of times in the Bible when God revealed something to people, particularly His prophets, through a dream (Genesis 20:3; 28:12; 37:5-11; 40:5; Daniel 2; 4; Matthew 1:20). The ability to interpret dreams was a special gift (Genesis 40:5-23; Daniel 4:19-27).

DRESS. Adam and Eve made clothing out of leaves (Genesis 3:7). Later, people made clothing out of animal skins, hair, wool, linen, and cotton (Genesis 3:21; 38:12; Proverbs 31:13; Isaiah 19:9; Matthew 3:4; 7:15).

Men wore an inner tunic (Exodus 28:4), an outer tunic (Luke 3:11), a mantle or cloak (Exodus 12:34), breeches, a girdle or belt (2 Kings 4:29; Acts 12:8), a cap (Exodus

28:40), and sandals (Matthew 3:11). Women wore similar clothing. Theirs, however, was longer and made of finer material. Women also wore veils and ornaments (Genesis 38:14; Isaiah 3:18-23).

DRINK. The Hebrew people drank water, milk, vinegar and oil, wine, and strong drink (Genesis 14:18; 24:11-18; Leviticus 10:9; Judges 4:19; Ruth 2:14; John 2:3). Strong drink was anything of an alcoholic nature, such as barley beer, cider, honey wine, date wine, and raisin wine.

Strong drink is frequently mentioned in the Bible and is warned against (Genesis 9:21; Proverbs 20:1; Isaiah 5:11; 24:20; John 2:1-11).

DROPSY. See *disease.*

DROUGHT. A period of dryness due to lack of rain. Little rain falls in Palestine from May to October (Psalm 32:4).

DRUSILLA (droo-SIL-ah). The daughter of Herod Agrippa I. She was first the wife of Azizus, king of Edessa, and later of Felix, the governor of Judea. Paul preached before Drusilla and Felix about judgment and righteousness (Acts 24:24-25).

DUMAH (DU-mah). 1. The son of Ishmael. The descendants of Dumah lived in the northwestern part of the Arabian peninsula (Genesis 25:14; 1 Chronicles 1:30; Isaiah 21:11-12).

2. A town in Judah, 10 miles southwest of Hebron (Joshua 15:52).

DURA (DYOO-rah). A plain of Babylon. King Nebuchadnezzar set up an image made of gold on this plain (Daniel 3:1).

DYSENTERY. A disease caused by the inflammation and ulceration of the large intestine (Acts 28:8).

EAR. When priests were consecrated or lepers cleansed, blood was put on their ears (Exodus 24:20; Leviticus 14:14). The Bible describes a disobedient person as having an uncircumcised or heavy ear; and an obedient person, an open ear (Isaiah 50:5; Acts 7:51).

EARTH. A word with a variety of meanings. 1. The world where we live (Genesis 1:1).

2. Dry land (Genesis 1:10).

3. The people who live in the world (Genesis 6:11).

4. Soil (Exodus 20:24).

5. Carnal or unspiritual things (John 3:31; Colossians 3:2).

EAST. The direction towards the sunrise. The Hebrews faced toward the rising sun to determine direction (Genesis 2:8; 3:24; Joshua 12:3).

EAST COUNTRY. The region east of Palestine, especially Syria and Arabia (Genesis 25:1-7).

EAST SEA. See *Salt Sea.*

EAST WIND. A hot, dry wind from the east (Genesis 41:23, 27; Ezekiel 17:7-10).

EASTER (Teutonic goddess of light and spring). By the eighth century the name Easter was applied to Christ's resurrection.

EBAL (EE-buhl). A mountain about 2,700 feet above the sea. It was separated from Mount Gerizim by the Valley of Shechem. Mount Ebal was the mount of cursing; Mount Gerizim was the mount of blessing (Deuteronomy 11:29; 27:12-26; 28; Joshua 8:30-35).

EBED-MELECH (EE-bed-MEE-lek, king's servant). An Ethiopian who heard that Jeremiah had been thrown into a dungeon. Ebed-melech obtained the king's permission to draw Jeremiah out (Jeremiah 38:7-13; 39:15-18).

EBENEZER (eb-uhn-EE-zur, stone of help). A memorial stone that Samuel set up between Mizpeh and Shen to show the place where the Israelites had defeated the Philistines (1 Samuel 7:12).

EBER (EE-bur, beyond). A descendant of Shem. The Hebrews, the Joktanide Arabs, and the Aramaeans descended from Eber (Genesis 10:21-30; 11:14-17; Luke 3:35).

EBONY. A heavy, hard, dark wood used for ornamental work (Ezekiel 27:15).

ECCLESIASTES (e-klee-zi-AS-teez, preacher). The name of this Old Testament book means "one who sits and speaks in the assembly or church." The author of the book reflects on the value of life. He points out that, in theory, there can be no gain in everyday life since the same fate comes to everyone (1:9). Therefore a person's source of satisfaction lies within, in the way the person uses his or her mind and body for work and for pleasure at the proper time (2:24; 3:1-9, 13; 5:18).

The writer also notes that enjoyment of the good things in life is a gift of God (2:24; 25; 3:13; 5:19). In everything a person does, he or she should remember God, the Creator. Since no one can keep the commandments or fear God perfectly, the author's final thought— that one's chief duty is to do these very things (12:13)—prepares the reader for recognizing his or her need for the Gospel.

Date: About 400 to 350 B.C.

Audience: Jews

Outline: 1. The things of this world are vain (1—6). 2. Happiness is found only in the fear of the Lord (7—12).

EDEN (EE-d'n, delight). The garden in which God put Adam and Eve (Genesis 2:15).

EDOM (EE-duhm, red). 1. The name given to Esau because he sold his birthright for a dish of red stew (Genesis 25:30).

2. The people who descended from Esau and their country, located in the southeastern part of Palestine (Judges 11:17; Numbers 34:3; Psalm 83:6). Later, the Greeks renamed this country Idumaea.

EDOMITES (EE-duhm-ights). The descendants of Esau (Deuteronomy 23:7). They lived in the land of Edom, a land which they had taken from the Horites (Deuteronomy 2:12). When the Israelites were on their way to Canaan, they asked permission of the Edomites to pass through their country. But the Edomites said no (Numbers 20:18-21). Saul fought against the Edomites, and David defeated them (1 Kings 11:15-16; 1 Samuel 14:47; 2 Samuel 8:13-14). The Edomites were constant enemies of Israel (1 Kings 11:14-22; 2 Chronicles 21; 25; Isaiah 34:5-8; 63:1-4; Jeremiah 49:17).

EDUCATION. In early times Hebrew children were taught about God and their nation by their parents. Later the Book of Deuteronomy was used as a textbook (Deuteronomy 4:9; 6:6-7). Moses and the prophets were also leaders in education. Before the exile those who were considered wise became teachers. The Book of Proverbs contains ideas about the education of that period.

After the exile Ezra added to the number of teachers (Ezra 8:16). He also encouraged people to read, something which only a few people had been able to do before (2 Kings

5:7; 22:8-10; 23:2). People who made their living at teaching taught in synagog schools.

Around 75 B.C. compulsory education was begun. Students learned their work by memorizing what their teacher said.

EGLON (EG-lahn, calflike). A king of Moab who captured Jericho and made Israel serve him for 18 years. Eglon was killed by Ehud, a judge of Israel (Judges 3:12-30).

EGYPT (EE-jipt). A country largely in northeast Africa with a small part in the Sinai Peninsula (Genesis 10:6). It is also called the country of Ham (Psalm 105:23, 27). Egypt is watered by the Nile River, the longest river in the world. It is divided into a narrow valley and delta, both of which are surrounded by desert. Egypt's rulers were called pharoahs. Its religion was polytheistic, that is, the people believed in many gods. Some of the well-known gods were Ptah, Ra, Thum, and Amon.

Egypt was a powerful kingdom during Old Testament times. For many years the Hebrew people were slaves there until God sent Moses to free them (Exodus 1—14). In New Testament times Egypt was a center of culture.

EGYPTIAN SEA. See *Red Sea.*

EKRON (EK-rahn). One of five chief Philistine cities. After the Philistines captured the ark of God, they brought it to Ekron (Joshua 13:3; 15:11, 45-46; Judges 1:18; 1 Samuel 5:10; 2 Kings 1:2-16; Jeremiah 25:20; Amos 1:8). Today this city is called Akir. It is located about 11 miles from Gath.

EL (EL, God; Divine Being). An old name for God that can be traced to the Canaanites. It is often used in forming other words, for example, El-Bethel. Elohim, the plural form of El, is the more common word for God in the Old Testament.

ELAH (EE-lah, terebinth). 1. The son of Baasha and fourth king of Israel. Elah was killed by Zimri (1 Kings 16:8-10).

2. The father of Hoshea, the last king of Israel (2 Kings 15:30; 17:1; 18:1).

3. A valley southwest of Jerusalem where David killed Goliath (1 Samuel 17:2, 19; 21:9).

ELAM (EE-luhm). A son of Shem (Genesis 10:22; 1 Chronicles 1:17). Elam's descendants lived east of Babylonia and ruled it during Abraham's time. At that time the capital of Babylonia was Shushan (see Isaiah 21:2; 22:6; Jeremiah 49:34-39; Ezekiel 32:24; Ezra 4:9; Acts 2:9).

EL-BETHEL (el-BETH-el, God of Bethel). The name Jacob gave to the altar he built at Bethel (Genesis 35:7).

ELDAD (EL-dad, God has loved). One of 70 elders whom Moses appointed to help him (Numbers 11:16, 26-29).

ELDER. In Biblical times old people were treated with great respect because of their wisdom and experience (Leviticus 19:32; Deuteronomy 32:7; Job 32:6). An elder was one of the older men in his family or tribe who, by right of being firstborn, became its head (Deuteronomy 22:15; Exodus 3:16; 19:7). The elder made all the major decisions for his family or tribe and was the leader in various activities (Genesis 24:2; 2 Samuel 12:17; Ezekiel 27:9). Each city also had an elder who was called the elder of the city (Deuteronomy 21:3; 22:18). The elders became rulers of the synagog.

In the New Testament the terms *elder* and *bishop* are used to mean the same thing. The elder or presbyter was a man the apostles appointed in each Christian church to be its spiritual leader (Acts 20:17, 28; 1 Timothy 5:17; Titus 1:5-9; 1 Thessalonians 5:12; 1 Peter 5:1-3).

ELEAZAR (el-i-AY-zur, God has helped). The third son of Aaron. Because Aaron's two older sons had died, Eleazar took over the job of chief priest from Aaron (Exodus 6:23; Numbers 20:25-28). He helped Joshua divide the Promised Land among the tribes (Joshua 14:1).

ELECT, ELECTION. Election is the eternal act of God, by which, out of His grace and for Christ's sake, He chooses from sinful people those whom He will save (the elect). God chose the people of Israel, not because of the peoples' own goodness, but because of His divine love (Deuteronomy 4:37; 7:7-8; 9:4-6; 10:15; 23:5). Although many of the people lost their faith and fell away from God, those who remained faithful to Him and trusted in Him received the blessings of election (Isaiah 4:3; 37:31-32). The Old Testament also talks about God choosing individuals (Nehemiah 9:7; Psalm 78:70; 105:26).

The gospels speak of Christ choosing disciples (Luke 6:13). They also note that the elect are the Messianic community, those who have faith in Christ as the promised Messiah and Savior (Matthew 24:22, 24; Mark 13:20-27).

The New Testament letters spell out the doctrine of election. No one deserves to be saved. God, however, chooses from eternity those whom He will save. Those whom He will save are brought to faith in Christ Jesus by the Holy Spirit and are kept in faith by Him. They are placed in the company of other elect (Romans 9—11; 1 Corinthians 1:27-31; Ephesians 1:4-14; 1 Peter 1:2). Election should not make the elect feel like they have "made it"; rather, their response will be thankfulness to God for His love and grace in choosing them (2 Peter 1:10). Those who are of the elect are described as members of God's church (Romans 8:33; 16:13; Colossians 3:12; Titus 1:1; 1 Peter 1:1; 2 John 13).

EL-ELOHE-ISRAEL (el-e-LO-he-IZ-rah-el, God, the God of Israel). The name of Jacob's altar near Shechem (Genesis 33:20).

ELEPHANT. An animal used in war. Their tusks supplied ivory, which was used to make such items as thrones (2 Chronicles 9:17, 21).

ELEVEN, THE. After Judas betrayed Christ and then killed himself, the remaining disciples were called the Eleven (Matthew 28:16; Mark 16:14; Luke 24:9, 33; Acts 1:26).

ELI (EE-ligh, high). A descendant of Aaron (Leviticus 10:12). Eli lived at Shiloh and was both a devoted high priest and judge of Israel (1 Samuel 1:17; 2:20-30; 4:18). Eli's sons, who were also priests, acted shamefully; they had no regard for the Lord or His work. When Eli failed to discipline them, divine judgment was spoken against him and his household (1 Samuel 2:12—3:13).

In a battle between the Israelites and the Philistines, Eli's sons were killed, and the ark of the covenant was captured. When Eli heard the news, he fell backwards, broke his neck, and died (1 Samuel 4). The priesthood passed from Eli's family to Zadok's (1 Kings 2:27).

ELI, ELI, LAMA SABACHTHANI (AY-lee, AY-lee, LAH-mah sah-bahk-TAH-nee). See *Eloi, Eloi, lama sabachthani.*

ELIAB (i-LIGH-ab, God is Father). David's oldest brother (1 Samuel 17:13-14, 28; 2 Corinthians 11:18).

ELIADA (i-LIGH-ah-dah, whom God notices). One of David's sons (2 Samuel 5:16). He is referred to as Beeliada in 1 Chronicles 14:7.

ELIAKIM (i-LIGH-ah-kim, whom God sets up). 1. The master of Hezekiah's household (2 Kings 18:18, 19:2; Isaiah 22:20). When Jerusalem closed its gates against the Assyrians, Eliakim was one of the men sent to receive a message from the leader of the invading army (2 Kings 18:18, 26-27). After reporting to Hezekiah what the Assyrian leader had said, Eliakim was then sent to the prophet Isaiah for advice (2 Kings 19:2; Isaiah 37:1-7). Isaiah highly praised him (Isaiah 22:20-25).

2. One of Josiah's sons. When he became king, he changed his name to Jehoiakim (2 Kings 23:34; 2 Chronicles 36:4).

ELIDAD (i-LIGH-dad, God has loved). A leader of the tribe of Benjamin who helped divide the land of Canaan among the tribes (Numbers 34:21).

ELIEZER (el-i-EE-zur, God is help). 1. Abraham's steward (Genesis 15:2-3).

2. Moses' younger son (Exodus 18:2-4; 1 Chronicles 23:15-17; 26:25).

3. A chief whom Ezra sent to ask the Levites and Nethinim to return to Israel (Ezra 8:16).

ELIHU (i-LEE-hyoo, my God is he). One of Job's three friends (Job 32—37).

ELIJAH (i-LIGH-jah, my God is Lord). A Tishbite and great prophet. When King Ahab, influenced by his wife Jezebel, made Baal worship the court religion, Elijah appeared on the scene. He predicted a time of no rain as punishment for forsaking the Lord. During the three years of dry weather, Elijah was fed by ravens at the brook Cherith. Later he lived in the house of the widow of Zarephath (1 Kings 16:29—17:24). Then God told him to go and show himself to Ahab.

Elijah proposed a test to see whether Baal or the Lord was the true God (1 Kings 18:1-19). On Mount Carmel two altars were prepared: one to Baal by his prophets, and the other to the Lord by Elijah. Only the altar of the Lord was consumed by fire. In this way God proved He was the only true God; Baal was a false one. Then the 450 prophets of Baal were put to death (1 Kings 18:20-40).

After this Jezebel plotted against Elijah's life. So Elijah fled to Horeb, where he heard the still, small voice of the Lord. Then Elijah was sent to anoint Hazael as king over Syria, Jehu as king over Israel, and Elisha as prophet in Elijah's place (1 Kings 19). Elijah pronounced God's judgment on Ahab for the murder of Naboth (1 Kings 21:17-29). At the end of his life, Elijah was taken to heaven in a whirlwind (2 Kings 2:1-12).

In the New Testament John the Baptizer is referred to as Elijah (Matthew 11:14; 17:10-13; Luke 1:17).

ELIM (EE-lim, large trees). An oasis in the desert where the Israelites camped during the Exodus (Exodus 15:27; 16:1; Numbers 33:9). There were 12 wells and 70 palms there.

Today it is the site of Wadi Gharandel.

ELIMELECH (i-LIM-uh-lek, my God is king). Naomi's husband (Ruth 1:1-3).

ELIPHAZ (EL-i-faz, God is gold). 1. The son of Esau and Adah (Genesis 36:4; 1 Chronicles 1:35-36).
2. The chief of Job's three friends. In his talks with Job, Eliphaz traced all suffering and distress to sin and told Job to make his peace with God (Job 3—8; 15:22-24). God rebuked Eliphaz for saying this and told him to make a sacrifice (Job 42:7-9).

ELISABETH. See *Elizabeth.*

ELISHA (i-LIGH-shah, God is salvation). The prophet who took Elijah's place as prophet to the Northern Kingdom. Elisha was the son of Shaphat and came from the tribe of Issachar. His prophetic work belonged to the reigns of Jehoram, Jehu, Jehoahaz, and Joash. During this time Elisha performed many miracles (2 Kings 2—9; 13).

ELISHAMA (i-LISH-ah-mah, God has heard). 1. The captain of the tribe of Ephraim at the Exodus and an ancestor of Joshua (Numbers 1:10; 2:18; 7:48, 53; 1 Chronicles 7:26).
2. Jehoiakim's scribe (Jeremiah 36:12, 20-21).

ELISHEBA (i-LISH-i-bah, God of oath). Aaron's wife (Exodus 6:23).

ELIZABETH (i-LIZ-ah-beth, God is oath). The wife of Zechariah and the mother of John the Baptizer (Luke 1).

ELIZAPHAN (el-i-ZAY-fan, God has protected). The chief of the Kohathites when the Israelites were in the wilderness (Exodus 6:22; Numbers 3:30). He and his brother Mishael removed the bodies of Nadab and Abihu from the camp (Leviticus 10:4)

ELKANAH, ELKONAH (el-KAY-nah, el-KO-nah, God has acquired).

Samuel's father (1 Samuel 1:1—2:21).

ELKOSH (EL-kahsh). The place where the prophet Nahum was born (Nahum 1:1).

ELNATHAN (el-NAY-ahm, gift of God). 1. The grandfather of Jehoiachin (2 Kings 24:8; Jeremiah 26:22).
2. Three men Ezra sent to Iddo to obtain priests for the house of God (Ezra 8:16).

ELOHIM (e-LO-him). See *El.*

ELOI, ELOI, LAMA SABACHTHANI (i-LO-igh, i-LO-igh, LAY-mah, say-BAK-thah-nigh, My God, my God, why have You forsaken Me?). Jesus' fourth cry from the cross (Psalm 22:1; Matthew 27:46; Mark 15:34).

ELYMAS (EL-i-mas, wise). See *Bar-Jesus.*

EMBALM. To prepare a dead body with spices so that it will be preserved from decay. The Egyptians were noted for embalming. When Jacob died, Joseph had the Egyptians embalm Jacob. Joseph was also embalmed when he died (Genesis 50:2, 26).

EMBROIDERY. The Hebrews and their neighbors did weaving, sewing, and artistic needlework (Exodus 38:23; Judges 5:30; Psalm 45:13-14). They embroidered the hangings of the temple and the priests' clothing (Exodus 26:36; 27:16; 28:33, 39; 39:29).

EMEROD (EM-ur-ahd). A hemorrhoid or tumor (Deuteronomy 28:27).

EMMANUEL (i-MAN-yoo-el). See *Immanuel.*

EMMAUS (e-MAY-uhs, hot springs). The village where two of Jesus' disciples were going on the day of Jesus' resurrection. It was near Jerusalem, although its exact location is unknown (Luke 24:13-33).

ENCAMPMENT. See *camp, encampment.*

ENCHANTMENT. The use of magic arts, spells, or charms. Balaam's omens, sorcery, and serpent charming are some examples of enchantment (Numbers 24:1; 2 Kings 9:22; Ecclesiastes 10:11; Isaiah 47:9-12). The Egyptians practiced enchantment, but it was forbidden to God's people (Exodus 7:11-22; 8:7; Deuteronomy 8:10-14).

ENDOR (EN-dawr, fountain of Dor). A village near Mount Tabor (Joshua 17:11; Psalm 83:10; 1 Samuel 28:7).

EN-GEDI (en-GEE-digh, fountain of wild goat). A town on an oasis on the western shore of the Dead Sea about 15 miles southeast of Hebron. It is fed by warm spring water (Joshua 15:62; 1 Samuel 24:1-7; Song of Solomon 1:14).

ENGRAVING. To cut or etch letters or a design on a surface. This was a well-known practice in Palestine and neighboring regions (2 Chronicles 2:14). Examples of engraved articles include the commandments, stones and signets, and idols (Exodus 20:4; 28:11, 36; 32:4, 16).

ENOCH (EE-nuhk, dedicated). 1. The first son of Cain (Genesis 4:7).
2. The father of Methuselah. After the birth of Methuselah, Enoch walked with God for 300 years, and then God took him to heaven (Genesis 5:18-24; 1 Chronicles 1:3; Hebrews 11:5; Jude 14).
3. A city built by Cain (Genesis 4:17).

ENOS, ENOSH (EE-nahs, EE-nash). The son of Seth and grandson of Adam (Genesis 4:26; 5:6-11; Luke 3:38).

ENSIGN (EN-sighn). 1. A signal displayed from the top of a pole (Isaiah 13:2).
2. A standard, or perhaps an emblem, given to each of the four divisions of the Israelite army at the time of the Exodus (Numbers 2:2).

EPAPHRAS (EP-ah-fras, lovely). A Christian at Colossae who visited Paul when he was in prison (Colossians 1:7-8; 4:12; Philemon 23).

EPAPHRODITUS (I-paf-ro-DIGH-tuhs, lovely). A Christian who carried the gifts of the church at Philippi to Paul while Paul was in prison at Rome (Philippians 2:25-30; 4:18).

EPHAH (EE-fah). See *measures 2d.*

EPHES-DAMMIM (EE-fes-DAM-im, end of Dammim). A place in Judah between Soco and Azekah. David fought Goliath there (1 Samuel 17:1). It is also referred to as Pas-dammim (1 Chronicles 11:13).

EPHESIANS, LETTER OF PAUL TO (i-FEE-zhuhns). This letter is commonly regarded as a circular letter that Paul wrote to the churches in Asia, the chief of which was Ephesus (1:1; 3:1; 4:1). In this letter Paul speaks about what the church is and its relationship to the Lord of the church. Ephesians 2:10 is a good summary of the entire book: "We are His workmanship, created in Christ Jesus for good works . . . that we should walk in them."
Date: About A.D. 52 to 56 or A.D. 59 to 61
Audience: Christian churches in Asia Minor
Outline: 1. The church is God's workmanship, created in Christ Jesus (1—3). 2. The church is created for good works (4—6).

EPHESUS (EF-uh-suhs). A city situated on the Cayster River about three miles from the Aegean Sea. Ephesus was the capital of the Roman province of Asia. It was a commercial city and melting pot of different people, languages, and backgrounds. The city was dedicated to the worship of the Phoenician goddess Astarte, also called Artemis or Diana.
Many Jewish people who had Roman citizenship lived in Ephesus

and had a synagog there (Acts 18:19). On one of his missionary journeys Paul began a Christian church there (Acts 19:20; 1 Corinthians 16:8).

EPHOD (EF-od, covering). An apronlike garment with shoulder straps and a belt. Made of gold, blue, scarlet, and fine-twined linen and beautifully adorned, it was one of the many garments worn by the high priests for worship (Exodus 29). Later, others also wore ephods (1 Samuel 2:18; 2 Samuel 6:14; 1 Chronicles 15:22).

EPHPHATHA (EF-ah-tha, be opened). Jesus spoke this when he healed a deaf man (Mark 7:34).

EPHRAIM (EE-fray-im). 1. The second son of Joseph and Asenath (Genesis 46:20). Jacob, Ephraim's grandfather, adopted both Ephraim and his brother, Manasseh, as his own sons. When the two sons were brought to Jacob on his sickbed, Jacob gave Ephraim the greater blessing, bestowing on him the birthright of the firstborn son (Genesis 48:8-20). Ephraim's descendants were numerous (Numbers 1:33; 26:37).

The tribe of Ephraim was given land west of the Jordan between Manasseh on the north and Dan and Benjamin on the south (Joshua 16). It became the heart of the Northern Kingdom (1 Kings 12; Isaiah 7:2; 11:13; Ezekiel 37:15-22).

2. A city near Absalom's sheep farm (2 Samuel 13:23).

3. A gate in Jerusalem (2 Kings 14:13; 2 Chronicles 25:23).

EPHRAIM, MOUNT. The central range of mountains in Samaria (Joshua 19:50; 1 Samuel 1:1).

EPHRATH (EF-rath, fruitful). An old name for Bethlehem-Judah (Genesis 35:16, 19; 48:7).

EPHRATHAH (EF-rah-tha). The wife of Caleb and mother of Hur (1 Chronicles 2:24, 50; 4:4).

EPHRATHITE (EF-rah-thight). An inhabitant of Bethlehem (Ruth 1:2).

EPICUREANS (ep-i-kyoo-REE-uhnz). The followers of Epicurus, a Greek philosopher who died in 270 B.C. Epicurus taught that the chief purpose of human beings is to achieve happiness. He denied life after death (Acts 17:16-32).

EPIPHANES (e-PIF-ah-neez). See *Antiochus 2*.

EPISTLE (i-PIS'l). A formal letter that contains Christian doctrine and instruction (Acts 15:30; Romans 16:22). The term refers particularly to the 21 New Testament books. These epistles are divided into Pauline and Catholic, or General, Epistles. The New Testament books are also called letters.

In 2 Corinthians 3:2-3 Paul referrs to Christians as epistles written by the Holy Spirit.

ERASTUS (i-RAS-tuhs, beloved). A convert of Paul. Erastus, who lived in Corinth, was with Paul at Ephesus (Acts 19:22; Romans 16:23; 2 Timothy 4:20).

ESARHADDON (ez-ur-HAD'n, Asshur has given a brother). A son of Sennacherib and ruler of Assyria from 681 to 669 B.C. (2 Kings 19:37; Isaiah 37:38). Esarhaddon was one of Assyria's greatest conquerors. He rebuilt the city of Babylon, defeated Egypt and made it pay tribute, and took Manasseh, the 14th king of Judah, captive (2 Chronicles 33:11).

ESAU (EE-saw, hairy). The firstborn of Isaac and Rebecca's twin sons (Genesis 25:25). Esau sold his birthright to his brother, Jacob, for a bowl of lentil stew (Genesis 25:29-34; 27:28-29, 36; Hebrews 12:16-17). Since lentil stew is red, Esau was referred to as Edom, which means red.

Esau married two Canaanite women and an Ishmaelite woman (Genesis 26:34; 28:9; 36:2). He tried to kill Jacob for tricking him out of Isaac's blessing (Genesis 27:41-45). Later he forgave his brother and warmly welcomed him back to Canaan (Genesis 33). The country of Esau's descendants is called Edom (Genesis 36).

ESCHATOLOGY (es-kah-TOL-o-ji, doctrine of last things). A study of the last things, such as death, resurrection, life after death, the second coming of Christ, judgment day, and heaven.

The Old Testament emphasizes the destiny of God's chosen people and the Day of the Lord (Isaiah 13:6, 9; 43:6; Joel 3:14; Amos 9:11-15; Zephaniah 1:7). The resurrection of the body and life after death is talked about in Isaiah 26:19-21 and Daniel 12:2. See also Job 19:25-26; Isaiah 53:10.

The New Testament emphasizes Christ's return to judge the world (Matthew 24:25; see also *Parousia*). It also talks about the resurrection of the body and the end times when the wicked shall be thrown into hell and those who believe in Christ shall enter the joy of the Father (Matthew 5:29-30; 25:31-46; Romans 8:11; 1 Corinthians 15).

ESDRAELON (es-dray-EE-lon). See *Jezreel, Valley of.*

ESHTAOL (ESH-tay-ol). A town 13 miles northwest of Jerusalem that was allotted to the tribe of Dan (Joshua 15:33; 19:41). Samson carried out his work in this area (Judges 13:24-25; 16:31).

ESHTEMOA (esh-ti-MO-ah). A village nine miles south of Hebron. It was given to the priests (Joshua 21:14; 1 Chronicles 6:57).

ESSENE (e-SEEN). A Jewish sect in existence from the second century B.C. to the second century A.D. Their chief colonies were around the Dead Sea.

Although the Bible does not speak of the Essenes by name, Josephus, Philo, and the Dead Sea scrolls do talk about this group. The Essenes lived a simple life of sharing everything among each other. They believed that people should remain unmarried. While against slavery and animal sacrifice, they practiced cleanliness and tried to keep the Law. The Essenes also believed in life after death.

ESTHER (ES-tur, Ishtar, Babylonian goddess; star). A Jewish orphan maiden who was the cousin of Mordecai, a minor official of King Ahasuerus (Xerxes I). Ahasuerus ruled Persia from 486 to 465 B.C. Esther became his wife, and when her people were going to be put to death, Esther saved them. Esther's Hebrew name was Hadassah, which means myrtle (Esther 2:7).

ESTHER, BOOK OF. This book is numbered among the Writings in the Hebrew Scriptures; it is the last of the historical books in the English Bible. The author of Esther was familiar with Persian government and the palace of Shushan. The book explains the origin of the Feast of Purim, or day of Mordecai (Esther 9:21-32).

Date: About 400 B.C.
Audience: Jews
Outline: 1. Esther becomes queen (1—2:17). 2. Situation of Jews; plot to kill them (2:18—4:3). 3. Counterplot to save Jews (4:4—8). 4. Jews delivered (9:1-19). 5. Deliverance commemorated (9:20-32). 6. Peace under Mordecai's administration (10).

ETAM (EE-tam, hawkground). Rock Etam was a place where Samson lived (Judges 15:8, 11).

ETERNAL LIFE. Eternal life begins when the Holy Spirit by grace brings a person to faith in Jesus Christ, the Son of God and Savior of the world (John 1:4; 10:10; 17:3;

Romans 6:23). Although the Christian already has eternal life, he or she will not experience it fully until the resurrection of the body and the life of the world to come (Matthew 25:46; John 6:54; Romans 2:7; Titus 3:7). Eternal life is forever.

ETERNITY. Without beginning or end. Eternity is described as "forever" or "from everlasting to everlasting" (Psalm 90:2). Only God is before and after all things (Jeremiah 1:5; Psalm 90; Revelation 1:8; 21:6). His reign, power, and glory are eternal (Psalm 29:10; Isaiah 44:6; 57:15).

ETHAM (EE-tham). The second place where Israel set up camp after leaving Egypt (Exodus 13:20; Numbers 33:6).

ETHBAAL (eth-BAY-uhl, with Baal). A king of Sidon who was the father of Jezebel (1 Kings 16:31).

ETHIOPIA (ee-thi-O-pi-ah, possibly means sunburnt). A country in eastern Africa, south of Egypt. Both Cush, the Hebrew name for this country, and Ethiopia refer to the same country (Genesis 10:6-8; 1 Chronicles 1:8; 2 Chronicles 12:3; 14:9; Ezekiel 30:9; Acts 8:27). The people of Ethiopia were merchants (Isaiah 45:14). They were also a strong military power (2 Chronicles 14:9-12). See also *Cush*.

EUCHARIST. See *Lord's Supper*.

EUNICE (YOO-nuhs, victorious). Timothy's mother (Acts 16:1; 2 Timothy 1:5).

EUNUCH (YOO-nuhk, bedkeeper). A castrated man. Eunuchs were court officials and guardians of women and children (2 Kings 20:18; Esther 1:10-15; Daniel 1:3; Acts 8:27). The Hebrews did not practice castration, nor did they permit eunuchs to enter the congregation (Deuteronomy 23:1).

EUPHRATES (yoo-FRAY-teez). A great river, 1,780 miles long, flowing from Armenia to the Persian Gulf. The Euphrates is one of the rivers that ran through Eden (Genesis 2:14). In the Old Testament it is frequently called the great river or the River (Genesis 15:18; Deuteronomy 11:24). It was regarded as an ideal boundary of Palestine and of David's conquests (Deuteronomy 11:24; Joshua 1:4; 2 Samuel 8:3; 1 Chronicles 18:3).

EURAQUILO (yoo-RAK-wi-lo, NE wind). A stormy wind found on the Mediterranean. It was also called the Northeaster and was responsible for shipwrecking Paul (Acts 27:14).

EUTYCHUS (YOO-ti-kuhs, fortunate). A young man who went to sleep while Paul was preaching and fell from a third story window to his death. Paul brought him back to life (Acts 20:9-10).

EVANGELIST (i-VAN-juh-list, publisher of good tidings). Someone who preaches the Gospel (Acts 8:4-40; 21:8; 2 Timothy 4:5). The office of evangelist is mentioned in Ephesians 4:11. At a later date, the name evangelist was given to the writers of the four gospels.

EVE (EEV, life). The first woman. God formed her out of Adam's side. She is the mother of all living beings (Genesis 2:18-25; 3—4).

EVIL. 1. Anything which is not in harmony with the divine order; that which creates disorder in the universe (Genesis 3; Job 2:10; Psalm 23:4; Proverbs 15:15; Luke 16:25). 2. See *sin*.

EVIL-MERODACH (EE-vil-mi-RO-dak, man of Marduk). The king of Babylon from 562 to 560 B.C. He reigned after Nebuchadnezzar (2 Kings 25:27; Jeremiah 52:31).

EXILE. See *captivity; dispersion*.

EXODUS (EK-so-duhs, a going out). The departure of Israel from Egypt (Exodus; Hebrew 11:22).

EXODUS, BOOK OF. The second book of the Pentateuch. The Israelites referred to it as "and these are the names'' because these are its opening words in Hebrew. The name Exodus comes from a Greek word that means going out. The Book of Exodus describes the way God brought His people Israel out of Egypt and made of them a nation. It also speaks of the covenant God made with Israel, the giving of the Law, and the establishment of the priesthood and system of sacrifice.

Date: 15th to 13th century B.C.

Audience: Israelites

Outline: 1. The Israelites set free from Egyptian rule (1—12:36). 2. Israel in the wilderness (12:37—18:27). 3. Organization of Israel at Sinai (19—40).

EXORCISM (EK-sawr-siz'm). The driving out of demons and evil spirits by the use of magical spells, charms, and ceremonies (Matthew 12:27; Mark 9:38; Acts 19:13).

EXPIATION (eks-pi-AY-shuhn). See *atonement; propitiation.*

EZEKIEL (i-ZEEK-yuhl, God strengthens). One of the Old Testament prophets. He was a son of Buzi and from a priestly family (Ezekiel 1:3). Ezekiel was taken into captivity to Babylon in 597 B.C. with Jehoiachin (Ezekiel 33:21; 40:1; 2 Kings 24:11-16). In Babylon, Ezekiel lived on the Chebar Canal, where he began his prophecies (Ezekiel 1:1, 3; 3:15).

EZEKIEL, BOOK OF. The prophet Ezekiel wrote this book while he was a captive in Babylon. His purpose was to comfort the house of Israel and to reassure God's people that they had not been forsaken. The last part of the book emphasizes the New Covenant. The book is full of imagery—for example, the sections about the valley of bones, the Good Shepherd, and the showers of blessings.

Date: About 593 to 571 B.C.

Audience: People of Judah

Outline: 1. Prophecies against Judah and Jerusalem before the destruction of the temple (1—24). 2. Prophecies against foreign nations, hostile to God and His people (25—32). 3. Chastened Israel will be restored, and the promised kingdom of God will come (33—48).

EZION-GEBER or **EZION-GA-BER** (EE-zi-on-GEE-bur, EE-zi-on-GAY-bur, backbone of giant). A place on the north end of the Gulf of Aqabah where the Israelites camped on their journey in the wilderness (Numbers 33:35-36; Deuteronomy 2:8). Later, Ezion-geber was a naval port and copper refining center of King Solomon (1 Kings 9:26; 22:48; 2 Chronicles 8:17). Today it is identified with Tell el-Kheleifeh. Its site has been excavated.

EZRA (EZ-rah, help). A Jewish priest, scribe, and prophet (Ezra 7:6-12). With the help of Artaxerxes, Ezra led a group of exiles back to Jerusalem around the year 459 B.C. Ezra reformed Jewish life, worship, and government. He read the Law in public and rebuilt the temple (Ezra; Nehemiah).

EZRA, BOOK OF. The 15th book of the Old Testament. It describes the activities of Ezra, the scribe, and records the Israelites' return to their home country and their separation from foreign customs and idolatry.

Date: About 400 B.C.

Audience: Jews

Outline: 1. Return of exiles and rebuilding the temple (1—6). 2. Ezra's reforms (7—10).

FABLE. 1. A story in which animals and other objects in nature are made to act and speak as if they were human beings (Judges 9:8-15; 2 Kings 14:9).

2. A myth or fictitious story (1 Timothy 1:4; 4:7: 2 Timothy 4:4; Titus 1:14; 1 Peter 1:16).

FACE. 1. Used both literally and figuratively. To fall on the face was an act of reverence, petition, or sorrow (Genesis 17:3; Numbers 14:5; Joshua 7:6).

2. The face of God is God in His active presence (Numbers 6:25-26). No one can see God's face and live (Exodus 33:20). To seek God's face means to worship Him (Psalm 27:8).

FAITH. That belief and trust in the promise of God in Christ Jesus, worked by the Holy Spirit, through which a person is declared just, brought into a right relationship with God, saved (Romans 5:1; 1 Corinthians 2:10-13; Ephesians 2:8). Faith can be pictured as the hand that receives the blessings of salvation which God, out of grace, has provided in Christ Jesus.

In the Old Testament faith is described by the words *believe, trust in*, and *take refuge in* (Genesis 15:16; Exodus 14:31; 2 Samuel 22:3; Psalm 28:7). In the New Testament the word *faith* occurs on nearly every page. It is described as belief and trust in Jesus Christ as the Lord, the one who paid for the sins of the world with His blood and His innocent suffering and death (Luke 24:46-48; John 3:16; 20:31; Acts 2:36; 16: 31; Romans 10:6-15; Galatians 2:20; 1 John 1:7).

The Holy Spirit works faith in Christ in the individual through the Gospel and the means of grace, the Word and sacraments (Romans 1:16; 10:17). Through faith in Christ, the individual dies, is buried, is raised, and lives with Christ (Romans 6:4, 8; Colossians 2:12; 3:3).

FALL. The fall of humanity into sin is described in Genesis 3. It was that act by which Adam and Eve turned away from God, yielded to temptation, and broke God's commandments. The fall involved not only Adam, but all of humanity, in sin, misery, and death (Romans 5:12-21).

As one man's fall affects all of humanity; so Christ's death and resurrection for the sins of the world brings God's grace to all (Romans 5:18).

FALSE PROPHET. A person, not sent by or responsible to God, who performs signs and wonders to lead people astray (Jeremiah 29:9; Ezekiel 13). See also *prophet*.

FAMILIAR SPIRIT. The spirit of a dead person or demon that mediums claimed they could call forth for consultation (Leviticus 19:31; 20:6, 27; Deuteronomy 18:11; 1 Samuel 28:3; 2 Kings 21:6).

FAMINE. A lack of food and drink caused by war or the absence of rain (Genesis 12:10; 26:1; 1 Kings 17:2; 2 Kings 6:25).

2. A lack of God's Word (Amos 8:11-12).

FAN. A fork to throw threshed grain into the air to clean it of chaff (Isaiah 30:24; Matthew 3:12). See also *agriculture*.

FARTHING. Two Roman bronze coins worth a penny or less (Matthew 5:26; 10:29; Luke 12:6).

FASTING. Partially or totally abstaining from food. Moses fasted on Sinai for 40 days and nights (Exodus 34:28). In the Old Testament fasting was a sign of religious humiliation. At first fasting was supposed to be done only on the Day of Atonement (Leviticus 16:29; 23:27-32). Later days of national disaster and the like were added.

The disciples of John fasted, but not those of Jesus (Matthew 9:14-17; Luke 5:33-39). Jesus fasted 40 days and nights in the desert (Matthew 4:2). He approved of fasting, but not if it were done for show (Matthew 6:16-18).

FATHER. This word has several meanings in the Bible. 1. It can mean one's own father (Genesis 19:31), an ancestor (1 Kings 5:11; Numbers 18:2; Matthew 3:9), or the founder of a community, tribe, or nation (Genesis 10:21; 17:4-5; 1 Chronicles 2:51; 4:14).

2. God as creator (Malachi 2:10; Isaiah 63:16) or Savior (Romans 8:15; Galatians 4:6). God is the Father of Jesus (Matthew 11:26; Mark 14:36).

3. A man who acts with fatherly kindness toward another person (Job 29:16; Isaiah 22:21) or a teacher (2 Kings 2:12).

4. A father in the faith (1 Corinthians 4:15).

FEAR. This word is used in different ways. It can mean reverence, terror, dread, trembling, or fright (Genesis 9:22; Deuteronomy 28:67; Job 41:33; Proverbs 29:25; Acts 10:2, 22). To fear God generally means to show awe and respect for His holiness (Psalm 34:11; Ecclesiastes 12:13).

FEAST. 1. A lavish and costly meal which people attended with great joyfulness (Daniel 5:1; Luke 5:29; John 2:1).

2. A time when the Jewish people celebrate their religious festivals. Their major feasts include (a) the Passover, or Feast of Unleavened Bread (Leviticus 23:5-8; Numbers 28:17-25); (b) the Feast of Weeks, Pentecost, Harvest, or First Fruits (Exodus 23:16; Numbers 28:26-31); and (c) the Feast of Tabernacles, or Booths (Leviticus 23:34-36; Deuteronomy 16:13-17).

Lesser festivals include (a) the Feast of Dedication, or Lights (John 10:22); (b) Purim (Esther 9:21-28); (c) the Feast of Wood Offering (Nehemiah 10:34); and (d) Sheep-Shearing (1 Samuel 25:4-11).

FELIX (FEE-liks, happy). A Roman procurator of Judea (Acts 23:26).

FELLOWSHIP. The basic idea of fellowship is that of sharing something in common. Christian fellowship shares the common bond of the Gospel, faith in Christ, and various spiritual gifts (1 Corinthians 13; Philippians 1:5-7; Philemon). It is created by God, who calls Christians into participation in Christ so that they share in His work, blessing, and glory (Romans 6:1-8; 14:8; 1 Corinthians 1:9; 1 John 1:3, 6-7). Through the work of the Holy Spirit believers have a oneness in Christ (John 17:11, 21-22; 2 Corinthians 13:14; Galatians 3:28; 1 John 1:7). The mark of fellowship is love (1 Corinthians 13; 1 Peter 1:22).

FESTIVAL. See *feast*.

FESTUS, PORCIUS (FES-tuhs, PAWR-shi-uhs). The Roman governor of Judea who came after Felix (Acts 24:27).

FETTERS. Chains for binding the feet of prisoners (Judges 16:21; 2 Chronicles 33:11; Psalm 105:18; Mark 5:4).

FIRE. A symbol of God's presence and a means of His judgment (Exodus 3:2; 19:18; 2 Peter 3:7). God's anger burns like fire (Psalm 79:5). Christ will appear in fire (2 Thessalonians 1:8).

Fire was used for cooking, for warmth, and to burn up sacrifices (Leviticus 21:6; 23:8; Isaiah 44:16; Jeremiah 36:22). It was to burn continuously on the altar (Leviticus 6:9-13).

FIRMAMENT. The expanse of sky dividing the primeval waters so that part were above it and part were below it (Genesis 1:6-7; Psalm 19:1; Ezekiel 1:22-26).

FIRSTBORN, FIRSTLING. The first one born of a mother's offspring (Exodus 12:12). 1. The oldest son received the birthright, a double portion of inheritance (Deuteronomy 21:17). Along with this he became the head of the family (Genesis 35:23; 43:33; 2 Chronicles 21:1-3). Sometimes the birthright was given to a younger son (Genesis 25:23; 49:4).

2. The firstborn of human beings and the firstling of animals belonged to God (Exodus 13:2, 15). The firstborn of man was given to God as a priest. When the Aaronic priesthood was established, the Levites took the place of the Israelites' firstborn (Numbers 3:12-15; 18:15-16).

Firstlings were given to the sanctuary. The clean were sacrificed; the unclean were either replaced by suitable sacrifices or killed (Exodus 13:2, 11-15; 22:30; 34:19-20; Leviticus 27:26-29).

FIRST FRUITS. The first ripe fruits, whether raw as in grain or fruit, or prepared, as in wine, oil, or flour. The first fruits were given to the priest as an offering for the Lord (Exodus 22:29; 23:19; 34:26; Leviticus 2:12; 23:10-12; Numbers 18:12).

FISH. The Sea of Galilee, filled with a great variety of fish, was the chief source of fishing for the people of Palestine (Luke 5:5). Once the fish were caught, they were sold in Jerusalem (2 Chronicles 33:14; Nehemiah 13:16).

The word *fish* is used figuratively for the Egyptians, the church, and captives (Ezekiel 29:4-5; Habakkuk 1:14; Matthew 13:48). The letters of the Greek word for fish became a symbol for "Jesus Christ, God's Son, Savior." See also *food 3*.

FISH GATE. A gate of Jerusalem near the fish market (2 Chronicles 33:14).

FISHER. The disciples were called fishers of men because they "caught" people with the Gospel (Matthew 4:19; Mark 1:17).

FLAGON (skin). A bottle or pitcher made of skin or earthenware (Isaiah 22:24).

FLESH. 1. The muscles or softer parts of any living thing (Genesis 41:2, 19; Job 33:21; Luke 24:39).

2. All beings have flesh (Genesis 6:13, 19; Acts 2:17; Romans 3:20).

3. Meat (Exodus 16:12; Leviticus 7:19).

4. Flesh as opposed to spirit (Job 14:22; John 6:52; 1 Corinthians 5:5).

5. Our ordinary human constitution (Genesis 2:23; Matthew 19:5-6; 1 Corinthians 6:16).

6. Human nature deprived of the Spirit of God and corrupted by sin (Romans 7:5; 8:5-8; 2 Corinthians 7:1; Galatians 5:16-20; 2 Peter 2:10).

FLOCK 1. Sheep (Luke 2:8).

2. Israel as a covenant nation (Isaiah 40:11).

3. The New Testament church (Matthew 26:31; Acts 20:28-29; 1 Peter 5:2-3).

FLOOD. 1. Water, especially a river or the sea (Exodus 15:8; Joshua 24:2; Psalm 66:6). A flood is also any overflowing, for example, the overflowing of a body of water (Isaiah 44:3; Nahum 1:8; Luke 6:48).

2. The Deluge in the time of Noah is referred to as the Flood. It is that event when God destroyed all living things on earth by water except the creatures in Noah's ark (Genesis 6—9).

FLUX. See *dysentery.*

FOOD. The people in Bible times ate various kinds of food. 1. Bread and water were the "stay and staff" of life (Isaiah 3:1). Bread was made mainly from wheat. Sometimes barley, spelt, millet, and lentils were also ground for bread or were eaten by the poor (Ezekiel 4:9-10).

Crushing the grain between two stones was one ancient method for grinding flour. The Canaanites used a rotary-type mill in which the cone of the upper millstone fit into a hollowed out spot in the lower millstone.

Once the grain was carefully sifted, it was ready to make into bread. Yeast, salt, olive oil, and water or milk were added to the flour to make the bread.

The people used different types of ovens to bake the bread. The simplest type was a slightly curved, circular sheet of iron which was heated over the fire. Then a thin layer of dough was placed on it to bake. Another type of oven was a dome of clay. The dough was placed under it, and then it was covered with fire. Community ovens were also used.

2. Vegetables, legumes, beans, and lentils were an important part of the Hebrew diet (Genesis 25:34; 2 Samuel 17:28). The people also freely ate melons, cucumbers, onions, garlic, and leeks (Numbers 11:5; Isaiah 1:8). Dill, mustard, and coriander seed provided strong flavoring for their foods (Exodus 16:31; Isaiah 28:25, 27; Matthew 13:31). Cinnamon bark, mint, cummin, and saffron flavored both food and wine (Exodus 30:23; Song of Solomon 4:14; Matthew 23:23). In addition to these items, parsley, celery, lettuce, and cabbage were grown.

One of the favorite dishes of the Israelites, which used many of the above items, was vegetable stew. Since good quality meat was scarce in Palestine, the people ate it only on special occasions (Luke 15:23; Exodus 12:3-10). At these times they might barbecue and serve whole animals (Genesis 18:7; Luke 15:23). Poorer quality meats were stewed or used to flavor vegetable stew.

3. Fish were taken mainly from the Sea of Galilee, the Jordan River, and the Mediterranean Sea (Matthew 4:18-31). They were roasted over charcoal or salted and dried for later use (John 21:9-13; Mark 8:7). Wild or domestic birds and their eggs also provided a good source of protein (Leviticus 11:13-19; Isaiah 10:14; Matthew 23:37; Luke 11:12; John 18:27).

4. Milk and milk products supplied the Israelites with protein, calcium, and fat. At mealtime the people, particularly the children, drank cow's, sheep's, or goat's milk (Genesis 18:8; Deuteronomy 32:14; 1 Samuel 6:7; Hebrews 5:12-13). They ate curds of milk and cheese made from sour milk (Genesis 18:8; 1 Samuel 17:18; Proverbs 30: 33). Cream skimmed from the top of sour milk was churned inside a goatskin to make butter. (Klinck)

FOOL. A person who has no wisdom or understanding or one who is lacking in morals or religion (Psalm 14:1; 92:6; Proverbs 12:15; Jeremiah 17:11; Luke 12:20).

FOOTMAN. A soldier who fights and marches on foot or a guard (1 Samuel 22:17; 2 Kings 13:7).

FOREIGNER. Among the Israelites, anyone who was not part of their nation was a foreigner (Exodus 12:45; Ephesians 2:12). The New Testament describes those who are not citizens of God's kingdom as foreigners (Ephesians 2:19; 1 Peter 2:11).

FOREKNOWLEDGE. God's eternal knowledge or foresight of all future events. See also *elect, election.*

FORERUNNER. Someone who prepares the way (Hebrews 6:19-20).

FORK. See *fan.*

FORGIVENESS. God's act whereby He ends the separation caused by peoples' sins and puts them back into a proper relationship with Himself. No one deserves to be forgiven, nor can anyone earn forgiveness (Matthew 18:23-25; Ephesians 2:8). Rather, forgiveness is a gift of God, given out of grace for Christ's sake (Mark 2:5, 7, 10; Luke 24:47; John 20:23; Ephesians 1:7; 1 John 2:12). As a result of Christ's forgiveness, we are to forgive our neighbor (Matthew 6:12-14; Ephesians 4:32). Recognizing and being sorry for our sins precedes forgiveness (Psalm 51; Isaiah 57:15; Jeremiah 14:20).

FORT, FORTIFICATION, FORTRESS. Cities in ancient times were fortified with walls built of brick and stone. Jerusalem, Samaria, and Damascus were well-known fortified towns. God's protection is often pictured as a strong fortress (2 Samuel 22:2; Psalm 31:3; Jeremiah 6:27).

FOUNTAIN. Springs of water were of great importance in Palestine (Genesis 16:7; Deuteronomy 8:7; 33:28; 1 Samuel 29:1). God, the Source of grace, is described as having or being the Fountain of life (Psalm 36:9; Jeremiah 17:13). Jesus told the woman at the well that the water He gives becomes a spring of living water (John 4:14).

FOWLER. A person who catches birds with a net or cords (Psalm 91:3; 124:7).

FRANKINCENSE (FRANGK-in-sens). A fragrant gum resin from certain types of trees. It was an ingredient in the oil used to anoint priests to their offices and in meal offerings (Exodus 30:34; Leviticus 2:1). Frankincense was also burned and poured on showbread (Leviticus 6:15; 24:7).

FRINGE. Tassels made of twisted blue thread that were fastened on to each corner of a garment. The Israelites wore these to remind themselves of the Law and their loyalty to the Lord (Numbers 15:37-40; Deuteronomy 22:12).

FRONTLET. Anything bound on the forehead. The Jewish people bound jewels or amulets between their eyes. Later they wore phylacteries (prayer bands) around their foreheads or on their left arms (Exodus 13:2-10, 11-16; Deuteronomy 6:4-9; 11:13-21; Matthew 23:5).

FULLER. A person who bleaches, cleans, thickens, or dyes cloth (Malachi 3:2; Mark 9:3). A fuller's field, the place where this work was done, lay outside the east wall of Jerusalem (2 Kings 18:17; Isaiah 7:3; 36:2).

FURLONG. See *measures 1i*.

FURNACE. People smelted iron, burned bricks, and melted silver and gold in furnaces (Exodus 9:8, 10; 19:18; Deuteronomy 4:20; Proverbs 17:3; Ezekiel 22:20). Bake ovens were called furnaces (Nehemiah 3:11). The New Testament pictures everlasting punishment as a furnace of fire (Matthew 13:42; 25:41).

FUTURE LIFE. See *eschatology; eternal life; eternity*.

GABBATHA (GAB-ah-thah). The place where Pilate held court and where Jesus was tried (John 19:13).

GABRIEL (GA-bri-uhl, man of God). The angel who interpreted visions to Daniel and announced the births of John the Baptizer and Jesus (Daniel 8:16-27; 9:20-27; Luke 1:11-22; 26-38).

GAD (GAD, good fortune). 1. Jacob's seventh son (Genesis 30: 9-11; 49:19).

2. The name of a tribe of Israel that descended from Jacob's seventh son (Numbers 1:24-25; 26:15-18). This tribe settled east of the Jordan River (Number 32). In 722 B.C. Tiglath-pileser, king of Assyria, took this tribe into captivity along with the other nine northern tribes (1 Chronicles 5:26).

3. The name of a prophet who helped and wrote about David (1 Samuel 22:5; 2 Samuel 24:11-24; 1 Chronicles 29:29).

4. A pagan god of fortune worshiped by the Canaanites (Isaiah 65:11).

GADARENES (gad-ah-REENZ). The people who lived in the city of Gadara, about six miles southeast of the Sea of Galilee, or in the town of Gerasa on the east coast of the Sea of Galilee (Matthew 8:28; Mark 5:1; Luke 8:26, 37).

GAIUS (GAY-yuhs). 1. A man of Macedonia who helped Paul at Ephesus (Acts 19:29).

2. A man from Derbe who helped Paul (Acts 20:4).

3. A Christian at Corinth who was baptized by Paul (1 Corinthians 1:4).

4. The person to whom the Third Letter of John was sent. Some scholars believe that some of these men may have been the same person.

GALATIA (gah-LAY-shi-ah). A region of central Asia Minor (modern-day Turkey) named after the Gauls, who settled there about the 3rd century B.C. After the Romans captured the area in 64 B.C., a Roman province called Galatia was formed. It included the region Paul visited on his first missionary journey (Acts 16:6; 18:23; Galatians 1:2).

GALATIANS, LETTER OF PAUL TO. Paul wrote this letter probably to the churches that started on his first missionary journey and soon after that journey was over (Acts 13:13—14:28). He stresses that one is saved by grace through faith and not by works.

Date: About A.D. 48

Audience: Christians of Galatia

Outline: 1. Defense of Paul's apostleship (1—2). 2. Defense of the Gospel of free grace, without works of the Law (3—4). 3. Practical applications (5—6).

GALILEAN (GAL-uh-lee-uhn). A person from Galilee. See also *Galilee.*

GALILEE (GAL-uh-lee, circle). The name of the northernmost province of the three provinces of Palestine. This name was already used in Old Testament times (Joshua 20:7; 1 Kings 9:11). It was given to the tribes of Zebulun, Asher, and Naphtali (Joshua 19:10-16, 24-39). The land was fertile, and a number of important trade routes crossed the area (Isaiah 9:1).

At the time of Christ, Galilee extended from Mount Hermon on the north to Mount Carmel on the south and from the Jordan River on the east to the Mediterranean Sea on the west. Herod Antipas was its ruler. Jesus performed the major part of His ministry there. The 12 disciples, except Judas Iscariot, were all from Galilee. The leaders of Judea hated Galileans, who were known by the way they talked (Mark 14:70).

GALILEE, SEA OF. A fresh-water lake fed by the Jordan River, which flows in at the north end and out at the south end. It is 13 miles long, 7 miles wide, and 160 feet deep at its deepest point. Its blue, fresh water is full of fish.

The Sea of Galilee is also referred to as the Sea of Chinnereth, or Chinneroth, the Lake of Gennesaret(h), and the Sea of Tiberias (Joshua 12:3; 13:27; Luke 5:1; John 6:1; 21:1).

GALL. 1. A bitter material produced by the liver (Job 16:13).

2. People thought that the poison of snakes was gall (Job 20:14).

3. A poisonous, bitter-tasting plant (Hosea 10:4).

4. Part of the drink the soldiers offered to Christ to lessen His suffering (Matthew 27:34).

5. A symbol for a bitter, painful experience (Jeremiah 8:14; Acts 8:23).

GALLEY. A low, flat-looking ship with a row of oars along each side. It was often rowed by slaves (Isaiah 33:21).

GALLIO (GAL-i-o). The Roman proconsul (governor) of Achaia from A.D. 51 to 52. He was the brother of the philosopher Seneca. Gallio refused to hear the Jews' case against Paul in Corinth (Acts 18:12-17).

GALLOWS. An instrument used to hang people. Gallows are mentioned nine times in the Book of Esther as a means of execution. Since death by strangulation was unusual in Persia, the word translated as *gallows* should probably be translated as *pole* or *stake*.

GAMALIEL (gah-MAY-li-uhl, reward of God). The grandson of Hillel, the great Jewish teacher, and one of Paul's most influential teachers (Acts 22:3). Gamaliel was a Pharisee and a member of the Sanhedrin (Acts 5:34). He gave wise advice to the other leaders at the trial of Peter and the other apostles (Acts 5:38-40).

Gamaliel is considered one of the greatest Jewish rabbis. He is referred to as "rabban" (our teacher).

GAMES. Children often played in the streets (Zechariah 8:5). They played make-believe and kept birds (Job 41:5; Matthew 11:16-17).

Adult "games" included merrymaking, telling riddles, playing music, dancing, racing, and using the bow and sling (1 Samuel 20:20; Judges 14:12-19; 20:16; Psalm 19:5; Jeremiah 15:17; Luke 15:25). Paul knew about Greek sports contests (1 Corinthians 9:24-27; 2 Timothy 2:5; 4:7-8). A board for an ancient game was found at Saul's castle in Gibeah. See also *dance; music.*

GATE. The door or entrance to the tabernacle, the camp of the Israelites, the temple, cities, houses, and prisons (Genesis 19:1; Exodus 27:16; 32:26; 2 Chronicles 8:14; Acts 19:17; 12:10). Markets and courts, or places of judgment, were often near gates because many people went back and forth or met to talk or do business there (Deuteronomy 17:5; Ruth 4:1-12; 2 Samuel 15:2; 2 Kings 7:1). A gate is a symbol of power (Genesis 22:17; Matthew 16:18). It also describes the beginning of something or the way to have access to something, for example, the gate of heaven, the gate of righteousness, the gates of the New Jerusalem, the gates of death (Genesis 28:17; Job 38:17; Psalm 118:19-20; Revelation 21:12, 21).

GATEKEEPER. Someone who watches the gate of a city, temple, palace, house, or other private entrance to make sure that no unauthorized person goes through (Psalm 84:10; Mark 13:34).

GATH (GATH, wine press). One of the five great Philistine cities (Joshua 13:3). Its site is unknown. Gath was the home of Goliath and one of the places where David hid from Saul (1 Samuel 17; 21:10). David later captured Gath (1 Chronicles 18:1).

GAZA (GAY-zah). The capital city of Philistia (Genesis 10:19). It was given to Judah when Canaan was divided (Judges 1:18). Gaza was the scene of Samson's death and the place near which Philip converted the treasurer of Ethiopia (Judges 16; Acts 8:26).

GAZELLE (gah-ZEL). The smallest of the Palestinian antelopes. This animal was ceremonially clean, that is, it was one of the animals the Israelites were allowed to eat (Deuteronomy 12:15, 22).

GEHENNA (gi-HEN-ah, valley of Hinnom). Gehenna was the name of a valley south of Jerusalem where the Hebrews offered their children to the false god Moloch (Joshua 15:8; 2 Kings 23:10; Jeremiah 7:31; 19:2-6). Later this place became a dump for unclean matter; fires burned in it continually. For this reason the New Testament writers used the word *Gehenna* to name the place of the eternal destiny of unbelievers (Matthew 5:22, 29-30; 10:28; 18:9; 23:15, 33; Mark 9:43, 45, 47; Luke 12:5). In this latter sense, Gehenna is identical with the lake of fire (Revelation 19:20; 20:10). See also *hell*.

GENEALOGY (jen-ee-AL-o-jee, birth record). The tracing forward or backward of the ancestral relationships of tribes and families (Genesis 35:22-26; Numbers 1:2, 18; 1 Chronicles 9:2; Nehemiah 7:5; Matthew 1:1-16; Luke 3:23-38). Genealogies often contain gaps (for example, in Exodus 6:16-24).

GENERATION. 1. Creating or procreating (Genesis 2:4).

2. Offspring or successions of offspring (Genesis 5:1).

3. Age as a period of time (Genesis 15:16; Deuteronomy 32:7; Psalm 45:17).

4. People of a specific historical period (Leviticus 3:17; Matthew 11:16; 17:17).

GENESIS (JEN-i-sis, beginning). The first book of the Pentateuch. As the book of beginnings, Genesis describes the origins of the physical universe, plants, animals, human life, and human institutions.

Date: 15th to 13th century B.C.

Author: Moses

Outline: 1. The creation of the world and the history of humanity: Adam, Noah and the Flood, and Shem (1—11:26). 2. History of the patriarchs: Abraham, Ishmael, Isaac, Esau, and Jacob (11:27—50).

GENNESAR, GENNESARET, GENNESARETH (ge-NEE-sahr, ge-NES-ah-ret, ge-NES-ah-reth). 1. The plain northwest of the Sea of Galilee (Matthew 14:34; Mark 6:53).

2. See *Galilee, Sea of.*

GENTILES. 1. Non-Hebrew nations of the world (Genesis 10:5; 14:1; Judges 4:2, 13, 16).

2. People outside the Jewish and Christian faith (1 Corinthians 5:1; 10:20).

GERASENES, GERGESENES (GER-ah-seenz, GUR-ge-seenz). See *Gadarenes.*

GERIZIM (GER-i-zim). A mountain about 2,850 feet high that stands opposite Mount Ebal. The blessings were read from Mount Gerizim; the curses, from Mount Ebal (Deuteronomy 11:29; 27:12). The Samaritans built a temple for themselves on Mount Gerizim (2 Kings 17:33; John 4:20).

GETHSEMANE (geth-SEM-ah-nee, oil press). An olive yard east of Jerusalem. It was the place of Jesus' agony and arrest (Matthew 26:36-56; Mark 14:26-52; Luke 22:39-54; John 18:1-13).

GIANTS. A person who is unusually tall and powerful. The Nephilim are the first giants mentioned in the Bible. They were on the earth in the days before the Flood and in Canaan when the spies went through the land (Genesis 6:4; Numbers 13:33).

Giants known as the Rephaim lived in Canaan, Edom, Moab, and Ammon. At the time of the conquest, Og, king of Bashan, was the only one left of this race. His iron bedstead was about 13 1/2 feet long (Genesis 14:5; 15:20; Deuteronomy 3:11; Joshua 12:4). The Anakim, another race of giants, were connected with the Rephaim because of their size (Numbers 13:22; Deuteronomy 2:10-12). When the Hebrews captured Hebron, the Anakim who escaped destruction found refuge in Philistine cities. Goliath of Gath was probably one of these remaining Anakim (1 Samuel 17:4).

GIBEAH (GIB-i-ah, hill). 1. A city of Benjamin a few miles north of Jerusalem. It was the birthplace of Saul and the place where he lived after becoming king (Judges 19:13-14; 1 Samuel 10:26; 15:34). Its modern-day site is Tell el-Ful. Excavation there has uncovered Saul's fortress-palace.

2. Gibeah at Kiriath-jearim. It was the place where the ark was kept after the Philistines returned it (2 Samuel 6:3-4).

GIBEON (GIB-ee-uhn, hill city). A city in Benjamin that was given to the Levites (Joshua 18:25; 21:17). Originally it was a Hivite city. At the time of the conquest, the people of Gibeon made a treaty with Joshua under false pretences. By doing this, they saved their city but brought slavery upon themselves (Joshua 9—10; 2 Samuel 21:1-9).

GIDEON (GID-ee-uhn, cutting down). The son of Joash of the tribe of Manasseh (Judges 6:11). While threshing wheat, the angel of the Lord called Gideon to deliver his people. That night Gideon tore down his father's altar to Baal and built one to the Lord. The townspeople wanted to kill Gideon for doing this, but his father told them to let Baal defend himself if he were a god. Because of this incident Gideon was known as Jerubbaal, which means let Baal contend (Judges 6:32).

Gideon defeated the Midianites and destroyed Succoth. When his people wanted to make him king, Gideon refused (Judges 6—8; Hebrews 11:32). He was also called Jerubbesheth, meaning contender with Shame (2 Samuel 11:21). Because of his work Gideon is regarded as one of the judges of Israel, even though he is not specifically called by that title.

GIHON (GIGH-hon, gushing forth). 1. One of the four rivers of Eden (Genesis 2:13).

2. A spring in the Kidron Valley near Jerusalem that supplied some of the water to that city. Hezekiah built the Siloam Tunnel to carry water from the Gihon to the pool of Siloam within the city walls of Jerusalem (2 Kings 20:20; 2 Chronicles 32:30).

GILBOA (gil-BO-ah). A mountain range overlooking the Valley of Jezreel. Saul and Jonathan died there while fighting the Philistines (1 Samuel 31).

GILEAD (GIL-i-ahd, to be rough). The name given to the land east of the Jordan River. It extended from the Sea of Galilee on the north to the Dead Sea on the south (Genesis 31:21-25; Deuteronomy 3:12-17).

GILGAL (GIL-gal, circle). The place

near Jericho that became Israel's base camp after the Israelites crossed the Jordan (Joshua 4:19-24; 9:6). Saul was crowned king of Israel at Gilgal and also had his kingship taken away there (1 Samuel 11:15; 13:4-15).

GLASS. By 1500 B.C. opaque glass was widely used by the Egyptians and Phoenicians (Job 28:17). Clear glass was made in Roman times (Revelation 21:18, 21).

GLEANING. The gathering of grain left in the fields or grapes left on the vines after harvest. According to Old Testament law, owners of fields and vineyards were to leave leftover grain, grapes, and fallen fruit for the poor (Deuteronomy 24:19-21; Ruth 2:2-3).

GLORY. 1. That which shows the greatness of someone or something. The glory of God is shown in and by His great miracles, His eternal perfection, His creation, and all His works (Psalm 8; Matthew 17:2; John 2:11). Most importantly, it is shown by His Son, our Lord Jesus Christ (John 1:14; 2 Corinthians 4:6). The glory of people is truly shown only by their relationship to God (2 Corinthians 3:18).

2. That which *is itself* the greatness of someone or something. Here glory is spoken of as a possession of, or even part of, someone or something. Scripture speaks of God's glory and of the glory awaiting believers in the life to come (Isaiah 42:8; Luke 2:9; Romans 8:18; Philippians 3:20-21).

GNOSTICISM (NOS-tuh-siz'm). A system of belief that reached its peak in the second to third century A.D. According to Gnostics, salvation came by hating the world and everything physical and by escaping to the spirit world. They said Jesus came not to save people from sin but to show them how to escape to this spiritual world.

Gnosticism was a problem for Christians during these first few centuries after Christ. Some of the books of the New Testament seem to have been written in part to fight against it (John; Colossians; 2 Peter; 1, 2, 3 John; Jude; Titus; Revelation).

GOAT. A valued animal that is mentioned many times in the Bible. Its hair was woven into cloth; its flesh and milk provided food; and the whole animal was used for sacrifice (Exodus 35:26; Leviticus 3:12; 4:24; 9:15; Deuternomy 14:4). See also *Azazel*.

Jesus used the goat as a symbol for those going to hell (Matthew 25:32-33).

GOD. The Being who is not limited in any way or by anything, who is not held by time or space, who possesses all power, knowledge, and wisdom, and who created the world and all people. God shows Himself through His creation, but because all people have fallen into sin, they exchange their knowledge of the true God for a lie and worship false gods (Romans 1:18-32; Acts 14:15-17; 17:22-31). Because of this, God chose to show Himself and His will to people through Jesus Christ so that they might know and believe in Him and be saved (John 1:14, 18; 2 Corinthians 4:6; 5:18-20).

The chief names for God in the Old Testament are Elohim and Yahweh (see *Jehovah*). God is all-powerful; He is a spiritual being. Yet, the Bible describes Him as though He were a human person so that people can somewhat understand Him and talk about Him. For instance, Psalm 145:16 speaks of God's "hand," even though God does not have hands as people do. Although Scripture often describes God as though He has a human body and human feelings or as acting in a human way (Genesis 3:8; Psalm 2:4; Zephaniah 3:17), the only way He is truly like people is in Jesus Christ (Isaiah 55:8-9).

The name God can rightly be used to refer to the entire Trinity or to any one of the three Persons of the Trinity (Ephesians 1:3; John 1:1; Acts 5:3-4). See also *gods, false; Holy Spirit; Jesus Christ; Trinity.*

GOD FEARERS. See *proselyte.*

GOD MOST HIGH. See *High, Most.*

GODS, FALSE. See *Artemis; Asherah; Ashtoreth; Baal; Baal-zebub; Chemosh; Gad 4; Hadad 1; Merodach; Milcom; Molech; Nehushtan; Rimmon; Sakkuth; Zeus.*

GOG. The prince of Rosh, Meshech, and Tubal. The prophet Ezekiel described him as invading Israel in the Last Days (Ezekiel 38:39. See Revelation 20:8-15).

GOLD. A precious metal Israel obtained from foreign lands (1 Kings 10:2; 22:48). The Israelites made ornaments, money, and temple furnishings out of gold (Genesis 24:22; Exodus 36:34-38; 1 Kings 10:2; 22:48). Gold was a symbol of purity and perfection (Job 23:10; Revelation 21:15, 21).

GOLGOTHA (GOL-go-thah). See *Calvary.*

GOLIATH (go-LIGH-uth). The Philistine giant whom David killed (1 Samuel 17).

GOMER (GO-mur). The unfaithful wife of the prophet Hosea (Hosea 1:3).

GOMORRAH, GOMORRA (go-MAHR-ah, submersion). A city that was destroyed by fire. It was on a plain that is now under the Dead Sea (Genesis 19:24, 28). See also *Sodom.*

GOOD. That which is right, helpful, or better than others of its kind. The only true good is from God; in fact, God *is* good, and everything He does is good (Exodus 18:9; Psalm 118:1; Jeremiah 32:40; Mark 10:18; Romans 7:12). Especially His plan of salvation is good. If a person wants to "do good," then he or she must have faith in and live for Jesus Christ (Romans 6; Galatians 5:24-26).

GOPHERWOOD. The type of wood Noah used to build the ark. Bible scholars are not certain what kind of wood this was, but some think it may have been something like cypress (Genesis 6:14).

GOSHEN (GO-shuhn). 1. The area in northeastern Egypt assigned to the Israelites (Genesis 46:28).

2. An area in southern Palestine, possibly named after the town of Goshen in the hills of Judah (Joshua 10:41; 15:51).

GOSPEL (good news). The Good News that God has forgiven all people because Jesus Christ has fulfilled the Law in their place and paid the penalty for their sin (Romans 1:16-17; 1 Corinthians 15:1-15; 2 Corinthians 5:18-20; Ephesians 2:8-9).

GOSPELS. The first four books of the New Testament. Matthew, Mark, Luke, and John each wrote one of the books. They are called gospels because they tell the Good News of how salvation was won for all people by Jesus Christ. The first three gospels are referred to as the synoptic gospels because they can be placed side by side for comparison. The writers of all four of the gospels are often referred to as evangelists.

GOVERNOR. Although this title is used for many officials in the Bible, it usually refers to someone who ruled a city or province and reported to the ruler above him (Genesis 42:6; Ezra 5:14; Luke 3:1).

GRACE. God's undeserved love and favor in Jesus Christ by which He is moved to forgive people's sins and grant them salvation (John 3:16; Titus 3:4-5). The word *grace* is sometimes used of a gift, quality, or virtue; saving grace, however, is none of these things. It is a quality within God. It is also referred to as God's steadfast love or faithfulness (2 Samuel 7:15; Nehemiah 9:17; Psalm 31:21; 42:8).

GRAPE. See *vineyard*.

GRASS. Used in the Bible as the general name for all small green plants (Matthew 6:30). Grass is also a symbol for the shortness of life (Psalm 90:5-6; James 1:10-11).

GRECIA, GREECE (GREE-shah, GREES). The name for the area in Bible times that included Macedonia, Achaia, and the islands of the Aegean Sea (Acts 20:2). Today Greece is the name of a modern country in southeastern Europe that is almost identical in location to the Greece of Bible times.

GRECIAN, GREEK (GREE-shuhn, GREEK). 1. The language of Greece, from which the original language of the written New Testament came.

2. A person who was born in or lived in Greece (Acts 17:12). When Jew and Greek are contrasted in the New Testament, the term *Greek* is used for a foreigner in general (Romans 1:16). Greek-speaking Jews were referred to as Hellenists.

GUILT. See *conscience; sin, II.*

HABAKKUK (hah-BAK-uhk, embrace). A prophet of Judah whose message of hope in God's grace is recorded in the Book of Habakkuk. Habakkuk prophesied about 600 B.C. while the temple was still standing (2:20).

HABAKKUK, BOOK OF. The eighth book of the Minor Prophets. Written by the prophet Habakkuk, the book contains a message of hope in God's grace despite the harshness of His judgment.

Date: 620 to 605 B.C.

Audience: People of Judah

Outline: 1. The terrible judgment to come through the Chaldeans (1). 2. The five woes with which God threatens Chaldea (2). 3. The Lord shall live: vision of the God of salvation (3).

HADAD (HAY-dad, thunderer?). 1. The name of the Aramean god of storm and thunder (like the Canaanite god Baal).

2. Possibly also a title, since several kings and princes of Edom had this name (1 Chronicles 1:46, 50; 1 Kings 11:14-25).

HADES (HAY-deez). In classical Greek this word refers first to a person and then to the place in the depths of the earth where the spirits of the dead go. The Hebrew word *Sheol* means about the same thing. In the New Testament Hades refers to the place of the dead (Luke 10:15; Acts 2:27; Revelation 6:8). See also *Gehenna; hell; Sheol.*

HAGAR (HAY-gahr, flight). Sarah's Egyptian servant. Hagar took Sar-

ah's place and had a son, Ishmael, for Abraham (Genesis 16; 21). Hagar represents slavery under the Law (Galatians 4:24-25).

HAGGAI (HAG-ay-igh, festive). A prophet around 520 B.C. during the days of Darius (1:1). Haggai was a leader in rebuilding the temple (Ezra 5:1). His prophecy is recorded in the Book of Haggai.

HAGGAI, BOOK OF. The 10th book of the Minor Prophets. The book contains four prophetic sermons concerning the rebuilding of the temple.

Date: 520 B.C.

Audience: Jews

Outline: 1. Haggai speaks against apathy and encourages the people to rebuild the temple (1). 2. Haggai speaks about the future glory of the house of God and the doom of the heathen (2).

HAGIOGRAPHA (hag-i-OG-rah-fah, sacred writings). The third main division of the Jewish Old Testament. Its Hebrew name is *Kethubhim,* which means writings. The Hagiographa include Ruth, Chronicles, Ezra, Nehemiah, Esther, Job, Psalms, Proverbs, Ecclesiastes, Song of Solomon, Lamentations, and Daniel.

HAIL. 1. A word of greeting or respect for a superior. The soldiers who mocked Jesus addressed Him with this word (Matthew 27:29).

2. Pellets of ice that fall from clouds like rain. God sent a plague of hail on Egypt (Exodus 9:18-29). People feared hail because it destroyed their crops and hurt or damaged other things (Psalm 78:47-48).

3. A symbol of God's judgment (Isaiah 28:2).

HAIR. In Old Testament times both men and women had long hair (2 Samuel 14:26). Nazirites, people who had made a special promise to God, were not supposed to cut their hair (Numbers 6:1-5). Samuel and

Samson were Nazirites. Baldness was disliked and was used as a symbol for God's anger or judgment (Isaiah 3:24; Jeremiah 47:5). In New Testament times long hair was for women only (1 Corinthians 11:14-15).

Scripture forbids or warns against certain ways of wearing one's hair (Leviticus 19:27; 1 Peter 3:3). It also mentions barbers and describes how hair was trimmed (Ezekiel 5:1; 44:20).

HALLEL (ha-LAYL, praise). The name given to certain psalms that played a special part in Israel's worship, for instance, Psalms 113 to 118. Jesus and His disciples probably sang the Hallel at the Last Supper.

HALLELUJAH (HAL-i-LOO-yah, praise the Lord). A call or command to praise God and His name. This word became an important part of the language of Israel's worship. It is found at the beginning and end of certain psalms, as well as in the Book of Revelation (Revelation 19:1, 3, 4, 6).

HALLOW. To set apart as holy, for special use for or by God (Exodus 20:11; Luke 11:2).

HAM (HAM, black; also the Egyptian name for Egypt). 1. The third son of Noah (Genesis 5:32). When Ham angered his father, Noah spoke a curse on Canaan (Genesis 9:21-27). Ham's sons were Cush, Mizraim, Put, and Canaan (1 Chronicles 1:18). Their descendants lived in South Arabia, Egypt, Ethiopia, and Canaan.

2. The poetic name for Egypt (Psalms 105:23, 27).

HAMAN (HAY-muhn). The wicked prime minister of Ahasuerus. Haman tried to have all the Jews in Persia killed (Esther 3:1).

HAMMER. 1. A tool used, much like today, for many tasks that required forceful blows, for instance, driving tent pins, tearing down buildings, shaping gold or other metals, and breaking rock (Judges 4:21; 1 Kings 6:7; Psalm 74:6; Isaiah 41:7).

2. A symbol of power or strength (Jeremiah 50:23).

HAMMURABI (ham-uh-RAH-bi). A king of Babylon who ruled during the 18th century B.C. He is known for the battles he fought, the cities he built, and the Code of Hammurabi, which was a set of laws he put together.

HANAMEEL, HANAMEL (HAN-ah-meel, HAN-ah-mel, God has pitied). The prophet Jeremiah's cousin. Before the siege of Jerusalem Jeremiah bought a field from him (Jeremiah 32:6-12).

HANANIAH (han-ah-NIGH-ah, Lord has favored). 1. The false prophet who opposed Jeremiah (Jeremiah 28:1-17).

2. The Hebrew name of Shadrach, one of the three men who was thrown into the fiery furnace because he would not worship the golden image King Nebuchadnezzar set up (Daniel 1:3-19; 3).

HAND. 1. Figurative for power, strength, or control (Exodus 13:3, 14, 16; 1 Samuel 23:20; Psalm 76:5). The phrase "hand of God" refers to God's actions or presence (1 Samuel 5:11; Ezra 5:22; 1 Peter 5:6). The open hand stands for generous giving (Deuteronomy 15:8; Psalm 145:16).

2. People gave directions by using their right hand for the south and their left hand for the north (Job 23:9; Acts 21:3).

3. The Bible speaks of the right hand as the place of honor and authority (1 Kings 2:19; Matthew 25:33; Acts 2:33).

4. Hands were used to give a blessing (Mark 10:16; 2 Timothy 1:6).

HANNAH (HAN-ah, grace). Samuel's mother (1 Samuel 1—2).

HARAN (HAY-rahn, road). 1. Abraham's brother (Genesis 11:26-31).

2. A city in upper Mesopotamia where Abraham went after leaving Ur (Genesis 11:31-32).

HARDNESS OF HEART. A condition of stubbornness and disobedience in which a person refuses to listen or change his or her mind (Exodus 7—10). Hardness of heart can prevent understanding and belief (Acts 19:9). People may harden their hearts against God or other people (Exodus 8:32; Deuteronomy 15:7). God sometimes confirms their hardness of heart as punishment (Exodus 10:1; Romans 9:18).

HARLOT. See *prostitute.*

HAROD (HAY-rod, fear). The spring or well where Gideon camped with his men (Judges 7:1).

HARP. See *music.*

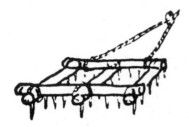

HARROW. A tool which farmers used. The harrow was a toothed instrument that animals dragged along the ground to break up clods of earth after plowing (Isaiah 28:24-25). See also *agriculture.*

HARVEST. See *agriculture; orchard; vineyard.*

HARVEST, FEAST OF. See *Pentecost 1.*

HASMONEANS (haz-mo-NEE-ahnz). See *Maccabees.*

HATE. 1. To dislike or regard as ugly or wrong; to have feelings toward someone or something that are the opposite of love (Psalm 45:7; Matthew 24:10).

2. To withdraw from or avoid someone or something so that a proper relationship with God can be kept (Amos 5:15; Luke 14:26; compare with Matthew 10:37-39).

HAZAEL (HAZ-ay-el, God sees). A great king of Syria whom God used to bring judgment upon Israel (1 Kings 19:15-18). Hazael followed Ben-Hadad II, ruling Damascus from about 840 to 800 B.C. Hazael captured Israel's land east of the Jordan, continually troubled Jehoahaz, and once even planned to attack Jerusalem (2 Kings 10:32-33; 12:17-18; 13:3-7, 22-25).

HAZOR (HAY-zawr enclosure). A city of northern Galilee near the headwaters of the Jordan River. Jabin was the ruler of Hazor when Joshua captured it (Joshua 11:1-14). Later it was given to the tribe of Naphtali (Joshua 19:36, 39). Another King Jabin of Hazor was defeated by Deborah and Barak (Judges 4).

HEAD. 1. A part of the body.

2. A whole person (Proverbs 10:6).

3. The capital of a country or region (Isaiah 7:8-9).

4. A leader in society (Isaiah 9:14-15).

5. The name for one who has authority over others (Ephesians 5:23).

6. The expression "upon the head" refers to guilt, responsibility, or duty (Joshua 2:19; Ezekiel 9:10).

7. The expression "lift up the head" or the action of lifting up the head means to restore or renew favor, life, strength, etc. (Genesis 40:20-21; Psalm 83:2).

HEAD OF THE CHURCH. Christ, who gives life, strength, and direction to every believer and who rules as the Head of the body, the church (Ephesians 1:22; 4:13-16).

HEADBAND. Probably a sash or other piece of cloth worn around the head (Isaiah 3:18).

HEAD STONE. See *cornerstone.*

HEAL. See *apothecary; disease.*

HEAR. 1. To receive sound by means of the ear (2 Samuel 15:10).

2. To listen to God's Word and will (Matthew 13:18).

3. To understand and follow God's Word and will (John 8:47; 10:27).

4. To listen to and approve as right (1 John 4:5).

5. God's "hearing" describes His action of answering prayer (Psalms 116:1).

HEART. 1. A symbol for the life of the whole body (Judges 19:5).

2. A word for describing the center of thought, understanding, decision-making, emotion, will, and conscience (Deuteronomy 29:4; Nehemiah 7:5; Isaiah 44:18; 65:14; Romans 11:21; 1 Corinthians 7:37). Some Bible translations use the word *mind* instead of *heart* to describe these things.

3. The place within us where Christ and the Spirit live (Ephesians 3:17; 2 Corinthians 1:22).

HEARTH (HAHRTH). 1. A portable fireplace or firepot (Jeremiah 36:22-23).

2. A fireplace on an altar (Ezekiel 43:15-16).

HEATHEN. See *barbarian; Gentiles.*

HEAVEN (HEV-uhn). 1. The layer of air surrounding the earth and everything in it (Daniel 7:13; Mark 14:62).

2. The upper or outer part of the universe and all that is in it; the firmament, especially the "waters above" (Psalms 148:4; Isaiah 40:22).

3. The invisible world or universe from which God rules (Ezra 1:2; Psalm 115:3); the home of angels (1 Kings 22:19; Mark 12:25). Christ rules from heaven and receives believers there (John 14:1-3; Acts 7:55; Hebrews 8:1). See also *paradise.*

HEBREW (HEE-broo). The language in which most of the Old Testament was written. Scripture refers to it both as a Canaanite language and as the language of the Israelites (2 Kings 18:26, 28; Isaiah 19:18). The language is closely related to ancient languages from the region of Palestine and is probably based on a Canaanite dialect adopted by the patriarchs.

The Hebrew alphabet, consisting only of consonants, came from the writing of the Phoenicians and was in existence by the 15th century B.C. About A.D. 600 to 800 scribes known as the Massoretes added vowel sounds to the Hebrew text of the Old Testament.

HEBREWS (HEE-broos). Abram is the first person in the Old Testament to be referred to as a Hebrew (Genesis 14:13). From that point on the name is given to his descendants in both the Old and the New Testaments. Hebrew is another name for a person of the nation of Israel just as a person who lives in the United States is referred to as an American.

The word *Hebrew* may come from a word that means to pass over, referring back to Abram's crossing of the Euphrates River after he had left home, or it may come from the name Eber, an ancestor of the Israelites (Genesis 10:21). In ancient writings from Bible times the Hebrew people are sometimes linked with people known as the Habiru.

HEBREWS, LETTER TO THE. Scholars are uncertain about who wrote this book. They think it could have been Paul, Barnabas, or Apollos. It is certain, however, that the letter was written to Christians, especially Hebrew Christians, who were in danger of falling from the faith (10:19-39).

Date: A.D. 65 to 70

Audience: Jewish Christians outside Palestine

Outline: 1. The pre-eminence of Jesus, the ultimate High Priest and Author of salvation, over angels, Moses, Joshua, and high priests (1—10). 2. Roll call of heroes and heroines of the faith (11). 3. Exhortation to faith and Godliness (12). 4. Exhortations to social and religious duties; closing (13—15).

HEBRON (HEE-brun, union). A city about 20 miles southwest of Jerusalem (Joshua 15:48). It was originally called Kiriath-arba (Genesis 20:2). Hebron played a large part in Abraham's life (Genesis 13:18; 18:23). The spies visited this place, Joshua conquered it, and David was anointed as king and ruled Judah from Hebron for more than seven years (Numbers 13:22; Joshua 10:36-37; 2 Samuel 2:4, 11).

HEDGE. A kind of fence or enclosure made of plants, often thorns (Isaiah 5:5; Hosea 2:6).

HEIFER. A young cow that has not produced a calf (Judges 14:18). A heifer is often used in metaphors (Jeremiah 46:20; 50:11). The Israelites used a red heifer for purification ceremonies and as a sin offering (Numbers 19).

HEIR. The individual to whom another person's wealth or possessions, the person's inheritance, is given after the person dies. When a man died, his inheritance was first divided among the sons of his legal wives (Genesis 21:10; 24:36; 25:5). The oldest son usually received a double share and became the head of the family (Deuteronomy 21:15-17). If the man had no sons, the inheritance was divided, in order, among his daughters, brothers, paternal uncles, or other relatives (Numbers 27:8-11).

HELL. Either the place of eternal punishment or the punishment itself. It is called Sheol in the Old Testament and Gehenna in the New Testament. Hell is described as eternal punishment, a fire that cannot be put out, a place where worms continually eat and fires continually burn the damned, a lake of fire, the outer darkness, and the furnace of fire where people cry out and grind their teeth (Isaiah 66:34; Matthew 13:42, 50; 25:30, 46; Mark 9:44; Revelation 20:14). Unbelievers are put in hell because they are under the wrath of God (John 3:36). See also *Gehenna; Hades.*

HELLENIST (HEL-en-ist). See *Grecian, Greek.*

HELMET. See *armor, arms.*

HEM. The edge, fringe, or border of a piece of clothing (Exodus 28:33-34; Matthew 9:20). The Pharisees wore especially long fringes because they wanted to show off their obedience to the command in Numbers 15:38-39 (Matthew 23:5).

HEMLOCK. See *gall 3; wormwood.*

HEPHZIBAH (HEF-zi-bah, my delight is in her). 1. The wife of Hezekiah (2 Kings 21:1).

2. The symbolic name God gave to Israel to show His love and mercy for the covenant people (Isaiah 62:4).

HERALD. 1. A messenger or someone who publicly announces decrees of the government or other news (Isaiah 41:27; Daniel 3:4).

2. Someone who spreads the Gospel, especially someone who preaches it (2 Peter 2:5).

HERD. See *cattle.*

HERDSMAN. A person in charge of cattle or pigs (Genesis 13:7; Matthew 8:30-33). The Israelites viewed this job favorably, but the Egyptians looked down on it (Genesis 46:34; 47:6).

HERESY (HER-uh-see, choice). In the New Testament world various schools of thought or belief were called heresies, that is, sects or parties within a larger system of belief

(Acts 5:17; 15:5). For instance, Sadducees, Pharisees, and Christians were all regarded as heresies, that is, sects or parties within Judaism (Acts 5:17; 15:5; 24:5, 14).

2. The word is used in connection with differences of opinion, goals, or belief that cause divisions within the church (1 Corinthians 1:10; 11:18-19).

3. The word is used as a name for false, harmful teachings (2 Peter 2:1).

HERMON (HUR-mun, holy mountain). A mountain about 9,100 feet high that stands approximately 30 miles southwest of Damascus and about the same distance northeast of the Sea of Galilee. Water runoff from the rain and snow on its slopes feeds the Jordan River.

Mount Hermon marked the northern extent of Israel's conquests east of the Jordan River (Deuteronomy 3:8). Some think it may be the mountain where the transfiguration of Christ took place (Mark 9:2). It is called Baal-hermon in Judges 3:3 because it was a major center of worship of that false god.

HEROD (HER-uhd, heroic). The family name of a line of rulers from Idumea (southern Palestine) who ruled in Palestine during New Testament times (55 B.C.—A.D. 93). 1. Although the line was begun by Herod Antipater, it was his son who was known as Herod the Great. Herod the Great was the Roman procurator of Judea in 47 B.C. and was king of the Jews for more than 30 years, from 37 to 4 B.C. To stay on the good side of Rome and of the people in Palestine, Herod rebuilt cities and temples, most importantly the temple at Jerusalem (John 2:20). To maintain his power he did many wicked things, often deceiving or killing people. He was the king who spoke to the Wise Men and had all the baby boys in Bethlehem killed (Matthew 2:1-18).

2. Herod Archelaus, the son of Herod the Great, was the ruler of Judea, Idumea, and Samaria from 4 B.C. to A.D. 6. (Matthew 2:22).

3. Herod Antipas, another son of Herod the Great, ruled Galilee and Perea from 4 B.C. to A.D. 39 (Luke 3:1, 19). He was the ruler during Jesus' lifetime. Herod was rich and sly. Jesus referred to him as "that fox" (Luke 13:32).

4. Herod Philip, yet another son of Herod the Great, is known only as the husband of Herodias. His brother Herod Antipas took Herodias from Herod Philip and married her himself (Matthew 14:3-4).

5. Herod Philip II was not the son of Herod Philip but of Herod the Great. Herod Philip was his half-brother. Herod Philip II ruled Iturea and other regions (Luke 3:1).

6. Herod Agrippa I, a grandson of Herod the Great, ruled different areas of the region of Palestine from A.D. 37 to 44. He persecuted Christians. An angel of the Lord killed him because of his pride and wickedness (Acts 12:1-23).

7. Herod Agrippa II was a son of Agrippa I and a great-grandson of Herod the Great. He was king of the territory east of Galilee from about A.D. 53 to 70. Paul was brought before him (Acts 25:13—26:32).

HERODIANS (hi-RO-di-ahnz). People who supported the Herods and the rule of Rome (Mark 3:6).

HERODIAS (hi-RO-di-as). Herod the Great's granddaughter. She left her first husband, Herod Philip, to marry her brother-in-law Herod Antipas (Matthew 14:3-4). Herodias caused the death of John the Baptizer (Matthew 14:6-12).

HEZEKIAH (hez-i-KIGH-ah, strength is the Lord). The 13th king of Judah. Hezekiah was the son of Ahaz and the father of Manasseh.

He returned Judah to the worship of the true God after a long period of idolatry (2 Chronicles 29—31). Under his direction many of the godly teachings of Solomon were written down (Proverbs 25:1). Judah prospered during his rule. Then Hezekiah became mixed up in a power struggle among Egypt, Assyria, and other nations.

Hezekiah strengthened the defenses of Jerusalem (2 Chronicles 32:5-8). He also supervised the building of the Siloam Tunnel to bring water into the city (2 Kings 20:20). When Sennacherib attacked, Hezekiah and the prophet Isaiah prayed to God for help, and God destroyed the attacking army (Isaiah 36—39).

HIEROGLYPHIC (high-ur-o-GLIF-ik, sacred carving). A system of picture writing used in Egypt and other ancient nations. It is one of the earliest forms of writing.

HIGH, MOST. A name for God (Psalm 9:2; 21:7; Luke 8:28). Melchizedek served God Most High (Genesis 14:18-20).

HIGH PLACES. 1. Places of worship located on high ground. They usually had some type of altar and often one or more buildings (2 Kings 12:31-32). Because the Canaanite high places brought the threat of idolatry and immorality, God commanded the Israelites to destroy them (Numbers 33:52). But the kings of Israel, beginning already with Solomon, rebuilt the high places, sometimes to worship the true God but more often to worship false gods (1 Kings 3:2, 4; 11:7; 2 Kings 17:7-20).

2. The term *high place* eventually became a general name for any place of worship, even one in a valley (Jeremiah 7:31). The place was considered high because of the lordship of the deity.

HIGH PRIEST. See *priest.*

HILKIAH (hil-KIGH-ah, portion is the Lord). One of Ezra's ancestors who was the high priest in the days of King Josiah (Ezra 7:17). Hilkiah found the book of the Law in the temple (2 Kings 22:4-14).

HINNOM (HIN-um). See *Gehenna.*

HIRAM (HIGH-ram, brother of exalted one). 1. The king of Tyre who sent cedar and workmen to David for his house and lumber and gold to Solomon for use in building the temple (2 Samuel 5:11; 1 Kings 9:11-14).

2. The workman who made all the bronze items in or around the temple (1 Kings 7:13-46). Both of these men were sometimes referred to as Huram.

HISS. 1. A way of showing surprise or contempt (1 Kings 9:8; Job 27:23; Jeremiah 19:8). It is sometimes translated as scoff.

2. A way of signaling or calling (Isaiah 7:18).

HITTITES (HIT-ights). The descendants of Heth (Genesis 10:15). The Hittites were a great nation that at one time ruled a large portion of the ancient Near East. They are frequently mentioned in the Old Testament (Genesis 26:34). Archaeologists have discovered remains of the Hittite civilization and have learned their language.

HOLY. That which is set apart to be used for or by God, or that which is recognized as partaking in God's holiness. God's very name is "Holy" because He is perfect in every way and is "high above," or set apart from, all things (Isaiah 57:15). God demands that His people be holy or set apart for Him (Leviticus 19:2; Numbers 15:40-41). The holiness of God is imparted to people through His act of choosing them in grace and through His other mighty acts (Deuteronomy 26:28-29). It culminates in the saving work of Jesus Christ (John

17:19; 1 Corinthians 1:4-9; 1 Peter 2:1-10). Jesus is called the Holy One of God (Mark 1:24).

HOLY LAND. See *Canaan 2*.

HOLY SPIRIT. The Third Person of the Trinity (Matthew 28:19; 2 Corinthians 13:14). The Holy Spirit works through and is sent by God the Father and God the Son (John 15:26; Acts 1:8). The Holy Spirit is God and performs the works of God (Genesis 1:2; Romans 8:9). He creates and sustains the universe and the church (Genesis 1:2; Job 33:4; Acts 2). Moreover each individual believer is created, or born again, through the Spirit, who works through water and the Word (John 3:3-8; 6:63; 1 Corinthians 12:3, 13).

The Holy Spirit lives in the hearts of believers, strengthening and encouraging them in the faith and building them up in the unity of the Spirit and in the unity of the body of believers, the church (Ephesians 4:1-6; 1 Corinthians 12; 2 Corinthians 1:22). The Holy Spirit also unites believers to God the Father and to Jesus Christ (Romans 8:14-17).

The Holy Spirit gave a special measure of understanding to the prophets, worked in a special way in certain leaders of God's people, and was given without measure to Jesus Christ (Judges 3:10; Isaiah 61:1; Luke 4:1; Colossians 1:19; 1 Peter 1:10-12; 2 Peter 1:21). The Holy Spirit dwells in believers (2 Timothy 1:14). He continues to give understanding of God and His will to believers and gives them all spiritual blessings (John 14:26; 16:13-15).

HOLY SPIRIT, SIN AGAINST. See *sin, unpardonable*.

HOMES. Shepherds, exiles, outcasts, and lepers often lived in caves found throughout the limestone ridges of Palestine (1 Kings 18:4; 19:9). People built temporary shelters, or

booths, by covering four upright poles with a network of sticks and leaves (Isaiah 1:8). Sometimes they made these shelters out of woven river reeds that they plastered with mud.

Nomadic people lived in tents, which were often woven from dark-colored goat or camel hair (Genesis 4:20). These tents were usually very large. They had several supporting poles, sloping sides that were held in place by cords anchored in the ground with stakes, and curtains to divide up the living space inside (Isaiah 54:2; Jeremiah 10:20).

In sections of Palestine where building stone was readily available, people built homes out of blocks of limestone. Mortar made from lime and sand held these blocks together. In some areas of the ancient world people built homes made from clay bricks (Genesis 11:3). They constructed doors from planks of wood or slabs of stone. The windows of their homes were usually very narrow; they were placed high up in the wall and fitted with wooden latticework (Proverbs 7:6). To make roofs for their homes, people laid beams across the tops of the walls. Then they covered these beams with a layer of branches laid crosswise, a layer of rushes and straw, and a layer of clay. More alternating layers of rushes and straw were added, and the roof was fin-

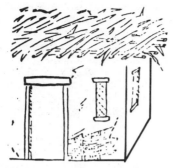

ished with a solid layer of clay. The walls extended about three feet above the roofline (Deuteronomy 22:8). The people often worked or stored things on their rooftops or went there to be alone or to enjoy cool breezes (Joshua 2:6; Acts 10:9). A stairway on the outside of the house led from street level up to the roof. Sometimes people built an upstairs room, or upper room, on one side of the building (2 Kings 4:10; Mark 14:15; Acts 1:13). They also might make the one main room into two levels, the upper level for living quarters and the lower one for sheep and goats.

The furnishings of a typical house included mats or rugs woven from wool, grass, or straw. These were used for mattresses at night and in place of chairs during the day. A stove or fireplace for heating and cooking was located in the middle of the house. Sometimes it was only a hole in the earthen floor. Spoons, forks, and other utensils and pots and pans were made of copper. Knives were made of bronze or iron and had wooden handles. Plates, cups, bowls, jugs, and other containers were made of pottery. People stored wheat in large, pottery jars. Other things were stored by hanging them from the roof beams.

Wealthier homes had furniture— couches, beds, chairs—more like today's furniture. Often these homes had walled courtyards or consisted of a series of rooms built around an open court. As the nation of Israel grew richer, the wealthy and powerful people built big, beautiful mansions and palaces (1 Kings 7:1-8; Amos 6:4-8). (Klinck)

HONEY. Wild honey, which was plentiful in Palestine, was eaten in various ways (Exodus 16:31; 1 Samuel 14:25). It was often a symbol of richness and plenty (Numbers 14:8).

HOOKS. Hooks were used for fishing, hanging curtains, leading animals or prisoners, pruning and trimming, and hanging meat (Exodus 26:37; 2 Chronicles 33:11; Job 41:1; Ezekiel 19:4; 26:37; 40:43; Joel 3:10).

HOPE. A feeling of peace and joy; a sense that something good will happen. The Christian's hope is centered in Jesus Christ (1 Timothy 1:1). It flows from the new, loving relationship a Christian has with God through faith in Jesus Christ (Romans 5:1-11). Faith, hope, and love are often linked in Scripture (1 Corinthians 13:7, 13; Hebrews 11:1; 1 Thessalonians 1:3; 5:8). The Christian hope looks beyond this life to the glory of heaven (2 Corinthians 4:16-18). It takes Christ's resurrection as the promise of God that the Christian will also be raised to life eternal (1 Corinthians 6:14). Christians who live in such hope are comforted in times of trouble and are motivated to live lives pleasing to God (Psalm 43:5; 1 John 3:1-3).

HOR (HAWR, mountain). 1. A mountain on the edge of Edom. Aaron died on Mount Hor (Numbers 20:22-29).

2. A mountain in northern Palestine, probably in Lebanon, that was used to mark the northern boundary of Canaan (Numbers 34:7-8).

HOREB (HO-reb, dryness). The mountain where the Law was given to Israel. Horeb and Sinai are names for the same mountain (Exodus 17:6).

HORN. At first people blew on animal horns to give signals. They also made containers out of animal horns (Joshua 6:5; 1 Samuel 16:1). Later they made horns out of metal (Numbers 10:2). The projecting corners of the altar in the tabernacle and the temple were called horns (1 Kings 1:50). The horn was a symbol of honor and strength (Daniel 7:7; Luke 1:69).

HORSE. The Hebrew people during Jacob's time were familiar with horses (Genesis 49:17). The Egyptians used horses, mainly for war (Exodus 14:9). The Israelites were ordered not to keep any horses captured in battle, and the rulers of Israel were directed not to keep large numbers of horses (Deuteronomy 17:16; Joshua 11:6). Later kings, however, did keep horses (1 Kings 1:5; 4:26).

HOSANNA (ho-ZAN-ah, save now). At Jesus' triumphant entry into Jerusalem the crowds chanted this as they waved palm branches (Matthew 21:9-15). Usage of the word may have originated with Psalm 118:25-26.

HOSEA (ho-ZAY-ah, salvation). A prophet at the time of Kings Uzziah, Jotham, Ahaz, Hezekiah of Judah, and Jeroboam II of Israel (Hosea 1:1). Isaiah, Amos, and Micah were other prophets at the same time as Hosea. Hosea's prophecy is recorded in the Book of Hosea.

HOSEA, BOOK OF. The first of the Minor Prophets as they appear in the Old Testament. The first three chapters are the key to the whole book. By discussing Hosea's marriage to the unfaithful Gomer, these chapters provide a clear picture of Israel's unfaithfulness and God's forgiveness. The rest of the book is a collection of largely unconnected sayings and prophecies.

Date: About 742 to 715 B.C.

Audience: Israelites

Outline: 1. Israel's unfaithfulness and God's forgiveness symbolized by Hosea's marriage (1—3). 2. Israel's sinfulness and need for repentance (4—6:3). 3. The punishment that must be given for sin (6:4—10:15). 4. God scolds His people and explains His anger (11—13). 5. Call to repentance and promise of forgiveness for the penitent (14).

HOSHEA (HO-SHEE-ah, salvation; same as Hosea). The last king of Israel. Hoshea gained the throne by joining with a foreign king to assassinate Pekah, who was then king of Israel (2 Kings 15:30). Hoshea placed himself under the control of Assyria by paying tribute to the king of Assyria, Shalmaneser V (2 Kings 17:3). When Hoshea stopped paying tribute, the Assyrians conquered Israel and took the people captive. Apparently Hoshea was not as wicked as other kings of Israel (2 Kings 17:2).

HOSPITALITY (hos-puh-TAL-uh-tee). The readiness to help strangers by giving them food, clothing, shelter, or whatever else they might need. Hospitality is commanded in the Levitical law and is encouraged elsewhere in the Old and New Testaments (Genesis 18:1-8; Leviticus 19:34; Job 31:32; Hebrews 13:2).

HOST. 1. A great number. The host of heaven refers either to the numerous stars and other heavenly bodies that people often wrongfully worshiped or to the angels and the company of saints in heaven (Deuteronomy 4:19; 1 Kings 22:19; Luke 2:13).

2. One of God's names is Sabaoth, or Lord of hosts. He is named this because He rules over the an-

gels, the stars, and all things (Genesis 28:12; Job 37—39; Isaiah 40:26).

3. Someone who shows hospitality.

HOUSE. 1. The name for a family line (Exodus 2:1; Luke 2:4).

2. The name for the place where God makes His presence known, for instance, at Bethel, which means house of God, in the tabernacle, and in the temple (Genesis 28:17; Exodus 34:26; 1 Kings 6:1).

3. See *homes*.

HULDAH (HUL-dah, weasel). A prophetess in the Old Testament. She was the wife of Shallum (2 Kings 22:14-20; 2 Chronicles 34:22-28).

HUMILITY. The opposite of pride; not thinking more of oneself than one should. Someone who is humble puts God and others ahead of self (Proverbs 15:33; Romans 12:3; see also Luke 18:9-14).

HUNTING. The Israelites hunted many types of wild deer, sheep, and birds (Deuteronomy 2:15, 22; 14:5; 1 Samuel 26:20). They used bows and arrows, slingstones, spears, nets, pits, and traps (Genesis 27:3; Job 41:28-29; Psalms 9:15).

HUR (HUR). 1. The man who helped Aaron hold up Moses' hands at Rephidim so that Joshua was able to defeat the Amalekites (Exodus 17:8-16).

2. A king of Midian (Numbers 31:8).

HYMN. A song telling about God and praising Him (Exodus 15:1-19; Deuteronomy 32:1-43; Judges 5; 1 Samuel 2:1-10; Psalms; Luke 1:46-55, 68-79). Christians are encouraged to worship God by using psalms, hymns, and spiritual songs (Colossians 3:16).

HYPOCRISY (hi-PAHK-ru-see). To play a part; to pretend to be what one is not. In the Bible hypocrisy usually describes a condition of pre-

tending to have faith when no faith is present in the heart at all (Matthew 23:28). It also refers to any type of trickery, lying, or falsehood (Mark 12:15).

HYSSOP (HIS-uhp). Although the Bible mentions this plant numerous times, it apparently is not always referring to the same type of plant. Exodus 12:22 seems to speak of a bushy plant that the Israelites used to sprinkle blood on the doorposts at the first Passover. John 19:29 mentions a long stalk or stem as part of the hyssop plant that was used to put the bitter drink to Jesus' lips while He hung on the cross. The plant was used in certain religious ceremonies and also as a symbol of purification, correction, and forgiveness (Leviticus 14:4, 6, 49; Numbers 19:6; Psalm 51:7).

IBEX (IGH-beks). Probably a large, light-colored antelope. Since the ibex was classed among the clean animals, the Israelites were allowed to eat it (Deuteronomy 14:5).

ICE. Snow and ice can be found on the higher mountains of Palestine, such as Mount Hermon (Jeremiah 18:14). Otherwise, although known to people in Palestine, snow and ice are rare except in the extreme north of the country (Job 6:16; 37:6, 10).

ICHABOD (IK-ah-bod, there is no glory). The son of Phineas and grandson of Eli. Ichabod was born after his father was killed in a battle with the Philistines, a battle in which the Philistines captured the ark of the covenant. Ichabod's mother named him as she did because she felt the glory had departed from Israel (1 Samuel 4:19-22).

ICONIUM (igh-KO-ni-uhm). A city on the southwestern edge of the central plain of Asia Minor (modern-day Turkey). Paul visited this city on his missionary journeys (Acts 13:51; 14:1-22; 16:2).

IDDO (ID-o). 1. The name of a wise man who wrote down the events of the reigns of Solomon, Rehoboam, Jeroboam, and Abijah (2 Chronicles 9:29; 12:15).

2. The grandfather of the prophet Zechariah (Zechariah 1:1, 7).

IDOL, IDOLATRY (IGH-dol, igh-DOL-ah-tree). A false god or anything that is placed ahead of the true God is an idol. Worshiping a false God or placing a thing or person ahead of God is called idolatry. Often idols had names and were represented by pictures or some type of statue or figurine made of various materials and in varying sizes (Genesis 31:34; Isaiah 40:19-20; Daniel 3:1). Idols and idolatry are forbidden and are spoken of as foolish, hateful, and horrible in Scripture (Exodus 20:4-5, 23; Isaiah 44:9-20; Ezekiel 37:23). Paul describes idols and idolatry as exchanging the truth about God for a lie (Romans 1:21-23, 25).

IDUMEA, IDUMAEA (id-yoo-MEE-ah). The Greek name for Edom, the area south of Judah (Mark 3:8).

IGNORANCE. A lack of knowledge. In the Bible ignorance is especially a lack of knowledge concerning the true God and His will. It is sometimes described as excusable and at other times as inexcusable (Ezekiel 45:20; Ephesians 4:18).

ILLYRICUM (i-LIR-i-kuhm). The name of a Roman province on the east coast of the Adriatic Sea, northwest of Greece. It was later called Dalmatia (2 Timothy 4:10). As far as we know, it is the northernmost part of Europe into which Paul traveled on his missionary journeys

(Romans 15:19). Today Illyricum is part of the country of Yugoslavia.

IMAGE. See *idol, idolatry.*

IMAGE OF GOD. People were originally created in the image of God (Genesis 1:26-27). Since God is a spiritual being and no person or thing can equal Him in any way, the likeness of people to God is spiritual, not physical, and is always "less than," not "equal to."

In the most proper sense, being created in the image of God means that people were created without sin. But this image was lost in the fall into sin. In the broader sense, the image of God refers to humanity's rationality and will and still remains in people, although the presence of original sin has also corrupted that likeness (Genesis 9:6; James 3:9). Christ is the image of God, and in Him we can see God (John 1:1, 14, 18; Colossians 1:15). Through Christ people regain the likeness to God (Romans 8:29).

IMMANUEL (i-MAN-yoo-uhl, God is with us). The name of the child whom the prophet Isaiah predicted would be born of a virgin (Isaiah 7:14; Matthew 1:22-23). This is an important prophecy predicting the birth of the Savior, Jesus Christ, the Promised One spoken of in many Old Testament prophecies (Isaiah 9:6-7; 11:1; Micah 5:2-3).

IMMORTALITY (im-awr-TAL-uh-tee). See *eschatology; eternal life.*

IMPUTATION (im-pyoo-TAY-shuhn). Placing the blame for something bad or the credit for something good on someone else. When Adam and Eve fell into sin, that sin was imputed to all, that is, the blame for it was placed upon all people. In the same way, when Christ paid the price for sin by His death and resurrection, that payment was imputed or credited to all who believe in Christ (Romans 5:12-21; 2 Corinthians 5:19-21).

INCARNATION (in-kahr-NA-shuhn). The term for what took place when the Son of God took on a human body and soul. The word itself does not occur in the Bible, but it is used properly in the Nicene Creed to describe Jesus' birth. See also *Jesus Christ.*

INCENSE. Any substance that gives off a sweet smell when burned. Incense played an important part in Israel's worship. It was burned on the altar of incense morning and evening, carried into the Holy of Holies on the Day of Atonement, and used at other times as well. The incense the Israelites used is described in Exodus 30:34-35. People also burned incense to worship false gods (Jeremiah 44:28).

Incense is a symbol for prayer or worship (Psalm 141:2; Revelation 5:8).

INCEST. Having sexual relations with members of one's own family. Incest is forbidden in Scripture (Leviticus 20:11-17, 19-21; 1 Corinthians 5:1).

INCORRUPTION (in-ko-RUP-shuhn). Freedom from physical decay or other imperfection. See also *eternal life.*

INDIA (IN-di-ah). The country on the east of the Persian Empire (Esther 1:1).

INHERITANCE. See *heir.*

INIQUITY (i-NIK-wi-tee). See *sin, II.*

INK. A substance used for writing. Ink was made by mixing charcoal or lampblack (a fine black powder) with water and plant gum (Jeremiah 36:18; 2 John 12).

INN. Places where travelers can sleep at night. Hebrew hospitality made inns and hotels in our sense practically unnecessary. The inns in Luke 2:7 and 10:34 were probably more like private homes than places of business.

INSPIRATION. (in-spuh-RAY-shuhn). The special way the Holy Spirit worked in certain people to cause them to act out, speak, or write God's Word (Micah 3:8; 1 Corinthians 2:13; 1 Peter 1:10-11). When the Holy Spirit did this, the person who was inspired, or motivated, to act, speak, or write was certainly under the direction of God's power, but he or she was not a robot (see Luke 1:1-4).

INTERCESSION. See prayer.

IOTA (igh-O-tah). See jot.

IRON. Iron is mentioned already in Genesis 4:22. The Hittite people passed the knowledge of ironworking to the Philistines. When David conquered the Philistines, the Israelites learned about ironworking as well. Tools, weapons, chariots, chains and shackles, and writing tools were all made from iron (Numbers 35:16; Joshua 6: 19, 24; 17:16; 1 Samuel 17:7; Job 19:24; Psalm 105:18). Iron is also a symbol of strength.

ISAAC (IGH-sahk, laughter). Abraham's only son by Sarah (Genesis 17:19). Isaac was the son of the promise, the one through whom God continued to work out His plan of salvation (Genesis 21:12). Isaac showed himself to be a faithful, obedient son when God ordered Abraham to sacrifice him (Genesis 22:1-18). Isaac married Rebekah and had two sons: Jacob and Esau. Rebekah and Jacob plotted together to trick Isaac into giving Jacob the blessing of the firstborn son (Genesis 24—27). Isaac died at Mamre (Genesis 35:27-29).

ISAIAH (igh-ZAY-yah, the Lord is salvation). A prophet of Judah during the reigns of Uzziah, Jotham, Ahaz, and Hezekiah (Isaiah 1:1). Isaiah lived in Jerusalem. The year that Uzziah died, Isaiah saw a vision in the temple (Isaiah 6). This is sometimes referred to as Isaiah's

call to be God's prophet. Isaiah married and had two sons (Isaiah 7:3; 8:3). Hezekiah sought the help of Isaiah when the Assyrians were about to attack Jerusalem (2 Kings 19:1-11).

ISAIAH, BOOK OF. This is the longest of all the prophetic books. It is about God's judgment and grace and contains many passages about the Promised Savior, much beautiful poetry, and history.

Date: 740 to 687 B.C.

Audience: Jews

Outline: 1. Introductory development of two themes: threat of judgment and promise of redemption (1—5). 2. Isaiah's vision: his commissioning to be God's messenger (6). 3. Immanuel: His messianic kingdom (7—12). 4. Judgment pronounced on foreign nations and apostate Jerusalem (13—23). 5. Judgment on the world and Jewish blessing: the Day of the Lord (24—27). 6. Jerusalem to be destroyed and restored (28—33). 7. Day of victory in God's kingdom (34—35). 8. Jerusalem delivered from Assyrians, destroyed by Babylonians (36—39). 9. The way of salvation through forgiveness opened for all sinners by the suffering servant and the way to glory (40—66).

ISCARIOT (is-KAR-i-ut). See Judas 2.

ISH-BOSHETH (ish-BO-sheth, man of shame). One of Saul's sons. He was originally called Eshbaal (1 Chronicles 8:33). Ish-bosheth ruled two years at Mahanaim but was defeated by David's men. Later he was assassinated (2 Samuel 2:8-32; 3; 4:5-12; 1 Chronicles 8:33).

ISHMAEL (ISH-may-uhl, God hears). 1. The son of Abraham and Sarah's maidservant, Hagar (Genesis 16:3, 15; 17:25). Sarah became jealous of her stepson and demanded that Abraham send him and his mother away. Abraham was disturbed by this, but trusting God's word to him, he sent them away (Genesis 21:8-20. See also Galatians 4:21-31). Ishmael's descendants became a great nation (Genesis 17:20; 25:12-16).

2. The man who assassinated Gedaliah and caused Jeremiah to flee to Egypt (Jeremiah 40:7—41:18).

ISHMAELITES (ISH-may-ul-ights). Descendants of Ishmael. The Ishmaelites were traveling desert merchants and traders for the most part (Genesis 37:25-28).

ISLE, ISLAND (IGHL, IGH-lahnd).
1. Dry land surrounded by water (Jeremiah 47:4; Acts 13:6).

2. Habitable land that once was water (Isaiah 42:15).

3. Coastal land, either beaches or islands, especially in the Mediterranean Sea area (Isaiah 20:6; 23:2).

4. Symbolic for faraway lands, whether islands or not (Isaiah 49:1). It often describes the majesty of God and the broad scope of Messianic prophecy (Psalm 97:1; Zephaniah 2:11).

ISRAEL (IZ-ray-el, God strives; he strives with God). 1. The name given to Jacob at Penuel after he wrestled with an intruder (Genesis 32:28).

2. The name of the nation composed of the descendants of Jacob and his 12 sons. Jacob and his sons founded the 12 tribes of Israel (Exodus 3:16). The name Israel is used more than 2,000 times in Scripture to refer to the Children, or nation, of Israel.

3. The name given to the 10 northern tribes of Israel after Solomon's death when they revolted under Rehoboam, and the kingdom split into two. The Northern Kingdom was called Israel to distinguish it from the Southern Kingdom, which was called Judah (1 Samuel

11:8). The capital of Israel was first Shechem and later Samaria (1 Kings 12:25; 16:24). When a remnant of the people returned to Palestine after the Babylonian exile, the name Israel was used again of all the descendants of Jacob and his sons (Ezra 10:10).

4. This name is also used to describe all those who follow in the faith of Abraham, Isaac, and Jacob and therefore are true Israelites, no matter what their physical descent (Psalm 73:1; Romans 9:6-8, 23-24; 11:13-36; Galatians 3:26-29).

ISRAELITES (IZ-ray-uhl-ights). See *Israel.*

ISSACHAR (IS-a-kahr, hired laborer). 1. The ninth son of Jacob, the fifth by his wife Leah. A tribe of Israel was made up of Issachar's descendants (Genesis 30:14-18). Jacob prophesied that Issachar's descendants would become slaves (Genesis 49:14-15).

2. The area southwest of the Sea of Galilee that was assigned to the tribe of Issachar. It included the Plain of Esdraelon, also called the Valley of Jezreel (Joshua 19:17-23; Judges 6:33).

ITALY (IT-ahl-ee). The name of the whole peninsula of land that begins with the Alps on the north and juts southeastward into the Mediterranean Sea. The city of Rome is on the western shore of this peninsula (Acts 18:2).

ITHAMAR (ITH-ah-mahr, palm coast). The youngest son of Aaron (Exodus 6:23). Ithamar was consecrated as a priest and directed the construction of the tabernacle (Exodus 28:1; 29:1-9; 38:21).

ITTAI (IT-ay-igh). A powerful man from Gath who was loyal to David and led 600 of his men against Absalom (2 Samuel 15:18-22).

ITUREA (i-tyoo-REE-ah). A hilly area in the mountains of Lebanon, north of Palestine. At one time warlike descendants of Ishmael lived there (Genesis 25:15-16). Later Iturea was also the name of a small Roman province (Luke 3:1).

IVORY. Both a symbol and a source of wealth, ivory was imported into Palestine and used to decorate houses and furniture (1 Kings 10:18; 22; Amos 3:15). People also made many objects and implements out of ivory and decorated with it.

J

JABBOK (JAB-uk, effusion). An eastern tributary of the Jordan River that runs through Gilead. It rises near Amman and flows through a deep canyon to join the Jordan about 23 miles north of the Dead Sea (Genesis 32:22).

JABESH-GILEAD (JAY-besh-GIL-i-uhd). A city east of the Jordan River and about 10 miles southeast of Beth-Shan in the territory given to the tribe of Manasseh. All the men of this city were destroyed because they did not obey the command of God to assemble at Mizpah (Judges 21:8-14). Later Saul freed the city from the Ammonites (1 Samuel 11:1-11). The people of this city remembered Saul and gave him a decent burial (1 Samuel 31:11-13).

JABIN (JAY-bin, he discerns). 1. A king of Hazor whom Joshua defeated (Joshua 11:1-14).

2. Another king of Hazor whose general, Sisera, was defeated by Deborah and Barak (Judges 4).

JACHIN (JAY-kin). 1. The name of several minor Old Testament characters, including a son of Simeon (Genesis 46:10).

2. Jachin and Boaz were the names of the two large pillars that stood in front of the temple (1 Kings 7:15-22).

JACOB (JAY-kuhb, supplanter). The son of Isaac and Rebekah and the younger twin of Esau (Genesis 25:21-26). Jacob bought the birthright from Esau for a pot of lentil stew and, with his mother's help, tricked Isaac into giving him the blessing of the firstborn son (Genesis 25: 29-34; 27:1-41). Then Jacob fled to Haran. On the way he had a vision of a ladder reaching to heaven (Genesis 27:42—28:22). At Haran Jacob worked for his Uncle Laban at least 20 years, 14 years to earn the right to marry Laban's daughters, Rachel and Leah, and six more to acquire flocks of his own (Genesis 29:1-30). Jacob had at least 12 sons and 1 daughter by his wives and his wives' maids. Leah was the mother of Reuben, Simeon, Levi, Judah, Issachar, Zebulun, and Dinah. Rachel was the mother of Joseph and Benjamin. Leah's maid, Zilpah, was the mother of Gad and Asher, and Rachel's maid, Bilhah, was the mother of Dan and Naphtali (Genesis 29:31—30:24; 35:16-26).

Jacob fled from Laban back to Palestine, wrestling with God one night on the way (Genesis 30:25—32:32). Jacob made friends again with his brother, Esau, and settled in Canaan (Genesis 33). Jacob worshiped the true God and was blessed by Him (Genesis 35:9). The story of Jacob's life overlaps in Genesis with the story of his son Joseph's life in Egypt (Genesis 42—46). Before he died, Jacob gave a prophetic blessing to each of his sons (Genesis 49).

2. The name is also used as a symbol for the Israelites (Numbers 23:10; Psalm 59:13).

3. The father of Joseph, and the paternal, earthly grandfather of Jesus (Matthew 1:15-16).

JADDUA (ja-DYOO-ah, known). The name of the last high priest mentioned in the Old Testament (Nehemiah 12:11, 22).

JAEL (JAY-uhl, wild goat). The wife of Heber. Jael killed Sisera, the general of Jabin's troops, with a tent pin (Judges 4:17-27).

JAH (JAH). The shortened form of the divine name YHWH (probably pronounced YAH-weh). YHWH occurs often in poetic sections of Scripture and is translated as either God or Lord. It is used frequently as part of proper names as well as other words, such as hallelujah.

JAHVE, JAHWE, JAHWEH (JAH-veh, JAH-weh). See *Jehovah*.

JAIR (JAY-ur, enlighten). One of the judges of Israel (Judges 10:3-5).

JAIRUS (JAY-uh-ruhs, the Greek form of the name Jair). The ruler of the synagog, probably at Capernaum, whose daughter was raised by Jesus (Mark 5:22; Luke 8:41).

JAMBRES (JAM-breez). The name of one of the Egyptian magicians who opposed Moses (2 Timothy 3:8-9; see also Exodus 7:9-13).

JAMES (JAMZ, the Hebrew form of this name is Jacob). 1. The son of Zebedee who was called away from the family fishing business along with his brother to be a disciple (Matthew 4:21). James, his brother John, and Peter formed the inner circle of disciples who were closest to Jesus. James witnessed the transfiguration of Jesus, the raising of Jairus's daughter, and Jesus' agony in Gethsemane (Matthew 26:37; Mark 5:37; 9:32). He was killed by Herod Agrippa I about A.D. 44. Jesus nicknamed James and his brother the sons of thunder (Mark 3:17).

2. James, the son of Alphaeus and Mary, another of the 12 disciples of Jesus (Mark 3:18; Acts 1:13). Often referred to as James the Less, he is distinguished from the other disciple named James as being either younger or smaller or both (Mark 15:40).

3. One of the brothers of the Lord (Matthew 13:55). He apparently did not believe in Jesus until after His resurrection, possibly being converted by one of Jesus'postresurrec-

tion appearances (John 7:5; Acts 1:13-14; 1 Corinthians 15:5, 7). James became a leader of the early church, especially the church at Jerusalem (Galatians 1:19; 2:12). He served as chairman of the Apostolic Council at Jerusalem (Acts 15:13, 19-23). It is generally thought that James wrote the Letter of James (James 1:1).

JAMES, LETTER OF. James wrote this letter to comfort the Jews outside Palestine who were undergoing trials. In the letter he warns them against spiritual laziness and having faith in name only—faith that takes no action.

Date: About A.D. 45

Audience: Jewish Christians

Outline: 1. Comfort (1). 2. Warning against indifference, faith without works, and dead orthodoxy (2—4). 3. Encouragement to patience and prayer: turn to the Lord, rest in Him, wait patiently for Him, and let life be attuned to His coming (5).

JANNES (JAN-eez). The name of an Egyptian magician who opposed Moses (2 Timothy 3:8-9. See Exodus 7:9-13).

JAPHETH (JAY-feth, beauty or enlarged). He was one of Noah's three sons and the father of Gomer, Magog, Madai, Javan, Tubal, Meshech, and Tiras (Genesis 6:10; 10:2). His descendants occupied the islands and coastlands of the Gentiles; they were the Indo-European peoples (Genesis 10:5). Japheth's obedient behavior brought him the blessing of his father (Genesis 9:20-27).

JAPHIA (jah-FIGH-ah, shining). 1. A king of Lachish whom Joshua put to death (Joshua 10:3-26).

2. One of the sons of King David (2 Samuel 5:15).

3. An ancient town located near Nazareth (Joshua 19:12).

JASHAR (JAY-shur, upright). The author of a lost poetical book that was used in writing the historical books of the Old Testament (Joshua 10:13; 2 Samuel 1:18).

JASON (JAY-suhn, healing). A Christian who showed Paul hospitality at Thessalonica and received harsh treatment from the Jews (Acts 17:5-9). He is probably the same person as the Jason mentioned in Romans 16:21.

JASPER. A type of quartz stained deep shades of red, brown, green, yellow, and the like. In ancient times jasper included other types of rock as well. Jasper was used for decorative purposes (Exodus 28:20; Ezekiel 28:13; Revelation 4:3).

JAVELIN (JAV-lin). A short, light spear. See also *armor, arms.*

JEBUS (JEE-buhs). The name of Jerusalem when occupied by the Jebusites (Joshua 15:63; 18:28; Judges 19:10). The city was small in comparison to the size of Jerusalem at Solomon's time. See also *Zion 1.*

JEBUSITES (JEB-yoo-zights). A mountain tribe of Canaan that lived at Jebus (Genesis 10:16; 15:21; Numbers 13:29; Joshua 11:3). Joshua killed their king and assigned their territory to Benjamin (Joshua 10: 23-27; 18:16, 28).

JECONIAH (jek-o-NIGH-ah, Lord establishes). A variant spelling of the name Jehoiachin. Jeconiah, or Jehoiachin, was a king of Judah (1 Chronicles 3:16-17; Jeremiah 24:1; 27:20; 28:4; 29:2). See also *Jehoiachin.*

JEDIDAH (ji-DIGH-dah, beloved). The mother of Josiah (2 Kings 22:1).

JEDIDIAH (jed-i-DIGH-ah, beloved by the Lord). The name Nathan gave to Solomon (2 Samuel 12:25).

JEGAR-SAHADUTHA (JEE-gahr-say-hah-DYOO-thah, heap of witness). The Aramaic name Laban gave to the heap of stones he piled up as a memorial covenant between him and Jacob. Jacob called it Galeed (Genesis 31:47-48).

JEHEZEKEL, JEHEZKEL (ji-HEZ-i-kel, ji-HEZ-kel, God strengthens). The head of the 20th division of priests (1 Chronicles 24:16).

JEHOAHAZ (ji-HO-ah-haz, Lord has laid hold of). 1. The son and successor of Jehu and 11th king of Israel (2 Kings 10:35; 13:1). Jehoahaz did what was evil in the sight of the Lord and continued the idolatry of Jeroboam. Because of this, God became angry with Israel and allowed Hazael, king of Syria, and Ben-hadad, his son, to campaign successfully against them (2 Kings 13:1-9).

2. The son and successor of Josiah and 17th king of Judah. His reign of three months was evil. After this time he was deposed by Pharaoh Neco and taken captive to Egypt (2 Kings 23:30-34; 2 Chronicles 36:1-4). In 1 Chronicles 3:15 and Jeremiah 22:10-12 he is referred to as Shallum. He is also called a lion's whelp (Ezekiel 19:1-4).

JEHOIACHIN (ji-HOI-ah-kin, Lord establishes). The son and successor of Jehoiakim and 19th king of Judah. During his short reign of three months and a few days he did that which was evil in the sight of the Lord. Then Nebuchadnezzar carried him away into captivity and put him into prison. When Evil-Merodach ascended the throne of Babylon a number of years later, he released Jehoiachin (2 Kings 24:8-16; 25:27-30; 2 Chronicles 36:9-10; Jeremiah 39:2; 52:28-34; Ezekiel 17:12). See also *Jeconiah.*

JEHOIADA (ji-HOI-ah-dah, Lord has known). The high priest at the time Athaliah usurped the throne. Jehoiada's wife hid the young prince Joash while Jehoiada planned and carried out the revolt that led to Athaliah's overthrow. Then Joash became the rightful king. Jehoiada was Joash's uncle, and while Jehoiada lived, Joash was faithful to the Lord (2 Kings 11:1—12:16; 2 Chronicles 22:10—24:22).

JEHOIAKIM (ji-HOI-ah-kim, Lord establishes) The son of Josiah and 18th king of Judah. His name was originally Eliakim. When his father died, the people put Jehoahaz, Jehoiakim's younger brother, on the throne. But when Pharaoh Neco took Jehoahaz captive to Egypt after three months, he made Eliakim, whose name he changed to Jehoiakim, the new king. Jehoiakim did what was evil in the eyes of the Lord and went back to idol worship. He also heavily taxed his people so that he could pay tribute to Pharaoah Neco.

In 605 B.C. Nebuchadnezzar defeated Neco in battle at Carchemish and advanced on Jerusalem. Jehoiakim then became Nebuchadnezzar's servant and paid tribute to him. Three years later Jehoiakim rebelled against Babylonian rule. When he died, his body received the burial of a donkey (2 Kings 23:34-37; 24:1-6; 2 Chronicles 36:4-8; Jeremiah 1:3; 22; 24—28; 35—37; 45—46; 52; Daniel 1:1-2).

JEHOIARIB (ji-HOI-ah-rib, Lord pleads). The head of the first division of temple priests (1 Chronicles 9:10; 24:7).

JEHORAM (ji-HO-ram). See *Joram 2.*

JEHOSHAPHAT (ji-HAHSH-ah-fat, the Lord has judged). The son of Asa and fourth king of Judah. Jehoshaphat reigned 25 years and is described as a good king. In the third year of his reign he sent princes and Levites to teach the people the Law. He made peace with Israel and removed the high places and idols out of Judah. After visiting Ahab, king of Israel, Jehoshaphat was persuaded to join armies with Ahab against the Syrians. On Jehoshaphat's return home the prophet Jehu rebuked him for joining forces with Ahab and Ahaziah. Jehoshaphat died around 850 B.C. and was succeeded by his son Jehoram (1 Kings 15:24; 2 Kings 8:18, 26; 2 Chronicles 17—21:1; Matthew 1:8).

JEHOSHAPHAT, VALLEY OF. A symbolic name for a valley where the Lord will gather all nations for judgment (Joel 3:2, 12).

JEHOSHEBA (ji-HAHSH-i-bah, the Lord is an oath). The wife of the high priest Jehoida and the daughter of Jehoram and sister of Ahaziah, both kings of Judah. When Jehoram was murdered, Jehosheba hid Joash, Jehoram's son, from Athaliah until Joash could safely be proclaimed king (2 Kings 11:2).

JEHOVAH (ji-HO-vah). A common English word for one of God's names. It is a combination of the Hebrew consonants YHWH (which were probably pronounced YAHweh and mean Lord) and the vowel points of *Adonai*, the word the Hebrew people said whenever they saw YHWH in the text. The Hebrews took seriously the commandment to keep God's name holy. That is why they spoke the word *Adonai* whenever they encountered God's name *YHWH* in their writings.

YHWH is derived from the verb *to be* and indicates God is eternal (Exodus 3:13-15). It is God's personal name for Himself, the one He uses when dealing with His people. To know the name *YHWH* is to know God manifesting Himself to His people in grace and love (1 Kings 8:43-44; Psalm 9:10; Jeremiah 16:21).

JEHOVAH-JIREH (ji-HO-vah-JIGH-re, the Lord will provide). The name Abraham gave to the place where he put Isaac on the altar (Genesis 22:14).

JEHOVAH-NISSI (ji-HO-vah-NISigh, the Lord is my banner). The altar Moses built at Rephidim as a memorial of the victory over Amalek (Exodus 17:15-16).

JEHOVAH-SHAMMAH (ji-HO-vah-SHAM-ah, the Lord is there). The name given to heavenly Jerusalem in Ezekiel's vision (Ezekiel 48:35; see also Revelation 21:3).

JEHU (Je-hu, Lord is he). 1. A prophet who rebuked Baasha and Jehoshaphat (1 Kings 16:1, 7, 12; 2 Chronicles 19:1-3).

2. The 10th king of Israel. He was a son of Jehoshaphat, a grandson of Nimshi, and a commander in Ahab's army. Because of Ahab's wickedness, God told Elijah to anoint Jehu king over Israel and commission him to destroy the house of Ahab (1 Kings 19:16-17).

After being anointed king, Jehu killed Jehoram of Israel (Ahab's son), Ahaziah of Judah, Jezebel (Ahab's wife), Ahab's heirs, and the prophets of Baal. Jehu, however, made no attempt to walk in the Lord's ways. He assembled all the people and said to them: "Ahab served Baal a little; but Jehu will serve him much" (2 Kings 10:18). Jehu also payed tribute to Shalmaneser III, king of Assyria (2 Kings 9—10; 2 Chronicles 22:7-9).

JEHUDI (ji-HYOO-digh, Jew). A messenger sent by the court of King Jehoiakim to ask Baruch for the scroll Jeremiah had written (Jeremiah 36:14-23).

JEPHTHAH (JEF-thah, he opens). One of the judges of Israel. Jephthah was an illegitimate son who was driven from home by his brothers, the legitimate heirs. Jephthah went to the land of Tob, where he lived until the elders of the tribes of Israel called him back to fight the Amorites. Jephthah rashly promised God that, if he were permitted to win the war with the Amorites, he would offer as a burnt offering whatever first came to him from out of his house when he returned home. Jephthah did defeat the Amorites and upon his return home was first greeted by his daughter, his only child. Because of his promise, Jephthah sacrificed her to the Lord. Jephthah judged Israel six years. Then he died and was buried in Gilead (Judges 11:1—12:7; Hebrews 11:32).

JERAHMEEL (ji-RAH-mi-el, God has mercy). One of the officers Jehoiakim sent to arrest Jeremiah and Baruch (Jeremiah 36:26).

JEREMIAH (jer-i-MIGH-ah, Lord exalts or appoints). One of the greatest Hebrew prophets. Jeremiah lived from about 640 to 587 B.C. He was the son of Hilkiah, a priest of Anathoth in the territory of Benjamin (Jeremiah 1:1). In the 13th year of King Josiah's reign Jeremiah was called to prophesy by a vision in which God told him he was "to destroy and to overthrow, to build and to plant" (Jeremiah 1:4-10).

Jeremiah continued in his prophetic office during the days of the last kings of Judah (Josiah, Jehoahaz II, Jehoiakim, Jehoiachin, and Zedekiah), approximately 41 years. He supported and probably assisted in Josiah's reforms (2 Kings 23). He warned Jehoiakim not to be friends with Egypt and depend on it because the Chaldeans would be successful in their attack against Jerusalem.

Jeremiah dictated a scroll of his prophecies to Baruch. When the scroll was eventually read to the king, he cut off a section at a time and threw it into the fire until the entire scroll was destroyed (Jeremiah 36).

In the days of Zedekiah, the princes persecuted Jeremiah (Jeremiah 37—38). After Jerusalem was captured in 605 B.C. by the Chaldeans, Nebuchadnezzar showed Jeremiah great kindness (Jeremiah 39:11-12). Jeremiah finally moved to Egypt, where he probably died (Jeremiah 43:6-7).

JEREMIAH, BOOK OF. A book of prophetic sermons and autobiographical and historical material written by the prophet Jeremiah.

Date: 627 to 587 B.C.

Audience: Israelites

Outline: 1. Jeremiah's call (1). 2. Warnings to Jews (2—29). 3. Promise of restoration of Israel (30—33). 4. Prophecies occasioned by Israel's leaders, Jehoiakim and Zedekiah (34—38). 5. Prophecies after the fall of Jerusalem (39—45). 6. Prophecies against other nations: Egypt, Philistia, Moab, Ammon, Edom, Damascus, Elam, Arabia, Babylon (46—51). 7. Prophecy fulfilled: Jerusalem's fall (52).

JERICHO (JER-uh-ko, place of fragrance or moon-city). A city near the Dead Sea about 825 feet below sea level and six miles west of the Jordan. Jericho has been examined by archaeologists and is regarded as the oldest known city in the world.

Joshua conquered Jericho and later gave it to the tribe of Benjamin (Joshua 2—6; 18:21). Later, during Ahab's reign, Hiel rebuilt the city (1 Kings 16:34). Jericho is frequently mentioned in the Scriptures (2 Kings 2:1-22; 25:5; Ezekiel 2:34; Matthew 20:29; Mark 10:46; Luke 10:30).

JEROBOAM (jer-o-BO-ahm, he pleads people's cause.) 1. Jeroboam I, the first king of Israel after the division of the kingdom. As a young man, Jeroboam was industrious and able. Consequently, Solomon, who was busy in building operations in Jerusalem, made Jeroboam superintendent over all the forced labor assigned to the house of Joseph (1 Kings 11:27-28). One day on the road outside Jerusalem, Jeroboam met the prophet Ahijah. Ahijah told him the kingdom would be divided, and Jeroboam would become king of 10 of the tribes (1 Kings 11:29-40).

When Solomon heard this news, he wanted to kill Jeroboam, and so Jeroboam fled to Egypt (1 Kings 11:40). After Solomon's death, Jeroboam did become king of the 10 northern tribes. He made Shechem his capital and Tirzah the place where he lived (1 Kings 12:1-25). Jeroboam was afraid the people would be won back to the house of David and kill him if they went to Jerusalem to worship, so he built worship centers containing golden calves in Bethel and Dan (1 Kings 12:25-33). The prophet Ahijah foretold Jeroboam's downfall (1 Kings 13;14).

2. Jeroboam II, the son and successor of Jehoash and the 13th king of Israel. Jeroboam was successful in war with Syria and other nations and extended Israel's territory. Amos prophesied during Jeroboam's reign against the moral corruption and idolatry which continued under Jeroboam. Hosea also began his prophetic work during Jeroboam's lifetime. Excavations at Samaria show the splendor of that time (2 Kings 14:23-29).

JERUSALEM (ji-ROO-sah-lem). The capital of the United Kingdom of Israel and Judah and of Judea. According to the Tell el Amarna letters it was originally called U-ru-sa-lim, which means city of peace. It sits on a 2,550-foot-high rocky plateau 33 miles east of the Mediterranean Sea and 14 miles west of the Dead Sea.

Jerusalem's water is supplied by the Gihon Spring in the Kidron Valley and by En-rogel, a spring near the join of the Kidron and Hinnom valleys. There are reservoirs within the city. During Hezekiah's reign a tunnel was cut in the rock to conduct water from the Gihon to the Upper Pool of Siloam (2 Chronicles 32:30).

The Jerusalem David took from the Jebusites consisted of only the southeast corner of present-day Jerusalem. Located on a hill south of Ophel, it was 1,250 feet long and 400 feet wide (1 Chronicles 11:4-8). Solomon extended its walls to protect his palaces and temple (I Kings 3:1; 9:15). Manasseh also extended the wall of Jerusalem (2 Chronicles 33:14). After it had been broken down by Nebuchadnezzar, Nehemiah rebuilt the wall out of old material, extending it on the north. Herod built or extended the walls as they were in the time of Christ. The modern walls of the city were built by Suleiman the Magnificent in A.D. 1542. The temple stood on Mount Zion.

In its history Jerusalem has been known by many different names. It is considered the Salem of Melchizedek (Genesis 14:18). It is also called Salem, Jebus, the city of David, Zion, the city of Judah, the city of God, the city of the great King, and the holy city (Judges 19:10-11; 1 Kings 8:1; 2 Kings 14:20; 2 Chronicles 25:28; Nehemiah 11:1; Psalm 46:4; 48:2; 76:2).

JERUSALEM, THE NEW. The city of God. It is described as coming down from heaven and as the mother of believers (Galatians 4:26; Revelation 21:2, 10. See also Hebrews 11:8-10; 12:22-24).

JESHUA, JESHUAH (JESH-yoo-ah, Lord is salvation). 1. See *Joshua.*

2. The head of the ninth division of priests (1 Chronicles 24:11; Ezra 2:36; Nehemiah 7:39).

JESHURUN (JESH-yoo-run, upright). A poetical name for Israel that represents Israel as a righteous people (Deuteronomy 32:15; 33:5, 26; Isaiah 44:2).

JESSE (JES-ee). The son of Obed and grandson of Ruth (Ruth 4:17,22; Matthew 1:5). David was the youngest of his eight sons (1 Samuel 16:11-13; 17:12).

JESUS CHRIST (JEE-zuhs KRIGHST). The Biblical names and titles for Jesus tell us who He is and what He does for humanity. Some of the most important of His names and titles are:

1. Jesus. The word *Jesus* is Greek for the Hebrew name *Joshua,* which means savior (Matthew 1:21, 25; Luke 1:31).

2. Christ. *Christ* is Greek for the Hebrew name *Mashiah,* which means anointed one. Jesus is fully anointed with the Spirit of God (John 3:34). Thus, He is the promised *Mashiah* or Messiah (Matthew 16:13-23; Luke 2:25-26; John 1:35-41). See also *Messiah.*

3. Logos. Jesus is referred to as Logos, which in Greek means word (John 1:1-14; 1 John 1:1; Revelation 19:13). This name is used in the New Testament to identify Jesus as the eternal Second Person of the Trinity. As the Logos, Jesus is the living Word of God who creates and preserves life (John 1:3; Psalm 147:15-18; Matthew 8:24-27; 9:1-8; Colossians 1:15-20). The Spirit of the

eternal Word also inspired the prophets of old (1 Peter 1:10-11).

4. Son of God. This title is applied to Jesus in a unique sense (Matthew 11:27; 16:16; 21:33-41; John 1:14, 18; 3:16-18). It says that Jesus as the Son is equal to God the Father (John 10:30; 12:45; 14:8-11; 17). He is the Second Person of the Trinity eternally born of God the Father (John 1:18; 3:16; Romans 8:3). He has the same characteristics, works, and honor as God the Father (Matthew 9:18; John 5:17, 21, 23, 25; 21:17; Colossians 1:15-20).

5. Son of Man. Jesus used this title to emphasize His humanity, especially in connection with His ministry (Luke 9:56; 19:10), power (Matthew 9:6; 12:8), death (Mark 14:21; Luke 22:48; John 3:14), resurrection (Matthew 17:9; Mark 9:9), ascension (John 6:62), and second coming and judgment (Matthew 25:31). As the New Man or New Adam, Jesus brought into existence the new humanity (Romans 5:12-21; 1 Corinthians 15:22; Philippians 2:5-11). As man, He shared in the flesh and blood of man (Romans 9:4; Hebrews 2:14). Jesus is God and man in one person (John 1:14; Colossians 2:9; 1 Timothy 2:5).

6. Servant of God. Jesus is the Servant of God because He did what God willed, especially saving humanity (Matthew 12:18; Mark 14:32-42; John 1:29; 4:34; 5:30). For this reason He is the ultimate fulfillment of Isaiah 53 (Mark 8:31; 10:33; Romans 4:25).

7. Savior. Jesus is the promised Savior (Luke 2:11, 22-23). Through His life, death, resurrection, and preaching He saves

those who believe in Him from sin, wrath, and death (Matthew 1:21; Luke 19:10; John 4:42; Acts 4:12; 11:14; 16:31; Romans 5: 9-10; 10:9-10; 2 Timothy 1:10).

8. Mediator. Jesus is the Mediator between God and people (Galatians 3:19; 1 Timothy 2:5; Hebrews 8:6; 9:15; 12:24). As Prophet, Priest, and King, Jesus brings people to God. (See also offices of Prophet, Priest, and King below.)

9. Lamb of God. Jesus is the Lamb of God sacrificed for the sins of the world (John 1:29, 36; Acts 8:32; 1 Corinthians 5:7; 1 Peter 1:19; Hebrews 7:27. See also Exodus 12; Isaiah 53:7).

The work of Jesus Christ may be described in terms of the three offices He fills. As *Prophet,* Jesus announces the kingdom of God through His words and actions. He reveals to people God's anger over sin and God's love in Him. Christ carries on His prophetic work today through the Gospel proclaimers of the church. As *Priest,* Christ fulfilled all righteousness and paid for the sins of all people by offering up to God the sacrifice of His own life, death, and resurrection in their place (Romans 4:25; 2 Corinthians 5:19; Hebrews 7). Now He continues to intercede for humanity before God the Father (Romans 8:34; 1 John 2:1). As *King,* Christ rules the whole world through His power (Matthew 28:18; Ephesians 1:22; Hebrews 1:3), the church on earth through His grace (Matthew 16:18-19; 28:19-20; Mark 16:15; Romans 1:16-17; 14:17-18), and the church in heaven through His glory (Matthew 25:34; John 17:24; 2 Timothy 4:18; Revelation 5:12-13; 21:4).

Further, the work of Jesus Christ may be described in terms of two states of being. During His state of *humiliation,* which began at the moment of the incarnation and continued through His death, Jesus in His human nature did not fully and always use all of the divine characteristics given to Him through His divine nature (Philippians 2:6-8). Beginning with His being made alive in the tomb and His descent into hell, Jesus in His human nature began to fully and constantly use all His divine characteristics (Philippians 2:9-11; Ephesians 4:8). This is called Christ's state of *exaltation.*

JETHRO (JETH-ro, excellence). A priest and prince of Midian and the father-in-law of Moses. After Moses fled from Egypt, he came to Midian, where he met Jethro. Jethro gave Moses his daughter Zipporah in marriage. Later, after Moses had led the Israelites out of Egypt and they were camping in the wilderness, Jethro came to Moses and gave him advice on how to govern the people (Exodus 18).

Jethro was probably a surname or title; Reuel or Raguel was his personal name (Exodus 2:18; Numbers 10:29).

JEW (JYOO). Originally someone who belonged to the tribe or Kingdom of Judah as opposed to those of the Northern Kingdom (2 Kings 15:36; 16:6). After the Babylonian Captivity, since the majority of the Israelites returning were from Judah, the meaning of the name Jew was extended. It was applied to anyone of the Hebrew race who returned from captivity.

Hebrew denotes those who descended from Abraham; Israel denotes those who descended from Jacob; and Jew denotes those who descended from the tribe or Kingdom of Judah. The word *Jew* is not applied to Gentile converts as *Israel* is. See also *Hebrews; Israel.*

JEZEBEL (JEZ-uh-buhl, unmarried or unexalted). Ahab's wicked wife (1 Kings 16:31). Jezebel's father was Ethbaal, the king of Tyre and Sidon and a priest of Astarte. Jezebel worshiped the gods of her father. Ahab built altars to Baal in Samaria to please Jezebel, and 450 prophets of Baal and Astarte were invited to eat at her table (1 Kings 16:31-32; 18:19). Jezebel killed the prophets of the Lord and opposed Elijah (1 Kings 18:13; 19:1). When Ahab coveted Naboth's vineyard, Jezebel planned and carried out a way to have Naboth put to death so that Ahab could take over (1 Kings 21).

Because of these murders and other wicked acts, Elijah prophesied that Jezebel would die and the dogs would eat her by the wall of Jezreel (1 Kings 21:23). Eleven years after Ahab's death, Jehu killed Jezebel, and Elijah's prophecy was fulfilled (2 Kings 9:7, 30-37).

JEZREEL (JEZ-ri-el, God sows). A city of Issachar about five miles north of Jerusalem (Joshua 19:18; 1 Samuel 29:1). The kings of Israel had a palace there (2 Samuel 2:9; 1 King 18:45-46; 21:1). Naboth's vineyard was nearby.

JEZREEL, VALLEY OF. A plain 20 miles long and 14 miles wide between the ridges of Gilboa and Moreh. It is better known as the Plain of Esdraelon (Joshua 17:16; Judges 6:33; Hosea 1:5).

JOAB (JO-ab, Lord is father). The son of David's half-sister Zeruiah and the brother of Asahel and Abishai (2 Samuel 2:18). Joab killed Abner out of vengeance for the death of his brother Asahel whom Abner had killed at the battle of Gibeon (2 Samuel 3:22-39). David made Joab commander-in-chief of the armies of all Israel as a reward for his part in the attack on Jebus (1 Chronicles 11:4-9). Under Joab's leadership, Israel defeated Syria, Edom, and Ammon (2 Samuel 10—12).

Joab arranged Uriah the Hittite's death according to David's orders (2 Samuel 11). He killed Absalom and Amasa (2 Samuel 18:9-15; 20:4-13). When Adonijah tried to take the throne, Joab sided with him against David (1 Kings 1). On his deathbed, David said he wanted Joab brought to justice for the unjust murders of Abner and Amasa. Solomon, carrying out this wish, had Joab put to death (1 Kings 2:28-34).

JOASH (JO-ash, Lord has given). 1. The son of Ahaziah and the eighth king of Judah (2 Kings 11:2). When Joash was a baby, his father was murdered. Joash was saved from the same fate by his Aunt Jehosheba, the wife of the high priest Jehoiada. Jehosheba hid Joash in the temple for six years. Then through Jehoiada's efforts, Athaliah was put to death, and Joash was rightfully crowned king.

Under the guidance of Jehoiada, Joash restored worship of the Lord. After Jehoiada's death, however, Joash turned his back on the Lord and led his people into idolatry. When Zechariah, Jehoiada's son, denounced Joash for his idolatry, Joash had him put to death. Joash reigned about 37 years. He was killed by his servants (2 Kings 11—12; 2 Chronicles 24).

2. The son of Jehoahaz and the 13th king of Israel. Joash followed in the sins of Jeroboam by continuing the worship of the calves at Bethel and Dan. He respected Elisha, however, and went to see him when the prophet was dying. Elisha told Joash to strike the ground with some arrows. The number of times Joash struck the ground symbolized the victories he would win over the Syrians, the Moabites, and Amaziah of Judah.

Joash reigned about 16 years. He died in peace, and his son, Jeroboam II, took the throne (2 Kings 13—14; 2 Chronicles 25).

JOB, BOOK OF. A book belonging to the wisdom literature of the Old Testament. It is a great literary masterpiece, containing dramatic, lyric, and epic poetry.

The book, named after its chief character, Job, gives an account of Job's suffering and the reasons for it. It asks the questions: How is the suffering of the righteous compatible with the concept of a just God? Is human conduct justly rewarded or punished on earth? Job concludes that as he knows God, so God knows him; that his redeemer lives and he shall see God; and that though God's rule is mysterious, He rules for best.

Date: Possibly 10th century B.C.
Audience: Israelites and Gentiles
Outline: 1. Job's love of God tested (1—2:10). 2. Job's love for himself exposed (2:11—37). 3. Job's lack of trust reproved by God (38—42:6). 4. Job's restoration (42).

JOBAB (JO-bab). A king who joined with Jabin and Hazor to fight Joshua (Joshua 11:1).

JOCHEBED (JOK-i-bed, the Lord is glory). The mother of Moses and Aaron (Exodus 6:20; Numbers 26:29).

JOEL (JO-el, the Lord is God). The son of Pethuel and author of the second book of the Minor Prophets (Joel:1). Little is known about Joel outside of his prophecy.

JOEL, BOOK OF. The second book of the Minor Prophets as they appear in the Old Testament. It was written by the prophet Joel.

The book opens with a description of a plague of locusts which Joel views as a punishment for sin. Joel urges the people to repent of their sins and has a vision of Judg-

ment Day. He also prophecies of the day when God would pour out His Spirit on all flesh (Joel 2:28-32). Peter quotes this prophecy in his Pentecost sermon (Acts 2:16-21).

Date: 800 to 600 B.C.; difficult to date with accuracy
Audience: Israelites
Outline: 1. Plague of locusts (1—2:17). 2. The Lord pities and gives spiritual blessings (2:18-27). 3. The valley of decision, the coming of the day of the Lord (2:28—3:21).

JOHANAN (jo-HAY-nuhn, the Lord is merciful). A Jewish chief who warned Gedaliah, the governor of Judah, of a plot to murder him (2 Kings 25:23; Jeremiah 40:8—41:16). Later Johanan led Jeremiah and some other countrymen to Egypt (Jeremiah 40—43).

JOHN (JON, the Lord has been gracious). 1. The father of the apostle Peter (John 1:42; 21:15-17).

2. John the Baptizer, the forerunner of Jesus. John was the son of Elizabeth and Zechariah, the priest, both of whom were descendants of Aaron (Luke 1:5-25, 56-80). Following the pattern of Elijah, John lived as a Nazirite in the desert (Matthew 11:12-14; 17:11-12; Luke 1:17). He began his ministry in the 15th year of Tiberias Caesar in the region around the Jordan (Luke 3:1-3). John preached the baptism of repentance and the coming of the kingdom of heaven (Matthew 3:1-12; Luke 3:4-14). He baptized Jesus in the Jordan and witnessed to Him as the promised Messiah (Matthew 3:13-17; Mark 1:9-10; Luke 3:21; John 1:24-42).

John rebuked Herod for living in sin with Herodias, his brother Philip's wife. This made Herod angry, so he put John in jail (Mark 6:17-20). Because of what John had said to Herod, Herodias also had a grudge against John and wanted to kill him. She told her daughter, who had pleased Herod with her dancing, to ask for the head of John the Baptizer on a platter. Her daughter did this, and Herod gave the order to behead John (Matthew 14:6-12; Mark 6:21-28).

Jesus highly praised John (Matthew 11:7-14; Luke 7:24-28).

3. John the apostle, a son of Zebedee and Salome and the brother of James (Matthew 4:21; 27:56; Mark 15:40; Acts 12:1-2). John was from Galilee, probably Bethsaida, and was a fisherman by trade (Mark 1:19-20; Luke 5:10; John 1:44). John the Baptizer introduced John to Jesus with the words: "Behold the Lamb of God!" (John 1:35-36). John followed Jesus and was called by Him to be an apostle (Mark 1:19-20; Luke 5:10; John 1:43; 2:2, 12, 23; 4:5). Jesus named John and his brother James, Boanerges, which means sons of thunder (Mark 3:17).

John was among the three whom Jesus chose to be with Him at the raising of Jairus's daughter, at His transfiguration, and at Gethsemane (Matthew 17:1; 26:37; Mark 5:37; 9:2; 14:23; Luke 8:51; 9:28).

One time when Jesus was rejected in a Samaritan village, John and James asked if Jesus wanted them to call down fire from heaven to burn the village. Jesus rebuked them (Luke 9:54). Another time John, James, and their mother asked Jesus for places of honor in His future kingdom (Matthew 20:20; Mark 10:35-45). John helped prepare the Passover for Jesus and His disciples on the night before Jesus' crucifixion (Luke 22:8).

John has been identified as the beloved disciple. At the Last Supper he sat next to Jesus (John 13:23). Later, when Jesus was taken prisoner, John followed the soldiers and was able to go along with Jesus into the court of the high priest (John 18:15-16). At the cross John stood near Mary, Jesus' mother. When Jesus asked John to look after Mary, John accepted the trust (John 19:26-27).

John was the first disciple to believe that Jesus had risen from the dead (John 20:1-10). With the other disciples, he saw the risen Christ on the night of His resurrection and again a week later (Luke 24:33-43; John 20:19-30). After a night of fishing with the disciples on the Sea of Galilee, John was the first to recognize Jesus as He stood on the beach (John 21:1-7). After Jesus' ascension John waited for some time in the Upper Room in Jerusalem with the other apostles, and after Pentecost he became a missionary with Peter (Acts 1:13; 3:1—4:22; 8:14-17; Galatians 2:9).

John lived to an old age. He wrote the fourth gospel, the three letters bearing his name, and the Book of Revelation.

JOHN, GOSPEL OF. It is generally believed that the apostle John, "the disciple whom Jesus loved," wrote this gospel. The author of the book was an eyewitness of the events he describes. His stated purpose for writing it is to show that Jesus is the Christ, the Son of God, so that those believing this might have life in His name (John 20:30-31). With this in mind, John presents the acts and words of Jesus, revealing the unique Person of Christ and His significance to the world.

John describes Jesus as the eternal Logos (1:1-18), the Messiah (1:41-51; 4:25-26; 6:14; 7; 10:22-25; 17:3), the Son of Man (3:12-15; 5:22-27; 6:62; 12:27-36), and the Son of God (3:16; 5:17-31; 8:58; 10:29-39; 14:1).

Date: A. D. 90 to 100

Audience: Christian Gentiles and Jews

Outline: 1. Jesus, the Word of God in the flesh (1:1-18). 2. The

Word is spoken to all Israel (1:19—4). 3. The Word is rejected by Israel (5—12). 4. The Word is received by the disciples (13—17). 5. The Word speaks God's grace and truth (18—20). 6. Conclusion: Jesus, Peter, and the beloved disciple (21).

JOHN, FIRST LETTER OF. According to the early church the apostle John wrote this letter near the end of the first century. He wrote it to warn against false teachers (Gnostics) and to strengthen his readers in their Christian loyalty. The keynote of the letter is faith and love.

Date: A.D. 90 to 100

Audience: Christians in Asia whom John knew

Outline: 1. The revelation (1:1-4). 2. "God is light and in Him is no darkness" (1:5—2:28). 3. "We are God's children now" (2:29—4:6). 4. "God is love" (4:7—5:12). 5. Apostolic teachings, the great certainties to which we hold (5:13-21).

JOHN, SECOND LETTER OF. John wrote this letter to encourage his readers to walk in light and to warn them against error. The "elect lady" may refer to a woman or a church.

Date: A.D. 90 to 100

Audience: Christians in Asia Minor

Outline: 1. Salutation (1—3). 2. Love one another and abide in the doctrine of Christ (4—11). 3. Conclusion and greetings (12—13).

JOHN, THIRD LETTER OF. This letter is addressed to Gaius and commends him for his Christian life and for his service to the evangelists John sent. In the letter John also censures Diotrephes for his bad conduct and praises Demetrius.

Date: A.D. 90 to 100

Audience: Gaius, a loyal Christian and gracious host to those who came to share the Gospel

Outline: 1. Acknowledges the hospitality and love Gaius showed to traveling evangelists (1—8). 2. Loveless conduct of Diotrephes will be dealt with (9—10). 3. Commends Demetrius (12). 4. Conclusion and greeting (13—15).

JOKTAN (JOK-tuhn, small). A person who descended from Shem through Eber (Genesis 10:25-30). He is the ancestor of 13 Arabian tribes.

JONA (JO-nah). See *John 1*.

JONAH (JO-nah, dove). A son of Ammitai of Gath-hepher and a prophet of Israel. Jonah predicted the recovery of the land of Israel to its ancient borders through the efforts of Jeroboam II. He also preached to Nineveh (2 Kings 14:23-25; Jonah 1:1). His prophecy is recorded in the Book of Jonah.

JONAH, BOOK OF. The fifth book of the Minor Prophets. It is typological in character. Its purpose is to teach that God's grace and mercy is not limited to Israel but extends to all (4:11).

The Book of Jonah differs from the other prophetic books. They are mainly prophetic with a minimum of narrative; Jonah is the opposite.

Date: 8th century B.C.

Audience: Israel

Outline: 1. Jonah flees from the presence of the Lord (1). 2. Jonah prays out of the belly of Sheol (2). 3. Jonah obeys, Nineveh repents and is spared (3). 4. Jonah's anger and God's question (4).

JONATHAN (JON-ah-thuhn, the Lord has given). The oldest son of King Saul (1 Samuel 13:16; 14:49; 1 Chronicles 8:33). Jonathan was a great military commander. He successfully fought the Philistines (1 Samuel 13—14).

Jonathan is best known for his devotion to David. Although Jonathan was the rightful heir to the throne, he stripped himself of his royal robe, girdle, and sword and pledged his loyalty to David (1 Samuel 18:4; 20:42). Later when Saul wished to kill David, Jonathan defended him from Saul's anger (1 Samuel 19:1-7; 20). Jonathan was killed with Saul in a battle with the Philistines at Mount Gilboa (1 Samuel 31:2-10; 2 Samuel 1:17-27).

JOPPA, JOPPE (JOP-ah, JOP-e, beauty). An ancient walled seaport about 34 miles northwest of Jerusalem. It was assigned to the tribe of Dan. Simon Peter did missionary work there (Acts 9—11). Joppa, which is mentioned in both the lists of Thutmose III and the Amarna Letters, is modern-day Joffa (Joshua 19:46; 2 Chronicles 2:16; Ezra 3:7; Jonah 1:3).

JORAM (JO-ruhm, the Lord is high). 1. The son of Ahab and the ninth king of Israel. With the help of the kings of Judah and Edom, Joram defeated the Moabites (2 Kings 3:1-27). He was also undoubtedly the king to whom Naaman came to be cured of his leprosy and who sent the Syrians home unharmed (2 Kings 5; 6:8-23). Jehu killed Joram and threw his body into Naboth's vineyard (2 Kings 9:14-26).

2. The son of Jehoshaphat and fifth king of Judah. Shortly after Joram became king, he killed all his brothers and some other princes of Israel. Joram married a daughter of Ahab who led him into idolatry. During his reign, Joram was harassed by the Edomites, the Philistines, and the Arabs (2 Kings 8:16-24; 2 Chronicles 21).

JORDAN (JAWR-d'n, downrusher). The most important river in Palestine. It flows in a fissure extending from between the Lebanon and Anti-Lebanon Mountains through the Sea of Galilee to the Dead Sea and beyond. The Jordan Valley is 160 miles long, 2 to 5 miles wide, and as much as 1,292 feet below sea level. The river is 3 to 10 feet deep and about 100 feet wide (Genesis 13:10; Joshua 2:7; Judges 3:28; Matthew 3:13).

JOSEPH (JO-zuhf, he adds). 1. The son of Jacob and Rachel (Genesis 30:22-24). Joseph was Jacob's favorite child (Genesis 37:3-4). When Joseph was 17, his father sent him to the place where his brothers were looking after their flocks. Because his brothers were jealous of Joseph, they sold him into slavery to a caravan of merchants going to Egypt (Genesis 37).

In Egypt Joseph became the slave of Potiphar, the captain of the pharaoh's guard. Falsely accused by Potiphar's wife, Joseph was put into prison for years. In prison Joseph became friends with the jailer. God gave Joseph the ability to interpret the dreams of the chief baker and chief butler who were in prison with Joseph. Two years later when the pharaoh had two prophetic dreams, the jailer remembered Joseph and told the pharaoh about him. After Joseph correctly interpreted the pharaoh's dream, the pharaoh made him a high officer in the kingdom (Genesis 39—41).

When famine struck the land and Joseph's brothers came to Egypt for food, Joseph saved them from starving (Genesis 42—45). Joseph arranged for his family to come to Egypt and settled them in Goshen (Genesis 47). Joseph died at 110 years of age. When the people of Israel left Egypt, they took Joseph's bones with them and buried them at Shechem (Joshua 24:32).

2. The husband of Mary, Jesus' mother (Matthew 1:16; Luke 3:23). Joseph was a carpenter who lived in Nazareth (Matthew 13:55). When he found out that Mary was expecting a child, Joseph was going to put her away without public exposure. But when an angel assured

Joseph that the child Mary was carrying was of the Holy Spirit, Joseph took her for his wife (Matthew 1:18-25). Joseph took Mary with him when he went to Bethlehem to be taxed. There Jesus was born (Luke 2:4-6).

Forty days after Jesus' birth, Joseph and Mary presented Jesus in the temple (Luke 2:22-40). When an angel warned Joseph in a dream that Herod was going to kill baby Jesus, Joseph fled with Mary and Jesus to Egypt (Matthew 2:13-18). After Herod had died and the danger was past, they returned to Nazareth (Matthew 2:19-23). When Jesus was 12 years old, Joseph and Mary took Him to Jerusalem (Luke 2:41-52).

3. Joseph of Arimathea, a member of the Sanhedrin and a secret disciple of Jesus. Jesus was buried in Joseph's new tomb (Matthew 27:57-60; Mark 15:42-46; Luke 23:50-53).

4. A "brother of the Lord" (Matthew 13:55; 27:56). He is the same as Joses (Mark 6:3; 15:40, 47).

5. The personal name of Barnabas (Acts 4:36).

JOSES (JO-seez, Greek for Joseph).
1. See *Joseph 4.*
2. See *Joseph 5.*

JOSHAPHAT (JOSH-ah-fat, the Lord has judged). A priest who blew the trumpet before the ark when it was brought to Jerusalem (1 Chronicles 15:24).

JOSHUA (JOSH-yoo-ah, the Lord is salvation. Later Jeshua, Jesus). 1. The helper and successor of Moses. Joshua, an Ephraimite, was the son of Nun (Exodus 33:11; Numbers 13:8, 16; 1 Chronicles 7:27). Joshua commanded the Israelites in their attack against the Amalekites (Exodus 17:8-16). As Moses' attendant, he went part of the way up Mount Sinai with Moses (Exodus 24:13; 32:17). Joshua was also in charge of the tab-

ernacle (Exodus 33:11).

As a leader of Ephraim, Joshua was among the spies sent to report on the land of Canaan. Of the 12 sent, only he and Caleb urged the people to go and take the land (Numbers 13; 14:7-10). Moses appointed Joshua as his successor (Deuteronomy 31; Joshua 1). On the death of Moses, Joshua made plans for crossing the Jordan.

After entering Canaan, Joshua conquered the land by leading the Israelites into a number of battles. Then he supervised the allotment of the conquered territory as it was divided among the tribes (Joshua). Joshua asked for and obtained for himself the town of Timnath-serah. He died at 110 years of age and was buried in Timnath-serah (Joshua 24:29).

JOSHUA, BOOK OF. The first book in the Hebrew division of the Old Testament known as the Former Prophets. In the English canon it is the first of the historical books.

The purpose of the book is to teach God's will for Israel and to show how He gave His people the land He had promised them.

Date: 15th to 13th century B.C.
Audience: Israelites
Outline: 1. The conquest of Canaan (1—12). 2. Division of the conquered land among the 12 tribes (13—22). 3. Last words and death of Joshua (23—24).

JOSIAH (jo-SIGH-ah, the Lord supports). The son of Amon and Jedidah and 16th king of Judah. Josiah came to the throne of Judah when he was eight years old and reigned for 31 years (2 Kings 22:1). In the eighth year of his reign he began to seek the God of David, and four years later he set about to suppress idolatry in Judah and Israel (2 Chronicles 34:3).

In his 18th year he decided to repair the temple. While engaged in this activity, workmen found the book of the Law and handed it over to Shaphan, the scribe, who read it to the king. Josiah gathered together "all the elders of Judah and Jerusalem. . . . the inhabitants of Jerusalem and the priests and the Levites, all the people both great and small; and he read in their hearing all the words of the book of the covenant which had been found in the house of the Lord" (2 Chronicles 34:29-30). This reading of the Law stimulated worship reforms anew.

In 609 B.C. Josiah's leadership was ended when Pharaoh Neco defeated and killed him in battle at Megiddo (2 Kings 22—23; 2 Chronicles 34—35).

JOT. The smallest letter in the Hebrew and Greek alphabets (Matthew 5:18).

JOTBATH, JOTBATHAH (JOTbath, JOT-bah-thah, pleasantness). One of the places Israel set up camp. It may have been near Ezion-geber (Numbers 33:33-34; Deuteronomy 10:7).

JOTHAM (JO-thuhm, Lord is upright). 1. The son of Gideon. When Shechem made Abimelech king, Jotham told the parable of the trees and bramble (Judges 9).

2. The 11th king of Judah. He began reigning as a regent of his father, King Uzziah, while Uzziah was a leper. Later he was the sole king. Jotham is described as good because he followed the Lord. He fortified Jerusalem, built fortresses in Judah, and fought successfully against the Ammonites (2 Kings 15; 2 Chronicles 27).

Jotham lived during the time of Isaiah, Hosea, and Micah (Isaiah 1:1; Hosea 1:1; Micah 1:1). He was an ancestor of Jesus (Matthew 1:9).

JOURNEY. See *measure 1h.*

JUBAL (JYOO-buhl). A son of Lamech and perhaps the inventor of

musical instruments (Genesis 4:19-21).

JUBILEE (JYOO-buh-lee, blast of trumpets). Every 50th year in Israel was to be celebrated as a year of jubilee. This year was announced by a blast on the trumpet. Three things characterized this year. First, the land rested for the year. Second, property that people had to sell because of poverty was to be returned to them. And finally, all Israelite slaves were to be set free (Leviticus 25:8-55; 27:16-25; Ezekiel 46:17).

JUDAEA (jyoo-DEE-ah). See *Judea.*

JUDAH (JYOO-dah, praise). 1. The fourth son of Jacob and Leah (Genesis 29:35). When Joseph's brothers were planning to kill Joseph, Judah suggested they sell him to the Ishmaelites instead (Genesis 37:26-27). Judah married a Canaanite woman and had three sons with her. After his two older sons and his wife had died, Judah had twin sons by his daughter-in-law Tamar (Genesis 38).

Judah became a leader of his family (Genesis 43:3-10; 44:16-34). Jacob bestowed the blessing of the birthright on Judah. This blessing is usually understood as a Messianic prophecy (Genesis 49:9-10).

2. The tribe that descended from Judah. It occupied the greater part of southern Palestine (Joshua 15:20-63). David and Solomon were two kings of Israel that came from the tribe of Judah. Jesus also came from the tribe of Judah through Boaz, Jesse, and David (Luke 3:23-32).

3. The Kingdom of Judah, which began when the 10 northern tribes withdrew from Rehoboam around 912 B.C. and lasted until 587 B.C. when Jerusalem fell. In 538 B.C. Cyrus permitted the Jews to return to their homeland (1 Kings 12—22; 2 Kings; 2 Chronicles 11–36; Ezra; Nehemiah).

JUDAS (JYOO-dahs). 1. See *Judah 1.*

2. Judas Iscariot, the disciple who betrayed Jesus (Matthew 10:4; Luke 6:16). Iscariot is thought to mean man of Kerioth. Judas was the treasurer for Jesus and the apostles (John 12:4-6; 13:29). He became greedy, however, and took money from the group money box for himself (John 12:3-9). Judas betrayed Jesus for 30 pieces of silver but then regretted his deed and hanged himself (Matthew 26:47-49; 27:3-5; Acts 1:17-18).

3. The brother of Jesus (Matthew 13:55; Mark 6:3). See also *Jude, Letter of.*

4. One of the 12 apostles. He was also apparently referred to as Thaddeus since this name appears in lists in the place that corresponds to Judas (Matthew 10:3; Mark 3:18). Judas was the son or perhaps brother of James (Luke 6:16).

5. A man in Damascus to whom Paul went after his conversion (Acts 9:11).

JUDE (JYOOD). See *Judas 3; 4.*

JUDE, LETTER OF. The author of this letter gives his name as Jude, the brother of James, and calls himself a bondservant of Jesus Christ. He is commonly identified with Judas, the brother of Jesus.

Date: A.D. 60 to 70

Audience: Anonymous

Outline: 1. Salutation (1—2). 2. Purpose of letter (2—4). 3. Solemn warning against false teachers (5—13). 4. The safeguard of the church (14—23). 5. Closing doxology (24—25).

JUDEA (jyoo-DEE-ah). The term used in Ezra 5:8 and 9:9 for the province to which the tribes of Judah and Benjamin returned. It is usually called Judah (Nehemiah 2:7).

At the time of Christ, Judea was the southern division of the three re-

gions into which the Roman province of Palestine was divided, the other two being Galilee and Samaria. Judea was about 55 miles long and wide. It was located east of the Jordan River and Dead Sea, from Beersheba in the south to 10 miles north of the Dead Sea in the north.

JUDGES. The governors, leaders, and deliverers of the Israelites between the time of Joshua and Saul. They included Othniel, Ehud, Shamgar, Deborah, Barak, Gideon, Abimelech, Tola, Jair, Jephthah, Ibzan, Elon, Abdon, and Samson. The high priest Eli and the prophet Samuel also functioned as judges. The activity of the judges is described in the Book of Judges.

JUDGES, BOOK OF. A historical book in the Old Testament that is placed among the Former Prophets, following the Book of Joshua. Taking its name from the title of the people who ruled Israel from the death of Joshua to the time of Samuel, the Book of Judges tells the story of the history of Israel during that period.

The book covers a period of about 300 years. Since more than one judge may have ruled in different areas at the same time, it is difficult to arrive at an exact chronology for the book.

Date: About 1375 to 1050 B.C.
Audience: Israelites
Outline: 1. Why God raised up judges (1—3:6). 2. What the judges did to deliver Israel (3:7—16). 3. How deeply Israel had fallen (17—21).

JUDGMENT. In the Old Testament the word *judgment* occasionally refers to the administration of justice (2 Samuel 15:4; 1 Kings 3). It usually refers, however, to keeping people in a right relation to the covenant (Isaiah 11:61). The prophets describe God as bringing judgment upon a disobedient people. The purpose of God's judgment is to purify, not destroy, His people. God's judgment preserves a faithful remnant (Isaiah 6:13).

God's judgments point to the final judgment, the Day of the Lord, the day when His judgment will come upon all who are unjust and disobedient. On that day God will vindicate His divine rule (Isaiah 25; Zechariah 14).

In the New Testament the word *judgment* sometimes refers to the administration of law (John 18:31; Acts 23:3). Usually it refers to the judgment of God and includes the salvation of believers (Luke 18:1-8; Romans 1:18-32; 1 Corinthians 11:29-32; 2 Thessalonians 1:5-10). God's judgment culminates in the Final Judgment (Matthew 11:20-24; 25:31-46; John 16:11; 1 Thessalonians 4:13-18). It belongs to God and is administered by Christ (Matthew 18:35; 25:3l-46; Romans 14:10). God's judgment is salvation to believers, condemnation to unbelievers (Matthew 25:31-46). God's judgment is based on whether an in-

dividual keeps the Law perfectly (Matthew 25). But since the Law has been fulfilled only by Christ, a person's relationship to Him is the decisive factor (Matthew 10:32-33; Romans 8:1-17; Galatians 5:13-25).

JUDGMENT HALL. See *praetorium*.

JUDITH (JYOO-dith, praised Jewess). Esau's wife (Genesis 26:34).

JULIUS (JYOOL-yuhs, soft-haired). A Roman centurion of the Augustan band who conducted Paul and other prisoners to Rome (Acts 27).

JUSTIFICATION. The gracious act of God by which He pronounces all people to be not guilty of their sin (2 Corinthians 5:19). The basis for His acquittal is that Jesus Christ fulfilled the Law in humanity's place and paid the penalty for all people's sin (Romans 5:12-20). An individual gains the benefits of Christ's substitutionary life and death through the instrument of faith, which God gives him or her by the Holy Spirit working through the Gospel (Romans 1:16; 3:21-25; 5:1; Ephesians 2:8-9). See also *reconciliation*.

JUTAH, JUTTAH (JYOO-tah, JUT-ah, extend). A town in Judah about 5 1/2 miles southwest of Hebron. It was assigned to the priests (Joshua 15:55; 21:16). It may be the same as the "city of Judah," where John the Baptizer was born (Luke 1:39). Today it is known as Yuttah.

KAB. See *measures 2b*.
KADESH (kay-DESH, consecrated). Known as En-mishpat in early times, Kadesh was in the desert about 70 miles south of Hebron (Genesis 14:7). Hagar fled to the region around Kadesh (Genesis 16:7, 14). Israel wandered in this area for 37 years, twice stopping to set up camp at Kadesh (Numbers 13:25-26; Deuteronomy 1:46). Miriam died at Kadesh (Numbers 20:1). There, rather than speaking to the rock as the Lord had told him to do, Moses struck it to bring forth water (Numbers 20:2-13). This displeased the Lord, and so the waters were called Meribah, which means strife. Kadesh is often called Kadesh-barnea (Numbers 32:8; Deuteronomy 2:14).
KADESH-BARNEA (KAY-desh-BAHR-ni-ah). See *Kadesh*.
KARKOR (KAHR-kawr, soft level ground). The place east of the Jordan River where Gideon attacked Zebah and Zalmunna (Judges 8:10).
KEDAR (KEE-dur, dark). 1. One of Ishmael's sons (Genesis 25:13; 1 Chronicles 1:29).
2. An Arabian tribe that descended from Kedar. The people of this tribe lived in black tents and had flocks and camels (Song of Solomon 1:5; Isaiah 21:13-17; 42:11; 60:7; Jeremiah 49:28-29).
KEDEMAH (KED-i-maa, eastward). Ishmael's son and the tribe that descended from him (Genesis 25:15; 1 Chronicles 1:31).

KEDESH (KEE-desh, sacred place). 1. A Canaanite city northwest of Lake Huleh that Joshua conquered during his northern campaign. Having captured the city, Joshua put its king to death (Joshua 12:22). Kedesh was given to the tribe of Naphtali and made a city of refuge (Joshua 19:37). Years later Tiglath-pileser captured it (2 Kings 15:29). Also called Kedesh-naphtali, it was the home of Barak (Judges 4:6).
2. A town in southern Judah, probably the same as Kadesh.
KEILAH (ki-IGH-lah). A city in the lowlands of Judah (Joshua 15:44). David delivered it from the Philistines (1 Samuel 23:7-13).
KENAZ (KEE-naz). A descendant of Esau and an ancestor of the Kenizzites (Genesis 15:19).
KENITES. A tribe of Midianites related to the Kenizzites (Genesis 15:19). The Kenites had extraordinary skill in metal work. Moses' father-in-law was a Kenite (Judges 1:16). Hobab the Kenite guided the Israelites on their march through the desert (Numbers 10:29-32; Judges 1:16; 4:11). The Kenites were on friendly terms with the Israelites. They settled in Wadi Arabah, near Hebron, in Naphtali, and in southern Judah (Numbers 24:20-22; Judges 1:16; 4:11; 1 Samuel 15:6; 27:10; 30:29).
KENIZZITES (KEE-niz-ights). Descendants of Kenaz (Genesis 36:11). The Kenizzites were a tribe that lived in southern Canaan before Israel. It seems that they were conquered by and merged with the Edomites (Genesis 15:19; Deuteronomy 2:12). Part of the tribe, however, may have merged with Judah. Caleb and Othniel were Kenizzites (Numbers 32:12; Joshua 14:6; 15:17).
KENOSIS (ki-NO-sis, emptying). A term applied to Jesus' humiliation. It means that during His earthly life

Jesus, according to His human nature, did not always and fully use the divine attributes communicated to His human nature (Philippians 2:7).

KERIOTH-HEZRON (KEE-ri-oth-HEZ-ron). A city in southern Judah (Joshua 15:25). Most likely Judas Iscariot came from there.

KETURAH (kuh-TYOO-rah, incense). Abraham's second wife. She was the mother of six sons, the ancestors of the eastern nations (Genesis 25:1-6; 1 Chronicles 1:32-33).

KEY. An Oriental key was made of a piece of wood. It had pegs to fit the corresponding holes in a wooden bolt (Judges 3:25; Isaiah 22:22). The key is a symbol of power and authority (Isaiah 22:22; Luke 11:52; Revelation 3:7).

The Keys of the Kingdom are power Christ gives to the church through the apostles to open heaven by forgiving the sins of penitent Christians or to close heaven by retaining the sins of the impenitent (Matthew 16:19; 18:18)

KID. A young goat. It was a favorite food item (Genesis 38:17; Luke 15:29). Kids were also used for sacrifice (Judges 13:15-19).

KIDNEY. An internal organ that, along with the fat around it, was used for a burnt offering (Exodus 29:13, 22; Leviticus 3:4-15). People regarded the kidney as the seat of emotion and desire (Job 16:13; Psalm 73:21; Proverbs 23:16).

KIDRON, BROOK. A valley and winter brook that begins northwest of Jerusalem. It then joins with the Valley of Hinnom and runs 20 miles to the Dead Sea. The Kidron was a burial ground and dumping place for destroyed idols and their altars (1 Kings 15:13; 2 Kings 23:6; 2 Chronicles 29:16; 30:14). When David was being chased by Absalom, he fled across the Kidron (2 Samuel 15:23). Jesus crossed over it on His way to Gethsemane (John 18:1).

KING. The Lord was the King of Israel (Deuteronomy 33:1-5; 1 Samuel 8:7; 10:19; 12:12). Later, the Israelites wanted to be like other nations and have a human king. So God allowed them to have kings to rule over them; nevertheless, these kings were accountable to the Lord. They were subject to democratic processes, the moral law, and prophetic warnings (2 Samuel 12; 1 Kings 12:16; 21:20-24).

Israel had kings to rule them from about 1020 to 587 B.C., beginning with Saul and ending with Zedekiah. Their kings had scepters, a crown, a throne, and a palace (1 Kings 2:19; 7:1-12; 2 Kings 11:12; Psalm 45:6). The kings' officers included such people as army officers, a captain of the bodyguard, a secretary, overseers, and counselors (1 Samuel 14:50; 2 Samuel 8:17; 15:12; 20:23-24; 1 Kings 4:6).

KINGDOM OF GOD. This theological term refers to the fact that God is the Creator of the world and everything in it and rules over all things with unlimited power. He especially rules over His people as their Creator, Redeemer, and Sanctifier.

The development of this concept can be traced through the Old Testament. God is described as King over the whole earth (Numbers 23:21; Deuteronomy 33:5; Psalm 47:7). Specifically, His Lordship over Israel, His chosen nation, is seen (1 Samuel 12:12; Isaiah 44:6). In turn, the Israelites hoped for the coming of the kingdom of God—they looked for a redeemer or messiah who would establish the kingdom of God.

During the time of the kings, these rulers were God's representatives, responsible to Him and ruling in His stead. David, for instance, was a type of ideal king or messiah, ruling the kingdom subject to God's will and law. None of the kings, however, not even David, were perfect representatives of God. Nor were the people of Israel perfect. Thus it became clear that the kingdom of Israel did not equal the kingdom of God.

The prophets pointed out that God's kingdom is really a spiritual kingdom that includes all nations (Isaiah 2:4; 9; 11; 61; Jeremiah 23:5-6; Zechariah 9:10). The New Testament pictures God's kingdom as the Holy Spirit in the hearts of His people. Numerous Bible passages speak of the rule of God (Matthew 12:28; Mark 4:11; Luke 9:27, 11:20).

When John the Baptizer said the kingdom of God was near, he was telling people that God was laying the foundation for His rule in human hearts through the Messiah. Jesus is that Messiah. He is the Fulfiller of the Kingdom and the One who brings God's kingdom to people (Matthew 12:28; Luke 9:27; 17:20-21). Jesus says: "The time is fulfilled and the kingdom of God is at hand; repent, and believe in the Gospel" (Mark 1:15). People enter the kingdom of God by repenting of their sins and believing in Jesus as their Savior (Matthew 18:3-4; John 3:3-5). As members of the kingdom of God, the Holy Spirit works in them, and they become more and more Christ-like (Matthew 5—7;

Luke 9:60-62).

The kingdom of God is, at times, spoken of as a future blessing and, at times, as a present reality (Matthew 7:21; 8:11; Luke 16:16; 17:20). The church proclaims the kingdom of God by witnessing to Christ.

KINGS, FIRST AND SECOND BOOK OF. At first, these were one book, the last in the division known as the Former Prophets. They were divided into two, however, in the Septuagint. They describe the religious history of Israel during the period of the kings and show that the Lord carries out His threats and keeps the promises of "His holy covenant."

First and Second Kings cover the time period from around 1000 to 560 B.C. Much of the historical material found in these books has been verified by archaeological finds.

Date: About 562 B.C.

Audience: Israel

Outline: 1. Solomon, David's co-regent and successor (1 Kings 1—2). 2. Solomon's reign (1 Kings 3—11). 3. Divided kingdom: kings of Israel and Judah (1 Kings 12—2 Kings 18). 4. Kings of Judah to Babylonian exile (2 Kings 18—25).

KINGS OF JUDAH AND ISRAEL. These kings can be divided into three groups: the kings of the United Kingdom of Israel, the kings of Judah, the Southern Kingdom, and the kings of Israel, the Northern Kingdom. 1. The kings of the United Kingdom and the approximate dates they ruled were

Saul	1030—1010 B.C.
David	1010—970
Solomon	970—931)

2. The kings of Judah and the approximate dates they ruled were

Rehoboam	931—915 B.C.
Abijah	915—913
Asa	913—873
Jehoshaphat	873—849

Johoram	849—843
Ahaziah	842
Athaliah	842—837
Joash	837—800
Amaziah	800—?
Uzziah	?—742
Jotham	750—735
Ahaz	735—715
Hezekiah	715—686
Manasseh	686—642
Amon	642—640
Josiah	640—609
Jehoahaz	609
Jehoiakim	609—598
Jehoiachin	598
Zedekiah	598—587

3. The kings of Israel and the approximate dates they ruled were

Jeroboam I	931—910 B.C.
Nadab	910—909
Baasha	909—886
Elah	886—885
Zimri	885
Omri	885—874
Ahab	874—853
Ahaziah	853—852
Joram	852—842
Jehu	842—815
Jehoahaz	815—798
Joash	798—782
Jeroboam II	793—753
Zechariah	753—752
Shallum	752
Menahem	752—741
Pekahiah	741—739
Pekah	?—731
Hoshea	731—722

KIRIATH-ARBA (KIR-i-ath-AHR-bah, city of Arba). An ancient name for Hebron (Genesis 23:2; Joshua 14:15; Judges 1:10; Nehemiah 11:25).

KIRIATH-JEARIM (KIR-i-ath-JEE-ah-rim, city of thickets). A Gibeonite town near Mount Jearim (Joshua 9:17). It was known by different names, for instance, Kiriath-arim, Baalah, Kiriath-baal, and Baale-judah. Kiriath-jearim was assigned to Judah first and then later to Benjamin (Joshua 15:60; 18:20).

The ark of the covenant remained there for 20 years (1 Samuel 6:19—7:2).

KISH (KISH). A Benjaminite; the father of Saul (1 Samuel 9:3; 10:11; Acts 13:21). Kish was the son of Abiel; however, the Bible sometimes refers to him as the son of Ner (1 Samuel 9:1; 1 Chronicles 8:33; 9:39).

KITTIM (KIGHT-tim). 1. The descendants of Javan. These people lived on Cyprus and other islands and on the coasts along the eastern part of the Mediterranean Sea (Genesis 10:4; Numbers 24:24; 1 Chronicles 1:7; Daniel 11:30). The name Kittim was applied to these places too (Isaiah 23:12; Jeremiah 2:10).

2. Macedonia or the Macedonian people. See also *Macedonia*.

KNEADING-TROUGH. A shallow dish made of clay or wood which was used to knead dough (Exodus 8:3).

KNEE, KNEEL. "To bend the knee" or kneel indicated an attitude of worship, prayer, awe, or subjection (Genesis 41:43; 2 Chronicles 6:13; Psalm 95:6; Isaiah 45:23; Matthew 17:14; Philippians 2:10).

KNIFE. In ancient times knives were made of flint (Joshua 5:2-3). The Philistines used metal knives. These did not become common in Israel until the time of the later kings. Knives were used for killing, cutting, pruning, and shaving (Leviticus 7:33-34; 1 Kings 18:28; Isaiah 18:5; Ezekiel 5:1).

KOHATH (KO-hath). One of Levi's sons (Genesis 46:11; Exodus 6:16-18; Numbers 3:17). His descendants, the Kohathites, were one of the three divisions of Levites. Moses and Aaron were Kohathites (Exodus 6:18-20).

KORAH (KO-rah, ice or baldness). A Levite who secretly plotted with Dathan and Abiram against Moses. As punishment for this, as well as to show that Moses was His appointed leader, God allowed the earth to open up and swallow Abiram and Dathan and their households and Korah and his servants. Korah's sons, however, were not destroyed (Numbers 16—17).

KORAHITE (KO-ra-ight). Someone who descended from the Levite Korah. Heman and Samuel were both Korahites (1 Chronicles 6:33-38). The Korahites became famous temple singers (1 Chronicles 15:17; 16:41-42; titles of Psalms 42; 44—49; 84—85; 87—88).

LABAN (LAY-buhn, white). Abraham's great-nephew and Rebekah's brother (Genesis 22:20-24; 24:29; 25:20). Laban lived at Haran (Genesis 11:31-32; 24:4, 10). He allowed Rebekah to go with Abraham's servant to Canaan to become Isaac's wife (Genesis 24). Later Jacob and Rebekah's son Isaac worked for Laban for 20 years. As payment for this service, Isaac received cattle and also his wives, Leah and Rachel (Genesis 29—31).

LABOR. The Bible describes labor as honorable (Psalm 128:2; Proverbs 21:25; 1 Thessalonians 4:11). God's work of creation is called labor (Genesis 2:2). Jesus points to God's continued work in the world, that is, His providential care, to defend working on the Sabbath (John 5:17). Laborers were protected by laws (Deuteronomy 24:14).

LACHISH (LAY-kish). A royal city of the Canaanites located at Tell ed-Duweir, 30 miles southwest of Jerusalem and 15 miles west of Hebron. It was one of the largest cities of ancient Judah. Under Joshua, the Israelites captured Lachish and killed its king (Joshua 10:3-35). Years later, shortly after the division of the kingdom, Rehoboam strengthened the defenses of Lachish (2 Chronicles 11:9). Amaziah, king of Judah, fled there and was slain (2 Kings 14:19). Around 701 B.C. Sennacherib, the king of Assyria, captured Lachish (2 Kings

18:14,17). Nebuchadnezzar destroyed Lachish along with Jerusalem two times, once in 598 B.C. and then again in 587 B.C. (2 Kings 24—25; Jeremiah 34:7). When the exiles returned from captivity, they once again lived in Lachish (Nehemiah 11:30). The city, however, never regained its former importance.

Archaeologists have found many important items at Lachish. One find, the Lachish Letters, are written in Hebrew and belong to Jeremiah's time.

LAHAI-ROI (lah-HIGH-roy). See *Beer-lahai-roi.*

LAISH (LAY-ish, lion). A city in the extreme north of Palestine. The people of the tribe of Dan captured it and renamed it Dan (Judges 18:7-29).

LAMB. A young sheep. Lamb's meat was used for food and sacrifices, particularly at Passover (Genesis 22:7; Exodus 12:3-5; 29:38-41; Leviticus 3:7; 2 Samuel 12:4). Lambs used for sacrifices had to be perfect, without blemish. They pointed to Christ, the Lamb of God, who takes away the sin of the world (John 1:29; Revelation 5:6, 8).

Christians, particularly children, are compared to lambs (John 21:15).

LAMENTATIONS. The English Bible places this book after the Book of Jeremiah. In the Hebrew Scriptures it appears between Ruth and Ecclesiastes. The book laments the destruction of Jerusalem and the suffering of the people there. It acknowledges that God is just in allowing suffering to result from sinfulness (1:18, 22; 2:17; 3:33; 4:13, 22). The five chapters are really five poems, of which the first four are based on letters from the Hebrew alphabet.

Date: After 587 B.C.

Audience: People of Judah (in captivity)

Outline: 1. First lament: Destroyed Jerusalem is personified as a humiliated, deserted widow (1). 2. Second lament: The catastrophe was a result of the Lord's anger (2). 3. Third lament: God's mercy, the conviction that judgment represents only the disciplinary aspect of His steadfast love, which cannot come to an end (3). 4. Fourth lament: Penitent realization of having offended a loving God is not in vain, for restoration will follow when the "punishment . . . is accomplished" (4). 5. Fifth lament: God accepts a sincere confession of guilt and can be moved to answer humble appeals to His mercy (5).

LAMP. A container holding liquid and a wick. Lamps were burned to give light (Exodus 27:20; 2 Kings 4:10). Lamps in the tabernacle and temple were made of gold (Exodus 25:31-40; 37:17-24). They burned olive oil (Exodus 27:20). In the Bible a lamp is also a symbol for God's Word, His guidance, and wise leaders (Psalm 18:28; 119:105; John 5:35).

LANCE, LANCET. A javelin or light spear (1 Kings 18:28; Jeremiah 50:41).

LANDMARK. An object, such as a stone or stake, that marked the boundary of an area of land. Landmarks were not to be removed (Deuteronomy 19:14; 27:17; Hosea 5:10).

LANGUAGE. Words, spoken or written to convey ideas. Language is a gift of God, but the differences in it are a result of sin (Genesis 11). Many languages were spoken during Old Testament times. Sumerian, Akkadian, Egyptian, Phrygian, Phoenician, Canaanite, and Hittite are only a few. The chief languages spoken in Palestine during New Testament times were Aramaic, Hebrew, Greek, and Latin (John 19:20).

LAODICEA (lay-ahd-i-SEE-ah). A wealthy city located in the Lycus Valley of Asia Minor. It was probably founded by Antiochus II and named by him for his wife (Colossians 2:1; 4:15; Revelation 1:11; 3:14-22).

LAPPIDOTH (LAP-i-doth, torches). Deborah's husband (Judges 4:4).

LAST DAY. See *judgment.*

LAST TIMES. See *eschatology.*

LATIN (LAT-in). The language spoken by the Romans (John 19:20).

LAVER (LAY-vur). A bronze basin of water in which priests washed their hands and feet before ministering at the altar or entering the sanctuary (Exodus 30:18).

LAW. 1. God's will for His creation, revealed to people in His judgments, words, rules, and acts (Exodus 20:1-17; 21:1; Deuteronomy 7:6-16; Psalm 19; 119; Isaiah 1:10).

2. The Torah, the first five books of the Old Testament (Matthew

5:17; Luke 16:16).

3. The Old Testament (John 10:34; 12:34).

4. The Ten Commandments given to Moses (Exodus 20:2-17; Deuteronomy 5:6-21; John 7:19). The commandments summarize God's requirements of people— what their relationship to God, to each other, and to the rest of creation should be (Leviticus; Deuteronomy).

Jesus showed respect and love for the Law. He pointed out its deeper meaning for people (Matthew 5:17-48). Paul emphasized that the Law shows the sinfulness of people because they can never keep it perfectly. Moreover, the Law is unable to provide victory over sin (Romans 3—7; Galatians). It does prepare one for the Gospel (Galatians 3:24). See also *appeal; judgment; righteousness.*

LAWYER. A professional interpreter of the Old Testament, often a scribe (Matthew 22:35; Luke 10:25).

LAYING ON OF HANDS. An act symbolizing dedication or blessing. It was used to dedicate priests to their office and animals to the Lord (Leviticus 1:4; Numbers 8:5-20). Through the laying on of hands blessings of various kinds were given and people were set apart for special service (Genesis 48:5-20; Mark 10:16; Luke 4:40; Acts 6:6; 13:3; 1 Timothy 4:14; 2 Timothy 1:6; Hebrews 6:2).

LAZARUS (LAZ-ah-ruhs, God has helped). 1. The brother of Mary and Martha. After Lazarus died, Jesus came to his town and brought him back to life (John 11-12).

2. The name of the beggar in the parable Jesus told about a rich man and a beggar (Luke 16:19-31).

LEAH (LEE-ah, languid). Laban's older daughter. Through a trick of her father, Leah was passed off on Jacob as his bride (Genesis 29—30;

49:31).

LEAVEN (LEV-uhn). A substance used to make dough rise (Exodus 12:15, 20; Matthew 13:33). The Israelites removed leaven from their houses during Passover and did not use it in meal offerings (Exodus; Leviticus 2:11). It was a symbol of corruption and moral influence, whether good or bad (Matthew 13:33; 16:6, 12; 1 Corinthians 5:6-8).

LEBANON (LEB-ah-nuhn, white). The snow-clad mountain ranges of Lebanon and Anti-Lebanon run 110 miles along the coast of Syria between the Taurus Mountains and the lower mountain ranges of Palestine. Some peaks reach 10,000 feet. Mount Hermon is the southern spur of the Anti-Lebanon range. The Lebanons formed the northern boundary of Palestine (Deuteronomy 1:7). They are known especially for their cedars (Judges 9:15; 1 Kings 5).

LEES. The sediment or thick portion of wine that falls to the bottom (Isaiah 25:6). "To settle on the lees" is an expression for a lazy, luxurious, unhampered, stupid life (Jeremiah 48:11; Zephaniah 1:12).

LEGION. 1. The largest single unit in the Roman army (about 6,000 men).

2. A great number (Matthew 26:53; Mark 5:9).

LEHI (LEE-high, jawbone). The place where Samson killed the Philistines with a donkey's jawbone (Judges 15:9-19).

LEMUEL (LEM-yoo-uhl, belonging to God). The unidentified king who wrote Proverbs (Proverbs 31:1-9). He may have been Solomon.

LEPROSY (LEP-ro-see). A dreadful skin disease. Leprosy usually began with scabs that scarred the skin and made the hair around the affected area turn white. Often raw flesh appeared (Exodus 4:6; Leviticus 13:10, 14-16, 24).

The leprosy referred to in the Bible probably included skin diseases other than what is commonly known as leprosy today (Leviticus 13:14). The leprosy of garments may have been mold or mildew (Leviticus 13:47-59; 14:33-37). Jesus healed lepers (Matthew 8:2-4; Luke 17:11-19).

LETTER. See *epistle*.

LEVI (LEE-vigh, joined). Jacob's third son by Leah (Genesis 29:34). Born in Haran, Levi went with his family on the return to Canaan. He joined his brothers in the plot against Joseph (Genesis 37). Levi had three sons: Gershon, Kohath, and Merari (Genesis 46:11; 1 Chronicles 6:16-48). He died in Egypt (Exodus 6:16).

LEVIATHAN (li-VIGH-ah-thuhn). A sea monster (Psalm 104:26). Poetical passages in the Bible describe it as somewhat similar to a crocodile or serpent (Job 41; Isaiah 27:1). Symbolically, Leviathan represents unrestrained power or evil (Job 3:8; Psalm 74:14; 104:26; Isaiah 27:1). See also *beast 4*.

LEVIRATE MARRIAGE (LEV-uhrayt MAR-ij). When an Israelite man died without any male children, the nearest male relative was supposed to marry the deceased's wife. The first son born of this union was then the heir of the woman's first husband (Deuteronomy 25:5-10).

LEVITES (LEE-vights). The descendants of Jacob's son Levi. Levi's three sons, Gershon, Kohath, and Merari, each became heads of a tribal family (Exodus 6:16-25; Leviticus 25:32; Numbers 35:2-8; Joshua 21:3). They became substitutes for the firstborn of their fellow Israelites in all duties pertaining to God (Numbers 3:11-13; 8:16). Their duty was to preserve the law of the Lord and His worship (Leviticus 10:11; Deuteronomy 17:18; 31:9-13). Each family descending from the three sons had different duties assigned to them (Numbers 3:5-39).

Aaron and Moses were Levites of the family of Kohath. The priests descended from this family through Aaron and his sons (Exodus 28:1; Numbers 18:7). They received no tribal territory but were assigned 48 cities and tithes (Leviticus 27: 30-33; Numbers 18:20-24; 35; Deuteronomy 10:9).

LEVITICUS (li-VIT-i-kuhs). The third book of the Pentateuch. Leviticus was the manual for the priesthood. The Book of Leviticus stresses the holiness of God and the demand for holiness that God expects from His covenant people: "You shall be holy; for I the Lord your God am holy" (Leviticus 19:2). The book also spells out the means for attaining this holiness. The barrier between a holy God and an unholy people is removed by making amends for sin. This is symbolized by the vicarious sacrifice of animals by the priests.

Date: 15th to 13th century B.C.

Author: Israelites

Outline: 1. Sacrifices and offerings (1—7). 2. Priests (8—10). 3. Cleanliness and holiness (11—22). 4. Feasts (23). 5. General rules (24—27).

LEVY. A tax. Solomon had the Israelites work four months a year for Hiram in Lebanon (1 Kings 5:13-18). Slaves also had to pay a levy (1 Kings 9:20-21).

LIBATION (ligh-BAY-shuhn). Pouring wine or some other liquid as an act of worship (Exodus 29:40-41; Jeremiah 44:17-25).

LIBERTINES (LIB-ur-teenz). Freedmen (Acts 6:9). They may have been Jewish people whom Pompey captured and allowed to return home as free people.

LIBERTY. Freedom, the opposite of slavery or bondage. Even though the Israelites often were in bondage, they prized liberty. Those who had become slaves were to be freed in the year of jubilee (Leviticus 25:8-17).

Old Testament prophecies about liberty have a spiritual meaning which is fulfilled in Christ (Isaiah 61:1, Luke 4:18; John 8:31-36). Jesus frees people from Satan, sin, death, judgment, fear, and the Law (John 1:29; Acts 26:18; Romans 6—8; Galatians 3). In matters that are neither commanded nor forbidden in God's Word, a Christian has freedom (Romans 14; 1 Corinthians 8).

LIBYA (LIB-ee-ah). A country in North Africa west of Egypt (Ezekiel 30:5; Acts 2:10).

LIBYANS (LIB-i-uhns). People who live in Libya (Jeremiah 46:9; Nahum 3:9).

LIEUTENANT (lu-TEN-uhnt). See *satrap.*

LIFE. A concept with various meanings. The Bible refers to the physical life of plants, animals, and humans as that quality which makes it possible for them to breathe, eat, grow, and reproduce (Genesis 6:17; Exodus 1:14; Job 3:20-21; Ecclesiastes 2:17).

2. The Bible also talks about the spiritual or eternal life of man. It is the gift of God which one has by grace through faith in Jesus Christ (Ephesians 2:8-10; John 17:3; 1 John 5:12). The person who believes in Jesus as Savior never dies (John 11:25-26).

3. Christ is the Source of all life (John 1:4; 11:25; Colossians 3:4).

LIGHT, DARKNESS. God made natural light. It is a blessing without which life as we know it cannot exist. Light is often used to describe God, the highest Good, from whom every good gift comes (James 1:17). Jesus is the Light of the world (John

1:4-9). God's Word and believers are spoken of as lights (Psalm 119:105; Matthew 5:14-16). Living a godly life is described in terms of putting on the armor of light or walking in the light (Romans 13:11-14; 1 John 1:7).

Darkness, on the other hand, is symbolic of evil and all the results of the power of evil: spiritual blindness, evil deeds, death, hell, and suffering (Job 10:21-22; Joel 2:2; Matthew 22:13; Luke 22:53; John 3:19-20; 1 John 1:6).

LIME. The mountains of Palestine contain a large amount of limestone. The Israelites burned this limestone to make lime plaster and the like (Isaiah 27:9; 33:12; Amos 2:1).

LINEAGE. See *genealogy.*

LINEN. A thread or cloth made from flax. Linen was used to make clothing, priestly garments, the temple veil, choir robes, and burial cloths (Genesis 41:42; Exodus 28:5-42; 2 Chronicles 3:14; 5:12; Mark 15:46). It was a symbol of wealth and purity (Luke 16:14; Revelation 19:8, 14).

LITTER. A couch or chair used to carry people (Song of Solomon 3:7; Isaiah 66:20).

LIVER. An internal organ of the body. The liver was used in sacrifice and for divination (Leviticus 3:4-15; Ezekiel 21:21; 29:13). It was thought to be the center of life and feeling (Proverbs 7:23).

LO-AMMI (lo-AM-ee, not my people). The symbolic name of Hosea's third son (Hosea 1:9).

LOANS. Something, especially money, that is lent. During Old Testament times the Hebrews were encouraged to make loans to their needy neighbors. If the Israelites became poverty-stricken, they could sell themselves as servants. After seven years, however, Israelite servants were to be released, and in the year of jubilee their debts were to be canceled (Leviticus 25:39-41; Deuteronomy 15:1-11).

The Israelites were not allowed to charge interest to other Israelites but could charge it to strangers (Leviticus 25:36-37; Deuteronomy 15:1-11). Charging interest on a loan was looked down upon (Nehemiah 5:7, 10; Psalm 15:5; Ezekiel 22:12).

LOGOS (LAHG-ahs). See *Jesus Christ.*

LOIN. Part of the back of the body between the hips and false ribs. Before walking or working, a man usually tied loose clothing at his loins.

LOIS (LO-is, pleasing). Timothy's grandmother (2 Timothy 1:5).

LONGIMANUS (lon-JIM-ah-nuhs). See *Artaxerxes 2.*

LORD. Various Hebrew and Greek names in the Bible are expressed by the English word *Lord.* 1. LORD (printed often in capital letters in the Bible) is God's personal name. It comes from the Hebrew word *Yahweh.* Some Bible versions use *Yahweh* instead of *LORD.*

2. Lord (capital *L* and the remaining letters lowercase) comes from the Hebrew word *'adon.* It means master or my master, my Lord, and denotes ownership by human beings or God (Genesis 24:14; Psalm 114:7).

3. *'Adonai* is the word the Israelites said whenever they saw the consonants of *Yahweh* (YHWH).

4. The Greek word *Kurios* is also translated as Lord. It is the word used for a human master or for God as the ruler (Matthew 8:25; 20:18; 21:9). It is also the word used for Christ, who by His death and resurrection is the Lord (Romans 14:9). See also *Jehovah; Jesus Christ.*

LORD OF HOSTS. See *host 2.*

LORD'S DAY. That day associated with the resurrection of Jesus and the outpouring of the Holy Spirit on the disciples (Acts 2:1-41). The Lord's day is the first day of the week. It was set aside for worship, although some people still observed the Sabbath (Acts 20:7; Revelation 1:10; see also Romans 14:5; 1 Corinthians 16:2; Galatians 4:10). See also *Sunday*.

LORD'S PRAYER. The prayer Jesus taught His disciples as a pattern for their prayers (Matthew 6:9-13; Luke 11:2-4).

LORD'S SUPPER. Christ instituted this supper on the night of His betrayal to replace the paschal feast. It is a memorial of His death for the sins of the world (1 Corinthians 11:26). In this meal Christ gives His body and blood together with the bread and wine (Matthew 14:22-24; Luke 22:19-20; 1 Corinthians 10:16-17; 11:20-26). Before going to the Lord's Supper, believers in Christ are to examine themselves to see whether they are truly sorry for their sins and truly believe in Jesus Christ as Savior (1 Corinthians 11:27-32). Christians who trust in the blessings Christ promises to give in this meal and partake of it in faith receive the forgiveness of sins, life and salvation, and a strengthening of their faith.

The Lord's Supper is also called the Breaking of Bread (Acts 2:42; 20:7; 1 Corinthians 10:16), Communion (participation, 1 Corinthians 10:16), Eucharist (blessing, 1 Corinthians 10:16), and the Lord's Table (1 Corinthians 10:21).

LO-RUHAMAH (lo-ryoo-HAY-mah). The symbolic name given to Hosea's daughter (Hosea 1:6, 8). It means "not pitied."

LOT, I. A way people in Bible times decided an issue or figured out the divine will in a matter (Joshua 18:6-28; Jonah 1:7; Matthew 27:35; Acts 1:26).

LOT, II (LOT, may mean covering). Haran's son; Abraham's nephew (Genesis 11:27-31). Lot went with Abraham to Egypt and Canaan (Genesis 13:1-7). In Canaan, Lot and his family settled in the Jordan Valley (Genesis 13:8-13). Before the Lord destroyed Sodom and Gomorrah, He sent two angels to help Lot and his family escape. Only Lot and his two daughters made it to safety (Genesis 19). Lot was an ancestor of Moab and Ammon (Genesis 19:36-38).

LOVE. Various types of love are referred to in the Bible. The Old Testament talks about God's steadfast love for His covenant people (Deuteronomy 7:7-9, 12). The Greek word *agape* represents God's undeserved love for sinful people (John 3:16; 1 John 4:8). This is the kind of love Christians are to have (Matthew 5:44-45; 1 Corinthians 13; 1 John 4). One may also have a noble, unselfish love or brotherly love (Matthew 10:37; John 5:20; Titus 3:15).

LOVE FEAST. A common meal early Christians shared with each other that was connected with the Lord's Supper (Jude 12; 2 Peter 2:13). These meals were held to express and deepen their brotherly love for each other.

LUKE (LYOOK). A doctor who was Paul's companion. Luke wrote the Gospel According to Luke and the Acts of the Apostles. From his writings it seems that he was a well-educated man. He was a Gentile Christian, probably a Greek, whom the New Testament mentions three times by name (Colossians 4:14; Philemon 24; 2 Timothy 4:11). It seems Luke accompanied Paul on his missionary journeys at times. In Acts 16:10 we learn that he joined Paul at Troas. Later, when Paul was on his third missionary trip, Luke joined him again at Philippi (Acts 20:5).

LUKE, GOSPEL ACCORDING TO. The third book of the New Testament. The vocabulary, style, and dedication to Theophilus indicate that Luke and Acts were written by the same person. Traditionally this person is Luke. At the beginning of the gospel, Luke says that he collected the information in it from eyewitnesses (1:2).

Date: A.D. 65 to 70
Audience: Gentiles
Outline: 1. Preface (1:1-4). 2. John and Jesus: Forerunner and Messiah (1:5—2). 3. The ministry of John (3:1-22). 4. Jesus' Galilean ministry (3:23—9:50). 5. Jesus' travel ministry (9:51—18:30). 6. Jesus' last days in Jerusalem (18:31—21:38). 7. Jesus' death, resurrection, and ascension (22:1—24:53).

LYCAONIA (lik-ay-O-ni-ah, wolf land). A high, rugged tableland of Asia Minor that was annexed to Galatia in 35 B.C. Paul visited this district and preached in three of its cities: Iconium, Derbe, and Lystra (Acts 13:51-14:23).

LYCIA (LISH-i-ah). A province of southwest Asia Minor (Acts 21:2; 27:5).

LYDIA (LID-i-ah). A woman in Philippi who made her living by selling purple dyes. She was Paul's first convert in Europe to Christianity. Paul stayed in her house when he was in Philippi (Acts 16;14-15, 40).

LYSIAS, CLAUDIUS (LIS-i-as KLAW-di-uhs). The chief captain of the Roman soldiers in Jerusalem. He rescued Paul from a mob and sent him to Caesarea (Acts 21—24).

LYSTRA (LIS-trah). A Roman colony in Lycaonia (Acts 14:6-21; 16:1-2; 2 Timothy 3:11).

MAACAH (MAY-ah-kah, oppression). 1. David's wife and Absalom's mother (2 Samuel 3:3; 1 Chronicles 3:2).

2. Rehoboam's wife, Abijah's mother, and Absalom's granddaughter (1 Kings 15:2, 10, 13; 2 Chronicles 11:20-22). She is also referred to as Micaiah (2 Chronicles 13:2).

MAASEIAH (MAY-ah-SEE-yah, work of LORD). 1. A captain who helped Jehoiada overthrow Athaliah (2 Chronicles 23:1).

2. The governor of Jerusalem during Josiah's reign (2 Chronicles 34:8).

3. A priest who was a co-worker of Ezra (Nehemiah 8:4; 12:41).

4. The father of the false prophet Zedekiah (Jeremiah 29:21).

MAAZIAH (may-ah-ZIGH-ah, may mean decision of the Lord). The head of the 24th division of priests (1 Chronicles 24:18).

MACCABEES (MAK-ah-beez, may mean hammer). A Hasmonean Jewish family that led a revolt against Antiochus IV, king of Syria. They won freedom for the Jews and ruled Judea from 166 to 63 B.C.

The term *Maccabaeus* was first given to Judas, the third son of the family. Later it was used of his entire family, as well as others who had a part in the rebellion. The history of the Maccabees is found in the Books of the Maccabees.

MACEDONIA (mas-i-DO-ni-ah). A country in the Balkan Peninsula north of Greece. Philip ruled Macedonia from 359 to 336 B.C., and his son Alexander the Great ruled it from 336 to 323 B.C. In 168 B.C. Macedonia became a Roman province. Paul often visited there (Acts 16:9-12; 17:1-15; 20:1-6; Romans 15:26; 1 Corinthians 16:5; 2 Corinthians 1:16; Philippians 4:15; 1 Timothy 1:3).

MACHAERUS (mah-KEE-ruhs, black fortress). A fortress that overlooked the Dead Sea. It was the prison of John the Baptizer.

MACHIR (MAY-kir, sold). The son of Manasseh (Genesis 50:23). The Machirites descended from him (Numbers 26:29).

MACHPELAH (mak-PEE-lah, double). A cave Abraham bought that was located in the western part of Hebron. Abraham, Sarah, Isaac, Rebekah, Jacob, and Leah were buried in this cave (Genesis 23; 25:9-10; 49:30-31; 50:13). A Mohammedan mosque now stands over the site.

MAGDALENE. See *Mary 3*.

MAGI (MAY-jigh). A title the Babylonians, Medes, and Persians gave to their priests and learned men (Daniel 1—2; 5). The Magi studied astrology and astronomy and interpreted dreams and omens. They were important men who advised rulers.

When Jesus was born, Magi (the wise men) came from the East to worship Him (Matthew 2:1-11). In New Testament times the words *Magi* or *Magos* were also applied broadly to anyone who used the methods of these priests and learned men from the East (Acts 8:9; 13:8).

MAGIC. The use of spells, charms, and the like that supposedly gives one powers to make things happen in an unusual way (Genesis 41:8; Exodus 7:11, 22; 8:7, 18; Acts 13:6-12). Magic includes necromancy (trying to tell the future by getting messages from the dead, 1 Samuel 28:8), exorcism (driving out evil spirits, Acts 19:13), dreams (Deuteronomy 13:1-4), shaking arrows (Ezekiel 21:21), divination (trying to tell the future through various means, Deuteronomy 18:10, 14), witchcraft (Leviticus 19:26; Isaiah 47:9), astrology (believing that the sun, moon, and stars affect peoples' lives, Daniel 2:27; 4:7), enchantment and telling the future (Deuteronomy 18:10, 14; Joshua 13:22; Acts 16:16), and divining by rods (Hosea 4:12).

MAGISTRATE. The chief official in a Roman colony (Acts 16:12-40).

MAGOG (MAY-gog, Gog's land). 1. People who descended from Japheth (Genesis 10:2; 1 Chronicles 1:5).

2. Gog's land is often identified with Scythia, the place where the Magog lived, or with Lydia (Ezekiel 38; 39:1, 11). The word *Magog* is also used symbolically for the final struggle of the forces of evil against the people of God (Revelation 20:7-9).

MAHALATH (MAY-hah-lath). 1. The daughter of Ishmael and wife of Esau (Genesis 28:9). She is also referred to as Basemath (Genesis 36:3).

2. The wife of Rehoboam (2 Chronicles 11:18).

3. The title of Psalms 53 and 88. The term probably refers to a familiar melody.

MAHANAIM (may-hah-NAY-im, two camps). A place east of the Jordan River on the boundary between Gad and Manasseh (Joshua 13:26, 30). After Jacob left Laban, the angels of God met him at Mahanaim (Genesis 32:2). Later Mahanaim was assigned to the priests as a Levitical city (Joshua 21:38). Ishbosheth ruled there, and when David was fleeing from Absalom, he went to Mahanaim (2 Samuel 2:8; 17:24; 1 Kings 2:8).

MAHER-SHALAL-HASHBAZ
(MAY-hur-SHAL-al-hash-baz, the
spoil speeds, the prey hastens). The
symbolic name Isaiah gave to his
second son (Isaiah 8:1-4).

MAHLON (MAH-lon, sickly). The
son of Elimelech and Naomi and the
first husband of Ruth (Ruth 1:2;
4:10).

MAID, MAIDEN. 1. A female servant or slave (Genesis 16:1).

2. A virgin (Deuteronomy 22:17)
or young woman (2 Chronicles
36:17; Jeremiah 2:32).

3. A prostitute (Amos 2:7).

MALACHI (MAL-ah-kigh, my messenger). A prophet who wrote the
last book in the Old Testament.
Nothing is known about Malachi except what is written in his book. He
is thought to have lived around the
time of Nehemiah (see Malachi
2:11-17 and Nehemiah 13:23-31;
Malachi 3:8-11 and Nehemiah
13:10-13).

MALACHI, BOOK OF. The 12th
book of the Minor Prophets, written
probably around Nehemiah's time.
It speaks to specific moral and religious abuses and to their under-
lying cause: religious apathy.

Date: About 450 B.C.

Audience: Jews

Outline: 1. Introduction (1:1-5).
2. Sins of the priests (1:6—2:9). 3.
Sins of the people (2:10—4:1). 4.
The rising of the Sun of Righteousness (4:2-6).

MALCHIJAH (mal-KIGH-jah,
LORD is king). 1. The head of the
fifth division of priests (1 Chronicles 24:1, 9).

2. A prince into whose dungeon
Jeremiah was thrown (Jeremiah
21:1; 38:1, 6).

MALCHUS (MAL-kuhs, king). A
servant of the high priest. On the
night Jesus was betrayed, Peter cut
off Malchus's ear in the Garden of
Gethsemane (John 18:30).

MALEFACTOR (MAL-uh-fak-tur).
One who does evil, a criminal (Luke
23:32-43; John 18:30).

MAMMON (MAM-uhn, wealth).
Riches, particularly those that make
people greedy and selfish (Matthew
6:24; Luke 16:9, 11, 13).

MAMRE (MAM-ri, perhaps meaning
strength). 1. An Amorite living at
Mamre. He helped Abraham (Genesis 14:13, 24).

2. A place where Abraham lived
that was near or in Hebron (Genesis
13:18; 14:13; 18:1; 35:27; 50:13).

MAN. A being that God created in His
own image and likeness (Genesis
1:26-27; 9:6; 1 Corinthians 11:7;
Colossians 3:10). He is dependent
upon God (Matthew 6:26-30; Acts
17:24-28). Man has a body (Matthew 6:25), flesh (Romans 1:3),
soul, spirit (Genesis 2:7; Matthew
10:28; Luke 9:56), and intelligence
(John 12:40; Romans 2:15).

Man fell into sin and lost the image of God (Genesis 3; Romans
5:15-21). As a result man refuses to
honor and thank God but worships
created things instead (Romans
1:19-25). Because of sin man also
dies (Romans 5:17). In His law God
shows man that he is a sinner, cut
off and turned in the opposite direction from his Creator (Romans
7:14-24). But out of grace, God
saves those who have faith in Jesus
as their Savior and conforms them
to His Sons's image (Romans 5:15-
21; 8:29; 1 Corinthians 15:48-49;
Colossians 1:15; 3:10).

MAN OF SIN. An enemy of Christ
who makes himself out to be greater
than God. He is found within God's
temple and shows himself as God.
He works with power and signs,
bringing rebellion against God, de-
ception, and delusion. The man of
sin will be uncovered at the end of
time when Christ comes in glory (2
Thessalonians 2:3-12; see also Daniel 7; 1 John 2:18; Revelation 13;

19). See also *antichrist*.

MAN, SON OF. See *Jesus Christ*.

MANASSEH (mah-NAS-e, cause to forget). 1. The first son of Joseph and Asenath (Genesis 41:50-51). Manasseh and his brother, Ephraim, were blessed by Jacob (Genesis 48:8-22).

2. The tribe that descended from Manasseh (Genesis 50:23; Numbers 26:28-34; Joshua 17:1).

3. The son of Hezekiah and 14th king of Judah. Manasseh was a wicked ruler. He brought back many forms of heathen worship. As punishment for his evil ways and idol worship, God let Manasseh's enemies, the Assyrians, carry him into captivity (2 Kings 21; 2 Chronicles 33; Jeremiah 47—49; Zephaniah 2:4-9; Matthew 1:10).

MANASSITES (mah-NAS-ights). People who descended from Manasseh (Deuteronomy 4:43; 2 Kings 10:33).

MANGER (MAYN-jur). A feeding place for cattle (Luke 2:7-16; 13:15).

MANNA (MAN-ah, what?). A special food God miraculously provided for the Israelites while they were in the wilderness. It was white and looked like hoarfrost (Exodus 16:14-36; Numbers 11:7-9; Deuteronomy 8:3; Joshua 5:12). Jesus is described as the true Manna from heaven (John 6:31-40).

MANOAH (mah-NO-ah, rest). Samson's father (Judges 13).

MARA (MAY-rah, bitter). The name Naomi gave to herself (Ruth 1:20).

MARAH (MAY-rah, bitter). A spring in the Wilderness of Shur where the Hebrews found water (Exodus 15:22-25; Numbers 33:8-9).

MARANATHA (mar-ah-NATH-ah). An expression meaning "Our Lord come!" See also *anathema maranatha*.

MARK (MAHRK). The writer of the second gospel. John was his Jewish name, and Mark was his Roman name. Sometimes he is referred to by both names: John Mark (Acts 12:12, 25; 13:5; 1 Peter 5:13). The young man mentioned in Mark 14:51-52 may be Mark.

John Mark's mother, Mary, had a home in Jerusalem (Acts 12:12-17). John Mark went with Barnabas, his cousin, and Paul, his spiritual father, on part of the first missionary journey (Acts 12:25; 13:1; Colossians 4:10; 1 Peter 5:13). He left them, however, before the trip was over and returned to Jerusalem (Acts 13:13). This resulted in an argument between Barnabas and Paul (Acts 15:36-41). As a result, Barnabas let Paul go on the second missionary journey without him, and Barnabas took John Mark and went to Cyprus (Acts 15:39). Later Mark became Paul's helper (2 Timothy 4:11; Colossians 4:10; Philemon 24).

According to tradition Mark presented Peter's story in his gospel (see 1 Peter 5:13). Mark is also said to have been the founder of the church of Alexandria.

MARK, GOSPEL ACCORDING TO. The second and shortest of the four gospels. According to tradition John Mark wrote this gospel to present Peter's story of Christ. The author of the book knows Jewish thought and life well. The book, however, is primarily addressed to Gentile Christians.

Date: About 65 A.D.

Audience: Gentiles

Outline: 1. Baptism and temptation of Jesus (1:1-13). 2. Early Galilean ministry (1:14—7:23). 3. Tour to Tyre and Sidon (7:24-30). 4. Later Galilean ministry (7:31—9). 5. Ministry in Perea (10). 6. Passion week and resurrection morning (11—16).

MARKET. A place in cities where goods were traded or sold and where people came together to visit (Psalm 55:11; Matthew 11:16; Luke 11:43; Acts 16:19).

MARRIAGE. A lifelong union between a man and a woman, instituted by God (Genesis 1:26-31; 2:18-25; Matthew 19:5). God provides blessings through marriage: children, help, and companionship (Genesis 1:28; 2:18-24; 29:32; 30:1). Sexual relations between a husband and his wife are God-pleasing (Proverbs 5:15-19; 1 Thessalonians 4:1-5; Hebrews 13:4).

The union of one man and one woman until one of them dies is God's ideal intention for marriage (Genesis 2:24; Proverbs 31:10-31; Matthew 19:5-6; 1 Timothy 3:2). Nevertheless, men in Bible times sometimes had more than one wife (Genesis 4:19; 30; 1 Kings 11:3).

The Israelites were not allowed to marry Canaanites or close relatives (Leviticus 18; 20; Deuteronomy 7:3-4). There were also certain legal restrictions on marrying people of other nations (Deuteronomy 23:3-8). After the exile Israelite men were told to divorce their foreign wives (Ezra 9—10).

Although divorce is not part of God's plan, it is allowed for certain reasons (Deuteronomy 24:1-4; Ezra 10:11-44; Matthew 19:3-9). Unless one's husband or wife has been sexually unfaithful, to divorce him or her is adultery (Matthew 5:31-32; 19:3-10; Mark 10:2-12; Luke 16:18).

In Bible times marriage customs differed from today. Fathers often picked wives for their sons. An engagement between a man and woman involved a legal agreement that was confirmed by an oath and dowry. After this the two were considered man and wife (Matthew 1:18-20). They did not live together as man and wife, however, until they were actually married. When the bridegroom took his bride from her father's house to his own, the people joined in a marriage celebration (Isaiah 61:10; Song of Solomon 3:11; Matthew 25:1-13).

The Scriptures picture the covenant union between God and Israel as a marriage (Isaiah 62:1-5; Jeremiah 2:2). In the New Testament the church is called the bride of Christ (Luke 5:34; 2 Corinthians 11:2; Revelation 21:2).

MARRIAGE, LEVIRATE. See *levirate marriage.*

MARS' HILL. See *Areopagus.*

MARTHA (MAHR-thah, lady). The sister of Mary and Lazarus (Luke 10:38-41; John 11; 12:2).

MARTYR (MAHR-tur, witness). A person who witnesses to his or her faith in Christ by dying for it (Acts 22:20; Revelation 17:6).

MARY (MAIR-ee, rebellion). Miriam in the Old Testament. In the New Testament a number of women are named Mary. 1. Mary, mother of Jesus. She was the wife of Joseph, a descendant of King David, and a relative of Elizabeth, John the Baptizer's mother (Matthew 1:18-25; Luke 1:27, 36; Romans 1:3).

Mary gave birth to Jesus at Bethlehem (Matthew 1:18, 20; Luke 2:1-20). At the proper time Mary and Joseph brought Jesus to the temple in Jerusalem for His presentation to the Lord (Luke 2:22-38). Shortly after the visit of the wise men, an angel warned Joseph in a dream to flee to Egypt because Herod was going to kill Jesus. So Mary and Joseph took Jesus and went to Egypt (Matthew 2:13-15). After Herod died, they returned to the land of Israel and lived at Nazareth (Matthew 2:19-23; Luke 2:39-40). When Jesus was 12 years old, Mary and Joseph took Him to Jerusalem for the Feast of the Passover (Luke 2:41-50).

Mary was at the wedding in Cana where Jesus performed His first miracle (John 2:1-12). When Jesus was dying on the cross, He asked John to look after Mary (John 19:25-27). After Jesus' ascension Mary met with other believers in the Upper Room for prayer (Acts 1:14).

Mary is called blessed among women (Luke 1:28, 42, 48). She carefully considered and thought about Jesus' mission and work and believed in His powers (Luke 2:51; John 2:3-5). Jesus stressed His spiritual relationship to Mary rather than His earthly one (Matthew 12:46-50; Luke 8:20-21; 11:27-28).

2. Mary, the wife of Clopas and mother of James and Joses (Matthew 27:56; Mark 15:40). She was one of the women at Jesus' crucifixion and burial (Matthew 27:56, 61; Mark 15:47). Early on the morning of Jesus' resurrection she went to His grave only to discover that He was not there; He had risen (Matthew 28:1; Mark 16:1; Luke 24:1).

3. Mary Magdalene, a woman who came from Magdala on the southwest coast of the Sea of Galilee. Mary became a devoted follower of Jesus after He cast seven demons out of her (Mark 16:9; Luke 8:1-2). She is often regarded as the sinful woman who anointed Jesus' feet and wiped them with her hair (Luke 7:37-50). No one knows this for sure, however, since the Biblical account does not name this woman. Mary was among the women who witnessed the crucifixion and burial of Jesus (Matthew 27:56, 61; Mark 15:40, 47; John 19:25). On the morning of His resurrection she went to His tomb (Matthew 28:1; Mark 16:1; Luke 24:1; John 20:1). She was the first person to whom the risen Lord appeared (Mark 16:9; John 20:11-29).

4. Mary of Bethany, the sister of Lazarus and Martha (John 11:1). While Martha prepared the dinner, Mary sat at Jesus' feet and listened to His teaching (Luke 10:38-41). On another occasion Mary anointed Jesus' feet with oil (John 12:1-8).

5. Mary, mother of John Mark and sister of Barnabas (Colossians 4:10). Mary lived in Jerusalem. When Peter was in prison, Christians met in her home to pray for his release. While they were gathered there, Peter surprised them by knocking at the door. After they had gotten over their amazement, they let Peter in and listened to him describe how the Lord had brought him out of prison (Acts 12:12-17).

MASTER. Various words in the Bible are translated as master. Consequently when the word *master* is used in English Bibles it may mean any of the following: master of a house or husband (Deuteronomy 22:22; Matthew 10:25); ruler, owner, or lord (Genesis 24:14, 27; 39:20; 2 Kings 19:4; Matthew 24:45); teacher (Matthew 23:10; Mark 9:5); superior or supervisor (Luke 5:5; 8:24).

MATTANIAH (mat-ah-NIGH-ah, Lord's gift). The original name of King Zedekiah (2 Kings 24:17).

MATTHEW (MATH-yoo, gift of the Lord). The son of Alpheus. Matthew, who was also referred to as Levi, was a tax collector at Capernaum. One day Jesus called him to be His disciple (Matthew 9:9-13; Mark 2:14-17; Luke 5:27-32). Along with the other 12 disciples, Jesus made Matthew an apostle (Matthew 10:3; Luke 6:15; Acts 1:13).

MATTHEW, GOSPEL ACCORDING TO. The first of the four gospels. Matthew wrote this account for Jewish converts to Christianity to show that Jesus was the Messiah promised in the Old Testament. It focuses on Jesus' teaching, whereas the gospel of Mark focuses on what Jesus did.

Date: A.D. 55 to 60

Audience: Jews

Outline: 1. The Messiah's birth and early years (1:1—4:16). 2. The Messiah's Galilean ministry (4:17—18:35). 3. The Messiah's Perean ministry (19—20). 4. The Messiah teaches in Jerusalem (21—25). 5. The Messiah's death and resurrection (26—28).

MATTHIAS (ma-THIGH-uhs, gift of Lord). The apostle whom the disciples chose to fill the place of Judas Iscariot after Judas killed himself (Acts 1:15-26).

MEASURES. Biblical measurements can be divided into three categories: length, dry ingredients, and liquids.

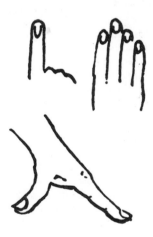

1. **LENGTH**
a. A fingerbreadth equaled about three-fourths of an inch.
b. A handbreadth equaled four fingerbreadths (about three and one-half inches).
c. A span was the distance from the tip of the thumb to the tip of the little finger when the fingers were stretched apart (about nine inches).
d. A cubit equaled two spans (about 18 inches).
e. A reed equaled six cubits (about nine feet).
f. A pace was the distance of one step (about 30 inches).
g. A little way (Genesis 48:7) was the distance one could walk in an hour (about three to four miles).
h. A day's journey was the distance traveled in one day (about 20 miles).
i. A furlong or stadium was about 600 feet.
j. A fathom was the distance between two hands when held wide apart (about five to six feet).
k. A mile was 1,000 paces (about 4,854 feet).
l. A Sabbath day's journey was 3,000 feet (Joshua 3:4).

2. **DRY MEASURES**
a. A handful was the amount that could be held in one hand.
b. A kab was equal to about two quarts.
c. A seah was equal to six kabs (about 10 to 12 quarts).
d. An ephah was equal to about a bushel.
e. An omer was one-tenth of an ephah (about five pints).
f. A homer was 10 ephahs, or the load of a donkey (about 10 bushels).
g. A choenix equaled about one quart.
h. A modius probably equaled about one peck even though Matthew 5:15 translates it as bushel.
i. A saton or measure equaled about a peck.
j. A cor equaled a homer (about 10 bushels).

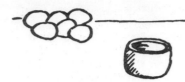

3.   LIQUID MEASURES
a.   A log was the amount displaced by six hen's eggs (about one pint).
b.   A hin equaled 12 logs (about six quarts).
c.   A bath equaled six hins (about nine gallons).
d.   A firkin was about 9 or 10 gallons.
e.   A sextarius was about one pint. (Klinck)

MEDAD (MEE-dad). One of the elders Moses chose to help him govern the people. Medad was a prophet (Numbers 11:26-27).

MEDAN (MEE-dan). The son of Abraham and Keturah (Genesis 25:2; 1 Chronicles 1:32).

MEDE (MEED). A person who came from Media (2 Kings 17:6; Esther 1:19; Isaiah 13:17).

MEDIA (MEE-di-ah). A country in Asia northwest of Persia and south of the Caspian Sea. The people who lived there were famous for the horses they bred. In 612 B.C. the Medes captured Nineveh. Under Nebuchadnezzar's rule, the Median Kingdom stretched from the Persian Gulf to the Caspian Sea (Esther 1:3, 14, 18; 10:2; Isaiah 21:2; Daniel 8:20).

MEDIATOR (MEE-di-ay-tur). A person who acts as a go-between (1 Samuel 2:25; Job 33:23; Isaiah 43:27). Christ is the Mediator of the new covenant. Through Him God and people are brought back into a right relationship with each other (1 Timothy 2:5; Hebrews 8:6; 9:15; 12:24). See also *Jesus Christ.*

MEDICINE. See *apothecary; disease.*

MEDITERRANEAN SEA (med-uh-tuh-RAY-ni-uhn). The sea that lies between Europe and Africa. It is also referred to as the sea, the Great Sea, the western sea, and the Sea of Philistines (Exodus 23:31; Numbers 13:29; 34:6; Deuteronomy 11:24; Acts 10:6).

MEDIUM. See *familiar spirit.*

MEGIDDO (mi-GID-o, place of troops). A city that overlooked the Plain of Esdraelon. It was situated on two important trade routes (Joshua 12:21; 17:11; Judges 1:27). Solomon strengthened its fortifications (1 Kings 9:15). When Ahaziah, king of Judah, was wounded by Jehu's men, he fled to Megiddo, where he died (2 Kings 9:27).

Megiddo was also the scene of a battle between Pharaoh Neco and King Josiah (2 Kings 23:29; 2 Chronicles 35:22). See also *Armageddon.*

MEHUJAEL (mi-HYOO-yay-el). Cain's grandson (Genesis 4:18).

MELCHIZEDEK (mel-KIZ-uh-dek, king of righteousness). The king of Salem (Jerusalem) and priest of God. Melchizedek blessed Abram and received tithes from him (Genesis 14:17-20). He is a type of Christ, the King-Priest (Psalm 110:4; Hebrews 5:6-10; 6:20; 7).

MELITA (MEL-i-tah, honey). The island where Paul was shipwrecked (Acts 28:1). Today it is thought that Melita is the island of Malta.

MEMPHIS (MEM-fis, place of good). An ancient city of Egypt located on the Nile River about 10 miles north of Cairo. The prophets spoke of it negatively, calling it Noph and Moph (Isaiah 19:13; Jeremiah 2:16; 44:1; 46:14; 19; Ezekiel 30:13, 16).

MENAHEM (MEN-ah-hem, comforter). The 16th king of Israel, who gained the throne by killing King

Shallum. Menahem paid tribute to Pul (Tiglath-pileser) to keep him from invading the land. He also practiced calf worship. The Scriptures evaluate Menahem's reign by saying that "he did what was evil in the sight of the Lord" (2 Kings 15:14—22).

MENE, MENE, TEKEL, AND PARSIN (MEE-ni, MEE-ni, TEK-il, and PAHR-sin). Four Aramaic words that suddenly appeared on a wall at Belshazzar's feast (Daniel 5:25-28). They probably mean "numbered, numbered, weighed, and divisions."

MEONENIM (mi-ON-i-nim, augurs). The diviners' oak that stood near Shechem (Judges 9:37).

MEPHIBOSHETH (mi-FIB-o-sheth, destroying shame). 1. The son of Saul and Rizpah (2 Samuel 21:8). 2. Jonathan's son. He was accidentally crippled after Saul's death. David honored Mephibosheth and provided for him by giving him Saul's estates (2 Samuel 4:4; 9:6-13; 16:1-4; 19:24-30; 21:7). He is also referred to as Meribaal (1 Chronicles 8:34; 9:40).

MERAB (MEE-rab, increase). Saul's daughter (1 Samuel 14:49).

MERATHAIM (mer-ah-THAY-im, double rebellion). A name for Babylon (Jeremiah 50:21).

MERCY. 1. The Hebrew word *hesed* means God's undeserved favor and love within the covenant relationship. See also *steadfast love*.
2. Various other Hebrew and Greek words are translated into English as "mercy." They convey the idea of compassion or sympathy, pity, pardon or forgiveness, and showing favor (Genesis 19:16; Deuteronomy 21:8; Psalm 4:1; Matthew 5:7; Colossians 3:12).

MERCY SEAT. The covering of the ark. It reminded the people of God's gracious act of "covering" sin (Exodus 25:17-22; 26:34; 37:6-9). On the Day of Atonement the high priest burned incense before the mercy seat and sprinkled blood on it. By doing this, he made atonement for his sins and the sins of the nation in the presence of the Lord, who appeared in a cloud upon the mercy seat (Leviticus 16). The blood of Christ, shed for the sins of the world, is the real atonement (Hebrews 9).

MERIBAH (MER-i-bah, strife). 1. A place where God gave Israel water from a rock. It was near Rephidim (Exodus 17:1-7).
2. Meribah of Kadesh. See *Meribath-kadesh*.

MERIBATH-KADESH (MER-i-bath-KAY-desh, Meribah of Kadesh). A place near Kadesh-barnea in the Desert of Zin. The people of Israel were thirsty there, so God told Moses to speak to the rock. But Moses struck the rock instead. Water flowed from it for the people to drink. Because of his disobedience, however, Moses was forbidden to enter the Promised Land (Numbers 20:1-13; Deuteronomy 32:51).

MERODACH (mi-RO-dak). Marduk, the chief god of the Babylonians (Jeremiah 50:2).

MEROM (MEE-rom, height). A place north of the Sea of Galilee where Joshua defeated the kings of northern Canaan (Joshua 11:5-7).

MESHACH (MEE-shak). The Babylonian name given to Mishael, one of Daniel's friends (Daniel 1:7). Because Meshach refused to worship the golden image King Nebuchadnezzar set up on the Plain of Dura, he was thrown into a fiery furnace (Daniel 3).

MESHULLAM (mi-SHUL-am, friend). A common name in the Old Testament. A number of men with this name lived during Ezra's time. Ezra sent one of them to get Levites for the temple in Jerusalem (Ezra

8:16).

MESHULLEMETH (mi-SHUL-i-meth, friend). The wife of King Manasseh of Judah and mother of Amon (2 Kings 21:19).

MESOPOTAMIA (mes-o-po-TAY-mi-ah, between rivers). The name applied to the upper part of the land between the Tigris and Euphrates rivers (Genesis 24:10; Deuteronomy 23:4; Judges 3:8-11; Acts 2:9; 7:2). The Hebrews called it Aram-Naharaim. Today it is Iraq.

MESSIAH (muh-SIGH-ah, anointed one). In the Old Testament this term describes any high official, such as a prophet, priest, or king, who was consecrated to his office by being anointed with oil. The term came to be used in a special sense, however, of a great prophet from David's family, anointed by God, and filled with His Spirit (Deuteronomy 18:15-18; 2 Samuel 7:12-14; Isaiah 11:2). This Messiah would deliver God's judgment on the wicked, restore God's kingdom to the people of Israel, and enable them to live perfectly as God's chosen people. Moreover, He would usher in a time of universal peace, goodwill, and well-being (Isaiah 11). Many nations would come to Him (Isaiah 11:10; 60:1).

The Old Testament also pictures the Messiah as the Savior and Suffering Servant, the one who would suffer and die for the sins of the people (Isaiah 25:9; 53; 63:1-5). He would be the Creator of a spiritual kingdom for all people (Isaiah 60; Jeremiah 33:15-26).

Jesus fulfills the Biblical prophecies concerning the Messiah. He is the Promised One of God (Luke 4:18; Acts 4:27). Through His threefold office of Prophet, Priest, and King, He ushers in God's spiritual kingdom. Through His suffering and death, He redeems people from their sins and brings peace and well-being between God and humanity (Luke 1:53; 7:18-25; John 3:16-21). See also *anoint; Jesus Christ.*

METHEG-AMMAH (MEE-theg-AM-ah). A town that David took from the Philistines (2 Samuel 8:1). It was probably Gath (1 Chronicles 18:1).

METHUSELAH (mi-THYOO-zuh-lah, man of dart). The son of Enoch, father of Lamech, and grandfather of Noah. He lived 969 years, which is the longest recorded age of any person (Genesis 5:21-27; 1 Chronicles 1:3; Luke 3:37).

MIBSAM (MIB-sam, sweet odor). The fourth son of Ishmael and grandson of Abraham (Genesis 25:13; 1 Chronicles 1:29).

MICAH (MIGH-kah, who is like Lord). A prophet from Moresheth-gath who wrote one of the shorter prophetic books in the Old Testament (Micah 1:1; Jeremiah 26:18). Micah began his work a little later than Hosea and Isaiah, prophesying during the reigns of Jotham, Ahaz, and Hezekiah.

MICAH, BOOK OF. The sixth book of the Minor Prophets. In his book Micah emphasizes God's judgment on the wicked and His salvation for all. He also foretells that the Messiah will be born in Bethlehem (Micah 5:2).

Date: 742 to 701 B.C.

Audience: The people of Judah and Israel

Outline: 1. Prophecies of doom against Samaria and Jerusalem (1—3). 2. Promises of deliverance because of God's covenant love and forgiveness which will come through David's line (4—5). 3. Israel's failure; God's faithfulness and salvation (6—7).

MICAIAH (MIGH-KAY-yah, who is like Lord). 1. A prophet who predicted the death of King Ahab (1 Kings 22:7-28; 2 Chronicles 18:6-

27).

2. The man who reported Jeremiah's prophecies to the Jewish princes (Jeremiah 36:11-13).

MICHAEL (MIGH-kuhl, who is like God). An archangel who fought for Israel (Daniel 10:13, 21; 12:1). Michael also disputed with the devil for Moses' body and defeated him and successfully fought the dragon Satan and the enemies of God's people (Jude 9; Revelation 12:7).

MICHAL (MIGH-kuhl, Michael). The daughter of Saul and wife of David (1 Samuel 14:49; 18:20-27). See also *Merab*.

MICHMAS, MICHMASH (MIK-mas, MIK-mash, treasury). A town near the Mount of Bethel, about seven miles north of Jerusalem. A notable battle between the Philistines and the Israelites occurred there. Through Jonathan's strategy the Philistines were defeated (1 Samuel 13—14). After the captivity Jewish exiles returned to Michmas and lived there (Nehemiah 11:31).

MIDIAN (MID-i-uhn, strife). One of the sons of Abraham and Keturah (Genesis 25:2).

MIDIANITES (MID-i-uhn-ights). A race of people that descended from Midian (Exodus 3:1; Numbers 22:4; Judges 7:13). They were merchants who lived south of Moab and east of the Gulf of Aqabah, although the boundary of their land did shift (Genesis 37:25-36). Moses fled from Egypt to Midian, where he married Zipporah (Exodus 2—4). The Midianites were defeated first by the Israelites and then by Gideon (Numbers 22—25; 31; Judges 6—8).

MIKLOTH (MIK-loth, rods). David's chief officer (1 Chronicles 27:4).

MILCAH (MIL-kah, counsel). A daughter of Haran, Abraham's brother, and the sister of Lot. Milcah married her uncle Nahor, and together they had eight children. Rebekah and Laban were her grandchildren (Genesis 11:29; 22:20-23; 24:15, 24, 47).

MILCOM (MIL-kom, their king). A heathen god who was worshiped by the Ammonites (1 Kings 11:5, 33; 2 Kings 23:13; Jeremiah 49:1, 3). Solomon introduced his worship into Israel. Milcom is sometimes identified with Molech. See also *Molech*.

MILE. See *measures 1k*.

MILETUM, MILETUS (migh-LEE-tuhm, migh-LEE-tuhs). A city on the seacoast of Ionia about 36 miles south of Ephesus. Paul stopped there (Acts 20:15, 17; 2 Timothy 4:20).

MILLENNIUM (1,000 years). The term applied to that period, before or after the final resurrection and judgment, when Christ will supposedly appear on earth with the saints and rule for 1,000 years. It is based on a misinterpretation of Revelation 20:1-7.

MINA (MIGH-nah). A Babylonian weight used in Palestine that was equal to about 60 shekels. A light mina was about 500 grams, and a heavy mina was about 1,000 grams (Ezekiel 45:12).

MINISTER. 1. A person who serves or waits on another. Joshua was Moses' minister (Exodus 24:13; Joshua 1:1).

2. A person who is active in service to God or the state. Priests performed a ministry (Exodus 28:43; Deuteronomy 10:8). Prophets and kings were also consecrated for sacred service. See also *king; priest; prophet*.

3. In the New Testament the usual word for ministry is *diakonia*, or service. All Christians are "ministers," or priests, and receive various gifts of the Holy Spirit (John 12:26; 1 Corinthians 12:4-13; 1 Peter 2:9; 4:10). The New Testa-

ment also identifies special ministries, however, in Word and Sacrament: apostles, evangelists, pastors, teachers, elders, bishops, and deacons (Luke 6:13; Acts 14:23; 21:8; Romans 12:7; 1 Corinthians 12:28-31; 2 Corinthians 6:13-10; Philippians 1:1; 1 Timothy 3:1-8; 5:17; 2 Timothy 4:5; James 3:1).

MIRACLE. An event that causes wonder; something that takes place outside of the laws of nature (John 4:48; Acts 2:19; 2 Corinthians 12:12).

The Old Testament describes a miracle as an extraordinary manifestation of God's presence (Numbers 16:30; Joshua 10:10-14; 2 Kings 20:8-11). God's people recognized the miracle as God's doing because of their faith in Him (Exodus 7—12; Judges 6:17-21, 36-40; 1 Kings 18:38-39).

The New Testament depicts miracles as acts of power, signs, and wonders (Luke 21:25; John 2:11; Acts 19:11). Their significance could be understood only by those who had faith in Jesus Christ (John 6:26; 11:25-27, 38-40; 20:30-31).

MIRIAM (MIR-i-uhm, rebellion). The sister of Moses and Aaron. After the Israelites had passed unharmed through the Red Sea, Miriam led the women, with timbrels and dancing, in a song of victory (Exodus 2:4-10). Miriam was a prophetess (Exodus 15:20-21). When she criticized Moses for marrying a Cushite woman, she was punished with leprosy. But Moses asked God to make her better, and Miriam was healed after seven days (Numbers 21:1-15). When Miriam died, she was buried at Kadesh (Numbers 20:1).

MISHAEL (MISH-ay-el, who is like God?). 1. Moses' uncle (Exodus 6:22; Leviticus 10:4-5).

2. The Hebrew name of Meshach, one of the three men thrown into the fiery furnace for refusing to worship the golden idol King Nebuchadnezzar set up on the Plain of Dura (Daniel 1:7; 3).

MISHMA (MISH-mah, hearing). A son of Ishmael and the founder of an Arabian tribe (Genesis 25:14; 1 Chronicles 1:30).

MITE (MIGHT). A small bronze or copper coin worth less than a penny (Mark 12:41-44; Luke 21:1-4).

MITRE (MIGH-tur). A turban worn by priests. The words "Holy to the Lord" were written on it (Exodus 28:4, 36-39; 29:6; 39:28-31; Leviticus 8:9).

MIZPAH, MIZPEH (MIZ-pah, MIZ-pe, tower). The heap of stones Jacob piled together in Gilead as a witness of the covenant between him and Laban. Laban called it Jegar-sahadutha; Jacob called it Galeed, which means cairn of testimony.

The Mizpah blessing, "The Lord watch between you and me, when we are absent one from the other," was spoken there (Genesis 31:44-49). The location may be that of Ramoth-gilead.

MIZRAIM (MIZ-ray-im). 1. Ham's son and the ancestor of the Egyptians (Genesis 10:6, 13-14; 1 Chronicles 1:8, 11-12). 2. The Hebrew word for Egypt (Genesis 45:20; Isaiah 11:11).

MOAB (MO-ab). Lot's son by his daughter (Genesis 19:30-38). Moab was the ancestor of the Moabites, people who lived on a well-watered tableland east of the Jordan (Numbers 21:13-15). The Moabites were the ones who refused the Israelites passage through their land when the Israelites were on their way to Canaan (Judges 11:17-18). Later they sent Balaam to curse Israel (Numbers 22—24). During the period of the judges Moab controlled Israel for 18 years (Judges 3:12-14).

David defeated the Moabites and made them pay tribute (2 Samuel 8:2, 12; 1 Chronicles 18:2, 11). The Moabites were enemies of Israel (2 Kings 1:1; 24:2; 2 Chronicles 20:1-30). The prophets spoke against them in a strong way (Isaiah 15—16; Jeremiah 9:26; 48; Ezekiel 25:8-11; Amos 2:1; Zephaniah 2:8-11). Ruth, the mother of Obed and an ancestress of Jesus, was from Moab (Ruth 1:4).

MOABITE STONE (MO-ub-ight). A two-by-four foot black asphalt stele erected around 850 B.C. by Mesha, king of Moab. The stone, which is inscribed with the Moabite language (a language that is almost the same as Hebrew), describes the events of 2 Kings 3:4-27.

MOLECH (MO-lek, king). A heathen god worshiped especially by the Ammonites. Sacrificing children to this god was a common worship practice. This practice was forbidden by Hebrew law (Leviticus 18:21; 20:1-5). Nevertheless, an altar was built to Molech in the Valley of Hinnom, and Manasseh worshiped him there, burning his sons as an offering to the god (2 Chronicles 33:6).

When Josiah was king, he stamped out idol worship and tore down the altar built to Molech (2 Kings 23:10). The prophets spoke strongly against the worship of Molech (Jeremiah 7:29-34; 19:1-13; Ezekiel 20:26-39; Amos 5:26). This god is also referred to as Moloch (Acts 7:43).

MONEY. In early times bartering, or trading one thing for another, was the system of exchange. Cattle, produce, and weighed metal were used for this (Genesis 13:2; 26:16; 1 Kings 5:11; 1 Chronicles 21:25). Coined money came into use after the exile (Ezra 1:4). To begin with, the Israelites used the coins of the country that had conquered them. During New Testament times coins from various countries were in use. See also *money-changer*.

MONEY-CHANGER. A person who for a fee changed foreign money into coins that could be used in the temple (Exodus 30:13-15; Matthew 21:12; Mark 11:15).

MONOTHEISM (MON-o-thee-iz'm, one God). The belief that there is only one God. See also *God; gods, false.*

MONTH. See *time.*

MOON. The principal light of the night, given to mark seasons, days, months, years, and signs (Genesis 1:14; Psalm 104:19; Joel 2:10; Matthew 24:29; Luke 21:25).

Many heathen nations worshiped the moon, but this practice was forbidden to the Israelites (Deuteronomy 4:19; 17:3). Nevertheless, during the period of the kings, moon worship was also practiced by some of the Israelites (2 Kings 23:5; Jeremiah 8:2).

MORASHTITE (mo-RASH-tight). See *Micah.*

MORDECAI (MAWR-di-kigh). A Benjaminite who was the uncle and foster father of Esther (Esther 2:5-7). Mordecai saved King Ahausuerus's life by letting him know through Esther about two men who were plotting to kill him (Esther 2:21-23). Mordecai also helped save the Jews from Haman's plot to destroy them (Esther 3—10). The Feast of Purim reminds the Jewish people of this deliverance.

MOREH (MO-re). An oak tree or plain near Shechem (Deuteronomy 11:30). Abraham camped there when he arrived in Canaan (Genesis 12:6).

MORESHATH-GATH (MO-resh-eth-GATH, possession of Gath). See *Micah*.

MORIAH (mo-RIGH-ah). The place where Abraham went to offer Isaac as a sacrifice to the Lord (Genesis 22:2). It probably is the hill in Jerusalem on which Solomon built the temple (2 Chronicles 3:1).

MORNING. See *time*.

MOSES (MO-ziz, drawn out or child). The great Hebrew leader, lawgiver, and prophet who delivered the Israelites from Egyptian slavery and prepared them for entrance into the Promised Land. Moses was born in Egypt to Israelite parents of the tribe of Levi. Since the pharaoh had ordered the death of all Hebrew baby boys, Moses' mother put him afloat in a basket on the Nile River. The pharaoh's daughter discovered baby Moses and adopted him as her own (Exodus 2:1-10). Moses received a fine education in the Egyptian court (Acts 7:22). This helped to prepare him for his later leadership of the Israelites.

When Moses was older, he killed an Egyptian who had struck one of Moses' Hebrew countrymen. The next day, fearing for his life, Moses fled to Midian.

Moses spent the next 40 years of his life in Midian. There he married Zipporah, the priest Jethro's daughter. Moses and Zipporah had two sons (Exodus 2:11-25). The time spent in Midian was a period of preparation for Moses. He grew familiar with wilderness life, its climate and resources. At the end of this period God spoke to Moses from a burning bush and called him as leader of Israel (Exodus 3—4).

In a series of 10 plagues Moses countered Pharaoh's attempt to keep the Hebrew people as slaves in Egypt. Finally, when the Lord passed over the Israelites but put to death all the firstborn of the Egyptians, Pharaoh said the Hebrew people could go. The Passover was instituted to remind the Israelites of this event (Exodus 5—15).

Moses led the Israelites through the Wilderness of Shur (Exodus 15:22-26). At Sin, God provided manna for the people to eat (Exodus 16). Next the Israelites traveled to Rephidim and from there to the wilderness at Sinai, where they set up camp (Exodus 17—19:2).

At Sinai, Moses received God's law for the people. It spelled out how they were to live in a covenant relationship with God (Exodus 20—25). There Moses also received instructions for building the tabernacle and regulations for the priesthood and the altar (Genesis 26:27; Exodus 28:29; 30). When Moses left the mountain and went back to the people, he found them worshiping a golden calf (Exodus 32).

God renewed the covenant with His people (Exodus 34). Then they began to build the tabernacle and make holy clothing for the priests (Exodus 35—38:40; 39).

Moses took a census of the people (Numbers 1—2). Later, at God's command, they left the wilderness at Sinai (Numbers 10). At various times Moses' actions or leadership were opposed. Miriam and Aaron spoke against him for marrying a Cushite woman. God punished Miriam with leprosy for this act. But when Moses asked God to heal her, God did so after seven days (Numbers 12). Later, Koran, Dathan, and Abiram also spoke out against Moses. Because of this, the Lord opened the earth and swallowed them up. In this way God showed the Israelites that Moses was indeed His chosen servant (Numbers 16—17).

When they left Mount Hor to go around the land of Edom, the people once again spoke against God and Moses, saying, "Why have you brought us up out of Egypt to die in the wilderness?" (Numbers 21:4-5). God punished them for their complaints and lack of trust by sending fiery serpents to bite them. Many of the people died. Moses prayed for the people and was told to set up a bronze serpent on a pole. Those bitten by real snakes would live if they looked at this bronze serpent (Numbers 21:6-9).

Because Moses sinned at Meribah, he was not allowed to enter the Promised Land. Joshua, the man Moses named as the new leader of the Israelites, would be the one to lead the people into Canaan. God did allow Moses to see the Promised Land, however, before his death (Numbers 20:27). Moses died on Mount Nebo (Deuteronomy 34).

Both the Old and New Testaments indicate that Moses wrote the first five books of the Old Testament called the Pentateuch (Genesis—Deuteronomy; Luke 24:27, 44; John 5:45-47). After his death, Moses' greatness was recognized by all (Jeremiah 15:1; Hebrews 3:2). Along with Elijah, Moses appeared on the Mount of Transfiguration with Jesus (Matthew 17:3-4). Moses is the great lawgiver with whom Christ is compared and contrasted (Acts 3:22; 2 Corinthians 3:12-18; Galatians 3—4; Hebrews 3).

MOTHER. The Israelites, unlike many other nations, held mothers in respect (Exodus 20:12). The word *mother* is sometimes used in a wider sense to mean grandmother or some other female ancestor (Genesis 3:20; 1 Kings 15:10) or a woman who acted kindly towards a person in need (Judges 5:7).

It is also used figuratively for nation, city, and the New Jerusalem (Isaiah 50:1; Galatians 4:26-31; Revelation 17:5).

MOTHER-OF-PEARL. See *alabaster.*

MOUNTAIN. Much of Palestine is hilly or mountainous. The best-known mountain range of Syria, the Lebanon range, formed the northwest boundary of the Promised Land (Deuteronomy 1:7; Joshua 1:4). The mountains consist of two ranges that begin at the northeast corner of the Mediterranean and extend northeast to southwest through Palestine. During the Greek period the name *Lebanon* was restricted to the western range while the eastern range was called the Anti-Lebanon. Often the peaks of mountains had names, for example, Mount Zion, Mount of Olives, Mount Hermon, Mount Tabor, and Mount Sinai. Many of these are no more than hills.

Mountains were places of refuge (Genesis 14:10). They were used as lookouts and as sites for assemblies, camps, and cemeteries (Judges 9:7; 1 Samuel 17:3; 2 Kings 23:16; Isaiah 18:3). Mount Ebal was the mountain from which the people recited the curses of the Law; Mount Gerizim, the blessings (Deuteronomy 27:4-26). Sinai and Zion were God's mountains (Exodus 24:13; Psalm 68:16; Isaiah 27:13).

Mountains symbolize strength, persons in authority, proud persons, the righteousness of God, and the Messianic reign (Psalm 36:6; 72:3; Isaiah 2:2, 14; Jeremiah 3:23).

MOURNING. During Bible times people showed grief for a dead person in the following ways: tearing their own clothing, putting on sackcloth and ashes, cutting their bodies, shaving their heads, crying loudly, and building fires (Genesis 37:34; Exodus 12:30; Leviticus 19:27-28; Deuteronomy 14:1; 2 Chronicles 16:14; Micah 1:10). Often professional mourners were hired (2 Chronicles 35:25; Matthew 9:23). Mourning lasted 7, 30, or 70 days (Genesis 50:3; Deuteronomy 34:8; 1 Samuel 31:13).

MULE. A cross between a horse and a donkey. It is not mentioned in the Bible before the time of David but was in common use then (2 Samuel 13:29; 18:9; 1 Kings 1:33, 38, 44; Ezra 2:66).

MURDER. The act of killing another person. Murder is forbidden (Exodus 20:13; Deuteronomy 5:17). During Old Testament times those who did take another person's life received the death penalty themselves (Genesis 9:6; Exodus 21:14). A person who killed someone else without meaning to do so could find freedom from the death penalty in cities of refuge (Numbers 35:9-34; Deuteronomy 19:1-10).

MUSIC. Music has existed from earliest times (Genesis 4:21). Folk music celebrated victories (Judges 5; 1 Samuel 18:6-7). Music was used at special occasions, such as feasts, weddings, and funerals (Genesis 31:27; 2 Samuel 19:35; Jeremiah 7:34; Matthew 9:23).

David organized a sacred choir and appointed instrumental musicians (1 Chronicles 6:31-48; 16). The use of these was continued by Solomon, Jehoshaphat, Hezekiah, Josiah, Ezra, and Nehemiah.

Various instruments were used in Biblical times, for example, lyres, harps, trumpets, pipes, flutes, oboes, timbrels, and cymbals. During the New Testament period people played flutes at funerals and to accompany dancing (Matthew 9:23; 11:7; Luke 7:32). Harps were symbols of praise (Revelation 5:8;

14:2). Music and hymns played an important role in the worship life of Israel (Matthew 26:30; Ephesians 5:19).

MYRA (MIGH-rah). A seaport of Lycia where Paul changed ships when he was being taken prisoner to Rome (Acts 27:5).

MYRRH (MUR). A yellow-brown resin used for perfume, embalming, and anointing (Exodus 30:23; Song of Solomon 3:6; Matthew 2:11; John 19:39; Revelation 18:13).

NAAMAH (NAY-ah-mah, pleasantness). 1. The wife of Solomon and mother of Rehoboam (1 Kings 14:21, 31; 2 Chronicles 12:13).

NAAMAN (NAY-ah-muhn, pleasantness). One of the commanders of Ben-hadad II. He was cured of leprosy by Elisha (2 Kings; Luke 4:27).

NABOTH (NAY-both). A man living in Jezreel who owned a vineyard near King Ahab's palace. When Naboth refused to sell Ahab his vineyard or exchange it for other land, Queen Jezebel plotted a way to get the land. She had Naboth stoned for blasphemy so that Ahab could take over the vineyard (1 Kings 21:1-24; 2 Kings 9:21-26).

NADAB (NAY-dab, liberal). 1. A son of Aaron. He was a priest who went up Mount Sinai with Moses. When Nadab and his brother offered a strange fire on the altar, they were killed (Exodus 6:23; 24:1, 9-11; 28:1; Leviticus 10:1-7; Numbers 26:60-61).

2. The second king of Israel. He was the son of Jeroboam and the one who succeeded him to the throne. Nadab "did what was evil in the sight of the Lord." He reigned over Israel two years. Then Baasha killed him and took over his throne (1 Kings 14:20; 15:25-31).

NAHOR (NAY-hawr, snoring). 1. Abraham's grandfather (Genesis 11:22-25; Luke 3:34).

2. Abraham's brother (Genesis 11:26-29; 22:20; Joshua 24:2).

NAHSHON (NAH-shon). A leader of the tribe of Judah in the wilderness (Numbers 1:7; 2:3; 7:12; 10:14). His sister married Aaron (Ex. 6:23).

NAHUM (NAY-hum, full of consolation). A prophet from Elkosh who prophesied to Judah between 663 and 606 B.C. (Nahum 1:1; 3:8-11). He wrote the Book of Nahum.

NAHUM, BOOK OF. The seventh book of the Minor Prophets. Written by the prophet Nahum, the book contains his prediction of the downfall of Nineveh, the capital of Assyria. Nahum insists that the Lord is a jealous God whose judgment will fall on those who oppose Him, but who is a stronghold to those who trust in Him (1:2-8).

Date: 663 to 612 B.C.

Audience: Ninevites

Outline: 1. God's majesty; threat of Nineveh's destruction (1). 2. Fall of Nineveh (2—3).

NAIN (NAY-in, beauty). A city in Galilee. Jesus raised a widow's son from death near Nain (Luke 7:11-17).

NAIOTH (NAY-oth, shepherd dwellings). A place in Ramah where Samuel and his prophets lived (1 Samuel 19:18—20:1).

NAKED, NAKEDNESS. Without any clothing, without an outer garment, or poorly clothed (Genesis 2:25; Matthew 25:36; John 21:7).

Figuratively the word naked depicts a lack of power or spiritual poverty (Genesis 42:9; Revelation 3:17).

NAME. In Biblical times a name often expressed something about the person named (Genesis 2:20; Isaiah 40:26). When an individual's name was changed, it reflected a change in the person's being. For instance, God gave Abram (exalted father) the name Abraham (father of a multitude) to show that He had established His covenant of grace with Abraham (Genesis 17:5; 35:10).

God's names reveal His nature

(Exodus 3:13-15), will (Psalm 22:22; John 17:6, 26), and attributes (Exodus 33:19; Psalm 8:1, 9; 1 Timothy 6:1). God is present where His name is present (Isaiah 18:7; 30:27).

NAOMI (nay-O-mi, my pleasantness). Ruth's mother-in-law (Ruth 1—2; 3:1; 4:3-17).

NAPHTALI (NAF-tah-ligh, my unresting). 1. A son of Jacob and Bilhah (Genesis 30:8; 46:24).

2. The tribe of Naphtali was given land in northern Palestine. Zebulun and Asher were to its west; the upper Jordan and Sea of Galilee to its east (Joshua 19:32-39). Barak came from this tribe (Judges 4:6). Naphtali was the first tribe captured by the Assyrians under Tiglath-pileser (2 Kings 15:29).

NATHAN (NAY-thuhn, he gave). 1. A prophet during the reigns of David and Solomon. When David consulted him about building the temple, Nathan told David to leave this job for his son (2 Samuel 7:1-7). Nathan also rebuked David for his adultery with Bathsheba (2 Samuel 12:1-14). When David grew old and Adonijah tried to get his throne, Nathan stepped in and through Bathsheba secured the succession for Solomon (1 Kings 1:8-45). Nathan also recorded the life of David and the history of the reign of Solomon (1 Chronicles 29:29; 2 Chronicles 9:29).

2. One of David's sons (1 Chronicles 3:5; Luke 3:31).

NATHANAEL (nah-THAN-ay-el, gift of God). One of Jesus' 12 disciples (John 1:45-51; 21:2). It is thought that Nathanael and Bartholomew were the same person.

NATIONS. In the Old Testament this word is often used for Gentiles, people who are not of the Jewish race (Exodus 34:24; Isaiah 43:9; Jeremiah 10:1-25).

NAVE. (NAYV). The Holy Place of the temple (1 Kings 6:3, 5, 17, 33;

2 Chronicles 3:4-5, 13).

NAZARENE (naz-ah-REEN). Someone who came from Nazareth. Jesus was a Nazarene (Matthew 2:23; Mark 14:67).

NAZARETH (NAZ-ah-reth). The town in Galilee where Mary and Joseph lived and where Jesus grew up (Mark 1:9; Matthew 4:13; Luke 1:26; 2:4, 51). Jesus is often referred to as Jesus of Nazareth (Luke 18:37; John 1:45-46; Acts 2:22).

NAZARITE, NAZIRITE (NAZ-ahright, NAZ-i-right, separated). An Israelite who bound himself or herself by a vow to be set apart from others for the service of God, either for life or for a set amount of time. Nazarites could not drink alcoholic beverages or cut their hair. They also had to avoid contact with the dead and abstain from eating unclean food (Numbers 6:1-21; Amos 2:11-12). Samson and John the Baptizer were both Nazarites (Judges 13; Luke 1:15).

NEAPOLIS (ni-ap-O-lis, new city). The seaport of Philippi to which Paul sailed after being given a vision to preach the Gospel in Macedonia (Acts 16:11).

NEBAT (NEE-bat, viewed). The father of Jeroboam I (1 Kings 11:26).

NEBO (NAY-bo). 1. The Babylonian god of learning (Isaiah 46:1).

2. The name of the mountain located in Moab that Moses climbed to view the Promised Land before he died (Deuteronomy 32:49-50; 34:1-5). See also *Pisgah, Mount.*

NEBUCHADNEZZAR, NEBUCHADREZZAR (neb-yoo-kuhd-NEZ-ur, neb-yoo-kuhd-REZ-ur, defend the boundary). Nabopolasser's son and the ruler of the Neo-Babylonian Empire from 605 to 562 B.C. In 605 B.C. Nebuchadnezzar defeated Pharaoh Neco at Carchemish. Then in 603 B.C. he made Judah his servant (Daniel 1:1; 2 Kings

24). After a few years of paying taxes to Nebuchadnezzar, Judah revolted. Nebuchadnezzar returned to Judah and in 587 B.C. destroyed Jerusalem and carried the people into captivity (2 Kings 24:11-16; 25:1-21). Nebuchadnezzar is frequently mentioned in the Old Testament (1 Chronicles 6:15; 2 Chronicles 36; Ezra 1:7; Nehemiah 7:6; Esther 2:6; Jeremiah 21—52; Daniel 1—5).

NEBUSHASBAN, NEBUSHAZ-BAN (neb-yoo-SHAS-ban, neb-yoo-SHAZ-ban, Nebo save). A rabsaris, an important officer in Nebuchadnezzar's court (Jeremiah 39:13).

NECHO, NECHOH, NECO (NEE-ko). See *pharaoh 8.*

NECROMANCY (NEK-ro-man-see). A form of witchcraft. A necromancer was a person who consulted the dead for information (Deuteronomy 18:11; 1 Samuel 28:1-25).

NEGEB (NEG-eb, dry). A grazing region lying south of Hebron (Genesis 12:9; 13:1; 20:1).

NEHEMIAH (nee-hi-MIGH-ah, the Lord comforts). The son of Hachaliah and the cupbearer of Artaxerxes Longimanus (Nehemiah 1:1; 2:1). When Artaxerxes found out that Nehemiah was distressed at Jerusalem's state of ruin, he allowed Nehemiah to return there. Nehemiah arrived in Jerusalem in the 20th year of Artaxerxes' reign, 444 B.C. Nehemiah became the governor of Judah (Nehemiah 2:1-10). He organized the Jewish community to carry out the task of rebuilding Jerusalem's walls (Nehemiah 1—4; 6). He also instituted reforms and restored worship and the Law (Nehemiah 5; 8—13).

NEHEMIAH, BOOK OF. Nehemiah is part of the third division of the Hebrew Scriptures known as the Writings. It describes how God restored the Law, worship, govern-

ment, and the walls of Jerusalem through the efforts of Nehemiah and other leaders after the Israelites' return from captivity.

Date: About 400 B.C.

Audience: Jews

Outline: 1. Rebuilding walls of Jerusalem (1—7:72). 2. Revival of house of Israel: spiritual rededication and political reformation (7:73—13).

NEHUSHTAN (ni-HUSH-tuhn, piece of bronze). This was the name Hezekiah gave to the brass serpent made in Moses' time. Hezekiah destroyed it because the people were worshiping it rather than the Lord (2 Kings 18:4).

NEIGHBOR. The Old Testament describes one's neighbor as someone who lives nearby or as a fellow Israelite (Exodus 11:2; Deuteronomy 15:1-11). The duty to love one's neighbor as oneself included both Israelites and foreigners (Leviticus 19:18-34).

The New Testament describes one's neighbor as every person for whom Christ died, that is, everyone (Luke 10:25-37). Because Christ died for all, love is to be extended to everyone (Matthew 5:43-48). Anything done to one's neighbor is done to Christ (Matthew 25:31-46).

NEPHILIM (NEF-uh-lim). See *giants.*

NER (NUR, lamp). 1. The son of Abiel, father of Abner, and uncle of Saul (1 Samuel 14:50-51; 26:5, 14; 2 Samuel 2:8, 12).

2. Saul's grandfather (1 Chronicles 8:33; 9:35-36, 39).

NERO (NEE-ro). The Roman emperor from A.D. 54 to 68. His full name was Nero Claudius Caesor Augustus Germanicus, but he was usually referred to as Caesar (Acts 25:11; Philippians 4:22).

NETHINIM (NETH-i-nim, dedicated). A group of servants or slaves who performed menial tasks in the temple (1 Chronicles 9:2; Ezra 2:43-58; 8:17-20; Nehemiah 7:46-56).

NEW BIRTH. See *conversion*.

NEW MAN. This term refers to the Christian believer who is created anew by God's grace. It is Christ who died and rose again who makes the existence of this new man possible (Romans 5:10; 8:34-39). By faith in Christ, the believer dies to the old life and rises to the new life, becoming a new creature (2 Corinthians 5:17; Galatians 6:15). Baptism works this conversion (Romans 6:1-4). The new man is a member of the church, Christ's body (Ephesians 2:15). His new life in Christ is shown in how he lives. It is constantly renewed in Christ (Romans 6:5-11; Colossians 3:10-11).

NEW TESTAMENT. 1. The books of the Bible from Matthew to Revelation.

2. The New Testament, or New Covenant, is a term describing the work of Christ, by whose life, death and resurrection God's grace is brought to all people (Jeremiah 31:31-34; 2 Corinthians 3; Galatians 4; Hebrews 7:20-22). The Holy Spirit brings people into this covenant by creating faith in their hearts by means of the Word (John 3:5; Romans 1:16-17; 15:16; 1 Corinthians 2:10; 2 Thessalonians 2:13). The Lord's Supper is the New Testament made visible (Matthew 26:26-28; 1 Corinthians 11:25). See also *covenant*.

NEW YEAR. See *time*.

NICANOR (ni-KAY-nawr, conqueror). One of the seven men chosen by the church in Jerusalem to look after the widows and the poor (Acts 6:5).

NICODEMUS (nik-o-DEE-muhs, victor over people). A leading Pharisee and member of the Sanhedrin. He visited Jesus one evening and talked with Him. Jesus told Nicodemus about the new birth neces-sary to enter the kingdom of God (John 3:1-21). When Jesus was on trial before the Sanhedrin, Nicodemus spoke up for Him, though in a roundabout way (John 7:50-52). After Jesus' death, however, Nicodemus helped Joseph of Arimathea with the burial (John 19:39-42).

NICOLAITANS (nik-o-LAY-uh-tuhns). A Gnostic sect in the churches at Ephesus and Pergamum. Their teachings were harshly spoken against by John (Revelation 2:6, 14-15).

NICOLAS, NICOLAUS (NIK-o-luhs, nik-o-LAY-uhs, victor over people). A proselyte at Antioch. He was one of the seven men chosen by the church at Jerusalem to take care of the widows and the poor (Acts 6:5).

NICOPOLIS (ni-KOP-o-lis, city of victory). A Roman town in Epirus that was founded by Caesar Augustus in 31 B.C. (Titus 3:12).

NILE (NIGHL). The main river of Egypt and Africa. It is 4,050 miles long. The Nile's yearly overflow leaves deposits of rich soil that make the land of northern Egypt fertile.

The people in ancient times worshiped the Nile as a god. Moses was placed on the Nile in a basket made of papyrus (Exodus 2:3). During one of the plagues the waters of the Nile were turned to blood (Exodus 7:20-21). The Nile was also famous for the papyrus that grows along its banks. From it, the people made papyrus writing material (Isaiah 19:7).

NIMROD (NIM-rod). A son of Cush. Nimrod was a hunter, builder, and founder of the kingdoms in Shinar (Genesis 10:8-12; 1 Chronicles 1:10; Micah 5:6). Many places in Mesopotamia were named Nimrod.

NINEVEH (NIN-uh-vuh). The capital of Assyria. It was located on the Tigris River and was founded by Nimrod (Genesis 10:9-11). Sargon

II, the ruler of Assyria from 722 to 705 B.C., made Nineveh the capital of Assyria. From 705 to 626 B.C. Nineveh was strengthened and made beautiful by Sennacherib, Esarhaddon, and Ashurbanipal. In 612 B.C. the city was destroyed by the Babylonians, Scythians, and Medes. Nineveh is mentioned numerous times in the Bible (2 Kings 19:36; Isaiah 37:37; Jonah; Nahum; Zephaniah 2:13; Matthew 12:41; Luke 11:30, 32).

NOAH (NO-ah, rest). The son of Lamech (Genesis 5:28-32). When Noah was 480 years old, God warned him that the world was going to be destroyed by water. Then He gave Noah instructions on how to build the ark. While building the ark, Noah warned people to repent of their wickedness (Genesis 6:1-9, 12-22; 1 Peter 3:20; 2 Peter 2:5). After 120 years God led Noah, Noah's wife, their sons, and their sons' wives into the ark. Then God directed the animals into the ark. When all were safely aboard, God shut the door. In this way He saved Noah and his family from the Flood, which destroyed everything outside the ark (Genesis 7—8).

After the rain stopped and the waters went down, Noah, his family, and the animals were allowed to leave the ark. Noah and his family repeopled the earth (Genesis 9:10). Noah lived to be 950 years old.

NO-AMON (no-AY-mon). See *Thebes.*

NOD (NOD, exile). The region east of Eden where Cain went to live after he had killed Abel (Genesis 4:16).

NORTHEASTER. See *Euraquilo.*

NOVICE (NOV-is). A recent convert to Christianity (1 Timothy 3:6).

NUMBERING. See *census.*

NUMBERS. The Hebrew people used letters of the alphabet for numbers.

Their numbers often had religious or symbolical meaning. For example, 10 was regarded as a sacred number, and 40 was a number of completeness (Exodus 20:3-7; 24:18; 1 Kings 19:8; Matthew 25:1-3).

NUMBERS. The fourth book of the Pentateuch. It is called Numbers because it records two numberings of the Israelites. The Hebrew name for this book is "In the Wilderness."

This book contains various laws, the numbering of the tribes, and the Israelites' journey from Sinai to Palestine.

Date: 15th to 13th century B.C.
Audience: Israelites
Outline: 1. Events leading to departure from Sinai (1—10:10). 2. Journey from Sinai to Moab (10:11—21). 3. Events in Moab; preparations for entering Canaan (22—36).

NUN (NUN, fish). Joshua's father (Exodus 33:11; 13:8; 1 Chronicles 7:27).

O

OATH. A solemn appeal to God, a person, or an object to witness the truth of a statement or the binding character of a promise (Genesis 21:23; Exodus 22:11; 2 Samuel 11:11; Matthew 5:34). Oaths of the covenant were worked out in a careful and detailed way (Genesis 21:28-31). Swearing by God's name showed loyalty to Him (Deuteronomy 6:13).

OBADIAH (o-bah-DIGH-ah, worshiper of the Lord). 1. One of Ahab's officers who was a friend to Elijah and the prophets of the Lord (1 Kings 18:3-16).

2. A prophet of Judah who wrote the Book of Obadiah (Obadiah 1:1).

OBADIAH, BOOK OF. The fourth book of the Minor Prophets as they appear in the Old Testament. It tells of Edom's destruction because of its constant hostility toward Israel.

Date: About 587 B.C.

Audience: Edomites

Outline: 1. Edom's sin and destruction (1-14). 2. Day of the Lord is near (15-21).

OBED (O-bed, worshiper, servant). The son of Boaz and Ruth and the grandfather of King David (Ruth 4:17, 21-22; 1 Chronicles 2:12; Matthew 1:5).

OBED-EDOM (O-bed-EE-dum). A man from Gath into whose home David had the ark of the covenant carried after Uzzah had been struck dead for touching it. The ark remained in Obed-edom's house for three months, and God greatly blessed Obed-edom and all his household (2 Samuel 6:10-12).

OBEDIENCE. The act of obeying. The complete, willing response to God is the duty of all people (Deuteronomy 4:30; Jeremiah 7:23; 1 John 5:2). Man disobeyed God, however, and fell into sin (Genesis 3). From that point forward the natural state of humanity is disobedience toward God (Romans 1:24; 5:19). Christ obeyed the Father and obtained the forgiveness of sins for all people (Romans 5:19; Philippians 2:8; Hebrews 5:8). Throughout the Bible obedience is linked to faith (Romans 1:5; 1 Peter 1:14). Christians show obedience in the home, to the state, in the church, and to others (Romans 13:1-7; Ephesians 5:21; 6:1; Hebrews 13:17; 1 Peter 3:6).

OBEISANCE (o-BAY-suhns). A bow or other bodily movement to show respect or obedience to God, an idol, an earthly ruler, or some other person (Genesis 43:28; Exodus 18:7; 2 Samuel 1:2; 2 Kings 5:18, Micah 6:6).

ODOR. Any smell, either pleasant or unpleasant (Genesis 8:21; Numbers 15:3-24; John 11:39).

OFFERING. See *sacrifice*.

OFFICES OF CHRIST. See *Jesus Christ*.

OINTMENT. Usually perfumed olive oil was used to dress the hair and make the skin smell sweet, to prepare bodies for burial, and to anoint people (Esther 2:3-12; Matthew 26:6-13; Luke 23:56). The balm of Gilead and eye salve were two medicines (Jeremiah 8:22; Revelation 3:18). See also *apothecary*.

OLD TESTAMENT. 1. The 39 books from Genesis to Malachi that make up the first part of the Bible. Most of the Old Testament was written in Hebrew except for a few sections in Ezra and Daniel, which were written in Aramaic.

2. The covenant of Moses. See also *covenant*.

OLIVE. See *orchard*.

OLIVES, MOUNT OF; OLIVET (AHL-i-vet). A ridge about one mile long on the eastern side of Jerusalem, separated from it by the Valley of Kidron. Gethsemane, Bethphage, and Bethany are on its slopes (2 Samuel 15:30; Zechariah 14:4; Matthew 21:1; 24:3; Mark 11:1; Luke 22:39; John 8:1; Acts 1:12).

OMEGA (o-MEG-uh). See *alpha*.

OMER (O-mur). See *measures 2e*.

OMNIPOTENCE (ahm-NIP-o-tuhns). All-powerful. Only God has limitless power and authority (Genesis 17:1; Matthew 19:26; Ephesians 1:21-22).

OMNIPRESENCE. (ahm-ni-PREZ-uhns). The attribute of being in all places at once. God is omnipresent; that is, He is everywhere (Psalm 139:7-10; Proverbs 15:3; Acts 17:27-28).

OMNISCIENCE (ahm-NISH-uhns). The term used to describe God's complete knowledge of all things (1 Samuel 2:3; Matthew 10:30; Acts 15:18; Ephesians 1:4).

OMRI (OM-righ). The sixth king of Israel, who reigned from about 886 to 874 B.C. Before gaining the throne, Omri was a general in the Israelite army of King Elah. During one battle news arrived that Zimri had killed Elah. At once the prophets and army proclaimed Omri the new king of Israel.

During his reign Omri moved the capital from Tirzah to Samaria. He is described as doing "evil in the sight of the Lord, . . . more evil than all who were before him" (1 Kings 16:16-28).

ON (ON). A city in the Delta of Egypt about 19 miles north of Memphis. It was called Heliopolis by the Greeks and is referred to as Beth-shemesh in Jeremiah 43:13. On was the main religious center for sun worship. Joseph's wife, Asenath, was the daughter of a priest of On (Genesis 41:45, 50).

ONESIMUS (o-NES-i-muhs, useful). Philemon's slave. It seems that Onesimus robbed his master and then ran away to Rome. In Rome he came in contact with Paul and became a Christian. Paul persuaded Onesimus to return to Philemon and wrote the Letter to Philemon on Onesimus's behalf (Colossians 4:9; Philemon).

ONESIPHORUS (on-i-SIF-o-rus, profit bringing). A Christian from Ephesus who ministered to Paul when Paul was in prison in Rome (2 Timothy 1:16-18; 4:19).

ONYX (ON-iks). A precious stone, perhaps some type of quartz, which was put on the high priest's shoulder pieces and breastpiece (Genesis 2:12; Exodus 28:9; 35:9; 1 Chronicles 29:2).

OPHRAH (AHF-rah). Gideon's hometown. It was located in Manasseh (Judges 6:11, 24; 8:27, 32).

ORACLE (AHR-ah-k'l). A place, such as the Holy of Holies, a message or word of God, a prophecy or some other way in which God communicated His will to His people (2 Samuel 16:23; 1 Kings 6; Isaiah 14:28; 15:1; Ezekiel 12:10; Acts 7:38; Romans 3:2; 1 Peter 4:11).

Heathen oracles are also mentioned in the Bible (Judges 17:1, 5; 8:27; 2 Kings 1:2). Israel is rebuked for consulting these false oracles (Hosea 4:12; Habakkuk 2:19).

ORCHARD. The place where fruit- or nut-bearing trees are grown. Olives, figs, dates, pomegranates, citrus fruit, almonds, and walnuts were among the fruits and nuts grown in Palestine.

The olive harvest began in August when the whitish fruit was knocked from the trees. The oil was taken out of the olives by placing the fruit in a stone basin or on a concave stone and then crushing it with another stone. Olive oil was used in ceremonial anointings, as fuel for lamps and torches, for anointing the body and head, and in salves for wounds (Exodus 27:20; 29:7; 1 Samuel 16:13; Luke 7:46; 10:34). The olive was a symbol for peace, wealth, and success (Genesis 8:11; Psalm 52:8).

Various types of figs were grown in Palestine (1 Kings 4:25; Psalm 105:33). The first crop was ready to harvest in May (Isaiah 28:4; Nahum 3:12). The regular crop was ready in late July or mid-August, and sometimes a third crop was ready in late fall (Amos 8:1). The sycamore fig had smaller fruit (Amos 7:14). Figs were dried for year-round use.

Date palms grew wild along the Mediterranean Sea, the Jordan Valley, and in desert oases. Dates were dried and caked for use in the winter. Palm tree branches were brought to Passover celebrations (Matthew 21:8; Mark 11:8; John 12:13).

Pomegranates are often mentioned in the Old Testament (Haggai 2:19). The people made wine from the juice of this fruit (Song of Solomon 8:2). In a number of passages the pomegranate is referred to as an apple (Proverbs 25:11; Song of Solomon 2:3, 5; Joel 1:12).

Almonds and walnuts were both common in Palestine. Almonds were particularly plentiful (Genesis 43:11; Exodus 25:33; Jeremiah 1:11). (Klinck)

ORDINATION (awr-duh-NAY-shuhn). The act of conferring a sacred office upon a person. Old Testament priests were ordained to office (Exodus 28:41; Numbers 3:3). Rams were sacrificed at these ordinations (Exodus 29:22-34; Leviticus 8:22-33).

In the New Testament, deacons, missionaries, and elders were or-

dained to office (Acts 6:6; 13:3; 14:23).

ORPHA (AWR-pah, fawn). The daughter-in-law of Naomi and sister-in-law of Ruth (Ruth 1:4-14).

OSNAPPAR (os-NAP-ur). The king of Assyria mentioned in Ezra 4:10. Osnappar is usually identified with Ashurbanipal, Sennacherib's grandson. Ashurbanipal ruled Assyria from 669 to 626 B.C.

OTHNIEL (OTH-ni-el, God's powerful one). The son of Kenaz and first judge of Israel (Joshua 15:17; 1 Chronicles 4:13). Othniel captured the town of Kiriath-sepher (Joshua 15:15-17; Judges 1:11-13). Later he delivered Israel from the Mesopotamians (Judges 3:8-11).

P

PACE. See *measures lf.*

PADAN-ARAM, PADDAN-ARAM (PAY-duhn-AY-ram, PAD-uhn-AY-RAM, plain of Aram). The plain surrounding Haran in Mesopotamia. It was the home of Rebekah and Laban (Genesis 25:20; 28:2-7; 31:18; 33:18; 35:9; 46:15).

PAGAN. See *Gentiles.*

PAGIEL (PAY-gi-el, meeting with God). The head person of the tribe of Asher when it was in the wilderness (Numbers 1:13; 2:27; 7:72, 77).

PALACE. See *architecture; homes.*

PALESTINE (PAL-uhs-tighn). The name comes from Philistia, the area along the coast where the Philistines lived (Psalm 60:8). The older name for this region was Canaan (Genesis 12:5). After the conquest it became known as the land of Israel (1 Samuel 13:19). The Book of Zechariah refers to it as the holy land (2:12), and during the Greco-Roman times it was called Judea.

Biblical Palestine was about 70 miles wide and 150 miles long. It lay south of the Lebanon Mountains, northeast of Egypt, north of the Sinai Peninsula, and east of the Arabian Desert. It was divided into five regions: the maritine plain on the west, the Shephelah, the central range, the Jordan Valley, and the eastern plateau.

Because of the variation in elevation from Mount Hermon's 9,101 feet above sea level to the Dead Sea's 1,290 feet below sea level, the

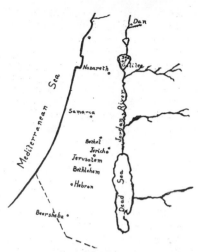

climate of Palestine varies greatly. The mean temperature of Jerusalem is 65 degrees F, whereas the Jordan Valley is tropical in climate. There are two seasons: winter (November—April) and summer (May—October). Winter is mild and rainy; summer is hot and dry.

In the days of Abraham, Palestine was inhabited by the Canaanites, Amorites, Hittites, Horites, and Amalekites. The Israelites conquered Palestine under Joshua and under the judges and kings. From 587 to 166 B.C. Palestine fell under foreign rule. Then the Maccabees reigned from 166 to 163 B.C., at which time the Romans took over until A.D. 325. During New Testament times Palestine was divided into three parts: Judea, Samaria, and Galilee.

PALSY. See *disease.*

PALTI (PAL-tigh, delivered). The man to whom Saul gave David's wife Michal (1 Samuel 25:44).

PAMPHYLIA (pam-FIL-i-ah, every race). A coastal plain along the Mediterranean in southern Asia Minor. Some of the people at Pentecost were from Pamphylia (Acts 2:10). On his first missionary trip Paul preached at Perga, the chief city of Pamphylia (Acts 13:13; 14:24; 15:38).

PAPER. See *papyrus.*

PAPHOS (PAY-foss). The capital city of Cyprus (Acts 13:6, 13).

PAPYRUS (pah-PIGH-ruhs). An 8- to 10-foot-high sedge or reedlike plant that grew along the Nile River in ancient times. The people of that time made paper from this plant (Job 8:11; Isaiah 18:2). Moses' ark was probably made of papyrus (Exodus 2:3).

PARABLE. A method of speech that compares two objects for the purpose of teaching a moral or religious truth (Matthew 15:14-15; Mark 13:28; 6:39). It is an earthly story with a heavenly or spiritual meaning. Although the events and characters in the parable are true to nature, not every detail of the story has a spiritual meaning. Rather there is only one main point of comparison (Matthew 15; Luke 15). Jesus often spoke in parables to teach the people about Himself and the kingdom of heaven.

A parable differs from a fable, myth, allegory, and proverb. See also *allegory; fable; proverb.*

PARACLETE (PAR-ah-kleet, comforter). One who is called to one's side or pleads one's cause before a judge. In 1 John 2:1 the term is used of Christ. He is the believer's Advocate with the Father; He pleads for the Christian before God. Elsewhere the word often refers to the Holy Spirit, who is the believer's Paraclete on earth (John 14:16, 26; 15:26; 16:7). It is He who indwells the Christian, bringing Christ and His work of salvation to remembrance; it is He who guides the believer into all truth.

PARADISE (PAR-ah-dighs, park). A park, orchard, or pleasure ground. The Garden of Eden was a paradise (Genesis 2:8-17; Revelation 2:7). In the New Testament the word *paradise* is used to describe heaven, the home of those who die in Christ (Luke 23:43; 2 Corinthians 12:4; Revelation 2:7).

PARBAR (PAHR-bahr, open place). Some building or place on the west side of the outer court of the temple (1 Chronicles 26:18).

PARDON. See *forgiveness; justification.*

PARMENAS (PAHR-mi-nas, faithful). One of the seven men chosen by the early church to look after widows and poor people (Acts 6:5).

PAROUSIA (pah-ROO-zhi-ah, presence or coming). A word used in the New Testament to describe the second coming of Christ in glory and power to judge the world at the end of time (Matthew 24:27-39; 1 Corinthians 15:23; 1 Thessalonians 4:15-17; James 5:8; 2 Peter 3:4; 1 John 2:28). See also *Advent of Christ 3; Day of the Lord 2; Jesus Christ; judgment.*

PARTHIANS (PAHR-thi-uhns). People who lived in southwest Asia, southeast of the Caspian Sea. Today that country is Iran. Parthians were present on the Day of Pentecost (Acts 2:9).

PASHHUR, PASHUR (PASH-ur). 1. A son of Immer. Pashhur was a priest. Because Jeremiah's prophecies angered Pashhur, he had the prophet put in stocks (Jeremiah 20:1-6).

2. The son of Malchiah. He was among the court princes in Zedekiah's reign who sought to put Jeremiah to death (Jeremiah 21:1; 38:1, 4).

PASSION (suffering). The sufferings of Christ, beginning with His agony in the Garden of Gethsemane and ending with His death on the cross (Acts 1:3). See also *Jesus Christ.*

PASSOVER. The first of three yearly festivals at which all the Jewish men were to come to the sanctuary (Exodus 23:14-17; Deuteronomy 16:16). It was instituted to keep alive the memory of the "passing over" of Israel when all the firstborn of Egypt were put to death (Exodus 12; 13:3-9). The ritual involved with this feast is described in Exodus 12:3-20. Passover began at sunset on the 14th of Nisan (Leviticus 23:5). Passover is also called the Feast of Unleavened Bread (Exodus 23:15; Deuteronomy 16:16).

Christ and the Lord's Supper are the Christian's Passover (Luke 22:1-20; 1 Corinthians 5:7).

PASTORAL EPISTLES. The name given to three of Paul's letters: 1 Timothy, 2 Timothy, and Titus. These letters show Paul's concern for the pastoral work of the church.

PATARA (PAT-ah-rah). A seaport on the southwest coast of Lycia (Acts 21:1).

PATMOS (PAT-mahs). A small island in the Aegean Sea off the southwest coast of Asia Minor. According to tradition the Emperor Domitian banished John there in A.D. 95 (Revelation 1:9).

PATRIARCH (PAY-tri-ahrk, fatherruler). The father or chief of a race. The name is given to the fathers of the human race both before and after the Flood (Genesis 4—5; 11). Scripture also gives this name to the founders of the Hebrew race and nation: Abraham, Isaac, Jacob, the 12 sons of Jacob, and King David (1 Chronicles 1:28, 34; Acts 2:29; 7:8-9; Hebrews 7:4).

PAUL (PAWL, little). The apostle to the Gentiles (Romans 11:13; Galatians 1:16; 2:2, 8-9).

Paul's given name was Saul. He was born in Tarsus to Jewish parents (Acts 21:39; 22:3). Paul's father was a Pharisee from the tribe of Benjamin (Philippians 3:5). He also held Roman citizenship, a privilege that he passed on to Paul (Acts 22:28; 23:6). Not too much is mentioned about Paul's relatives. From Acts 23:16 we learn that he had a sister and a nephew. Paul also mentions three relatives, two of which were Christians before Paul and well known among the apostles (Romans 16:7, 11).

As a child, Paul was schooled in reading, writing, arithmetic, and particularly in religion. Later he went to Jerusalem and became a student of Gamaliel, a famous teacher known for his tolerant ways (Acts 5:35-40; 22:3). As a student of Gamaliel, Paul studied the Holy Scripture and its various interpretations by famous rabbis. After this Paul likely returned to Tarsus, where he learned the trade of tentmaking (Acts 18:3).

Paul was present at the stoning of Stephen, the first Christian martyr (Acts 7:58; 9:13; 26:10-11; Galatians 1:13). Owing to his intense hatred of the Christians, a sect whom he thought to be a serious threat to the Jewish religion, Paul began to treat Christians in a cruel and harsh way. He sought them out in Jerusalem and other cities and then had them put in prison or even put to death (Acts 8:1-3; 9:1-2, 13-14; 22:1-5; 26:9-12).

One day while Paul was on his way to Damascus to arrest the Christians there, the glorified Jesus appeared to him and asked Paul why he was persecuting Him. Paul became a Christian and, a few days later, was baptized by Ananias (Acts 9; 22:1-16; 26:1-20; 1 Corinthians 15:8-10; Galatians 1:12-16; Ephesians 3:1-8).

Then Paul went to Damascus, where he met with the Christian disciples and preached in the synagogs about Jesus, the Son of God (Acts 9:15; 26:16-20). After this Paul went to Arabia (Galatians 1:17). Upon his return to Damascus, Paul continued to preach the Gospel but was forced to flee because of angry enemies who were trying to kill him (Acts 9:23-25). Paul then went to Jerusalem, and from there, he set sail for Tarsus (Acts 9:26-30. See also Acts 15:41). It seems that Paul spent a number of years there.

Barnabas brought Paul to Antioch to help him in serving the Christian church there (Acts 11:25). When the church at Antioch heard that the believers in the church at Jerusalem were suffering from a famine, they took up a collection for them and appointed Paul and Barnabas to take it to them (Acts 11:29-30). Soon after their return from Jerusalem, Paul and Barnabas were sent on the first missionary trip to Asia Minor. John Mark went along with them on part of this journey (Acts 13—14). When they returned to the church at Antioch, they reported to it how "God had opened a door of faith to the Gentiles" (Acts 14:28).

Not long after this, Jewish Christians from the church in Jerusalem came to Antioch. They said that Gentile converts must keep the Law. Paul went up to Jerusalem and attended the council, which reached a decision regarding Jewish laws for Gentile Christians (Acts 15).

Paul made two other missionary journeys, traveling to Asia Minor, Macedonia, and Greece (Acts 16—20). After his last trip, he went to Jerusalem for a visit. There he was almost killed by a mob. Roman soldiers came to break up the crowd and arrested Paul. Before taking him away, however, they allowed Paul to speak to his angry countrymen. Paul recounted to them his family background and how God had chosen him to tell others about Christ, the promised Messiah (Acts 21:37—22:21).

Paul was then sent before the Sanhedrin (Acts 22:30—23:10). Upon learning of a plot to kill Paul,

the Roman officer in charge sent Paul to Caesarea. There Paul was brought before Felix, the Roman governor of Judea. Paul was kept under house arrest for a few years. When the new governor of Judea arrived to replace Felix, Paul was brought before him. His name was Festus. Paul appealed to his Roman citizenship and asked to be sent to Rome to be heard by the emperor (Acts 25:6-12). Before he was sent to Rome, however, Agrippa and his sister, who were visiting Festus, asked to hear Paul speak. After listening to Paul, Agrippa declared that he thought Paul was innocent. But since the appeal to Rome had already been made, Paul had to be sent there (Acts 26).

And so Paul was sent to Rome (Acts 27—28). It seems likely that Paul was set free after his first trial and made additional missionary journeys (Philippians 2:24; 1 Timothy 1:3; 3:14; 2 Timothy 4:20; Titus 3:12; Philemon 22).

According to tradition Paul died in Rome around A.D. 67 (2 Timothy 1:8, 15; 4). He is the author of most of the letters in the New Testament.

PAULUS (PAWL-uhs). See *Sergius Paulus.*

PEACE. A word often used in the Bible in a variety of ways. It can mean a period of calm and quiet as opposed to war (Matthew 5:9; 2 Corinthians 13:11; 1 Timothy 2:2). It is also used to describe that state of spiritual tranquility and harmony that God gives when He brings one into a right relationship with Himself (Numbers 6:26). Christ is the Christian's peace with God (Ephesians 2:14-17). Through His death on the cross He has earned the forgiveness of sins for all people, making peace between God and people (Colossians 1:20). This peace is worked in believers by the Holy

Spirit through faith and shows itself in their lives (John 20:19, 22; Romans 12:18; 14:19; 1 Corinthians 7:15; Galatians 5:22; Ephesians 4:3; 1 Thessalonians 5:13).

PEACE OFFERING. An animal that was sacrificed to God as a thank offering for some blessing, as a result of some promise or vow made to God, or as an expression of love for God (Leviticus 3; Judges 20:26; 2 Samuel 24:25). See also *sacrifice.*

PEDAIAH (pi-DAY-yah, the Lord saved). 1. The grandfather of King Jehoiakim (2 Kings 23:36).

2. Zerubbabel's father (1 Chronicles 3:19).

PEKAH (PEE-kah, opening). The 18th king of Israel. Pekah gained the throne by murdering Pekahiah. He aligned himself with the king of Damascus against Jotham, king of Judah. Pekah reigned about 20 years and then was killed by Hoshea, who became the next king (2 Kings 15:25-31; 16; 2 Chronicles 28:5-15).

PEKAHIAH (pek-ah-HIGH-ah, the Lord opens). The 17th king of Israel. He took over the throne from his father, Menahem. He ruled about two years and then was murdered by Pekah, who wanted his throne (2 Kings 15:22-26).

PELEG (PEE-leg, division). A son of Eber (Genesis 11:16-19; 1 Chronicles 1:19, 25). "In his days the earth was divided" (Genesis 10:25). This statement may refer to the time God confused the language and scattered the descendants of Noah.

PEN. Either a stylus or graving tool used for cutting letters on stone or a reed pen used for writing on papyrus (Job 19:24; Psalm 45:1; Jeremiah 8:8; 3 John 13).

PENCIL. A tool that a carpenter used for marking lines (Isaiah 44:13).

PENKNIFE. A small knife used to sharpen reed pens (Jeremiah 36:23).

PENNINAH (pi-NIN-ah, coral). One of Elkanah's two wives (1 Samuel 1:2-6). His other wife was Hannah.

PENNY. See *denarius; farthing.*

PENTATEUCH (PEN-tah-tyuk). The first five books of the Old Testament: Genesis, Exodus, Leviticus, Numbers, and Deuteronomy. The Hebrew people called this collection of books the Torah, or the Law. Both the Old Testament and the New Testament speak of these books as being written primarily by Moses (Joshua 8:31; Ezra 6:18; Luke 24:27; John 5:45-47).

PENTECOST (PEN-ti-kawst, 50th day). 1. The Jewish Feast of Weeks, which was celebrated 50 days after the Feast of Passover (Exodus 34:18-26; Deuteronomy 16:10). It is also known as the Feast of Harvest and the day of First Fruits (Exodus 23:16; Numbers 28:26).

2. The 50th day after Easter Sunday. On this day the Holy Spirit was outpoured on the disciples, and many people came to faith in Christ (Acts 2; 1 Corinthians 16:8). This first Pentecost fell on the same day as the Feast of Harvest.

PENUEL (pi-NYOO-uhl, face of God). The place, east of the Jordan, where Jacob wrestled with God (Genesis 32:31; Judges 8:17; 1 Kings 12:25).

PERDITION (pur-DISH-uhn). See *Gehenna; judgment.*

PERDITION, SON OF. A phrase used to refer to two people in the New Testament. Jesus calls Judas Iscariot by this title (John 17:12). Paul uses the same title to refer to the "man of sin" (2 Thessalonians 2:3).

PEREZ-UZZA (PEE-rez-UZ-ah, breach of Uzzah). The name David gave to the place where Uzzah was struck dead for touching the ark of the covenant (2 Samuel 6:8; 1 Chronicles 13:11).

PERGA (PUR-gah). A city of Pamphylia. Paul and Barnabas passed through Perga on their first missionary journey. This is also the place where John Mark left them to return home (Acts 13:13; 14:25).

PERGAMOS, PERGAMUM (PURgah-mus, PUR-gah-muhm). A city in Mysia in Asia Minor. It is the third of the seven churches of Asia mentioned in the Book of Revelation (1:11; 2:12-17). Today it is called Bergama.

PERSIA (PUR-zhah, land of Aryans). To begin with, Persia was only the land around the Persian Gulf. Cyrus II, also known as Cyrus the Great, built the Persian Empire by conquering Media and Babylonia. This empire dominated Asia from 539 to 331 B.C.

Cyrus allowed the Hebrew exiles in Babylonia to return to their land (2 Chronicles 36:22-23; Ezra 1; Isaiah 41:2; 44:28; 45). Darius I gave them permission to rebuild the temple at Jerusalem (Ezra 6). Darius's son, Xerxes I, was the next Persian ruler. He was probably the same person as the Ahasuerus mentioned in Esther 1:1. Under Artaxerxes I, Ezra was allowed to lead more exiles back to Jerusalem. Nehemiah was also permitted to return to Jerusalem, where he organized the rebuilding of the city walls (Ezra 7—8; Nehemiah 2:1-8).

PETER (PEE-tur, rock). One of the 12 disciples and a leader in the early church. He received the name Peter from Jesus at their first meeting. Peter's given name, however, was Simon or Simeon (Matthew 4:18; Mark 1:16; John 1:41; Acts 15:14). He was also referred to as Cephas, which means rock (John 1:42; 1 Corinthians 1:12). Peter was the son of Jonas or John (Matthew 16:17; John 1:42; 21:15-17). He lived in Bethsaida, where, together with his brother Andrew, he made his living as a fisherman on the Sea of Galilee (Matthew 4:18; Mark 1:16; Luke 5:1-11; John 1:44).

Peter was first introduced to Jesus by Andrew and called to discipleship by Jesus at the Sea of Galilee (Matthew 4:18-22; Mark 1:16-20; John 1:40-42). Later, along with the other 11 disciples, Jesus called him to be an apostle (Matthew 10:2-4; Mark 3:13-19; Luke 6:13).

Because of Peter's personality, he seemed to be a natural leader among the disciples. On one occasion he walked on the sea towards Jesus. As his doubts began to grow, however, he began to sink, and Jesus had to put out His hand to save Peter (Matthew 14:25-33). At Caesarea Philippi, when Jesus asked the 12 disciples what they thought of Him, Peter answered, saying, "You are the Christ, the Son of the living God" (Matthew 16:16). Jesus praised Peter for his God-given confession of faith and said that He would build His church on it (Matthew 16:13-19; Mark 8:27-29; Luke 9:18-20). When Jesus began to tell the disciples about how He must suffer and die, Peter rebuked Him and said, "God forbid, Lord! This shall never happen to You." Jesus sharply scolded Peter for this (Matthew 16:21-23).

Along with James and John, Peter was a member of the inner circle of disciples (Matthew 16:15-16; 17:1). He was present at Jesus' transfiguration, in the Garden of Gethsemane, and at the high priest's palace, where Jesus was taken after His arrest (Matthew 17:1; 26:37, 69; Mark 9:2; 14:33, 66; Luke 9:28; 22:54; John 18:16). While in the courtyard of the high priest's palace, Peter denied Jesus three times (Matthew 26:69-75; Mark 14:70-72; Luke 22:59-62; John 18:26-27).

Peter was the first of the 12 disciples to whom Jesus appeared after

His resurrection (Luke 24:34; 1 Corinthians 15:5). On Pentecost, Peter preached the Spirit-inspired message to the crowds of listening people (Acts 2). He was also one of the chief leaders in the early church (Acts 1—12; 15). According to tradition Nero had Peter put to death in Rome around A.D. 65.

PETER, FIRST LETTER OF. Peter wrote this letter to the Christians suffering persecution in five provinces of Asia Minor: Pontus, Galatia, Cappadocia, Asia, and Bithynia (1:1). In his letter Peter tries to encourage them by stressing the comfort and hope they have in Jesus Christ, their Savior.

Date: About A.D. 62

Audience: Christians in Asia Minor

Outline: 1. The Christian hope and its effect on life (1—2:10). 2. Christian life (2:11—3:22). 3. Patience during troublesome times (4). 4. Duties of elders and people (5).

PETER, SECOND LETTER OF. A general letter written to warn its readers against false teachers and to remind them of the truths they had been taught about Jesus so that they might grow in His grace amd trust His promises.

Date: About A.D. 62 to 63

Audience: Most likely the Christians of the five provinces of Asia Minor

Outline: 1. Salutation (1:1-2). 2. The greatness of the Christian hope (1:3-11). 3. The certainty of the Christian hope (1:12—2). 4. Warnings in view of judgments (3).

PHANUEL (fah-NYOO-el, face of God). The father of the prophetess Anna (Luke 2:36).

PHARAOH (FAIR-o, great house). The title of Egyptian rulers (Genesis 12:15; 41:39, 42; Acts 7:10). At birth individual names were given to the pharaohs, for instance, Pharaoh Neco and Pharaoh Hophra. A

number of these Egyptian rulers are referred to in the Bible.

1. Pharaohs are mentioned in connection with Abraham and Joseph (Genesis 12:14-20; 40—41). The names of these pharaohs are unknown.

2. Also unknown is the name of the pharaoh of the oppression. He may have been Seti I or Thutmose III.

3. Another pharaoh is mentioned when the Children of Israel left Egypt under Moses. This ruler may have been either Rameses II or Amenhotep II.

4. Another pharaoh defeated the Canaanites of Gezer and gave the city as a dowry to his daughter, Solomon's wife (1 Kings 3:1; 7:8; 9:16).

5. Pharaoh Shishak, who began ruling Egypt during the latter part of Solomon's reign, used the division of the kingdom after Solomon's death for his own benefit. While the country was politically weakened, he invaded Jerusalem (1 Kings 14:25-26; 2 Chronicles 12:2-9).

6. Zerah invaded Judah in the days of King Asa but was defeated by him (2 Chronicles 14:9-15; 16:8).

7. Before Tirhakah became pharaoh, he did battle with Sennacherib, king of Assyria (2 Kings 19:9).

8. Pharaoh Neco killed King Josiah and, when Josiah's son, Jehoahaz, became king, Neco dethroned him and carried him off to Egypt. Next Jehoiakim was made king. In 605 B.C. Nebuchadnezzar, king of Babylonia, defeated Neco at Carchemish (2 Kings 23:29-35; 24:7; 2 Chronicles 35:20—36:4; Jeremiah 46:2).

9. Pharaoh Hophra was the ruler of Egypt while Jeremiah was a prophet in Judah. Jeremiah spoke against him (Jeremiah 44:30).

PHARAOH'S DAUGHTER. 1. The woman who found baby Moses on the Nile River and raised him as her own child (Exodus 2:5-10).

2. One of Solomon's wives (1 Kings 3:1).

PHARISEES (FAR-uh-see, separated). One of the three leading Jewish parties during Jesus' time. It is believed that this strict and influential sect had its beginning during the time of the Maccabees.

The Pharisees believed that people had the ability to do good or evil, and that, by keeping the Law in an outward manner, they could of themselves earn God's favor. For this reason they stressed keeping God's law and the oral law and put great emphasis on observing such rituals as washing, tithing, and fasting. They also avoided contact with non-Pharisees. They believed in the existence of angels and taught the immortality of the soul, two doctrines disputed by their rival party, the Sadducees (Matthew 9:11-14; 12:1-8; 16:1-12; 23; Luke 11; Acts 15:5; 23:6-8).

PHILADELPHIA (fil-ah-DEL-fi-ah, brotherly love). A city of Lydia in Asia Minor. It was the location of one of the seven churches addressed in the Book of Revelation (Revelation 1:11; 3:7-13).

PHILEMON (fi-LEE-mun, friendship). One of Paul's converts who lived in Colossae and had a church in his house. Paul addressed a letter to Philemon when he sent Philemon's runaway slave, Onesimus, back to him (Philemon).

PHILEMON, LETTER OF PAUL TO. A letter Paul wrote to Philemon in behalf of Philemon's runaway slave, Onesimus. In the letter Paul asks Philemon to forgive Onesimus and receive him back as a brother in the faith.

Date: A.D. 52 to 56 or 59 to 61
Audience: Philemon

Outline: 1. Greetings (1-3). 2. Thanks for Philemon's faith and love, and a prayer that they continue (4-7). 3. Paul's plea for Onesimus, his child in Christ (8-21). 4. Greetings from Paul's fellow workers; benediction (22-25).

PHILIP (FIL-uhp, lover of horses). 1. One of the 12 apostles. He came from Bethsaida on the Sea of Galilee and was likely a close friend of Andrew and Peter (John 1:44; 12:21). Philip was called to be a disciple near Bethany beyond the Jordan (John 1:41-43). Some time later Jesus called him to be an apostle (Matthew 10:3; Mark 3:18; Luke 6:14).

When Jesus was about to perform the miracle of feeding the 5,000, He tested Philip's faith by asking, "How are we to buy bread, so that these people may eat?" (John 6:5-7). On the day of Jesus' triumphal entry into Jerusalem, Philip brought some Greeks who wished to meet Jesus to Him (John 12:20-23). While Jesus was talking to His disciples on the night before He was crucified, He told them that by knowing Him they knew the Father. Philip, however, did not understand this and asked Jesus to show them the Father (John 14:8-12). The last information the New Testament gives about Philip is that he was among the apostles in the Upper Room after Jesus' ascension (Acts 1:13).

2. The evangelist who came from Caesarea. Philip was one of the seven men chosen to look after the needs of widows and the poor in the early church.

Philip preached the Gospel in Samaria. He cast out demons and healed sick people just as the apostles did. God used him to bring the Ethiopian eunuch to faith in Christ (Acts 6:5; 8:4-40; 21:8-9).

PHILIPPI (fuh-LIP-igh). A Macedonian city that was made a Roman colony by Octavius and granted citizenship privileges. Paul visited this city and made various converts there, among whom were Lydia and the Philippian jailor (Acts 16:12; 20:6; Philippians 1:1; 1 Thessalonians 2:2).

PHILIPPIANS, LETTER OF PAUL TO. A letter Paul wrote while he was in prison to thank the Philippians for sending a gift to him through Epaphroditus. In the letter Paul expresses his joy in Christ and offers the Philippians spiritual advice for the Christian life.

>Date: A.D. 52 to 56 or 59 to 61
>Audience: Christians at Philippi
>Outline: 1. Salutation, thanksgiving, and prayer (1:1-11). 2. News from prison (1:12-26). 3. Admonition (1:27—2:18). 3. The apostle's action on the Philippians' behalf (2:19—3:1). 4. Apostolic warning and admonitions (3:2—4:9). 5. Thanks for the gift (4:10-23).

PHILISTIA (fuh-LIS-ti-ah). The land of the Philistines, an area along the coast of Canaan about 50 miles long and 15 miles wide. It extended from Joppa to south of Gaza and had five great cities: Gaza, Ekron, Ashdod, Ashkelon, and Gath (Joshua 13:2-3; 1 Samuel 6:17).

The Philistines were a non-Semitic people who came from Caphtor (or Crete) around 1175 B.C. They were a warlike people, knowledgable in making iron tools and weapons. Since Israel did not have these types of weapons until the time of David, the Philistines dominated them during the period of the judges (Judges 13:1). Israel was set free from Philistine control by various deliverers, such as Shamgar, Samson, and Samuel (Judges 3:31; 13—16; 1 Samuel 7:1-14). Later, the Philistines were defeated by Jonathan and conquered by David, who

made them pay tribute (1 Samuel 13—14; 17—18). The Philistines regained their power during the period of the divided monarchy (1 Kings 15:27; 2 Chronicles 21:16; 28:18).

PHILISTINES (fuh-LIS-tinz). The people of Philistia. See also *Philistia.*

PHILOSOPHY (fuh-LOS-o-fee). The study of humanity's thinking about the meaning of life. In the Bible the word *philosophy* is used only in Colossians 2:8. Other passages in the New Testament, however, refer to various philosophical movements. The Epicureans and Stoics are mentioned in Acts 17:18. A chief threat to Christianity came from Gnostic (Colossians 2:8) and syncretistic thought (1 Corinthians 1:18-25; 1 Timothy 6:20).

PHINEAS (FIN-i-uhs). 1. The son of Eleazar and grandson of Aaron. Phineas ran a spear through an Israelite man and the Midianite woman he had brought into the camp. This ended a plague that had been sent as a judgment against the idolatry into which the Midianite women were leading the Israelites. For this reason God promised Phineas and his descendants an everlasting priesthood (Numbers 25:1-8; 31:6; Joshua 22:13; Judges 20:28). Except during the time of Eli, the descendants of Phineas held the high priesthood until A.D. 70.

2. A wicked son of Eli. Both he and his brother were unfaithful priests who were killed by the Philistines (1 Samuel 1:3; 2:34; 4:11-22).

PHOEBE (FEE-bi, pure; radiant). A deaconess at Cenchrea. She was perhaps the first deaconess of the Christian church and was highly spoken of by Paul (Romans 16:1-2).

PHOENICIA (fi-NISH-i-ah, bloodred, purple, or palm). A country along the Mediterranean coast, about 120 miles long, that went from Arvad to the Ladder of Tyre. In the New Testament it extended to Dor.

The people who lived in Phoenicia were Semitic in background. They were well-known seagoers who founded Carthage and places in Spain and may even have reached England. They were also famous shipbuilders and carpenters (1 Kings 5:6; Ezekiel 27:9). Phoenicia was a trading center of the nations (Isaiah 23:3; Ezekiel 27:25). Because the Phoenicians went to other lands and people from other lands came to Phoenicia, the Phoenician culture—its alphabet, dyes, numbers, weights, measures, and architecture—spread.

The Phoenicians worshiped the idols El, Baal, Anath, Astarte, and Ashera. Jezebel, Ahab's wife, brought this worship to Israel (1 Kings 16:31; 18:19). Hiram, one of the Phoenician kings, was friendly with David and Solomon (2 Samuel 5:11; 1 Kings 5:1-12; 2 Chronicles 2:3-16). Another Hiram, a craftsman and architect, helped Solomon build the temple (1 Kings 7:13-47; 2 Chronicles 2:13-14). After Elijah had told King Ahab about a coming drought, Elijah fled to Phoenicia, where a widow looked after him (1 Kings 17:9).

Jesus visited the regions of Phoenicia and healed a Syrophoenician woman there (Mark 7:24-30). Paul visited the Christians in Phoenicia (Acts 15:3; 21:2-7).

PHRYGIA (FRIJ-i-ah). A province in Asia Minor that once included the greater part of Asia Minor. It was obtained by Rome in 133 B.C. Paul visited Phrygia on several of his missionary journeys (Acts 2:10; 16:6; 18:23).

PHYLACTERY (fi-LAK-tur-ee). See *frontlet.*

PIECE OF GOLD OR SILVER. A certain amount of precious metal, either in coin or uncoined form. The phrases "a piece of gold" or "a piece of silver" are used in the Bible because the exact amount of money is unknown. In the Old Testament the original text often said "1,000 of silver," or "1,000 of gold" (Genesis 20:16). In the New Testament a piece of silver commonly meant a drachma (Luke 15:8-9), shekel, or denarion (Matthew 26:15; 27:3-9).

PILATE (PIGH-laht, armed with javelin). Pontius Pilate, the fifth procurator or representative of the Roman government in Judea (A.D. 26—36). Although Pilate found Jesus innocent of the accusations brought against Him, he nevertheless gave in to the peoples' wishes and condemned Jesus to death on the cross (Matthew 27; Mark 15; Luke 3:1; 13:1; 23; John 18—19; Acts 3:13; 4:27; 13:28; 1 Timothy 6:13).

PILGRIMAGE. 1. The Jewish people were expected to make the pilgrimage or trip to the temple in Jerusalem for the great feasts (Deuteronomy 16:16; Psalms 120—134; Acts 2:5-11).

2. In the New Testament Christians are referred to as pilgrims on the road to heaven (Hebrew 11:13; 1 Peter 2:11).

PILLAR. 1. A monument that marked a sacred spot or a grave or was put up as a memorial (Genesis 28:18; 31:45; 35:20; 2 Samuel 18:18).

2. Pillars or columns that supported buildings (Judges 16:25-30; 1 Kings 7; 2 Kings 11:14).

3. A pillar of cloud by day or fire by night that guided the Israelites during the Exodus and showed God's presence (Exodus 13:21; 14:19-24).

PINNACLE. Something shaped like a wing on a building, roof, battlement, or temple. The devil took Jesus to the pinnacle of the temple and said to Him, "If You are the Son of God, throw Yourself down" (Matthew 4:5; Luke 4:9).

PIPE. A musical instrument of the woodwind category (Genesis 4:21; Job 21:12; 30:31; Psalm 15:4). See also *music.*

PISGAH, MOUNT (PIZ-gah). Part of the Abarim mountain range that looks out over Jericho. (Numbers 21:20; 23:14; Deuteronomy 3:17; 4:49; 34:1; Joshua 12:3; 13:20). It is near Mount Nebo, the mountain from which Moses viewed the Promised Land (Deuteronomy 3:27).

PISHON (PIGH-shon). One of the four rivers of Eden (Genesis 2:11).

PISIDIA (puh-SID-i-ah). An area in southern Asia Minor north of Pamphylia. Paul visited there on his first two missionary journeys (Acts 13:14; 14:24).

PIT. 1. A hole that was dug for a well or cistern. Often these holes were used for prisons, burials, or traps (Genesis 37:24; 2 Samuel 23:20; Psalm 28:1; Isaiah 24:22; Ezekiel 19:8).

2. The word *pit* is also used in the Old Testament to mean death, grave, or existence beyond death (Job 33:18-30; Psalm 28:1; 30:3; Isaiah 14:15, 19). See also *abyss; sheol.*

PITCH. Asphalt or bitumen (Isaiah 34:9). Pitch was used to make vessels watertight (Genesis 6:14; Exodus 2:3; Isaiah 34:9).

PITHOM (PIGH-thom, dwelling of Atum, sun-god). An Egyptian store-city in Goshen. It held supplies of grain for armies and perhaps for caravans (Exodus 1:11).

PLAGUE. Something that causes trouble or suffering (Exodus 11:1). Often a plague was a quickly spreading disease that made many people severely ill or caused them to die (1 Samuel 5; 2 Samuel 24:13-25). The 10 plagues on Egypt were the means God used to convince the pharaoh to let the Israelites go (Exodus 7—12).

PLANE. A tree that grows along the water in Syria and Mesopotamia. The word *plane* is sometimes translated as chestnut or pine (Genesis 30:37; Isaiah 41:19; 60:13; Ezekiel 31:8).

PLEDGE. 1. Something given to be held as security for a loan (Deuteronomy 24:10-13, 17). See also *loans.*

2. A wager (2 Kings 18:23; Isaiah 36:8).

PLEIADES (PLEE-yah-deez, cluster). The stars in the constellation Taurus (Job 9:9; 38:31; Amos 5:8).

PLOW. See *agriculture.*

PLOWSHARE. A stone or the point of a plow (1 Samuel 13:20; Isaiah 2:4; Micah 4:3). See also *agriculture.*

POETRY. Features of Hebrew poetry include its rhythm, parallelism, alliteration, and rhyme or other word plays. Job, Psalms, Proverbs, Ecclesiastes, Song of Solomon, and sections in the prophets are examples of Hebrew poetry.

POMEGRANATE (POM-gran-it). See *orchard.*

PONTIUS (PON-shuhs). See *Pilate.*

PONTUS (PON-tuhs, sea). A region of northeast Asia Minor. During New Testament times it was a Roman province (Acts 2:9; 1 Peter 1:1). Aquila, one of Paul's helpers, came from Pontus (Acts 18:2).

POOR. The Old Testament speaks negatively about those who beg (Psalm 37:25; Proverbs 20:4). Laziness, some great trouble or disaster, and cruel or unjust treatment are cited as causes of being poor (Judges 10:6-17; Proverbs 10:4; 14:23; Isaiah 5:8; Matthew 23:14).

Although it is true that God promises to bless His people (Deuteronomy 28:1-14) and that hard work and wisely managing one's resources often benefit the person who does so, poor people were still present in Israel throughout its history. Laws protected the poor. For instance, when crops were harvested, some of the yield was to be left for the fatherless and widows (Leviticus 19:9-10; Deuteronomy 24:19-22). Every seventh year fields and orchards were to lie fallow so the poor could eat (Exodus 23:11; Leviticus 25:6). During the year of jubilee, land that people sold because they needed the money was to be returned to them (Leviticus 25:8-30). The poor were to receive their wages on time, and they were not to be charged interest (Exodus 22:25-27; Deuteronomy 24:14-15).

Scripture praises the person who has mercy on the poor (Psalm 41:1; Proverbs 14:21; 29:7).

PORCH. A passageway from a street to the inner hall (Matthew 26:71) or an area protected by a roof, such as a veranda, a colonnade or portico, or a vestibule or hall (Judges 3:23; 1 Chronicles 28:11; John 5:2).

POST. A messenger or courier (Esther 8:10, 14; Job 9:25).

POT. A clay or metal vessel used for holding liquid or dry ingredients (Judges 6:19; 2 Kings 4:38; Job

41:20, 31; Lamentations 4:2).

POTIPHAR (POT-uh-fur, who is of the sun). The captain of the pharaoh's guard during Joseph's time (Genesis 37:36; 39:1).

POTIPHERA (po-TIF-ur-ah, who is of the sun). The Egyptian priest of On, whose daughter, Asenath, became Joseph's wife (Genesis 41:45, 50; 46:20).

POTTAGE. A stew made of meat and vegetables (Genesis 25:29-30, 34; 2 Kings 4:38-40; Haggai 2:12).

POTTER, POTTER'S FIELD, POTTER'S WHEEL, POTTERY. See *trade*.

POUND. In the Old Testament a pound was equal to about 50 shekels (1 Kings 10:17; Ezra 2:69; Nehemiah 7:71). In the New Testament it equaled about 100 drachmas (Luke 19:13-25).

POVERTY. See *poor*.

PRAETORIAN GUARD (pri-TO-ri-uhn). The bodyguard and household of the emperor in Rome (Philippians 1:13).

PRAETORIUM (pri-TO-ri-uhm). The headquarters of a general.   2. The palace in Jerusalem occupied by Pontius Pilate (Matthew 27:27; Mark 15:16; John 18:28).

3. Herod's palace at Caesarea (Acts 23:35).

PRAYER (PRAIR). Speaking with God. Moses' prayers were largely intercessory, that is, speaking to God on behalf of the people (Exodus 32:11-13, 31-32; Numbers 11:11-15; Deuteronomy 9:18-21). The psalms are examples of the covenant people's prayers to their covenant God. These prayers are usually a result of some experience seen in its spiritual depth and are often closely related to sacrifice (Genesis 12:8; 26:25) and the temple (1 Kings 8:30, 33; Psalm 5:7).

The New Testament teaches that prayer is to be spoken in the name of Jesus since sinful people cannot approach God on their own merits (John 14:13; 15:16). They can do so only through Christ, who has bought humankind back from their sins and put them in a right relationship with God (Galatians 4:1-7). Christ taught the disciples the Lord's Prayer (Matthew 6:9-13; Luke 11:1-4). It is an example of proper approach and manner for speaking to God. Christ intercedes for believers before the Father (Romans 8:34; Hebrews 4:14-16; 7:25). The Holy Spirit who dwells within all Christians also intercedes for them according to the will of God (Romans 8:15-16, 26-27).

Prayers can be formal (Psalms; Matthew 6:9-13; 26:30; Luke 23:46) or spoken freely from one's own thoughts and concerns (John 17; Luke 18:13; 1 Thessalonians 5:17). They can be said together by a large group of believers or alone by an individual (Matthew 6:6; 14:23; Acts 1:14; Philemon 4); they can be said at set times and places (Acts 2:42; 6:4; 16:13) or at all times and places (Ephesians 6:18; 1 Thessalonians 5:17; 1 Timothy 2:8).

The Bible mentions various ways in which prayers can be said: with uplifted hands, while kneeling, while lying flat on the ground, or while standing (1 Kings 8:54; Psalm 28:2; Matthew 6:5; 26:39; Acts 9:40; 1 Timothy 2:8).

PREACHER, PREACHING. One who speaks God's message or the act of speaking for God.

In the Old Testament prophets proclaimed God's message—the Law and the Gospel. They spoke about God's will for people, proclaimed His judgment on those who had sinned, and spoke His promises (Ezekiel 20:46; Jeremiah 11:6).

In the New Testament preaching centered in the person and work of Jesus Christ (Acts 2:14-40; 3:11-26). Again, the message included both the Law and the Gospel (Matthew 4:17; Luke 3:3-14; 4:18; Acts 2:14-40; 17:22-31).

PREDESTINATION (pri-des-tuh-NAY-shuhn). God's act before the beginning of the world in choosing from sinners those whom He would save (Ephesians 1:4-5). God does this by (1) providing for the salvation of the world through Christ, (2) offering the merits and benefits of Christ's work to individuals through the Word and Sacrament, (3) working faith in the hearts of individuals through the Holy Spirit, (4) graciously receiving those who are sorry for their sins and who trust and believe in Christ as their Savior, (5) making individuals more and more holy by the Holy Spirit's work in them, (6) protecting them from the work of the devil and the sinful world, (7) keeping them in the faith until the end through the work of the Holy Spirit in Word and Sacrament, and (8) saving these individuals eternally (Matthew 20:16; 22:14; Mark 13:20-22; Acts 13:48; Romans 8:28-30; 9:11; 11:15; Ephesians 1:4-5; 2 Thessalonians 2:13; 2 Timothy 1:9; 2:10, 19; 1 Peter 1:2).

PRESBYTER (PREZ-buh-tur). See *elder*.

PRIEST. One who represents the people before God. Originally individuals or heads of families carried out the work of a priest (Genesis 4:3-4; 12:7; 13:18; 26:25; 33:20). Then through Moses God appointed Aaron and his sons and their descendants as priests (Exodus 28:1). Aaronic priests had to meet up to high standards (Leviticus 21:16-24). Consecrated for this task, they wore special clothing in the sanctuary, taught the people, and inquired of God's will (Exodus 28—29).

The priesthood was grouped into 24 divisions, each serving a week

at a time (1 Chronicles 24:1-19). Kings, judges, and prophets also made sacrifices to God (Judges 6:17-21; 13:15-20; 2 Samuel 6:17; 1 Kings 18:30-38).

The chief priest, or high priest, was in charge of all the other priests. He offered the sin offering, made sacrifice on the Day of Atonement, and discovered the will of God through Urim and Thummin (Leviticus 4; 16; Numbers 27:21; Nehemiah 7:65). The high priest wore the regular priestly clothing plus breastplate, ephod, girdle, and miter (Exodus 28). See also *Aaron*.

In the New Testament Jesus Christ is the only high priest. Since He sacrificed Himself for the sins of the people and this sacrifice need never be repeated, there is no longer a need for the Levitical priesthood; it has been done away with in Christ (John 14:6; 1 Timothy 2:5-6; Hebrews 5:7-10). See also *Jesus Christ (office of priest)*.

The New Testament also teaches the priesthood of all believers. Christians share in Christ's priestly activity by bringing the Gospel to people (Ephesians 2:18; Hebrews 10:19-25; 13:15; 1 Peter 2:5, 9; Revelation 1:5-6).

PRIEST, HIGH. See *priest*.

PRINCE. A ruler or chief person, such as the head of a family or tribe, a king, a ruler, a governor, a magistrate, a satrap, or a royal descendant (Genesis 25:16; Numbers 22:8; 1 Samuel 9:16; 18:30; 2 Kings 10:13; 2 Chronicles 12:5-6; Esther 1). The Messiah is called the Prince of Peace (Isaiah 9:6). The devil is called the prince or ruler of demons (Matthew 9:34).

PRINCIPALITY (prin-suh-PAL-uh-tee). 1. Rule or ruler (Ephesians 1:21; Titus 3:1).

2. Order of angels (Romans 8:38; Ephesians 3:10; 6:12; Colossians 1:16, 2:15).

PRISCA, PRISCILLA (PRIS-kah, pri-SIL-ah, little old woman). Wife of Aquila. Priscilla and her husband were tentmakers and Christian friends of Paul, whom they helped on a number of occasions (Acts 18:2, 18; Romans 16:3; 2 Timothy 4:19). They had a church in their house and together taught Apollos more about the Christian faith (Acts 18:26; 1 Corinthians 16:19).

PRISON. A place where persons who are suspected of committing a crime or who have been accused of one are kept. 1. The oldest prisons mentioned in the Bible were wells or dungeons (Genesis 37:24; Jeremiah 38:6-13). During the period of the kings prisons were located in the palace or in private houses (1 Kings 22:27; Jeremiah 32:2; 37:15). The Herods and Romans had royal prisons (Luke 3:20; Acts 12:4; 23:10, 35).

2. Another word for abyss, the place where Satan lives (1 Peter 3:19; Revelation 20:7).

PROCHORUS (PROK-o-ruhs, leader of chorus). One of the seven men chosen by the early church to look after widows and probably the poor in general (Acts 6:5).

PROCONSUL (pro-KAHN-suhl). The governor of a Roman province administered by the Senate (Acts 6:5).

PROMISE. The most important promise in the Bible is God's assurance that He would send a deliverer, or Messiah, to save His people (Genesis 3:15; 12:3; Romans 4:13; 9:8; Galatians 3:14-19). The promises in the Old Testament concerning the Messiah are fulfilled in Christ Jesus (Acts 13:23, 32-33; Romans 1:2-3; 15:8; Galatians 3:14; 2 Corinthians 1:20). Those who believe in Jesus as their Savior are called heirs of the promise (Romans 4:16; Galatians 3:16, 26-29; 4:28). By God's grace, through faith, they receive many blessings, including the forgiveness of sins, the indwelling of the Holy Spirit, and life everlasting (1 Corinthians 3:16; Galatians 3:1-14; 1 John 1:7).

PROPHET (PRAHF-it, seer; announcer; spokesman). A person called by God to speak for Him to the people. Prophets spoke God's Word of judgment, calling people to account for their sins (2 Samuel 12; Isaiah 58:1; Ezekiel 3:17), and His Word of mercy (Isaiah 40; 53). Their work involved forthtelling and, to a lesser degree, foretelling. They constantly emphasized God's work in the course of history, particularly His plan of salvation through the Messiah, Jesus Christ.

The Old Testament prophets came from all walks of life (Amos 1:1). Many of them wrote books of the Bible which have been named for them. The Old Testament also mentions schools of prophets (1 Samuel 19:19-20; 2 Kings 2:3-5; 4:38; 6:1).

PROPITIATION (pro-pish-i-AY-shuhn, cover; incline toward). The act of keeping God from being angry by satisfying His justice and holiness so that He can forgive sins.

Sin causes a separation between God and people; it is necessary that human guilt be removed in order to restore a right relationship between them. In the Old Testament the sacrificial system served this function, although God also forgave people without sacrifices being offered (Leviticus 14:18; 17:11; 19:22; Isaiah 6:7; 27:9; Ezekiel 16:63). These sacrifices pointed forward to the supreme sacrifice of God's Son, Jesus Christ, who died for the sins of the world. Christ's death and resurrection once and for all removed the barrier between God and all people (Romans 3:25; 1 John 2:2; 4:10).

PROSELYTE (PRAHS-uh-light). A stranger or foreigner in the land of Israel who obeyed certain of its rules (Exodus 20:10; Leviticus 17:10, 15; 18:26; 20:2, 22:18; 24:16). Although there were exceptions (Deuteronomy 23:3, 8), proselytes could become part of Israel if they underwent the rite of circumcision (Exodus 12:48-49).

In the New Testament proselytes included people who observed some or all features of the Jewish religion (Matthew 23:15; Acts 13:43) and those who simply feared God (Acts 10:2).

PROSTITUTE (PRAHS-tuh-tyoot). A person who offers sexual favors for money, especially a woman who offers herself to a man for money. There were both common and religious prostitutes in the ancient world (Deuteronomy 23:17-18; Hosea 4:14). The Scripture often speaks of prostitutes and prostitution as a symbol for disobedience and unfaithfulness (Exodus 34:15; Ezekiel 16; Hosea 4:15). The sin of prostitution is forbidden in Scripture many times (Leviticus 21:7, 9, 14; 1 Corinthians 6:18-20).

PROVERB (PRAHV-urb). Generally a short saying expressing a familiar or useful truth (Genesis 10:9; 1 Samuel 10:12; Deuteronomy 28:37; Proverbs).

PROVERBS, BOOK OF. A book in the Bible containing proverbs and practical advice that "men may know wisdom and instruction" (1:2). It notes that a wise person recognizes God in all things.

Date: 10th century B.C.

Audience: Believers in God and His promises

Outline: 1. Introduction (1:1-7). 2. Praise of wisdom (1:7—9). 3. Proverbs of Solomon (10—22:16). 4. Words of the wise (22:17—24:22). 5. Sayings of the wise (24:23-34). 6. Proverbs of Solomon (25—29). 7. Words of Agur (30). 8. Words of Lemuel (31:1-9). 9. Good wife (31:10-31).

PROVIDENCE (PRAHV-uh-duhns). The activity of God whereby He preserves, governs, and directs His entire creation (Job 9:5; Psalm 104:10-25; 145:15; Matthew 4:4; 6:26-28; Luke 12:6-7; Acts 17:25-28; Hebrews 1:3).

PROVINCE. A unit of a country, for instance, the provinces of the Roman Empire. Persian provinces were called satraphies (Ezra 2:1; 5:8; Acts 23:34; 25:1).

PSALMS, BOOK OF (song of praise; poem sung to music of stringed instruments). The longest book of the division of the Hebrew Scriptures known as the Writings. The authors of the various psalms are given in their titles. Bible scholars think the titles of the psalms may refer to musical directions or instruments, melodies, or liturgical instructions or occasions. Some think these titles may be simply descriptive. In the Hebrew Psalter the psalms are divided into five books.

Date: Pre-exile and during reigns of kings

Audience: Worshipers of the true God

Outline: 1. Book 1 (1—41). 2. Book 2 (42—72). 3. Book 3 (73—89). 4. Book 4 (90—106). 5. Book 5 (107—150).

PSALTERY (SAWL-tur-ee). A stringed musical instrument (1 Samuel 10:5; Psalm 57:8; 71:22; Daniel 3:5). See also *music.*

PTOLEMY (TAWL-i-mee). The common name of the Macedonian kings who ruled Egypt after the death of Alexander the Great in 323 B.C. until 30 B.C., the year of Cleopatra's death.

PUBLICAN (PUHB-li-kuhn). A person who collected taxes for the Roman government. The Romans used a tax-farming system, employing the natives of a particular country or area to collect taxes for them. For instance, in Palestine the publicans were usually Jews. Publicans had two marks against them. Not only were they collecting taxes, but they were doing this for Rome, a government hated by their fellow countrymen because of its control over their land. As a result publicans were also looked down upon, even hated, by their own countrymen (Matthew 9:10; 18:17; Luke 3:12-13; 19:2).

PURIM (PYOO-rim). A Jewish festival commemorating the deliverance of the Jews by Esther (Esther 3:7; 9:24-32). The name comes from Pur, meaning lot (Esther 9:24-26).

Q

R

QUART. See *measures 2; 3*.

QUEEN OF HEAVEN. A Semitic goddess of fertility. She was likely Astarte of Canaan or Ishtar of Babylonia (Jeremiah 7:18; 44:17-25).

QUEEN OF THE SOUTH. The queen of Sheba (Matthew 12:42; Luke 11:31. See also 1 Kings 10:1-13; 2 Chronicles 9:1-12).

QUIRINIUS, PUBLIUS SULPICIUS (kwigh-RIN-i-uhs PUB-li-uhs sul-PISH-UHS). The governor of Syria at the time Caesar Augustus issued the decree for the census in which Joseph enrolled (Luke 2:2).

QUIVER (KWIV-ur). See *archery*.

RAAMSES (ray-AM-seez). 1. A store-city the Hebrews built in northeast Eygpt while they were slaves there (Exodus 1:11). It was the capital of the 19th dynasty. It is also referred to as Rameses (Genesis 47:11; Exodus 12:37; Numbers 33:3, 5).

RABBI (RAB-igh, my master). A title of respect the Jewish people gave to their spiritual leaders and instructors (Matthew 23:7-8; Mark 10:51; John 1:38, 49; 3:2, 26; 6:25). John explains *rabbi* and *rabboni* as meaning master (4:31; 9:2; 11:8; 20:16).

RABBONI (ra-BO-nee). See *rabbi*.

RABSARIS (RAB-sah-ris, chief eunuch). The title of Assyrian officials who held high positions in the court (2 Kings 18:17; Jeremiah 39:3, 13).

RABSHAKEH (RAB-shah-ke, chief officer). The title of Assyrian military officials who held high positions (2 Kings 18:17-37; 19:4-8; Isaiah 36; 37:4, 8).

RACHEL (RAY-chuhl, ewe). The favorite wife of Jacob; mother of Joseph and Benjamin. Rachel was the younger daughter of Laban, Jacob's uncle. This made her Jacob's cousin (Genesis 29—35; Jeremiah 31:15).

RADDAI (RAD-ay-igh, trampling). One of David's brothers (1 Chronicles 2:14).

RAHAB (RAY-hab, broad). A woman who had a house on the wall of Jericho during the time of the conquest. For her help in hiding Israelite spies in her home, Rahab's life and the lives of her family were spared (Joshua 2:1-21; 6:17-25). She is likely the Rahab who married Salmon and became the mother of Boaz, an ancestor of Jesus (Ruth 4:21; Matthew 1:5).

RAHAB (RAY-hab, violent one). A mythical monster representing sea power and violence (Job 26:12; Psalm 89:10). The name is also applied to Egypt (Psalm 87:4; Isaiah 30:7).

RAIN. The rainy season in Palestine extends from October through April. The early rain occurs in October and November (Psalm 84:6; Isaiah 30:23; Jeremiah 5:24) and the late rain comes in March and April (Job 29:23; Proverbs 16:15; Jeremiah 3:3; Zechariah 10:1).

In the Bible rain is often a picture word for teaching and counsel, for the Word, for righteousness and peace, for blessings on believers, for judgments that destroy, and for nagging (Deuteronomy 32:2; Job 20:23; 29:21-25; Psalm 72:6; 84:5-6; Proverbs 19:13; Isaiah 55:10; Ezekiel 38:22).

RAINBOW. The sign of God's covenant with Noah. The rainbow is a reminder that God will never again flood the whole earth (Genesis 9:12-17).

RAM. A male sheep. The ram was a source of food and sacrifice (Genesis 15:9; 22:13; 31:38). The skins of rams were used as coverings for the tabernacle; their horns, for trumpets (Exodus 26:14; Joshua 6:4-20).

RAMAH (RAY-mah, height). 1. A town of Benjamin five miles north of Jerusalem. It was near Deborah's palm tree and Rachel's tomb (Joshua 18:25; Judges 4:5; 19:10-15; 1 Kings 15:17-22; Jeremiah 31:15; 40:1; Matthew 2:18). Benjaminites lived in Ramah after the captivity (Ezra 2:26; Nehemiah 7:30). Today it is called el-Ram.

2. A town in the mountains of Ephraim. It was the birthplace of Samuel and the place where he lived and was buried. In 1 Samuel 1:1 it is called Ramathaim-zophim to distinguish it from other towns of similar name. It may be the same as Arimathea, a place mentioned in the New Testament.

RAMESES (RAM-i-seez). See *Pharaoh 3*.

RAMOTH-GILEAD, RAMOTH IN GILEAD (RAY-moth-GIL-i-uhd, heights of Gilead). An Amorite city east of the Jordan and a Levitical city of refuge in Gad (Deuteronomy 4:43; Joshua 20:8; 21:38). It was the home of Jephthah and the place where Solomon's tax gatherer lived (Judges 11:34; 1 Kings 4:13). King Ahab was killed there (1 Kings 22:1-38). It was also known as Ramah, Ramath-mizpeh, and Mizpah or Mizpeh (Joshua 13:26; Judges 10:17; 2 Kings 8:29).

RANSOM. The price paid for getting someone or something back (Exodus 21:30. See also 1 Corinthians 6:19-20).

RAPHAEL (RAF-ay-el). An archangel.

REAP. See *agriculture*.

REBA (REE-bah, fourth). A Midianite king who, at Moses' command, was killed by Israel in Moab (Numbers 31:8; Joshua 13:21).

REBECCA, REBEKAH (ri-BEK-ah, noose). The daughter of Bethuel, wife of Isaac, and mother of

Esau and Jacob (Genesis 22:23; 24; 25:21-26).

RECONCILIATION (rek-UN-sil-i-AY-shuhn). The removal of the barrier, caused by sin, between God and humanity. Christ's death on the cross for the sin of the world is the way this barrier was removed. An individual appropriates the forgiveness earned by Christ for himself or herself by grace through faith (Acts 10:43; 2 Corinthians 5:18-19; Ephesians 2:16).

RECORDER. An official of high rank who wrote down important events and kept the public documents (2 Samuel 8:16; 20:24; 1 Kings 4:3; 2 Kings 18:18, 37; 1 Chronicles 18:15; Isaiah 36:3, 22).

REDEEMER, REDEMPTION (ri-DEEM-ur, ri-DEMP-shuhn). The buying back of humanity from sin and death by Christ, who paid the price with His perfect obedience and His sacrificial death on the cross (Romans 3:24; Galatians 3:13; Ephesians 1:7; 1 Peter 1:18-19; 1 Corinthians 6:19-20).

RED SEA. Body of water, 1,350 miles long, extending from the Gulf of Suez to the Indian Ocean. It has two arms: the Gulf of Suez and the Gulf of Aqabah. The name *Red Sea* may refer to either the Gulf of Suez (Numbers 33:10-11), the Gulf of Aqabah (1 Kings 9:26), the entire Red Sea (Exodus 23:31), or nearby lakes. The sea Israel crossed when leaving Israel should be translated as "Reed Sea." It was likely a body of water near Goshen. Many people identify it with the Bitter Lakes.

REED. Tall grasses, flags, or rushes. A reed is used as a picture word for uncertain support, fickleness, and weakness or helplessness (2 Kings 18:21; Isaiah 36:6; 42:3; Matthew 11:7; 12:20; Luke 7:24).

REFINER. Someone who worked with precious metals (Jeremiah 6:29; Malachi 3:2-3). See also *trade.*

REFUGE, CITIES OF. Six Levitical cities designed to provide temporary shelter for those who had accidentally killed someone (Numbers 35:6, 11-32; Deuteronomy 4:43; 19:1-13; Joshua 20). They were Kadesh (Naphtali), Shechem (Ephraim), Hebron (Judah), Golan (Manasseh), Ramoth-gilead (Gad), and Bezer (Reuben). See also *murder.*

REGENERATION (ri-jen-ur-AY-shuhn). To be born again, restored, renewed, completely made over. Regeneration is an act of God the Holy Spirit, who works through Word and Sacrament to bring a sinful, self-centered person into union with Christ Jesus through faith (John 1:13; 3:1-12; 1 Peter 1:23).

REHOBOAM (ree-ho-BO-am, enlarger of people). Son of Solomon and Naamah (1 Kings 14:21, 31; Matthew 1:7). Rehoboam was the last king of the United Kingdom of Israel. When he took over after his father's death, Rehoboam refused to listen to the people and lower their taxes. So the 10 northern tribes rebelled and made Jeroboam their king. Rehoboam became the first king of the Southern Kingdom of Judah, the two remaining tribes (1 Kings 12; 14; 2 Chronicles 10—12). Rehoboam made his kingdom and cities stronger. In the fifth year of Rehoboam's reign, however, King Shishak of Egypt captured the fortified cities of Judah and Jerusalem (1 Kings 14:25-27).

RELIGION. Humanity's recognition of its relationship to a supreme being and the expression of that relationship in faith, worship, and life. Religion may be true or false (Acts 17:22; 26:5; Romans 1:18-25; James 1:26-27).

REMISSION, REMIT. God's gracious forgiveness of sin and the guilt of sin through Christ's sacrificial death on the cross. Remission of sin is offered in Baptism, the Lord's Supper, and the Gospel and is received by grace through faith (Matthew 26:28; Mark 1:4; Luke 1:77; Acts 2:38; 10:43; Hebrews 9:22). The function of remitting and retaining sins is given to the church (John 20:23). See also *forgiveness.*

REMNANT (REM- nuhnt). Something left over. 1. People who survived a period of deep trouble (Joshua 12:4; 13:12).

2. The small number of people that survives God's judgment and remains faithful to Him. Because of God's love for His people, believers will be added from all peoples to form the church (Isaiah 10:20-23; 11:11-12; Jeremiah 32:38-39; Zephaniah 3:13; Zechariah 8:12; Romans 9:27).

REPENTANCE (ri-PEN-tuhns). A total change of heart and life that God works in an individual who does not believe or trust in Him by turning him or her around to one who does believe and trust in Him. Repentance includes both sorrow for one's sins and faith in Christ through whom forgiveness is granted (Jeremiah 31:18-19; Mark 1:4; Luke 3:3, 8; Acts 5:31; 26:29).

REPHIDIM (REF-i-dim). A place between Sin and Sinai where Israel camped (Exodus 17:1; 19:2; Numbers 33:14-15).

RESIN (REE-sen). An Assyrian city built by Nimrod. It was probably a suburb of Nineveh (Genesis 10:11-12).

RESURRECTION (rez-uh-REK-shuhn). A return to life after one has died. Because Christ rose from the dead, believers can be sure they too will rise from the dead and enjoy eternal life with Christ. The Bible describes the resurrected body as a spiritual body (Romans 6:3-11; 1 Corinthians 15). All people, both believers and nonbelievers, will rise from the dead (2 Colossians 5:10).

REUBEN (ROO-ben, see a son). Jacob's firstborn son by his wife Leah (Genesis 29:32). Reuben brought mandrakes to his mother, which she used to get Jacob to make her pregnant so she could have another child (Genesis 30:14-16). Reuben sinned by having sexual relations with his father's concubine (Genesis 35:22; 49:3-4). When his brothers wanted to kill Joseph, Reuben spoke up and suggested that they throw him into a pit instead. Reuben's intention was to release Joseph and let him return home (Genesis 37:22, 29-30).

Many years later when Joseph, whom they did not recognize, asked his brothers to bring Benjamin to Egypt, Reuben assured his father of Benjamin's safety (Genesis 42:36-38).

The tribe of Reuben settled east of the Jordan River, an area suited for raising flocks and herds (Numbers 1:20-21; 3; Joshua 13:15-23). In her song Deborah refers to the Reubenites' lack of help in the battle with Sisera (Judges 5:15-16). A number of years later the Assyrians took the Reubenites away into captivity (1 Chronicles 5:26).

REUBENITES (ROO-ben-ights). Descendants of Reuben (Numbers 26:7; Joshua 1:12).

REUEL (ROO-el, God's friend). One of Esau's sons and the ancestor of the Edomite clan (Genesis 36:4, 10, 13, 17; 1 Chronicles 35:37).

REVELATION (rev-uh-LAY-shuhn). The way in which God makes Himself and His ways known to people. God reveals something of Himself to all people through nature, their consciences, and history. God reveals Himself and His will in a special way to particular people at particular times through visions, phenomena, dreams, angels, words, prophecies, and by appearing in human form (Genesis 16:9; 18:9; 28:12-16; Exodus 3:4; 19:18; Isaiah 6). In particular, God reveals Himself through the Bible and Jesus Christ, the Word made flesh.

REVELATION, BOOK OF. The last book of the New Testament. John wrote Revelation to seven churches in Asia Minor while he was an exile on the island of Patmos (1—3). The book is apocalyptic in nature, that is, it is written in picture language. Its divine message is conveyed through the use of symbols and visions. Dealing with the past, present, and future, the purpose of the book is to prepare people for the great trouble and misery that they will face as God's people.

Date: A.D. 90 to 100

Audience: Seven churches in the Roman province of Western Asia Minor

Outline: 1. Introduction (1:1-8). 2. First three visions: the church and the powers of this world (1:9—11:19). 3. Last four visions: Christ and the powers of darkness (12:1—22:5). 4. Conclusion (22:6-21).

REWARD. Something given in return for something done. Being paid is a reward for work (Luke 10:7; 1 Timothy 5:18). God's punishment is the reward for people's sinfulness (Revelation 22:12; 2 Peter 2:12-15). The Bible also speaks about the reward of grace. Although people do not deserve it, God graciously provides for their salvation through Christ Jesus. Those who believe in Jesus receive life and salvation (Romans 3:27-31; Ephesians 4:8). This new life shows itself in fruits of faith, the way in which God crowns His work in the believer (Matthew 6:4; Mark 9:41; Luke 6:23; 1 Corinthians 3:14; Colossians 3:24).

REZIN (REE-zin). Last king of Damascus. Rezin ruled Syria from 735 to 732 B.C. He aligned his country with Israel against Judah. Tiglath-

Pileser, king of Assyria, besieged Damascus and when he finally captured it, killed Rezin and took his people into captivity (2 Kings 15:37; 16:5, 9; Isaiah 7:1-9; 8:6-8).

RHODA (RO-dah, rose). A young woman who worked in the home of Mary, John Mark's mother. When Peter was miraculously released from prison and went to Mary's home, Rhoda opened the door when he knocked on it (Acts 12:12-15).

RHODES (RODZ, roses). An island at the southwestern tip of Asia Minor that is famous for its huge statue of Helios (Ezekiel 27:15). Rhodes was a center for commerce, literature, and art. Paul stopped there once (Acts 21:1).

RIDDLE (dark or hidden saying). In the Bible a riddle is any saying in which the meaning is not at first clear (Judges 14:12-19; Daniel 8:23). Proverbs, musical meditations, oracles, parables, and hard questions are all riddles (Numbers 12:8; Judges 14:12-19; 1 Kings 10:1; 2 Chronicles 9:1; Psalm 49:4; Proverbs 1:6).

RIGHT HAND. A phrase for describing God's activity in carrying out His purposes (Exodus 15:6; Psalm 98:1). Jesus' session to the right hand of God shows Jesus' power (Acts 2:25; 7:55-56; Hebrews 1:3).

RIGHTEOUS. That which is right (Matthew 27:19; Philippians 1:7) or in accordance with the Law and ceremonies (Mark 2:17; Luke 5:32; Romans 5:7). The term is particularly used to describe people who are in a right relationship with God through faith (Genesis 15:6; Romans 1:17).

RIGHTEOUSNESS (RIGH-chuhsness, the quality of rightness). God is holy and right in His nature because He is God. He makes His righteousness known to people through His work in their behalf (Jeremiah 23:6; Hosea 2:19). He saves them from their earthly and spiritual enemies (Isaiah 40—55).

Jesus is our Righteousnes, the one who puts us in a right relationship to God (Romans 1:16-17; 3:21-26; 1 Corinthians 1:30; 1 Peter 2:24).

RIMMON (RIM-un, thunderer). An Assyrian storm god (2 Kings 5:18).

RING. A piece of jewelry (James 2:2; Luke 15:22). When rings were engraved with the symbol of the owner, they became symbols of power and authority. They were used as seals and signets (Genesis 41:42; Esther 3:10, 12; 8:2, 8, 10; Daniel 6:17).

RIVER. A flowing body of water, such as a stream, a channel, or a brook (Genesis 2:10-14; Psalm 119:136; Ezekiel 32: 6; Amos 6:14). The word *river* is also a picture word for a great deal of good or evil (Job 20:17; Psalm 36:8; 69:2; Isaiah 43:2). See also *Euphrates; Nile.*

ROAD. A path, a well-traveled road, or a highway made by a ruler or by people (Numbers 20:17; 21:22; Deuteronomy 19:3).

The Romans built an elaborate network of roads across their empire. The ones in Palestine were used by traders, armies, and travelers. Some well-known roads were those extending from Jerusalem to Jericho and beyond, from Jerusalem to Joppa, from Damascus to Ptolemais, from Ptolemais to Egypt, and from Galilee to Judea.

ROD. A branch, stick, staff, or shoot. A shepherd's rod was a sturdy club which he used for guiding, defending, and counting his flock (Leviticus 27:32; Psalm 23:4; Ezekiel 20:37).

A rod or shoot is a picture word for the Messianic ruler (Isaiah 11:1). Rod is also a picture word for power and great trouble (Job 9:34; Psalm 2:9).

ROE. See *gazelle; roebuck.*

ROEBUCK. A small deer (Deuteronomy 14:5; 1 Kings 4:23). See also *gazelle.*

ROMAN (RO-mahn). 1. A person who was born in Rome or had Roman citizenship. See *citizen 2.*

2. A Roman official (John 11:48; Acts 28:17).

ROMAN EMPIRE. See *Rome.*

ROMANS, LETTER OF PAUL TO. A letter Paul wrote from Greece to the Romans, whom he planned to visit (Acts 20:2, 3; Romans 1:1, 10, 11; 15:14-33). In this letter, Paul explains the Gospel in detail, describing the righteousness of God which justifies sinful humanity by grace through faith.

　Date: A.D. 56

　Audience: Christians at Rome

　Outline: 1. Introduction (1:1-15). 2. Sinfulness of humanity (1:16—3:31). 3. Justification through redemption in Christ (4—8). 4. Gospel creates new Israel out of Jew and Gentile (9—11:36). 5. Justification and Christian life (12:1—15:13). 6. Paul's plans, greetings, and warning (15:14—16).

ROME (ROM). The capital of the Roman Empire, situated on the Tiber River in Italy about 17 miles from the Mediterranean Sea. Rome was founded in 753 B.C. From 753 to 509 B.C., it was a monarchy; from 509 to 531 B.C., a republic; and from 31 B.C. until its fall, an empire.

The Roman Empire extended

over the whole Mediterranean world, providing a large network of roads, peace, trade, and a common government. This aided in the spread of the Gospel.

Under Augustus, the provinces of the empire were divided into senatorial provinces ruled by a proconsul (Acts 13:7; 18:12; 19:38) and imperial provinces ruled by a governor (Matthew 27:2; Luke 2:2; Acts 23:24).

Under Roman rule, cities, reservoirs, aqueducts, roads, and public buildings were constructed in Palestine. The Bible refers to four emperors: Augustus (Luke 2:1), Tiberius (Luke 3:1), Claudius (Acts 11:28), and Nero (Acts 25:11-12).

ROSE. Many authorities believe roses grew in Palestine during Bible times. The identity of the flower mentioned in Song of Solomon 2:1 and Isaiah 35:1, however, is unknown.

RUE (RU). A plant grown for its use in medicine and seasonings (Luke 11:42).

RUFUS (RU-fuhs, red). Son of Simon of Cyrene (Mark 15:21). The Rufus mentioned in Romans 16:13 may be the same person.

RUHAMAH (roo-HAH-mah). Hosea's daughter. Her name means "she has received mercy" (Hosea 2:1, see also Romans 9:25; 1 Peter 2:10). See also *Lo-ruhamah*.

RUSH. See *reed; papyrus.*

RUTH (ROOTH, may mean friendship). A woman from Moab who married Mahlon, a son of Elimelech and Naomi. When both Ruth and Naomi's husbands died, Ruth decided to return to Judah with Naomi. She told Naomi: "Where you go I will go, and where you lodge I will lodge; your people shall be my people and your God my God" (Ruth 1:16). Ruth married Boaz and became the mother of Obed, an ancestor of both David and Jesus (Ruth; Matthew 1:5).

RUTH, BOOK OF. One of the books in the division of the Old Testament known as the Writings. This book tells the story of Ruth, the woman from Moab who became the ancestor of David and Christ (Ruth; Matthew 1:5).

Date: 900 to 700 B.C.

Audience: People of Israel and Gentiles

Outline: 1. Ruth comes to live in Bethlehem (1). 2. Ruth meets her future husband (2). 3. Ruth becomes Boaz's wife (3—4:17). 4. Ruth becomes David's ancestor (4:18-21).

S

SABAOTH (SAB-ay-ahth, hosts). A Hebrew name for God that means Lord of hosts. See *host 2*.

SABBATH (SAB-ahth, rest; cessation). The weekly day of rest corresponding to the seventh day upon which God rested after creation (Genesis 2:3; Exodus 20:11; 31:17). The first time the Sabbath is mentioned by name occurs at the time when a double amount of manna was given on the sixth day to the people of Israel in the Wilderness of Sin. When they told Moses what had happened, he said: "This is what the Lord has commanded: 'Tomorrow is a day of solemn rest, a holy Sabbath to the Lord' " (Exodus 16:23). The command to keep the Sabbath holy was repeated on a number of occasions (Exodus 20:8-11; Leviticus 19:3, 30; 23:3; Deuteronomy 5:12-15).

The people observed the Sabbath by stopping their work, by gathering together for worship, and by increasing their offerings (Exodus 16:29; 20:10; 35:3; Numbers 15:32-36; 28:9-10; Amos 8:5). The penalty for not observing the Sabbath was death (Exodus 31:15).

The Day of Atonement on the 10th day of the seventh month was also a Sabbath (Leviticus 23:32).

The Sabbath day is a picture for the believer's entrance into God's rest fulfilled in Christ (Colossians 2:16; Hebrews 4).

SABBATH DAY'S JOURNEY. See *measures 1I*.

SABBATICAL YEAR (sa-BAT-i-kuhl yeer). Every seven years the Jewish people observed the Sabbatical year. During this year the land rested, the poor received what grew, and people in debt were released from what they owed (Exodus 23:10-11; Leviticus 25:2-7; Deuteronomy 15:1-18).

SABEANS (sah-BEE-uhnz). Semitic people who lived in southwest Arabia. The Sabeans or people of Sheba ran caravans in the Middle East. The Bible describes them as murderous bandits and slave dealers (Job 1:15; Joel 3:8). The queen of Sheba who visited Solomon was queen of the Sabeans (1 Kings 10; 2 Chronicles 9; Matthew 12:42; Luke 11:31).

SACKCLOTH. Coarse cloth made out of goat's hair and woven into sacks (Genesis 42:25). People wore sackcloth to mourn a death (Genesis 37:34; 2 Samuel 3:31; 2 Kings 6:30; Nehemiah 9:1; Job 16:15; Matthew 11:21; Revelation 11:3).

SACRAMENT (SAK-rah-ment). A word the church uses to describe a sacred act instituted by God where there are visible means connected to His Word. In a sacrament God offers, gives, and seals to the individual the forgiveness of sins earned by Christ. See *Baptism; Lord's Supper*.

SACRIFICE (SAK-ruh-fighs). An act of worship where a person presents an offering to God. Sacrifices were practiced from ancient times and expressed thankfulness to God (Genesis 4:3-4; 8:20-22). They were offered on many occasions, for example, on a pilgrimage, at a time of rejoicing, when making a treaty, before battle, and after God had appeared to an individual (Genesis 12:7; 31:54; 1 Samuel 1:3; 7:9; 20:6).

Sacrifices were offered for various purposes. Among the main ones mentioned in the Old Testament are the sin offering (Leviticus 4), the trespass offering (Leviticus 5:15—6:7; 14:12; Numbers 6:12), the burnt offering (Leviticus 1; 6:8-13), the peace offering (Leviticus 7:11-34), the meal and drink offerings (Leviticus 5:11-12; 6), and the red heifer offering (Numbers 19). Offerings were sacrificed upon the altar morning and evening, at each Sabbath and new moon, and at the three leading festivals (Exodus 29:38-42; Numbers 28—29).

All sacrifices point to and are fulfilled in Christ, the Lamb of God sacrificed for the sins of the world (Hebrews 9:10-28).

SADDUCEES (SAD-yoo-seez). One of the three leading Jewish religious parties at the time of Christ. Although a small group, they were influential. Unlike the Pharisees, the Sadducees believed only what was in the written law; they were opposed to tradition and denied belief in the resurrection, angels, and spirits (Mark 12:18; Luke 20:27; Acts 23:8). They stressed moral freedom. Both John the Baptizer and Jesus spoke against them (Matthew 3:7-8; 16:6, 11-12).

SAINT. 1. Those faithful to God in the Old Testament are called saints (2 Chronicles 6:41).

2. People, such as priests, who were set apart for God's service (Psalm 106:16; 1 Peter 2:5).

3. Members of the Jerusalem congregation (Acts 9:13; 1 Corinthians 16:1).

4. Those who believe in Christ (Romans 1:7; 1 Corinthians 1:2; 2 Corinthians 1:1).

SAKKUTH (SAK-uth). A false god worshiped by Israel (Amos 5:26).

SALAMIS (SAL-ah-mis). A city on Cyprus that Paul visited on his first missionary journey (Acts 13:5).

SALEM (SAY-lem, peace). The city of which Melchizedek was king. It

was probably Jerusalem (Genesis 14:18; Psalm 76:2; Hebrews 7:1-2).

SALMON (SAL-muhn). The father of Boaz (Ruth 4:21; Matthew 1:4; Luke 3:32).

SALOME (sah-LO-mi, of Solomon). 1. The wife of Zebedee and mother of James and John (Mark 15:40). Salome was among the women who witnessed the crucifixion of Jesus (Matthew 27:56). Later she anointed His body for burial (Mark 16:1).

2. The daughter of Herodias. Salome's dancing pleased Herod so much that he granted her request for the head of John the Baptizer (Matthew 14:6; Mark 6:22).

SALT. Salt was used as a seasoning and preservative and for sacrifices (Leviticus 2:13; Numbers 18:19; Job 6:6; Isaiah 30:24; Matthew 5:13).

Lot's wife was turned to salt (Genesis 19:26). The site of Shechem was sown with salt to keep it from producing vegetation (Judges 9:45; Ezekiel 47:11). The disciples of Christ are called the salt of the earth (Matthew 5:13; Mark 9:50; Luke 14:34).

SALT SEA. The name given to the Dead Sea because of its high salt content. Fed by the Jordan River, the Salt Sea is 46 x 9 1/2 miles long, 1,292 feet below sea level, and 1,300 feet deep. Since there is no outlet, the water is bitter and buoyant (Genesis 14:3; Numbers 34:3; Joshua 15:2). It is called by various names: Sea of Arabah (Joshua 3:16; 12:3), East Sea (Ezekiel 47:18; Joel 2:20), Sea (Ezekiel 47:8), and Former or Eastern Sea (Zechariah 14:8).

SALVATION (sal-VAY-shuhn). Deliverance from any type of evil, both physical and spiritual (Exodus 14:13, 30; Deuteronomy 28:29; Job 22:29; Isaiah 49:25). Spiritual deliverance or salvation includes rescue from sin (Matthew 1:21; Acts 4:12; Hebrews 2:10), death (Romans 6:9; 8:2; 1 Corinthians 15:54-57), evil (Galatians 1:4; 2 Timothy 4:18), and the power of darkness (Colossians 1:13). It is a gift of God's grace through faith in Christ (Acts 16:31; Romans 5:1) and marks the entrance into spiritual, eternal life (John 5:24; Colossians 3:9-10).

SALVE. See *ointment.*

SAMARIA (sah-MAIR-i-ah, watch-mountain). 1. The capital city of the Northern Kingdom of Israel. It was built by Omri on a tableland five and a half miles northwest of Shechem. Samaria is repeatedly rebuked for its luxury and evil ways (1 Kings 17—19; 21; 2 Kings 3:3-9; Isaiah 7:9; Jeremiah 31:5; Ezekiel 23:33; Hosea 8:5-6; Amos 3:1-12). Today it is called Sebastiyeh.

2. The entire area occupied by the Northern Kingdom of Israel, or the Ten Tribes (1 Kings 13:32).

3. The region where the Samaritans lived after they returned from captivity. See also *Samaritans.*

SAMARIA, MOUNTAINS OF. See *Ephraim, Mount.*

SAMARITANS (sah-MAR-uh-tuhns). In 2 Kings 17:29 a Samaritan refers to a person belonging to the Ten Tribes, or the old Northern Kingdom of Israel. Later Samaritans included a small leftover group of Jewish people who returned to Samaria after the captivity along with peoples from Babylonia, Syria, Elam, and other Assyrian lands (2 Kings 17:24-34). Since all these people intermingled, they were despised by their Jewish neighbors to the south (Nehemiah 4:1-3; Matthew 10:5; John 4:9-26; 8:48).

SAMOS (SAY-mahs, height). A mountainous island off the coast of Lydia. Paul stopped at Samos on his third missionary journey (Acts 20:15).

SAMOTHRACE, SAMOTHRA-CIA (SAM-o-thrays, sam-o-THRAY-shah). An island between Troas and Neapolis where Paul and his party spent the night on their voyage to Macedonia (Acts 16:11).

SAMSON (SAM-s'n, sunlike). A judge of Israel for 20 years. He was the son of Minoah from the tribe of Dan and a Nazirite from birth. Samson married a Philistine woman named Timnath. But later, when Timnath's father gave her to another, Samson burned the Philistine fields in revenge. Then the Philistines tried to capture him, but Samson broke the ropes binding him and, taking a donkey's jawbone, killed 1,000 Philistine men. Samson also performed great feats of strength. On one occasion he carried the heavy gates and two posts of the city of Gaza to the top of the hill that is before Hebron.

Samson fell in love with a Philistine woman named Delilah. She tricked him into telling her the source of his strength and then betrayed him into the hands of her countrymen. They cut off Samson's hair, blinded him, and put him to work grinding in the mill at the prison of Gaza.

On one occasion when the Philistines were making public sacrifice to their god Dagon, they called for Samson to make sport of him. Since his hair was beginning to grow, Samson was again fulfilling his Nazirite vow. He prayed to God, asking Him for strength one more time. Then Samson pushed against the pillars that supported the roof and brought the whole temple to Dagon down, killing himself and about 3,000 Philistines who were present (Judges 13—16; Hebrews 11:32).

SAMUEL (SAM-yoo-uhl, God has heard). Samuel is often referred to as the last of the judges and the first of the prophets after Moses (1 Samuel 3:20; 7:6; Acts 3:24). He was a Levite, the son of Elkanah and Hannah (1 Samuel 1:19-20). When he was still young, Samuel's mother brought him to Eli the priest, who educated Samuel and took care of him (1 Samuel 3).

Samuel anointed both Saul and David as kings of Israel (1 Samuel 10; 16:13). When Samuel died, all Israel mourned for him; the people buried him in Ramah, his home city (1 Samuel 25:1).

SAMUEL, FIRST AND SECOND BOOK OF. Two historical books of the Old Testament that tell the history of Israel from the time of Eli to David's old age. Although these books are named for Samuel, he was not their author (1 Samuel 25:1; 28:3).

Date: About 930 B.C.

Audience: Israelites

Outline: 1. Samuel as judge (1 Samuel 1—7). 2. Saul as king (1 Samuel 8—2 Samuel 1). 3. David as king (2 Samuel 2—24).

SANBALLAT (san-BAL-uht, Sin [the moon-god] has given life). A Persian officer who tried to defeat Nehemiah's plans for rebuilding the walls of Jerusalem (Nehemiah 2:10; 4:1-9; 6:1-14; 13:28).

SANCTIFICATION (sangk-tuh-fi-KAY-shuhn). The Hebrew word for sanctification means separation from the world and that which is sinful and consecration to a sacred purpose by the Lord (Exodus 31:13; 1 Chronicles 15:14; 2 Chronicles 5:11; 29:15).

In the wide sense the Greek word for sanctification includes the entire process of God's grace whereby spiritually dead people, through the work of the Holy Spirit in the Word and Sacrament, are reborn to spiritual life and made perfect in life eternal (Acts 26:18; Ephesians 5:26; 2 Thessalonians 2:13; Hebrews

10:14).

In the narrower sense, sanctification is the spiritual growth, worked by God the Holy Spirit, that follows after a person has come to faith in Christ; it does not include justification itself (Romans 6:15-23; Galatians 5:22-23; Philippians 2:13; 2 Peter 3:18).

SANCTUARY (SANGK-tyoo-er-ee). A holy place set aside for the worship of God. The sanctuary was the earthly place where God chose to dwell among His people. The Promised Land, the tabernacle, the whole temple, and particularly the Holy of Holies in the tabernacle and temple are called sanctuaries (Exodus 15:17; Leviticus 4:6; 1 Kings 6:16; 2 Chronicles 20:8). Judah is also God's sanctuary (Psalm 114:2).

The author of the Letter to the Hebrews explains that the earthly sanctuary was only a type of the true sanctuary—access to God made possible through Christ, the believer's High Priest (Hebrews 8:1-5; 9:1-8).

SANHEDRIN (SAN-hi-drin, council). The highest Jewish court during the Greek and Roman periods for enforcing Mosaic law. Often referred to as the council, it was made up of the high priest, elders, and scribes, the maximum number being 71. The high priest was in charge of the Sanhedrin. During Jesus' time, this council had jurisdiction over Palestine (Matthew 5:22; 26:59; Mark 14:55; 15:1; Luke 22:66; John 11:47; Acts 4:15; 6:12).

SAPPHIRA (sa-FIGH-rah, beautiful). The wife of Ananias. Within a period of a few hours, both she and her husband fell dead at Peter's feet because they had lied (Acts 5:7-10).

SARAH (SAIR-ah, princess). The wife of Abraham and mother of Isaac (Genesis 11:29; 21:2-3). Her given name was Sarai, but God changed it to Sarah (Genesis 17:15-

16). When Sarah's maid, Hagar, became pregnant with Abraham's child, she began to think she was better than Sarah. Sarah, in turn, treated Hagar cruelly and sent her away (Genesis 16:5-16; 21:9-21).

When Sarah was 90, God kept His promise to her and Abraham and blessed them with a son, Isaac. Sarah lived 127 years. After she died, Abraham buried her at Machpelah (Genesis 23). The writer of Hebrews praises Sarah for her great faith (Hebrews 11:11). See also *Abraham.*

SARAI. See *Sarah.*

SARDIS (SAHR-dis). One of the seven churches to which the Book of Revelation is addressed (Revelation 1:11; 3:1-6). Sardis was a city of western Asia Minor located about 50 miles east of Smyrna. It was known for its manufacture of textiles, gold jewelry, and minted coins. Sardis was also a patron of the mystery cults.

SARGON II (SAHR-gahn). One of the kings of Assyria. He was born in 772 B.C. and died in 705 B.C. In 722 B.C. he took over the throne from his brother Shalmaneser V and completed the conquest of Samaria begun by Shalmaneser (2 Kings 17:5; Isaiah 20:1).

Sennacherib, Sargon's son, succeeded Sargon to the throne.

SATAN (SAY-tahn, adversary). 1. When used as a common noun, the word *Satan* refers to an enemy or opponent (1 Samuel 29:4; 1 Kings 5:4; 11:14; Psalm 17:13; 38:20).

2. When the Scriptures use *Satan* as a proper noun, they are referring to the chief of the fallen angels, beings of great power (Matthew 8:28-29; 9:34; Luke 11:18). Satan is the enemy of God, humanity, and all that is good (Job 1:6, 12; 2:1; Zechariah 3:1).

Satan is named and described in other ways. He is called an enemy

(Matthew 13:39; 1 Peter 5:8), a murderer and liar (John 8:44), Abaddon, or Apollyon, the angel of the bottomless pit (Revelation 9:11), Beelzebul (Matthew 12:27), Belial (2 Corinthians 6:15), the devil (Matthew 25:41; 1 Peter 5:8), the dragon (Revelation 12), the evil, or wicked, one (Ephesians 6:16; 1 John 2:13), the prince of this world (John 6:11), the prince of power of the air (Ephesians 2:2), and a serpent (Revelation 12:9).

SATRAP (SAY-trap). An official person in the Persian Empire who was sent by the Persian king to rule several small provinces that had a combined government. These provinces were called satrapies, and the satrap had complete civil and military control over them.

SAUL (SAWL, asked). The first king of Israel. Saul was the son of Kish and came from the tribe of Benjamin (1 Samuel 8—9). Samuel anointed him to be king of Israel, and then later, after Samuel had brought all the tribes of Israel together, the people chose Saul by lot to be their king (1 Samuel 9:27; 10:1-13, 17-27). Under Saul's leadership, the Israelites defeated the Ammonites, Philistines, Moabites, Zobah, and Amalekites (1 Samuel 11—14).

When Saul disobeyed by offering the burnt offering himself rather than waiting for Samuel to do it, Samuel rejected him as the one from whom the kingdom of Israel would be established (1 Samuel 13:1-14). As Saul's power declined and David's popularity grew, Saul became jealous of David (1 Samuel 16—31). In a battle between the Israelites and Philistines, Saul was seriously wounded and killed himself by falling on his own sword (1 Samuel 31).

SAVIOR (SAYV-yur). 1. One who saves from danger or evil (2 Kings

13:5).

2. In Psalm 106:21 God is referred to as Israel's Savior. Jesus is called our Savior (Luke 2:11; John 4:42; 1 Timothy 1:1; 2 Peter 1:1). See also *Jesus Christ; salvation.*

SAW. See *trade.*

SCAB. See *disease.*

SCALES. See *disease; weight.*

SCAPEGOAT. See *Azazel.*

SCHISM (SIZ'm). See *heresy.*

SCOURGING (SKURJ-ing). 1. Severe punishment with a whip of cords or thongs (Joshua 23:13; Matthew 23:34; 27:26; Mark 15:15; John 19:1; Hebrews 11:36). A person could be whipped no more than 40 times (2 Corinthians 11:24). It was unlawful to scourge a Roman citizen (Acts 22:24-25).

2. Some great trouble or plague or a tongue lashing (Job 5:21; 9:23; Psalm 91:10; Isaiah 10:26).

SCRIBE. A person who copied records, books, and the like before printing presses were invented. In Jewish times scribes served as recorders, secretaries, and clerks (1 Chronicles 24:6; 27:32).

After the exile, scribes faithfully copied the Scriptures to preserve them for future generations. They became interpreters of the Law and powerful leaders in Israel (Ezra 7:6, 11; Nehemiah 8:1-13; 13:13; Matthew 16:21; 26:3; Acts 4:5).

SCRIPTURE. Something that is written down. The Old Testament and New Testament of the Bible are called Scripture.

SCROLL. A book made of sheets of skins, papyrus, or parchment sewn together to make a strip about 11 inches wide and many feet long. These sheets were rolled on sticks to make a book, a roll, or a scroll (Isaiah 34:4; Jeremiah 36; Ezekiel 3:1-3; Revelation 5; 10:1-10).

SCROLLS, DEAD SEA. Very old manuscripts first found in A.D. 1947 in caves around the Dead Sea. These manuscripts contained parts of the Old Testament, commentaries, and other writings.

SCURVY. See *disease.*

SEA. A large, deep body of water (Genesis 1:26; Exodus 10:19; Deuteronomy 30:13; Job 12:8). See also *Galilee, Sea of; Mediterranean Sea; Merom; Red Sea; Salt Sea.*

SEAL. A stamp or a ring with a raised design on it that was used to make an impression on something. People in authority used seals to secure or authenticate various items (Job 38:14). At the request of some Pharisees, Pilate sealed Jesus' tomb so that His disciples could not break into it and take His body without someone knowing about it (Matthew 27:66).

SECOND COMING OF CHRIST. See *advent of Christ 3; eschatology; Parousia.*

SECT (SEKT). A religious party that has its own set of beliefs. The Pharisees (Acts 15:5) and the Sadducees (Acts 5:17) were two sects of Judaism in Jesus' day. Some of the people in early New Testament times referred to Christians as a sect of the Nazarene (Acts 24:5, 14).

SEER (SEE-ur). See *prophet*.

SELAH (SEE-lah, may mean lift up). This word is often found in the Psalms (Psalm 9:16) as well as in Habakkuk 3:3, 9, 13. The meaning of the word is uncertain, although it may be an instruction for singers or musicians.

SELEUCIA (si-LYOO-shi-ah). A seaport of Syrian Antioch about 16 miles west of Antioch. It was founded by Seleucus Nicator. Paul and Barnabas sailed from Seleucia on their first missionary journey (Acts 13:4).

SENATE. See *Sanhedrin*.

SENNACHERIB (suh-NAK-ur-ib, Sin, the moon-god, has increased brothers). The son of Sargon II and the king who ruled Assyria from 705 to 681 B.C. After taking over the throne, Sennacherib dealt with revolts throughout his empire and extended the conquered territories of Assyria as far as the Mediterranean. During Hezekiah's reign, he invaded Judah. The Lord, however, saved Jerusalem by sending His angel to strike down the Assyrian army, forcing Sennacherib to return home (2 Kings 18—19; Isaiah 36—37).

In his annals Sennacherib describes his victories in Judah.

SEORIM (si-O-rim). The head of the fourth division of priests (1 Chronicles 24:8).

SEPHARVAIM (sef-ahr-VAY-im). A place near Riblah. The Assyrians brought people from Sepharvaim to colonize Samaria (2 Kings 17:24-34; 18:34; 19:13; Isaiah 37:13).

SEPTUAGINT (SEP-tyoo-ah-jint). The Greek translation of the Old Testament, prepared at Alexandria, Egypt, in the third century B.C. The abbreviation for this translation is LXX, which means 70.

SEPULCHER, SEPULCHRE (SEP-uhl-kur). See *burial*.

SERAIAH (si-RAY-yah, soldier of Lord). 1. One of the men sent to arrest Jeremiah and Baruch (Jeremiah 36:26).

2. A prince who was taken captive to Babylon when Jerusalem fell (Jeremiah 51:59-64).

SERAPHIM (SER-ah-fim). An order of angels. Isaiah saw seraphim standing around God's throne (Isaiah 6:2-7).

SERGIUS PAULUS (SUR-ji-uhs PAWL-uhls). The Roman proconsul of Cyprus, a senatorial province in Paul's time (Acts 13:7-12).

SERPENT. A snake, a creature that creeps on its belly (Genesis 3:14). A number of serpents are mentioned in the Bible, for instance, the asp or perhaps cobra (Deuteronomy 32:33), the adder (Genesis 49:17), and the viper (Job 20:16).

Serpents are a symbol of evil, great harmfulness, and poison (Genesis 49:17; Psalm 58:4; Proverbs 23:32; Matthew 23:33). They are described as subtle and wise (Genesis 3:1; Matthew 10:16). A serpent deceived Eve (Genesis 3). The bronze serpent Moses attached to the top of a pole when the Children of Israel were in the wilderness was a type of Christ (Numbers 21:4-9; John 3:14). When an Israelite who had been bitten by a real snake looked at the bronze serpent, he or she was healed.

SERUG (SEE-rug, branch). Father of Nahor and ancestor of Abraham (Genesis 11:20, 23; 1 Chronicles 1:26; Luke 3:35).

SERVANT. A general term used of both slaves and persons who worked for wages. The Israelites acquired slaves through purchase and war (Leviticus 25:44-45; Numbers 31:25-47). When slaves had children, their children also were slaves (Genesis 14:14; Ecclesiastes 2:7).

Israelites became slaves through poverty, theft, and birth (Exodus 21:1-11; 22:3; Leviticus 25:39, 47; 2 Kings 4:1). Old Testament laws protected servants (Exodus 20:10; Leviticus 25:55). Often they were treated as members of the household (Genesis 24; 30; 32:16; 1 Samuel 9:5, 8).

In New Testament times it was common practice for people to have slaves and servants (Mark 1:20; 14:66; John 18:10-18; Acts 12:13-15). Jesus was kind to servants (Matthew 8:5-13), often referring to them in His parables (Matthew 18:23-35; 24:45-51; Mark 13:34-37; Luke 20:9-16).

The New Testament stresses that faith in Christ removes the barrier between master and servant (Galatians 3:28; Philemon).

SERVANT OF THE LORD, OF CHRIST, OF THE CHURCH. 1. Any agent of the Lord, such as Abraham, Moses, and the prophets (Exodus 4:10; Psalm 105:42; Zechariah 1:6). Chiefly, however, the term is used as a title for Christ (Romans 1:1; 2 Corinthians 11:23; Colossians 4:12; Titus 1:1; 2 Peter 1:1; Revelation 1:1).

2. Ministers in the church (Colossians 4:7; 1 Thessalonians 3:2).

SERVANT, SUFFERING. Jesus is the fulfillment (Matthew 12:18; Luke 22:37) of the suffering servant spoken about in the Old Testament (Isaiah 42:1-4; 52:13—53:12).

SETH (SETH). 1. The third son of Adam and Eve (Genesis 4:25-26; 5:3-8; 1 Chronicles 1:1; Luke 3:38).

SEVEN. A number the Scriptures use symbolically for plenty or completeness (Genesis 4:15, 24; Matthew 18:21-22).

Seven can mean seven or another number rounded off to seven (1 Samuel 2:5; Matthew 12:45). Often seven and multiples of seven are used for religious cycles (Genesis

2:2). See also *Jubilee; numbers; Sabbath.*

SEVENTY, THE. Disciples sent on a special mission by Jesus (Luke 10).

SHABBETHAI (SHAB-i-thigh, of the Sabbath). A Levite during Ezra's time who favored the position that the Israelites should divorce their foreign wives. Shabbethai also played a chief role in rebuilding the temple and reading the law (Nehemiah 8:7).

SHADRACH (SHAY-drak). The Babylonian name given to Hananiah, one of Daniel's three friends (Daniel 1:7). Shadrach was thrown into the fiery furnace for refusing to worship the statue that King Nebuchadnezzar had set up (Daniel 3).

SHADES (silent ones). The dead in Sheol (Job 26:5; Psalm 88:10; Proverbs 2:18; 9:18).

SHALLECHETH (SHAL-i-keth, casting out). The west gate of the temple (1 Chronicles 26:16).

SHALLUM (SHAL-uhm, pacified). 1. The 15th king of Israel. After killing Zechariah, Shallum ruled for one month and then was killed himself by Menahem (2 Kings 15:10-15).

2. The son of Zadok, a high priest, and an ancestor of Ezra (1 Chronicles 6:12-13; Ezra 7:2). In 1 Chronicles 9:11 and Nehemiah 11:11 he is referred to as Meshullam.

3. Husband of the prophetess Hulda (2 Kings 22:14; 2 Chronicles 34:22). He was probably Jeremiah's uncle (Jeremiah 32:7).

4. Another name for Jehoahaz II, the son of Josiah. He was king of Judah (1 Chronicles 3:15; Jeremiah 22:11).

5. A ruler of half of Jerusalem who, with his daughters, helped repair the walls of Jerusalem (Nehemiah 3:12).

SHALMAN (SHAL-muhn). See *Shalmaneser 2.*

SHALMANESER (shal-muhn-EE-zur). The title of a number of Assyrian kings. 1. Shalmaneser III, the first Assyrian king to come into conflict with the Israelites, ruled Assyria from 859 to 824 B.C. He conquered the Hittites as far as the Mediterranean. The Syrian league was formed to stop him in the west. Among others, Ben-hadad of Damascus and Ahab of Israel opposed him. Nevertheless, Shalmaneser defeated Hazael, Ben-hadad's successor, and made Israel pay tribute.
2. Shalmaneser V was the king of Assyria from 727 to 722 B.C. He besieged Samaria. The city likely fell to him shortly before his death, or it may have fallen to his successor, Sargon. After the fall of Samaria, the 10 northern tribes were carried into captivity (2 Kings 17:3; 18:9). In Hosea 10:14, Shalmaneser is referred to as Shalman.

SHAMGAR (SHAM-gahr). The son of Anath. Over a period of time he killed 600 Philistines with an ox-goad, preparing the way for the deliverance of Israel by Deborah and Barak (Judges 3:31).

SHAMMUA, SHAMMUAH (sha-MYOO-ah, fame). 1. A Reubenite spy (Numbers 13:4).
2. A son of David and Bathsheba (2 Samuel 5:14; 1 Chronicles 14:4). In 1 Chronicles 3:5 he is referred to as Shimea.

SHAPHAN (SHAY-fan, rock badger). A scribe and secretary during Josiah's reign. When the book of the Law was found, Shaphan first read it privately and then took it to King Josiah (2 Kings 22:8-10). After hearing its contents, Josiah sent Shaphan, along with some others, to ask Huldah the prophetess what it meant (2 Kings 22:14-20).

SHAPHAT (SHAY-fat, he has judged). The father of the prophet

Elisha (1 Kings 19:16; 2 Kings 3:11).

SHAREZER (shah-REE-zur, protect king). The son and murderer of Sennacherib, the Assyrian king (2 Kings 19:37; Isaiah 37:38).

SHARON (SHAIR-uhn, plain). 1. A coastal plain between Joppa and Carmel. It was about 50 miles long and 6 to 12 miles wide (1 Chronicles 27:29; Isaiah 33:9; 35:2; Acts 9:35).

SHAVEH (SHAY-ve, plain). A place, probably near Jerusalem, where Melchizedek met Abraham (Genesis 14:17).

SHAVSHA (SHAV-shah). One of David and Solomon's scribes (1 Chronicles 18:16). He is probably the same person as the secretary Seraiah, the secretary Sheva, and the secretary Shisha (2 Samuel 8:17; 20:25; 1 Kings 4:3).

SHEALTIEL (shi-AL-ti-el, I have asked God). A son of Jeconiah, or Jehoiachin, or possibly of Neri (1 Chronicles 3:17; Matthew 1:12; Luke 3:27). Shealtiel was probably the legitimate successor of Jehoiachin, and when Shealtiel died, the right to the throne passed to Zerubbabel (Ezra 3:2; 1 Chronicles 3:17-19).

SHEAR-JASHUB (SHEE-ahr-JAH-shub, remnant shall return). A symbolical name Isaiah gave to his son (Isaiah 7:3).

SHEBNA, SHEBNAH (SHEB-nah, tenderness). King Hezekiah's secretary and the steward of his house. Isaiah rebuked him (2 Kings 18:18-26, 37; 19:2; Isaiah 22:15-25; 36:3, 11, 22; 37:2).

SHECHEM (SHEE-chem, shoulder). 1. A town in the hill country of Ephraim in the pass between Mount Ebal and Mount Gerizim. Shechem was a Levitical city of refuge (Genesis 12:6; 35:4; Joshua 20:7; Judges 9:7; Acts 7:16).
Shechem was the first place Abraham camped after leaving

Haran. Although the Canaanites were in the land at that time, the Lord appeared to Abraham and told him He would give the land to Abraham's descendants (Genesis 12:6-7). Later, Jacob bought ground at Shechem, and Joseph was eventually buried there (Genesis 33:18-20; Joshua 24:32). Today it is the site of Tell Balatah, located near Neapolis and Nablus.

SHEEP. Sheep were domesticated early (Genesis 4:2). The patriarchs and their descendants herded flocks of these animals (Genesis 12:16; Exodus 10:9; 1 Chronicles 27:31). Sheep were valuable property, since they were a source of food, clothing, and tribute (Leviticus 13:47; 1 Samuel 14:32; 2 Kings 3:4). They were also used as sacrifices in worship (Exodus 20:24; Leviticus 9:3). The sheep's horns were used for trumpets and as containers for liquids (Joshua 6:4; 1 Samuel 16:1). Sheep-shearing time was an occasion for great festivity (1 Samuel 25:4, 11, 36).

Sheep and shepherds are often used in a figurative way in the the Bible (2 Chronicles 18:16; Psalm 23; 119:176; Matthew 9:36; John 10).

SHEEPFOLD. An enclosure where sheep were kept, especially at night, for protection and when they were to be sheared (Numbers 32:16; Judges 5:16; 1 Samuel 24:3; Psalm 78:70; John 10:1).

SHEEP GATE. One of the gates of Jerusalem (Nehemiah 3:1, 32; 12:39).

SHEKEL (SHEK-uhl, weight). 1. A weight used for metals. It weighed about half an ounce (Exodus 30:13; 2 Samuel 14:26).
2. A coin (Matthew 17:27).

SHEM (SHEM). One of Noah's sons (Genesis 5:32; 10:1; Luke 3:36). Shem received a blessing from God:

from his line of descent would come the chosen people (Genesis 9:21-27). Shem is the ancestor of the Hebrews, the Aramaeans, and the Arabs.

SHEMAIAH (shi-MAY-yah, Lord has heard). 1. One of God's prophets. Shemaiah told Rehoboam, king of Judah, not to attempt regaining control of the 10 northern tribes of Israel, which had revolted (1 Kings 12:22; 2 Chronicles 11:2; 12:5, 7, 15).
2. The father of the prophet Uriah (Jeremiah 26:20).
3. A false prophet among the exiles in Babylonia who opposed Jeremiah (Jeremiah 29:24-32).
4. One of the men Ezra sent to Iddo to ask for Levites and temple ministers (Ezra 8:16).

SHEMER (SHEE-mur, guardian). A person who owned a hill in Samaria that Omri, king of Israel, bought (1 Kings 16:24).

SHEMINITH (SHEM-i-ninth, eighth). A musical term. It may refer to an octave, a scale, or the strings of an instrument (1 Chronicles 15:21; titles of Psalms 6 and 12).

SHEMUEL (shi-MYOO-uhl, heard of God). The Hebrew version of the name Samuel. Various people in the Old Testament are named Shemuel, among them, the prophet Samuel (1 Chronicles 6:33).

SHENAZAR, SHENAZZAR (shi-NAY-zahr, shi-NAZ-ur, Sin [the moon-god] protect). A son of Jehoiachin (Jeconiah), who was likely born in captivity (1 Chronicles 3:18).

SHEOL (SHEE-ol, perhaps meaning dig or ask). 1. The Old Testament name for the place where people go when they have died. It is translated in a number of ways, for instance, as grave and as the realm of the dead, a place full of darkness where the dead are (Deuteronomy 32:22;

Job 7:9; 17:16; 11:8; Psalm 89:48; Isaiah 38:10).

2. The people who are in Sheol (Isaiah 14:9). See also *eschatology; eternal life; Gehenna; Hades; hell.*

SHEPHATIAH (shef-ah-TIGH-ah, Lord has judged). 1. One of David's sons (2 Samuel 3:4; 1 Chronicles 3:3).

2. A prince who was among those who advised Zedekiah to put the prophet Jeremiah to death (Jeremiah 38).

SHEPHELAH, THE (shi-FEE-lah, low). The land between the central highlands of Palestine and the Mediterranean plain (1 Kings 10:27; 1 Chronicles 27:28; 2 Chronicles 1:15; 9:27; 26:10; Jeremiah 17:26; 32:44; Obadiah 19).

SHEPHERD. A person who makes his living by looking after sheep. The shepherd was an important person in Bible times (Genesis 29:6-7; 30:29-30; Exodus 2:16-22). He led his sheep to pasture and water; he looked after them and protected them from danger (Genesis 29:7; Exodus 2:16; 1 Samuel 17:34; Psalm 23; John 10:1-15). When a sheep was lost, the shepherd went out to search for it (Psalm 119:176;

Luke 15:1-7). At night, he brought the sheep home, checking to see they were all there by counting them as they passed under his shepherd's rod (Leviticus 27:32; Ezekiel 20:37).

Shepherding was often dangerous work (Genesis 31:40; 1 Samuel 17:34; John 10:11-13). For this reason a shepherd equipped himself with a sheepskin mantle, a crook, and a pouch in which he carried his slingshot, his food, and the oil for medicating scratches, cuts, and bruises on his sheep. Frequently, he was assisted in his work by a dog (Job 30:1). The chief shepherd, overshepherd, or overseer was the person in charge of a number of shepherds and the flocks for which they cared (1 Chronicles 27:30-31).

The word *shepherd* is also used figuratively in the Bible. God, a king, ministers, and Christ are all referred to as shepherds (Psalm 77:20; Isaiah 44:28; 56:11; Jeremiah 23:4; 31:10; John 10:14; Acts 20:28-30; Hebrews 13:20).

SHEREBIAH (sher-i-BIGH-ah, Lord has sent heat). A Levite who joined Ezra at Ahava on his return to Jerusalem. Ezra entrusted him with the gifts for the temple (Ezra 8:18, 24). Later, Sherebiah sealed the covenant with Nehemiah (Nehemiah 8:7; 9:4-5; 10:12; 12:8, 24).

SHESHBAZZAR (shesh-BAZ-ur, may mean sun god or guard lord). A prince of Judah at the time Cyrus made the decree allowing the Jews to return to Jerusalem. Cyrus made Sheshbazzar a governor and gave him the sacred vessels for the temple. Sheshbazzar also helped lay the foundation of the temple in Jerusalem. He is often identified with Zerubbabel (Ezra 1:8; 5:14, 16).

SHIBAH (SHIGH-bah, seven; oath). A well that Isaac's servants dug at Beersheba (Genesis 26:31-33).

SHIELD. See *armor, arms.*

SHIGGAION, SHIGIONOTH (shi-GAY-yahn, shig-i-O-nahth, wandering). A musical term perhaps referring to the music or meter of a piece (title of Psalm 7; Habakkuk 3:1).

SHIHOR (SHIGH-hawr, black). See *Nile.*

SHILOH (SHIGH-lo, peace). 1. A place about nine miles north of Bethel. It was the site of Israel's early sanctuary and the place where the ark of the covenant was kept for about 300 years (Joshua 18:1, 8-10; Judges 21:19-23). Eli and Samuel lived at Shiloh and ministered in the temple there (1 Samuel 3). Shiloh was also the home of the prophet Ahijah. He was the one who told Jeroboam that God was going to make him king over the 10 northern tribes (1 Kings 11:29-34; 14:1-18). By Jeremiah's time it seems that Shiloh lay in ruins (Jeremiah 7:12-14; 26:6-9).
2. A word of uncertain meaning. Many people think it refers to the Messiah (Genesis 49:10).

SHIMSHAI (SHIM-shigh). A scribe and leader in Samaria who wrote a letter to Artaxerxes complaining about the rebuilding of the temple (Ezra 4:8-9, 17, 23).

SHINAR (SHIGH-nur). An alluvial plain of southern Babylonia where the cities Babel, Erech, Accad, and Calneh were located (Genesis 10:10; Daniel 1:2). The tower of Babel was built on this plain. During Abraham's time, Amraphel was king of Shinar (Genesis 14:1, 9). Many years later, some of the Jews were taken captive to Shinar (Isaiah 11:1; Zechariah 5:11).

SHIP. See *boats.*

SHITTAH, SHITTIM (SHIT-ah, SHIT-im, acacia). A tree that grew in the Jordan Valley, in the wilderness of Sinai, and in the area around the Dead Sea. The acacia was one species of shittah tree. Its wood was hard, fine grained, and insect repelling. The Hebrews used acacia wood to build the tabernacle, the ark, the altars, the tables, and the bars and pillars (Exodus 25:5-28; 26:15-37; Isaiah 41:19).

SHITTIM (SHIT-im, acacias). The last place Israel camped before entering Palestine. From Shittim Joshua sent spies to look over the defenses of Jericho, and then Israel broke camp to cross over the Jordan (Numbers 25:1; Joshua 2:1; Micah 6:5). In Numbers 33:49 it is referred to as Abel-shittim.

SHOBAL (SHO-bal). The son of Hur and founder of Kiriath-jearim (1 Chronicles 2:50; 4:1-2).

SHOBI (SHO-bigh, one who leads captive). An Ammonite who brought food and other provisions to David and the people with him when they stopped at Mahanaim (2 Samuel 17:27).

SHOE. Leather sandals usually fastened to the foot with straps known as thongs (Exodus 3:5; Joshua 5:15; Isaiah 20:2). Many times the Bible uses the word *sandal* rather than shoe (Exodus 12:11; Amos 8:6; Matthew 3:11).

SHOWBREAD. A translation for the Hebrew words that literally mean bread of the presence (Exodus 25:30; 35:13; 39:36). The showbread consisted of 12 loaves of fresh, unleavened bread that were placed in two stacks on the table of

acacia wood in the Holy Place every Sabbath. The old loaves were eaten by the priests (Exodus 25:30; 1 Samuel 21:1-6; Matthew 12:3-4).

SHUA (SHU-ah, wealth). A Canaanite who was Judah's father-in-law (1 Chronicles 2:3).

SHUAH (SHU-ah, depression). A son of Abraham and Keturah (Genesis 25:2). An Arab tribe, probably the Shuhites, descended from him.

SHUR (SHOOR, wall). A region in the wilderness south of Palestine and east of Egypt. The Israelites marched through this area for three days after crossing the Red Sea (Genesis 16:7; 25; 18; Exodus 15:22).

SHUSHAN (SHU-shan, lily). The capital of Elam and later, under Cyrus, one of the capitals of the Persian Empire (Nehemiah 1:1; Esther 1:2; Daniel 8:2). It was called Susa by the Greeks. Today it is called Shush.

SHUSHAN-EDUTH (SHU-shan-EE-duth, lilies of the Testimony). The title of Psalm 60. Although its meaning is uncertain, it may be a musical term, perhaps referring to the melody.

SIDON (SIGH-d'n, fishery). An ancient Canaanite city situated on the Mediterranean coast about 22 miles north of Tyre. It was assigned to the tribe of Asher, but they never succeeded in conquering the Canaanite

people living there (Judges 1:31; 10:12; 18:7, 28). When Solomon was building the temple, he hired people from Sidon to cut timber for it (1 Kings 5:6; 1 Chronicles 22:4).

The Sidonians worshiped the false goddess Ashtoreth. Their religion corrupted the Israelites, who began to worship Ashtoreth also (1 Kings 11:5). Jezebel, Ahab's wife, came from Sidon. Under her influence, Ahab built an altar to Baal in Samaria and worshiped him (1 Kings 16:31). Sidon was spoken against by the prophets (Jeremiah 27:3; Joel 3:4-6).

Sidon is also mentioned in the New Testament. Christ visited there, and Paul stopped at the port at Sidon (Matthew 15:21; Acts 27:3). Today it is called Saida.

SIEGE. Surrounding a city with an army in order to capture it. In Israel's early days, sieges lasted only a short time (Judges 9:46-55; 2 Samuel 20:15). Later siege engines, protected ladders, and battering rams were built to help the army take over the city (2 Chronicles 26:14). See also *armor, arms; army; war.*

SIEVE (netted or shake). A utensil made of rushes, horsehair, or string that was used for sifting materials, such as grain (Isaiah 30:28; Amos 9:9).

SIGNET. See *ring.*

SILAS (SIGH-lahs, sylvan). An important member of the Christian church in Jerusalem. Silas went with Paul to Antioch to tell the Christians there the decision of the Jerusalem council (Acts 15:22, 27, 32). He also accompanied Paul on the second missionary journey (Acts 16—18). Silas is also referred to as Silvanus (2 Corinthians 1:19; 1 Thessalonians 1:1; 2 Thessalonians 1:1; 1 Peter 5:12).

SILOAH, SILOAM (si-LO-ah, si-LO-am, shooting forth; sent). A pool at Jerusalem on the southern side of the temple. It received its water from En-rogel through a 1,780-foot tunnel built during Hezekiah's reign (John 9:7). In Isaiah 8:6 it is referred to as Shiloah and in Nehemiah 3:15 as Shelah. Today it is called Birket Silwan.

SILVANUS (sil-VAY-nuhs). See *Silas.*

SILVER. A precious metal used from early times for money, ornaments, crowns, trumpets, vessels, and items in the tabernacle (Genesis 23:16; 24:53; 44:2; Exodus 26:19; 27:10; 38:19; Numbers 10:2; Job 28:15; Zechariah 6:11). Some idols were also made of silver (Psalm 115:40).

SIMEON (SIM-ee-uhn, hearing). 1. One of Jacob and Leah's sons (Genesis 29:33). Simeon and his brother Levi killed the people of Shechem because of what one of them had done to Dinah, their sister (Genesis 34:24-31). During Israel's famine Joseph kept Simeon hostage in Egypt in order to make sure the rest of his brothers would return (Genesis 42:24). When Jacob was dying, he foretold that the tribe of Simeon would be scattered in Israel (Genesis 49:5-7).

2. The tribe of Simeon. Members of this tribe descended from Simeon (Numbers 1:22-23). The tribe of Simeon received cities and villages in Judah and in the neighborhood of Beer-sheba (Joshua 19:1-9; 1 Chronicles 4:28-33).

3. A righteous and devout man to whom God revealed that he would not die until he had seen the Christ child. When Mary and Joseph brought the baby Jesus to the temple, Simeon came in and recognized Him as the promised Messiah. He uttered the blessing known as the *Nunc dimittis* (Luke 2:25-35).

4. Simeon Niger, a Christian at Antioch (Acts 13:1).

5. See *Peter.*

SIMON (SIGH-muhn, hearing). 1. See *Peter.*

2. Simon the Canaanite, or Simon the Zealot, one of the apostles (Matthew 10:4).

3. A brother of Jesus (Matthew 13:55; Mark 6:3).

4. A Pharisee who invited Jesus to his home for a meal. While Jesus was there, a woman came in and anointed His feet (Luke 7:36-50).

5. Simon of Cyrene, the man who carried Jesus' cross for Him (Matthew 27:32; Mark 15:21; Luke 23:26).

6. Simon Magus, a sorcerer of Samaria. When Simon saw that the Holy Spirit was given through the laying on of hands, he tried to buy the power from the apostles. Peter sharply rebuked him for this and told him to repent (Acts 8:9-24).

7. A tanner at Joppa. Peter stayed at his house for many days (Acts 9:43).

SIN, I (SIN). A desert plain lying inland from the Red Sea. The Israelites passed through the Wilderness of Sin on their way from the Red Sea to Mount Sinai (Exodus 16:1; 17:1; Numbers 33:11-12).

SIN, II. Sin is both doing what God forbids and failing to do what He commands (Romans 1:18-32; 1 John 3:4). Since God's law tells us what He wants us to do and not to do, sin is breaking God's law. It is a condition as well as an act.

When Adam and Eve yielded to the devil's temptation and fell into sin, they lost the image of God; they were no longer holy and innocent. Because of their sin, they came under God's just anger and curse. Also by their act of disobedience, sin entered the world and through it, misery, suffering, and death came upon the entire human race (Genesis 3; Psalm 51:5; Romans 3:9-23; 5:21; 6:6-17; 7:21-23).

From Adam all people receive both hereditary guilt (Romans 5:12) and a total corruption of the human nature, called original sin. Original sin is the evil condition of our nature that we have by being born of human parents also corrupted by sin. It consists of an alienation from God (Romans 1:18-24; 8:7) as well as a natural liking for doing evil (Romans 1; 7:14). It expresses itself in actual sinful deeds contrary to God's will as found in His law (Romans 3:20; 4:15; 7:7; James 4:12-17; 1 John 3:4).

Sin is against God (Genesis 39:9; 2 Samuel 12:13; Psalm 51:4). Because of original sin, people by nature cannot fear, love, or trust in God or love their neighbor (1 John). Because of sin everyone deserves temporal and eternal death. "The wages of sin is death" (Romans 6:23). Only through faith in Christ, who both kept God's law perfectly and suffered the punishment for the sins of the world, does one escape the results of sin. "But the free gift of God is eternal life in Christ Jesus our Lord" (Romans 6:23).

SIN OFFERING. See *sacrifice; Atonement, Day of.*

SIN, UNPARDONABLE. A sin that excludes the possibility of repentance. The Bible often refers to this sin as the sin against the Holy Spirit. This sin is committed when the Holy Spirit has clearly revealed the divine truth to the sinner, and yet, the sinner still consciously persists in his or her evil ways, opposing God and His will. It is the rejection of the Gospel by a hardened sinner who has been convinced of its truth (Matthew 12:31; Mark 3:29; Luke 12:10; 1 John 5:16).

SINAI (SIGH-nigh, may possibly mean thorny or Sin, the moon-god). The mountain on which the Law was given. Mount Sinai was probably a peak in the mountain range

Horeb (Exodus 3:1; 17:6; Deuteronomy 1:6; 4:10). The Ten Commandments were given from its peak, and the covenant between the Lord and Israel was ratified at its base (Exodus 20:1—24:8; Acts 3:38). The location of Mount Sinai is uncertain.

The Sinai Peninsula lies between the Red Sea, the Gulf of Aqaba, and the Gulf of Suez.

SIRAH (SIGH-rah, recession). A well about one mile north of Hebron. Here, Joab killed Abner (2 Samuel 3:26).

SISERA (SIS-u-rah). A Canaanite who was the captain of the army of King Jabin of Hazor. Under Deborah's direction Barak united his forces and met with Sisera in battle. When Sisera's forces were killed or scattered, he ran away on foot. Jael, the wife of Heber, killed Sisera while he slept (Judges 4—5; 1 Samuel 12:9; Psalm 83:9).

SISTER. 1. Full sister or half sister (Genesis 20:12; Deuteronomy 27:22).

2. Wife (Song of Solomon 4:9).

3. A woman of the same tribe (Numbers 25:18).

4. A female fellow Christian (Romans 16:1).

SLEEP. 1. Physical rest (Psalm 4:8; Proverbs 24:33; John 11:13).

2. Death (1 Kings 1:21; Psalm 13:3; Jeremiah 51:39; John 11:11).

3. Spiritual laziness or stupidity (Romans 13:11; 1 Thessalonians 5:6).

SMYRNA (SMUR-nah, myrrh). An ancient Ionian city about 40 miles north of Ephesus. After lying in ruins for a number of years, it was rebuilt by Alexander the Great in 320 B.C. John addresses the church at Smyrna in the Book of Revelation (1:11; 2:8-11).

SNAIL. 1. A lizard (Leviticus 11:30).

2. Snail (Psalm 58:8).

SNOW. Snow is common in the hilly country of Palestine (2 Samuel 23:20; Isaiah 55:10). It is often mentioned in poetical sections of Scripture and in metaphors (Job 37:6; 38:22; Psalm 51:7; 147:16; Isaiah 1:18; Matthew 28:3).

SODOM (SAHD-uhm). A city, along with Gomorrah, Admah, Zeboiim, and Zoar, that was located in the plain of Siddim (Genesis 13:12). Although the exact site of Sodom is unknown, many think it was located on the southeast end of the Dead Sea. In Genesis 14:2 it is described as a royal city. Abraham's nephew Lot lived there (Genesis 13:11-13). When God destroyed Sodom because of its wickedness, only Lot and his two daughters escaped (Genesis 19). The Bible repeatedly uses Sodom as an example of wickedness (Deuteronomy 29:23; Isaiah 1:9; 3:9; Jeremiah 50:40; Ezekiel 16:46; Matthew 10:15; Romans 9:29; 2 Peter 2:6). In Revelation 11:8 Sodom and Egypt are referred to as "the city of Sin."

SOJOURNER (so-JYOOR-nur). See *foreigner; proselyte.*

SOLDIER (SOL-jur). See *army.*

SOLOMON (SAHL-o-muhn, peaceable). Third and last king of the United Kingdom of Israel. Solomon was the son of David and Bathsheba. When Solomon was born, Nathan named him Jedidiah, which means beloved of the Lord (2 Samuel 12:24-25; 1 Kings 4:1; 1 Chronicles 3:5). After Solomon was made king, he put to death those who had plotted to take the throne from him: his brother Adonijah and Adonijah's followers Joab and Shimei. He also removed Abiathar, the priest, from office (1 Kings 1:5-40; 2).

Solomon married numerous women, one of whom was the daughter of the Egyptian pharaoh (1 Kings 3:1). Early in his reign Solomon was faithful to the Lord. He worshiped the Lord, offering up burnt offerings and praying to Him. When God told Solomon in a dream to ask whatever he wished of Him, Solomon chose wisdom so that he could rule his kingdom better (1 Kings 3:3-12). God answered his request, blessing Solomon with "wisdom and understanding beyond measure. . . . He was wiser than all other men" (1 Kings 4:29-31).

With the help of King Hiram of Tyre, Solomon built the temple in seven years. He also built a palace for himself (1 Kings 5—8; 2 Chronicles 2—7). Solomon showed wisdom in government and commerce (1 Kings 4:2-19; 10:11-29; 2 Chronicles 9:10-22). He also had interests and abilities in botany and zoology (1 Kings 4:33). In addition to this, Solomon was a great writer. Among other writings, the Book of Proverbs and Psalms 27 and 127 were likely written by him.

In his old age, however, Solomon began to fall away from the Lord. Under the influence of his foreign wives, he was tempted to worship others gods; he built altars to Chemosh and Molech and worshiped Ashtoreth. The Lord grew angry with Solomon. As judgment on Solomon's idolatry, God said He would take the Kingdom of Israel from Solomon's descendants. Only one tribe would remain for them to rule (1 Kings 11:1-13).

SOLOMON, SONG OF. The full title of this book of the Old Testament is "The Song of Songs Which is Solomon's" (1:1). It is also called "Canticles," which comes from the Latin for "Song of Songs." Historically Bible scholars have interpreted this book in a number of ways, for example, allegorically.

The allegorical interpretation was developed in the 18th century. According to it the bride represents the church and the bridegroom represents Christ (Isaiah 54:5; 62:5; Jeremiah 2:2; Hosea 2:19, 20; Matthew 9:15; John 3:29; 2 Corinthians 11:2; Ephesians 5:25-32; Revelation 19:7; 21:2).

Date: During the united monarchy

Audience: People of its time

Outline: 1. Mutual and yearning of the lovers (1:2—2:7). 2. The bride is invited to the fields (2:8—3:5). 3. "Solomon" arrives in majesty (3:6—5:1). 4. The bridegroom comes unexpectedly while the bride is in bed (5:2—6:3). 5. Mutual praises of the other's beauty (6:3—8:4). 6. The lovers are united and declare their undying love for each other (8:5-14).

SOLOMON'S PORCH. 1. A covered colonnade attached to Solomon's palace (1 Kings 7:7).

2. A colonnade on the east side of Herod's temple (John 10:23; Acts 3:11; 5:12).

SON. 1. A male child; one's immediate descendant (Genesis 27:1).

2. A descendant further removed than one's own child (2 Kings 9:20; Malachi 3:6).

3. A spiritual son (2 Kings 2:3; 1 Timothy 1:18; 2 Timothy 2:1).

4. An address to a younger person (1 Samuel 3:6).

5. A member of a profession (Nehemiah 12:28).

6. A follower (Numbers 21:29).

7. An adopted son (Exodus 2:10).

8. A native (Lamentations 4:2).

9. See *Jesus Christ.*

SON OF GOD. 1. Adam (Luke 3:38).

2. Angels (Job 38:7).

3. Believers (Romans 8:14; 2 Corinthians 6:18; Galatians 4:1-7). See also *adoption.*

4. See *Jesus Christ.*

SON OF MAN. 1. A human being (Numbers 23:19; Job 25:6; Psalm 8:4; Daniel 8:17).

2. Used in a Messianic sense in Daniel 7:13-14. Jesus applies the

term to Himself numerous times. See also *Jesus Christ.*

SONG. See *music; Psalms, Book of.*

SONG OF ASCENTS (DEGREES). See *Ascents, Song of.*

SONG OF SONGS. See *Solomon, Son of.*

SONSHIP. See *adoption; Son of God.*

SOOTHSAYER (SOOTH-say-ur). A person who says that he or she can tell the future (Deuteronomy 18:10, 14; Daniel 2:27).

SOPHERETH (so-FEE-reth, secretariat). A name or title given to some of Solomon's servants (Ezra 2:55; Nehemiah 7:55).

SORCERER (SAWR-sur-ur). See *magic.*

SOSTHENES (SOS-thi-neez, savior). A ruler of the synagog at Corinth (Acts 18:17). He may have been the man mentioned in 1 Corinthians 1:1, who was Paul's coworker.

SOUL, SPIRIT (sometimes translated life or ghost). The word *soul* comes from the Hebrew word *nephesh* and the Greek word *psuche.* The soul is not separate from the body; rather it is that which gives it life: it animates the flesh. It is the inner person as distinguished from the flesh (Job 14:22). Through the breath of God, people and animals become living beings or souls (Genesis 2:7, 19). The soul is described as living and dying and as life itself (Genesis 12:13; 44:30; Judges 16:30; Isaiah 53:12; Ezekiel 18:4; Acts 20:10). The soul departs at death (Genesis 35:18; Luke 12:20). The soul is the seat of the appetites, emotions, and passions (Deuteronomy 12:20; Psalm 107:9; Matthew 22:37; Luke 12:19; John 12:27). It can be lost and saved (Mark 8:35-36).

Spirit is a translation of the Hebrew word *ruah* and the Greek word *pneuma.* It is often translated as breath or wind (Job 15:30; 2 Thessalonians 2:8). The spirit of life is created and preserved by God (Job 10:12; 27:3; Zechariah 12:1). It is those inner aspects of one's personality and the seat of one's moral character (Ezekiel 11:19; 18:31; Mark 2:8; 1 Corinthians 5:3-5). The spirit returns to God at death (Ecclesiastes 12:7; Matthew 27:50; John 19:30). The Spirit of God gives special gifts to people (Exodus 31:3; Job 32:8).

At times soul and spirit are used as synonyms (Luke 1:46-47); at other times they are contrasted (1 Corinthians 15:44-45). Both demonstrate one life principle from two points of view. See also *death; eschatology; eternal life; Holy Spirit.*

SPAN. See *measures 1c.*

SPELT. An inferior type of wheat (Exodus 9:32; Isaiah 28:25; Ezekiel 4:9). See also *food 1.*

SPICES. Pleasant-smelling gums, barks, and the like that were used during Biblical times in ceremonies, in medicines, for embalming, for anointing, and for grooming oneself (Genesis 37:25; 43:11; Song of Solomon 4:14; Mark 16:1; John 19:39-40).

SPIDER. A spider's web is a picture word for the foolishness of wickedness (Job 8:14; Isaiah 59:5).

SPINNING. See *trade.*

SPIRIT. See *soul, spirit; Holy Spirit.*

SPIRIT, HOLY. See *Holy Spirit.*

SPIRITUAL GIFTS. Gifts and abilities that the Holy Spirit gives to Christians to equip them for service in the church (1 Corinthians 12).

SPOIL. See *booty.*

SPOT. 1. A mark or blot that spoils an animal or person (Genesis 30:32-39; Leviticus 13:2-39).

2. A physical or moral flaw (Leviticus 13; 21:17-24; Deuteronomy 32:5).

STADIUM (STAY-di-uhm). See *measure 1:*

STAFF. See *rod.*

STAIRS, STAIRWAY. See *homes.*

STANDARD. See *ensign 2.*

STAR. The Bible speaks of a star as any heavenly body except the sun and the moon. The Israelites recognized stars as the work of God and observed them from patriarchal times (Genesis 1:16). For instance, God told Abraham his descendants would be as numerous as the stars, and Joseph dreamed the sun, the moon, and 11 stars had bowed down to him (Genesis 15:5; 37:9).

Stars are also used as picture words for brightness, multitudes, and important persons (Genesis 22:17; 37:9; Numbers 24:17; Psalm 147:4; 148:3; Daniel 8:10; 12:3; Revelation 6:13). The star of the East led the wise men to Bethlehem after Jesus was born (Matthew 2:2-10). See also *astrologers.*

STEADFAST LOVE. The Hebrew word for this is *hesed.* Although difficult to translate into English, *hesed* has the basic sense of that lovingkindness, mercy, and faithfulness of God expressed in the act by which He chose Israel, established a covenant relationship with the people of Israel, promised them salvation, and bound Himself to loving them and showing them mercy. Those who have been called by grace into this covenant relationship with God respond in love to God and their fellow human beings (Genesis 24:12-27; Exodus 20:6; Psalm 5:7; 26:3; Jeremiah 16:5). Often this word is translated by lovingkindness or mercy as well as steadfast love. See also *grace; love; mercy.*

STEPHEN (STEE-vuhn, crown). One of the seven deacons chosen by the early church to minister to the needs of the Greek-speaking widows and probably the poor in general. Stephen himself was likely a Greek-speaking Christian. The New Testament describes him as a man of great faith, wisdom, and power

(Acts 6:3-8). Some people who belonged to the Synagog of the Freedmen, as well as Jews from Cyrene, Alexandria, Cilicia, and Asia, debated with Stephen. Accusing him of blasphemy against Moses and God, they stirred up the people to bring Stephen before the council (Acts 6:9-15).

Stephen gave a remarkable defense, explaining that Christianity was the fulfillment of Jewish history. His words angered his accusers, who took him outside the city and stoned him to death. The young man Saul (Paul) watched the proceedings and approved of Stephen's death (Acts 7—8:1).

STOICS (STO-iks, porch scholars). A school of Greek philosophy founded by Zeno. Stoics taught that virtue was the highest good. Through it they believed that one's actions were brought into harmony with nature and universal reason. Their religion was pantheistic, that is, they believed God is in everything.

Stoics were known for their austere ethics, for their rigid control of feelings, and for hiding their emotions. They were unmoved by pleasure or pain. When Paul was in Athens, he talked with some Stoics (Acts 17:18-32).

STRAIGHT STREET. A street of Damascus (Acts 9:11).

STRONG DRINK. Any alcoholic beverage (Numbers 28:6). It was usually made from grapes, barley, honey, or dates. Strong drink was forbidden to priests before they entered the sanctuary and to Nazirites (Leviticus 10:9; Numbers 6:3; Judges 13:4, 7; Luke 1:15).

STUMBLING BLOCK. 1. In Old Testament usage a stumbling block is any object that causes a person to fall (Leviticus 19:14).

2. In the New Testament Jesus and the cross are described as stumbling blocks (1 Corinthians 1:23). God's way of salvation through Jesus and the cross does not meet people's expectations or wishes. Individuals cannot be saved through their own reason or works, only by grace through faith in Christ's redeeming work for them. This is a "stumbling block" for them.

3. An occasion for inner conflict or sin (Romans 14:13; 1 Corinthians 8:9).

SUCCOTH (SUK-ahth, booths). 1. The place east of the Jordan near Damiyeh where Jacob built a house for himself and booths for his cattle on his return from Mesopotamia to Canaan (Genesis 33:17). Later, it was assigned to the Gadites (Joshua 13:27). During the time of Gideon, Succoth was an important town. When the people of Succoth refused to help Gideon, he punished the town severely (Judges 8:5-16).

2. The first place Israel camped after leaving Rameses (Exodus 12:37; 13:20; Numbers 33:5-6).

SUFFERING. A result of the alienation between God and people caused by sin (Job 10:2; Psalm 51:4). Although the root cause for suffering is spiritual, people suffer both physically and morally (Genesis 3:16; Job; Matthew 27:27-30; 39-44). Christ paid the penalty for the sins of the world by suffering and dying on the cross (Psalm 22; Matthew 27:45-46). Since it will not be until the next life that the effects of sin are totally removed, Christians still suffer in this world. Christian suffering, however, is understood by faith (Romans 8:24; 2 Corinthians 1:5-14). Suffering teaches Christians to rely on and trust in God. Paul writes: "We felt that we had received the sentence of death; but that was to make us rely not on ourselves but on God who raises the dead; He delivered us from so deadly a peril . . . [that] on

Him we have set our hope that He will deliver us again" (2 Corinthians 1:9-10). People who do not believe in Christ will suffer eternally.

SUN. The greater light of the day created and preserved by God (Genesis 1:16; Psalm 74:16; 104:19; Jeremiah 31:35; Matthew 5:45). The sun helps crops and vegetation to grow but also burns them (Deuteronomy 33:14; Jonah 4:8). In Old Testament days both the Hebrews and other nations worshiped the sun (2 Kings 21:3, 5; 23:5; Job 31:26-27).

The sun is also a picture word for the glory of Christ, heavenly beings, and the saints (Matthew 13:43; 17:2; Revelation 1:16; 10:1; 12:1).

When a person died before he or she reached old age, it was compared to the setting of the sun at midday (Jeremiah 15:9; Amos 8:9; Micah 3:6). A darkened sun was symbolic of some great disaster or trouble (Ezekiel 32:7; Joel 2:10, 31).

SUNDAY. The first day of the week. At first, the early Christians worshiped on both the seventh day of the week, the Sabbath, and the first day of the week, the day upon which Christ rose from the dead. Eventually they stopped meeting on the seventh day. The word *Sunday* is of pagan origin. See also *Lord's Day.*

SUPPLICATION (SUP-li-KAY-shuhn). A prayer for mercy or favor in some special need (1 Kings 8:28-54; Job 8:5; Psalm 6:9; Ephesians 6:18). See also *prayer.*

SUSA (SYOO-sah). See *Shushan.*

SWEARING. See *oath.*

SWORD. See *armor, arms.*

SYCAMORE (SIK-ah-mor). A fig tree. It was valued for its small, edible fruit and light, durable wood (1 Kings 10:27; 1 Chronicles 27:28; Psalm 78:47; Luke 19:4). See also *orchard.*

SYMEON (SIM-ee-un). See *Peter; Simeon 4.*

SYNAGOG (SIN-ah-gog, led together). A Jewish place for worship and for social gathering. The synagog served as the place for worship and instruction in both God's law and the civil and moral law. The synagog as a meeting place and building likely began during the captivity when people could not get to the temple in Jerusalem for worship (Ezra 8:15; Nehemiah 8:2; 9:1).

The furnishings of the synagog included a chest for the sacred books, a reading platform with a lectern, seats for the congregation, and lamps and trumpets. The ruler of the synagog, the attendant, and the almoner were the officers in charge of the synagog. When the people came for worship, they observed the following order of service: a reading from the Shema, prayer, a reading from the Law, a reading from the prophets, and the benediction. See also *education.*

SYRACUSE (SIR-ah-kyoos). A leading city on the east coast of Sicily where Paul stayed for three days on his voyage to Rome (Acts 28:12).

SYRIA (SIR-i-ah). In the Old Testament Syria was called Aram. It was that territory bounded by the Taurus Mountains, the Euphrates River, the Arabian Desert, and the Mediterranean Sea. David conquered it, but under Solomon it became independent (2 Samuel 8; 10; 1 Kings 11:23-25). Syria was a continual enemy of the Israelites (1 Kings 15:18-20; 20; 22; 2 Kings 6:8-33; 7; 9:14, 15; 10:32, 33; 13).

SYRIAC (SIR-i-ak). The language spoken in Syria; Aramaic (Daniel 2:4).

SYROPHENICIAN, SYROPHOENICIAN (sigh-ro-fi-NISH-uhn). A person who lived in northern Phoenicia. The Syrophoenicians were absorbed into the Syrian kingdom (Mark 7:26).

T

TAANACH (TAY-ah-nak). A Canaanite city about five miles southeast of Megiddo. Joshua conquered Taanach and gave it to Manasseh and the Kohathite Levites (Joshua 12:21; 17:11; 21:25). The battle between Barak and Sisera was fought near Taanach (Judges 5:19).

TABEEL (TAY-bi-el, God is good). The father of the one whom Rezin of Syria and Pekah of Israel proposed to put on the throne of Judah as their puppet king (Isaiah 7:6).

TABERAH (TAB-i-rah, burning). A place in the wilderness where Israel camped. Here the fire of the Lord burned some people who complained. Taberah is also called Kibroth-hattaavah (Numbers 11:3, 34; Deuteronomy 9:22).

TABERNACLE (TAB-ur-nak'l). 1. See *tent of meeting*.

2. The movable sanctuary in the form of a tent. God directed Moses to make the tabernacle so that He would have a place to live as King among His people (Exodus 25:8-9). Because it contained the ark and two tables, the tabernacle was sometimes referred to as the tent, or tabernacle, of witness (Exodus 38:21; Numbers 9:15; 17:7; 18:2). Other

names for it include the tent of meeting or the tabernacle of congregation, the house of the Lord, the sanctuary, and the temple (Exodus 23:19; 25:8; 29:42, 44; 1 Samuel 1:9; 3:3).

A description of the tabnernacle is found in Exodus 25:10—27:19. The tabernacle stood in a court that was 100 cubits long by 50 cubits wide. The court was enclosed by acacia pillars five cubits high that had silver bands and hooks connected at the top by silver-covered rods. From these rods hung sheets of fine linen, embroidered on the east entrance. The frame of the tabernacle was 30 cubits long by 10 cubits wide by 10 cubits high. It was made of gold-covered acacia wood, covered on the outside with double blankets of skin and on the inside with embroidered linen tapestry. The tabernacle was divided into the Holy and Most Holy Places by a linen veil embroidered with cherubim.

The altar of burnt offering stood in the court between the court entrance and the tabernacle. A laver (the place where priests washed) stood halfway between the altar and the tabernacle. The table of showbread, the golden candlestick, and the altar of incense were kept in the Holy Place, while the ark of the covenant was kept in the Holy of Holies.

The tabernacle was set up at Sinai the second year after the Israelites left Egypt (Exodus 40:2, 17). During the time of the conquest the tabernacle was stationed at Gilgal and Ebal (Joshua 4:9; 8:30-35). Later, it was stationed at Shiloh, Nob, and Gibeon (Joshua 18:1; 1 Samuel 4:17, 22; 21:1; 1 Chronicles 16:39; 21:29). Under David the ark of the covenant was moved to the new tabernacle in Jerusalem. When the temple was built, the ark was placed

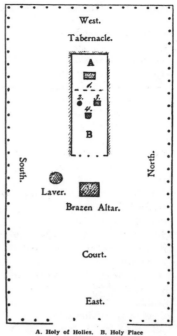

A. Holy of Holies.   B. Holy Place
1. Ark of the Covenant   3. Table of Showbread
2. Candlestick   4. Altar of Incense

in it (2 Samuel 6:17; 1 Chronicles 15:1).

TABERNACLES, FEAST OF. The third yearly festival of the Jewish people, commemorating the tent life of Israel. The people celebrated this festival by building booths or huts from the branches of fruit and palm trees (Exodus 23:16; Leviticus 23:34-43; Deuteronomy 16:13-15; 31:10-13; Nehemiah 8). Other names for this festival are the Feast of Ingathering, the Feast of the Lord, and the Feast of Booths (Exodus 23:16; Leviticus 23:34, 39).

TABITHA (TAB-i-thah, gazelle). See *Dorcas.*

TABLE. 1. See *showbread; tabernacle.*

2. A table spread with food (Judges 1:7; 1 Kings 2:7; Matthew 15:27; Mark 7:28; Luke 16:21).

3. See *Lord's Supper.*

4. A table the moneychangers used for their business (Matthew 21:12).

5. Stone tablets on which the Ten Commandments were written (Exodus 24:12; 31:18).

TABOR (TAY-bur). A limestone mountain in Galilee about six miles east of Nazareth (Joshua 19:22). It is 1,843 feet above sea level. Barak gathered 10,000 men together on Mount Tabor (Judges 4:6-14). Gideon's brothers were murdered there (Judges 8:21).

TAHATH (TAY-hath, that which is beneath). One of the places in the wilderness where Israel camped (Numbers 33:26-27).

TALENT. The largest metal weight in Bible times (Matthew 25:14-30). A talent of gold was worth about 15 times as much as a talent of silver. A talent of silver represented wealth; a talent of gold meant fabulous riches. (Klinck)

TALITHA CUMI (tah-LIGH-thah KOO-mi). An Aramaic expression that means maiden get up (Mark 5:41).

TAMAR (TAY-mur, palm tree). 1. The wife of Er, son of Judah. When she was left a widow, Tamar tricked her father-in-law, Judah, into making her pregnant. She became the mother of Perez and Zerah (Genesis 38:6-26; Numbers 26:20-21; Matthew 1:3).

2. Absalom's sister (2 Samuel 13; 1 Chronicles 3:9).

3. The daughter of Absalom and mother of Maacah (2 Samuel 14:27; 2 Chronicles 13:2).

TAMBOURINE (tam-boo-REEN). See *timbrel.*

TANNER. See *trade.*

TAPHATH (TAY-fath, drop). Solomon's daughter (1 Kings 4:11).

TARES. Probably a poisonous plant known as the bearded darnel. It is a grass that cannot be distinguished from wheat until the two are full

grown (Matthew 13:25-30).

TARSHISH (TAHR-shish, foundry; refinery). 1. A place on the Mediterranean, perhaps in Spain or Tunisia (2 Chronicles 9:21; 20:36-37; Psalm 72:10). Jonah fled to Tarshish (Jonah 1:3).

2. The "ships of Tarshish" were large, seagoing ships which carried refined ore or other cargo (1 Kings 9:26; 10:22; 22:48; 2 Chronicles 9:21).

TARSUS (TAHR-suhs). The chief city of Cilicia, located on the Cydnus River. It was a free city and a great commercial center. Known for its educational system, its schools were almost as good as those of Athens and Alexandria. Tarsus was the home of Paul, who no doubt benefited from all his city had to offer (Acts 9:11, 30; 11:25; 21:39; 22:3).

TAXES. Under the judges the Israelites paid taxes to support the priests and tabernacle.

Under the kings taxes were collected from various sources to support the kingdom. These included the following:

1. Taxes in kind levied on the produce of fields and flocks (1 Kings 4:7-28)

2. Military service (1 Samuel 8:12; 1 Chronicles 27:1)

3. Special gifts (1 Samuel 10:27; 16:20)

4. Duties paid by merchants (1 Kings 10:15)

5. Tribute and services exacted by subject people (Judges 1:28-36; 2 Samuel 8:6, 14)

6. Monopoly of certain trade (1 Kings 9:28; 22:48)

Under the Persian Empire, the satraps paid a fixed sum into the royal treasury. This sum was collected from the people by tribute, customs, and toll (Ezra 4:13, 20). The priests, Levites, and Nethinim, however, were exempt (Ezra 7:24).

The Egyptians and Syrians sold the right to tax to the highest bidder at auction. That person who promised to collect the most revenue from a province was authorized to do so and given military power to enforce his demands.

The Romans practiced tax farming (Matthew 17:24; 22:17). See also *census; publican.*

TEKOA, TEKOAH (ti-KO-ah). A town in Judah about six miles south of Bethlehem (2 Samuel 14:2, 4, 9). It was fortified by King Rehoboam and was the home of the prophet Amos (2 Chronicles 11:6; Amos 1:1). Today it is Tekia.

TEL-ABIB (tel-AY-bib, grain heap). A place on the Chebar Canal where Ezekiel lived (Ezekiel 3:15).

TEMAN (TEE-muhn, south). 1. Esau's grandson and a prince of Edom (Genesis 36:11,15,42; 1 Chronicles 1:36).

2. A district in northern Edom where Teman's descendants lived (Ezekiel 25:13; Amos 1:12). The people of Teman were noted for their wisdom (Job 2:11; Jeremiah 49:7).

TEMPLE. David wanted to build the temple so the Lord would have a permanent house instead of a tent. With this in mind, he gathered together the materials for it (2 Samuel 7; 1 Chronicles 17; 22; 28:12-19; 29:1-9). But it was Solomon, his son, who actually built the temple

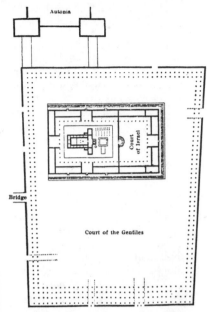

on Mount Moriah with the help of Hiram of Tyre. The temple proper was 60 cubits long, 20 cubits broad, and 30 cubits high. It was built of stone from a quarry. The roof was made of cedar; the floor was carved with cypress overlaid with gold; and the inside walls were lined with carved cedar overlaid with gold.

The Holy of Holies, or inner sanctuary, was a cube, each side measuring 20 cubits. It contained two cherubim made of olive wood and overlaid with gold and the ark with the mercy seat.

The Holy Place, separated from the Holy of Holies by a cedar door and a veil, was 40 cubits long, 20 cubits wide, and 30 cubits high. It contained an altar of incense made of cedar and overlaid with gold, 10 golden seven-lamp candlesticks, and 10 tables for showbread.

On the east, west, and south sides of the temple was a three-story building containing rooms for officials and storage. On the north side before the front entrance was a portico with two pillars, Jachin and Boaz.

The temple had two courts: the inner, or upper court for the priests, containing the altar of burnt offering and a molten sea, and around this inner court, the outer court for Israel (1 Kings 6—8; 2 Chronicles 3—7). This temple, known as Solomon's temple, was burned by the Babylonians. Zerubbabel's temple was larger than Solomon's but less magnificent (Ezra 3—6).

Herod rebuilt, enlarged, and made Zerubbabel's temple more beautiful. Herod's temple had an outer court where Gentiles often gathered, a court of women, and an inner court. The gate called Beautiful was on the east side of this temple (Acts 3:2). See also *nave*.

TEMPLE SERVANTS. See *Nethinim*.

TEN COMMANDMENTS. The Ten Commandments were given by God to Moses on Mount Sinai and written on tablets of stone (Exodus 20; 31:18; 32:15-19; Deuteronomy 10:1-5). The Ten Commandments form the basis of God's law. In the Old Testament they are also referred to as the words (Exodus 20:1; 34:28). In the New Testament they are called commandments (Matthew 19:17; Ephesians 6:2). Jesus' interpretation of the commandments is found in Matthew 5:17-48; 19:16-22; Mark 2:24-27; and Luke 6:1-10; 13:10-16. Perfect love is the fulfillment of the commandments (Matthew 22:35-40).

TENT OF MEETING. A provisional tent where the Lord met with His people (Exodus 33:7-11; 34:34-35).

TERAH (TEE-rah, ibex). 1. The father of Abraham, Nahor, and Haran (Genesis 11:26; 1 Chronicles 1:26; Luke 3:34). Terah, who lived in Ur of the Chaldees, served idols (Joshua 24:2). He moved with Abraham and Lot from Ur to Haran, where he died at the age of 205.

2. A place in the wilderness where Israel camped (Numbers 33:27-28).

TERAPHIM (TER-ah-fim). Household idols. They were figurines in human form which varied in size (Genesis 31:19, 32-35; 1 Samuel 19:13).

TERTIUS (TUR-shi-uhs, third). Paul's scribe. At Paul's dictation Tertius wrote down Paul's letter to the Romans (Romans 16:22).

TERTULLUS (TUR-TUL-uhs, little third). The Roman lawyer hired by Jewish authorities to prosecute Paul before Felix (Acts 24:1-8).

TESTAMENT. 1. Will (Hebrews 9:16-17).

2. Covenant (Hebrews 8:6-10).

3. The books of the Bible pertaining to the Old Covenant (Genesis—Malachi) and the New Covenant (Matthew—Revelation). The Old and New Covenants are more accurate descriptions for the Old and New Testaments. See also *covenant*.

TESTIMONY. 1. Divine commands (Deuteronomy 4:45; 6:17).

2. The Decalog or divine law as found in the ark. The two tables of the law are called the tables of testimony (Exodus 25:16).

3. Legal evidence; witness (Ruth 4:7).

TETRARCH (TET-rahrk, ruler of one quarter). One who ruled over a small territory (Matthew 14:1; Luke 3:1; Acts 13:1).

THADDAEUS (tha-DEE-uhs, wise). See *Judas 4*.

THEBES (THEEBZ). An ancient city of Upper Egypt referred to as No in the Bible. Thebes was built on both sides of the Nile and is well known for its temples and other ruins (Jeremiah 46:25; Ezekiel 30:14-16; Nahum 3:8).

THEOCRACY (thee-OK-rah-si, ruled by God). The form of government in the Old Testament where God Himself ruled His people and where all power and authority rested in Him (1 Samuel 8:4-9; 12).

THEOPHILOS (thee-OF-uh-luhs, friend of God). An unknown person, perhaps an official, to whom Luke and Acts are addressed (Luke 1:3; Acts 1:1).

THESSALONIANS, FIRST LETTER OF PAUL TO. Paul wrote this letter to the Thessalonians while he was in Corinth. His purpose for writing the letter was to encourage the Thessalonians to good conduct and to comfort them concerning those who had died.
Date: A.D. 50
Audience: Christians at Thessalonica
Outline: 1. Thanksgiving for Word of God in Thessalonica (1). 2. Paul's ministry at Thessalonica (2). 3. Paul's concern and intercession for Thessalonians (3). 4. Instructions ''to supply what is lacking in their faith'' (4—5).

THESSALONIANS, SECOND LETTER OF PAUL TO. Paul wrote his second letter to the Thessalonians to correct their wrong ideas about the return of Christ.
Date: A.D. 50
Audience: Christians at Thessalonica
Outline: 1. Thanksgiving and prayer (1). 2. Admonition concerning the coming of the Lord (2). 3. Exhortations and benediction (3).

THESSALONICA (thes-ah-lo-NIGH-kah, victory of Thessaly). A city on the Thermaic Gulf in Macedonia. Thessalonica was a commercial city, a chief port of Macedonia, and a free city in the Roman Empire. It was ruled by politarchs (Acts 17:1-8). Today it is known as Salonika.

THOMAS (TOM-ahs, twin). One of the 12 disciples. He was also known as Didymus, the Greek name for twin. Thomas showed great love for Jesus. When the other apostles were unable to talk Jesus out of going to Bethany to heal Lazarus because of the danger, Thomas said, "Let us also go, that we may die with Him" (John 11:16). Thomas doubted Jesus' resurrection since he was not present with the other apostles when Jesus showed Himself to them (John 20:24-25). Later, Thomas was with the apostles when Jesus appeared again; Thomas exclaimed, "My Lord and My God" (John 20:28). Thomas was with the apostles after the ascension (Acts 1:13). According to tradition Thomas preached in Parthia.

THORNS AND THISTLES. There are 22 Hebrew words for thorns, thistles, briers, etc., which grow in great quantities in Palestine (Genesis 3:16). Figuratively, thorns and thistles are descriptive of a waste place, wickedness, divine visitation, a messenger of Satan, and troubles (Numbers 33:55; 2 Samuel 23:6; Proverbs 22:5; 24:31; 2 Corinthians 12:7).

THRESHING, THRESHING FLOOR. See *agriculture.*

THUNDER. In Palestine thunder is rare in the summer. In Bible times, when thunder did occur, it served as a sign from God (1 Samuel 12:17-18). Thunder accompanied the giving of the Law (Exodus 19:16; 20:18). Thunder is described poetically as the voice of God and is a picture word for glory and power (Exodus 19:16; Job 37:2; Psalm 18:13; Revelation 8:5).

THYATIRA (thigh-ah-TIGH-rah, burning incense). A city of Asia Minor on the Lycus River in northern Lydia. It was known for its purple dyeing and weaving. Lydia, a seller of purple dye at Philippi, was from

Thyatira (Acts 16:14). One of the seven churches mentioned in the Book of Revelation was in Thyatira (Revelation 2:18-29).

TIBERIAS (tigh-BEER-i-uhs). A city built by Herod Antipas on the western shore of the Sea of Galilee. Herod named the city after the ruling emperor at that time: Tiberius Caesar. After A.D. 70, Tiberias became a center for Jewish learning, and later the Sanhedrin was transferred there (John 6:l, 23; 21:1). Today it is called Tabariyeh.

TIBERIUS, SEA OF. See *Galilee, Sea of.*

TIBERIUS (tigh-BEER-i-uhs). Tiberius Caesar was the second emperor of the Roman Empire. He was born in 42 B.C. and was the reigning emperor at the time of Christ's death (Luke 3:1; John 19:12, 15).

TIBNI (TIB-nigh). Omri's unsuccessful competitor for the throne of Israel (1 Kings 16:21-22).

TIGLATH-PILESER III (TIG-lath-pigh-LEE-zur, trust is [Ninip] the son of E-Sarra). The Assyrian king who ruled Assyria from 745 to 727 B.C. He extended the Assyrian Empire and was recognized as king even in Babylon, where he was referred to as Pul (2 Kings 15:19; 1 Chronicles 5:26). Tiglath-pileser broke the coalition of Uzziah, king of Judah, and made him pay tribute. Later, when Ahaz was king of Judah, Pekah of Israel and Rezin of Syria joined forces to conquer Judah. Ahaz paid Tiglath-pileser a large sum of money to defend him and his country from the armies of Pekah and Rezin (2 Kings 16:7-10).

TIGRIS (TIGH-gris). One of two rivers of Babylonia, the other one being the Euphrates.

TIMBREL (TIM-bruhl, beat or strike). A percussion instrument used to mark time (Genesis 31:27; Psalm 81:2). It is also called a tabret and a tambourine.

TIME. Time and seasons are mentioned early in the Bible (Genesis 1:5, 14-16; 8:22; Exodus 34:21; Psalm 74:17). Ancient people calculated time by dating such things as important events, the reign of kings and rulers, and natural phenomena like earthquakes (Exodus 12:40; 1 Kings 6:1; 2 Kings 3:1-2; Amos 1:1; Luke 3:1-2). They followed a lunar year, consisting of 354 days, 8 hours, and 38 seconds. The lunar year was divided into 12 lunar months with seven intercallary months added over 19 years.

The Hebrew month began with the new moon. Before the exile the Hebrews used numbers to name the months; after the exile, they used names. The sacred year began with Nisan (March—April); the secular year, with Tishri (September—October). Months were divided into weeks of seven days. The week ended with the Sabbath (Exodus 20:11; Deuteronomy 5:14-15).

The day was reckoned from either sunset to sunset or dawn to darkness (Genesis 1:5; 8:22; Exodus 12:18; John 11:9). It was divided into morning, noon, and evening (Psalm 55:17). Night was the time of darkness. It was divided into periods called watches (Exodus 14:24; Judges 7:19; Mark 13:35; Luke 12:38).

Sundials were used to divide the day (2 Kings 20:11; Isaiah 38:8). Hours are first mentioned in Daniel 3:6 and 5:5.

TIMNATH-SERAH (TIM-nath-SEE-rah, double portion). A city in Ephraim given to Joshua as his inheritance. It was his home and burial place (Joshua 19:50; 24:30). In Judges 2:9 it is called Timnath-heres.

TIMOTHY (TIM-o-thee, venerating God). Paul's companion, assistant, and friend whom he affectionately spoke of as his "beloved and faithful child in the Lord'' (1 Corinthians 4:17). Timothy's mother was a devout Jewish woman; his father was a Greek (Acts 16:1-3). When he was a child, his mother, Eunice, and grandmother Lois instructed Timothy in the Jewish religion (2 Timothy 1:5; 3:15). Through Paul's witness to the Gospel, Timothy became a Christian (1 Corinthians 4:17; 1 Timothy 1:2). After his conversion, Timothy became active in Christian work at Lystra and Iconium. When Paul visited Lystra on his second missionary trip, he found Timothy well spoken of by the Christians in these places (Acts 16:1-2). Paul decided to take the young man with him, and Timothy was set apart for church work by the laying on of hands (1 Timothy 4:14; 2 Timothy 1:6). Paul also circumcized Timothy in order not to offend the Jews (Acts 16:3).

Paul frequently mentions Timothy in his writings (Philippians 1:1; Colossians 1:1; 1 Thessalonians 3:2; 2 Thessalonians 1:1; Philemon 1). He also addresses two letters, 1 and 2 Timothy, to his friend. According to tradition, Timothy was a bishop at Ephesus.

TIMOTHY, FIRST LETTER OF PAUL TO. Paul wrote this letter to Timothy while Timothy was in charge of the church at Ephesus. In the letter Paul gives Timothy instructions for his office and warns him against false teachers.

Date: A.D. 62 to 63
Audience: Timothy and Christians in churches of Ephesus
Outline: 1. False doctrine at Ephesus (1). 2. Rules for worship (2). 3. Presbyters and deacons (3). 4. False teachers (4). 5. Attitude toward members (5). 6. Social questions (6).

TIMOTHY, SECOND LETTER OF PAUL TO. Paul wrote this letter to encourage Timothy to be

faithful in his work and to urge him to come to Rome with Mark.

Date: A.D. 64
Audience: Timothy, also to be shared with churches at Ephesus
Outline: 1. Salutation and thanksgiving (1:1-5). 2. Paul tells Timothy to rekindle the gift of God that is within him (1:6-18). 3. Paul's charge to Timothy (2:1—4:5). 4. Paul's request of Timothy (4:9-22).

TIRZAH (TUR-zah, delightfulness). A city that originally belonged to the Canaanites. Joshua captured Tirzah and killed its king (Joshua 12:24). Jeroboam I made Tirzah his capital, and it remained the capital of the kings of Israel until Omri built Samaria. Tirzah was located five miles east of Samaria and is probably modern-day Tell el-Far'ah.

TISHBITE (TISH-bight). Elijah is referred to as a Tishbite, someone from the town of Tishbe or a town similar to that name (1 Kings 17:1; 21:17; 28).

TITHE (TIGHTH). A 10th part of one's income. Abram gave tithes to Melchizedek; Jacob promised tithes to God (Genesis 14:20; 28:22; Hebrews 7:2, 6).

According to Mosaic law a 10th of all produce of the land and herds was sacred to the Lord (Leviticus 27:30-33). This tithe was used to support the Levites (Numbers 18:21-24). A 10th of it went for the priests (Numbers 18:25-32). Additional tithes were used for festivals and for the poor (Deuteronomy 12:5-18; 14:22-29). The Pharisees also tithed mint, anise, cummin, and rue (Matthew 23:23).

TITTLE. A small line or dot used to tell one Hebrew letter from another (Matthew 5:18; Luke 16:17).

TITUS (TIGH-tuhs). A Gentile convert to Christianity who became Paul's friend and helper. Titus went with Paul and Barnabas to Jerusalem at the time of the council. Since

Titus was born of Greek parents, he was uncircumcized (Galatians 2:3-5). This offended the Judaizers at the council; however, the church refused to make Titus submit to circumcision, siding with Paul, who maintained the freedom of Gentiles from the Mosaic law (Galatians 2:1, 3-5). Titus was sent to Corinth to solve the problems there and then rejoined Paul in Macedonia (2 Corinthians 2:13; 7:6, 13-14; 8:6, 16; 12:18). Later Titus was left behind in Crete to organize the churches there. Paul wrote his letter to Titus while Titus was in Crete (Titus 1:4-5). The last mention of Titus indicates that he went to Dalmatia (2 Timothy 4:10). According to tradition Titus was the bishop of Crete.

TITUS, LETTER OF PAUL TO. Paul wrote this letter to Titus while Titus was in charge of the churches on Crete. The letter is a manual for ministers and congregations.

Date: A.D. 63

Audience: Titus and Christians he was serving

Outline: 1. Christian ministers (1). 2. Instructions for church members (2). 3. Non-Christians and false teachers (3).

TOMB. See *burial.*

TOOTH. In the Bible a tooth illustrates the law of retaliation (Exodus 21:24; Matthew 5:38). When referred to in a figurative way, teeth also mean plenty or oppression (Genesis 49:12; Proverbs 30:14). The teeth of beasts are figurative for cruelty (Deuteronomy 32:24; Job 4:10). Cleanness of teeth is a picture of famine; gnashing of teeth, a picture of rage or despair (Job 16:9; Amos 4:6; Matthew 8:12).

TORCH. A light that could be carried from place to place (Judges 7:16; Ezekiel 1:13; Daniel 10:6; John 18:3).

TOWER OF BABEL. See *Babel 2.*

TOWN CLERK. An official in Ephesus who was second in rank to the president of the council (Acts 19:35-41).

TRADE. In Palestine trades were often carried out in the home. Mats and baskets were handwoven from straw or rushes. Wool, flax, and cotton were washed, combed, and spun into yarn. Then the yarn was woven on a loom into material.

Carpentry was also carried out in the home. The carpenter made agricultural machinery, woodwork for the house, furniture, and wooden utensils. Because of the lack of good timber in Palestine, its carpenters could not produce as fine a product as carpenters from countries where good wood was plentiful. When David built his palace and when Solomon built the temple, they hired carpenters from heavily wooded Phoenicia, where the carpenter's trade had reached its height (2 Samuel 5:11; 1 Kings 5:2-8).

Other trades in Bible times were those of the potter and brickmaker. Since Palestine has a good supply of clay, many items were made from it (Genesis 24:14-20; Leviticus 6:28; 1 Kings 17:12). Clay was dug from a field that became known as potter's field because of it. Pottery was roughly shaped by hand or worked on a potter's wheel, then dried and baked in a kiln (Jeremiah 18:3-6). Brick was molded in wooden molds and then baked in loosely built stacks or in kilns (Exodus 9:8-10).

Metal casting and forging, tanning, stonecutting, gem cutting, leather working, and tent making were other common trades in Bible times. The leather worker made sandals, parts of armor, aprons, belts, shoes, and purses (Genesis 3:21; 2 Kings 1:8, Matthew 3:4). Tentmakers used such items as knives, shears, and needles and thread to make their tents. The best tents were woven of goats' hair and were usually dark in color. (Exodus 25:4; Acts 18:3). (Klinck)

TRADITION (trah-DISH-uhn). 1. Interpretations of the Old Testament law (Matthew 15:1-9; Galations 1:14).

2. Apostolic teaching or truths handed down in the church by those who were witnesses to Christ (Luke 1:2; Romans 6:17; 1 Corinthians 11:2; 15:3-9; 2 Peter 2:21).

TRANSFIGURATION (trans-fig-yoo-RAY-shuhn). The name given to the time when Jesus was visibly glorified in the presence of His three disciples. Jesus' transfiguration likely occurred on Mount Hermon (Matthew 17:1-13; Mark 9:2-13; Luke 9:28-36).

TREASURE. Anything that is collected in storehouses, for instance, grain, wine, gold, or silver (1 Kings 14:26; 15:18; Matthew 2:11; 6:19).

Figuratively, treasure depicts God's resources in nature, God's peculiar people, piety, the Gospel, and Christ-centered wisdom and knowledge (Exodus 19:5; Deuteronomy 28:12; Isaiah 33:6; 2 Corinthians 4:7; Colossians 2:3).

TREASURY. The place in the temple where gifts were received (1 Chronicles 9:26; Mark 12:41; Luke 21:1; John 8:20).

TRESPASS. See *sin, II.*

TRIAL. A testing, usually accomplished by a painful process, for the purpose of purifying or achieving good (Psalm 7:9; Zechariah 13:9; 1 Peter 1:6-7).

TRIBE. The 12 tribes of Israel (Jacob's name in Genesis 32:28) came from Jacob's 12 sons, with Joseph's sons, Ephraim and Manasseh, forming two tribes (Genesis 48:5; Numbers 26:5-5l; Joshua 13:7-33; 15—19). No tribal territory was given to Levi. The heads or elders of each tribe had great influence (1 Samuel 8; 2 Samuel 3:17; 2 Kings 23:1).

TRIBULATION (trib-yoo-LAY-shuhn). See *suffering.*

TRIBUTE. 1. See *taxes.*

2. Temple tax (Matthew 17:24).

TRINITY (TRIN-uh-tee). The church's term for the coexistence of the Father, Son, and Holy Spirit in the unity of the Godhead: three distinct Persons in one Divine Being, or Essence. The term *Trinity* does not occur in the Bible, but many passages support the doctrine of the Trinity (Deuteronomy 6:4; Isaiah 48:16; Matthew 3:13-17; 28:19; John 10:30; 2 Corinthians 13:14; 1 Timothy 2:5).

TROAS (TRO-as). A city of Asia Minor in the district of Mysia about six miles south of ancient Troy. It was founded by Alexander the Great (Acts 16:8-11; 20:5-10; 2 Timothy 4:13).

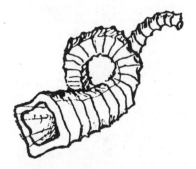

TRUMPET. A wind instrument made of metal or from the horn of a ram or goat (Numbers 10:2). Trumpets were played to provide music; they were also sounded in battle and for other signals, such as an alarm or when a new king took the throne (Judges 3:27; 1 Kings 1:39; Isaiah 18: 3; Hosea 8:1; Amos 3:6; 1 Thessalonians 4:6).

TRUTH. That which is eternal, ultimate, secure, steadfast, reliable. God is truth; He cannot lie (Psalm 31:5; Isaiah 65:16; John 17:3; 2

Timothy 2:13; Hebrews 6:18). Everything that comes from God is true (Psalm 33:4). God has made known all that humanity needs to know for life and salvation. Truth is manifested supremely in Christ (John 1:14, 17; 14:6). The Holy Spirit imparts the truth of Christ (1 John 2:20-22). God's Word is truth (John 17:17-19; 2 Corinthians 4:2; Galatians 5:7; Ephesians 1:13; James 1:18).

TUBAL-CAIN (TYOO-buhl-kayn, Tubal the smith). A son of Lamech who worked in brass and iron (Genesis 4:22). Tubal-cain represents the ancestor of all metalworkers.

TURTLE, TURTLEDOVE. A common type of pigeon in Israel that poor people used for sacrifices (Genesis 15:9; Luke 2:24).

TYCHICUS (TIK-i-kuhs, fortune). A disciple, messenger, and spokesman of Paul (Acts 20:4; Ephesians 6:21-22; Colossians 4:7-8).

TYRE, TYRUS (TIGHR, TIGH-ruhs, rock). An important Phoenician city on the Mediterranean Coast. It was built partly on the rocky mainland and partly on an island. Alexander the Great constructed a causeway to connect the two parts.

Tyre was a powerful merchant city (Isaiah 23:8). David formed an alliance with Tyre (2 Samuel 5:11; 1 Kings 5:1; 2 Chronicles 2:3). A number of the prophets spoke against Tyre and its inhabitants (Isaiah 23:1-17; Jeremiah 27:3; Ezekiel 26—28). Jesus visited its region and was well received (Matthew 15:21; Mark 7:24). Paul once stayed in Tyre for seven days (Acts 21:3-4).

UNBELIEF. A lack of faith; the rejection of God's promises and threats as found in His Word, and especially the refusal to believe and trust in Christ (John 3:36; Romans 11:20; Hebrews 3:19).

UNCIRCUMCISED. 1. Those who have not submitted to the Jewish rite of circumcision; Gentiles (Genesis 34:14; Judges 14:3; 1 Samuel 14:6; Romans 4:9).

2. Ears that do not hear the truth (Jeremiah 6:10; Acts 7:51).

3. Hearts that are not open to God (Leviticus 26:41; Jeremiah 4:4; Acts 7:51). See also *circumcision.*

UNCLEAN. 1. A number of food items were considered unclean in Bible times: animals that did not part the hoof and chew the cud; animals and birds that ate blood or the flesh of dead bodies; insects that did not have hind legs for jumping; and water creatures without scales or fins (Leviticus 11—15; Numbers 19; Deuteronomy 14).

2. Other forms of ceremonial uncleaness included leprosy, sexual discharge, and contact with the dead (Leviticus 11:24-40; 13—15; 17:15; Numbers 19:16-22).

UNICORN (YOO-nuh-kawrn). See *wild ox.*

UNKNOWN GOD. While Paul was in Athens, he found an altar with the inscription "To an unknown god" (Acts 17:23). This was an altar built to appease any god that may have been overlooked.

UNLEAVENED. Bread without yeast. The Israelites ate unleavened bread at Passover as a reminder of the Exodus (Exodus 12:8; 13:3-10).

UNRIGHTEOUS. See *righteous; unbelief.*

UPPER CHAMBER, ROOM. See *homes.*

UR (UR). Abraham's native city. It was located in southern Babylonia near Uruk and was called Ur of Chaldees (Genesis 11:28, 31; 15:7; Nehemiah 9:7). Today it is Tell Mugheir.

URIAH (yoo-RIGH-ah, flame of Lord). 1. A Hittite, the husband of Bathsheba. After David committed adultery with Bathsheba, he arranged to have Uriah placed on the front line of battle so that Uriah would be killed (2 Samuel 11; Matthew 1:6).
2. A prophet who was put to death by Jehoiakin after he predicted the destruction of Judah (Jeremiah 26:20-23).

URIM AND THUMMIM (YOO-rim and THUM-im, lights and perfections). Objects placed in the breastpiece of the high priest. Their exact nature is unknown. They were used, however, to determine the will of the Lord (Exodus 28:30; Leviticus 8:8; Numbers 27:21).

UZ (UZ). The land of Job. Although its site is uncertain, Bible scholars usually locate it in the Arabian Desert next to Edom (Job 1:1; Jeremiah 25:20; Lamentations 4:21).

UZZAH (UZ-ah, strength). Son of Abinadab. When the oxen of the cart bearing the ark stumbled, Uzzah was struck dead for putting out his hand and touching the ark of God (2 Samuel 6:3-11; 1 Chronicles 13:7-11).

UZZIAH (u-ZIGH-ah, Lord is strength). Also known as Azariah, he was the son of Amaziah and the 10th king of Judah. Uzziah became king at the age of 16 and ruled Judah for 52 years (2 Kings 14:21-22). He fought successfully against the Me-

hunim, the Arabs, and the Philistines. He strengthened his kingdom by developing agriculture, fortifying Jerusalem, and organizing the army (2 Chronicles 26:1-15). "And his fame spread far. . . . But when he was strong, he grew proud to his destruction" (2 Chronicles 26:15-16).

Uzziah decided to burn incense to the Lord and went into the temple with that in mind. The priests told him to leave, for only they were set apart to burn incense. When Uzziah became angry with them, God struck him with leprosy. Uzziah remained a leper until the day he died (2 Chronicles 26: 16-22).

VANITY 1. Unprofitableness (Ecclesiastes 1:2).

2. That which is empty, nothing, worthless, futile, such as idols and lies (2 Kings 17:15; Psalm 4:2; Isaiah 41:29).

3. Human help is vain (Psalm 60:11).

4. Sin (Psalm 119: 37; Romans 8:20).

VASHTI (VASH-tigh). The wife of Ahasuerus. She was the queen of Persia (Esther 1:9-22).

VEIL. 1. See *dress.*

2. The curtain that separated the Holy Place from the Most Holy Place in the tabernacle and temple (Exodus 26:31-35; 2 Chronicles 3:14; Matthew 27:51).

VINE. 1. See *vineyard.*

2. Figuratively, a vine often depicts both Israel and happiness and contentment (1 Kings 4:25; Psalm 80:8; 128:3; Micah 4:4). Apostate Israel is pictured as wild grapes or a strange vine (Isaiah 5:2; Jeremiah 2:21). An empty vine is a picture of spiritual unfruitfulness (Hosea 10:1). The vine of Sodom refers to godless people (Deuteronomy 32:28-33). The vine and branches is a picture of Christ and believers (John 15:1-6).

VINEYARD. The soil of Israel has always been good for cultivating grapes. When the Israelites arrived in Canaan, they expanded the grape industry already there (Numbers 13:23-27). They cleared the land of stones, terraced it, planted choice

shoots, and carefully cultivated and trained them (1 Kings 4:25; Isaiah 5:1-2; Hosea 2:12; Micah 1:6). Often they built a wall around the vineyard and erected a tower (Isaiah 5:1-7; Song of Solomon 2:15).

When harvesting began in June, bunches of grapes were gathered in baskets and taken to the winepress (Jeremiah 6:9; Revelation 14:14-20). The winepress was usually cut from solid rock, 6 to 12 feet in diameter and 1 to 2 feet deep, with a trench leading to a smaller container. Grapes were put in the winepress and trampled by men until the juice flowed into the lower container. This was one method of pressing grapes.

The grape juice was taken to the peoples' homes and allowed to ferment. The lees, or dregs, were poured off, and then the wine was stored in large jars of stone or bottles of goatskins (Matthew 9:17).

Fresh grape juice was also boiled down to make grape honey. Grapes were eaten raw in season or dried in the sun to make raisins (1 Samuel 25:18). (Klinck)

VINTAGE (VIN-tij). A time of joy (Judges 9:27; Isaiah 16:10; Jeremiah 25:30). See also *vineyard.*

VIPER. See *serpent.*

VIRGIN MARY (VUR-jin MAIR-ee). See *Mary 1.*

VISION. An inspired dream or apparition (Numbers 24;4. Isaiah 6; Ezekiel 1; 8—10; Daniel 7—8; Acts 10:9-16; 26:13-19; 2 Corinthians

12:1-4).

VOW. A voluntary promise to God either to do or not to do something. The Mosaic law did not require vows, but it did regulate them (Leviticus 27; Numbers 30; Deuteronomy 23:18-23).

WAGES. In early times wages were often paid in kind (Genesis 29:15, 20; 30:28-34). According to Mosaic law a hired person was to receive his wages at the end of the day (Leviticus 19:13; Deuteronomy 24:14-15; Matthew 20:8). Withholding wages was condemned (Jeremiah 22:13; Malachi 3:5). See also *labor; servant.*

WALL. 1. See *homes.*

2. In Bible times city walls were often made of clay (Psalm 62:3; Isaiah 30:13). Fortified cities, however, were surrounded by enormous stone walls (Nehemiah 4:3; Isaiah 2:15; Zephaniah 1:16).

3. In the Bible walls are a symbol of strength, protection, and salvation (Isaiah 26:1; Jeremiah 15:20; Zechariah 2:5). See also *fort, fortification, fortress.*

WAR. Before going to war, the Israelites consulted God's will and sought His help through prayer and sacrifice (Judges 1:1; 20:2; 1 Samuel 7:9; 14:37; 1 Kings 22:6).

As they were about to enter into battle, the Israelites, their commander, or a priest gave a shout or battle cry (1 Samuel 17:52; Isaiah 42:13). Fighting was carried on by hand-to-hand combat (2 Samuel 1:23; 2:18). Strategies employed included double attacks, ambushes, surprise attacks, false retreats, and night attacks (Genesis 14:15; Joshua 8:12; Judges 7; 20:36; 2 Kings 7:12). Some wars were decided by a single combat (1 Samuel 17).

After a battle, countrymen and enemies (if they were on their own soil) were buried and mourned (2 Samuel 3:31-39; 1 Kings 11:15). Triumph was expressed, captives were killed or sold into slavery, and the booty was equally divided (Deuteronomy 20:16-18; Joshua 10:24; 1 Samuel 30:24-25; 31:9; Amos 1:6, 9). See also *armor, arms; army.*

WASHING. Cleanliness is stressed in the Bible. Frequent bathing or washing was necessary because of the warm climate. After a journey the people washed the dust from their feet, and before meals they washed their hands (Genesis 18:4; Exodus 30:19, 21; Judges 19:21; Matthew 15:2; Mark 7:3; Luke 7:37-44; 11:38; John 13:5-14).

WATCH. 1. A guard (Judges 7:19; 2 Kings 11:5; Nehemiah 4:9; Matthew 27:62-66).

2. A lookout (1 Samuel 14:16; 2 Samuel 13:34; 2 Kings 9:17; Isaiah 21:8).

3. The Hebrews divided the 12 hours of night into three watches (Exodus 14:24; Judges 7:19; Lamentations 2:19); the Romans, into four (Matthew 14:25; Mark 13:35; Luke 12:38).

WATER. Because of the scarcity of water in Israel, it was greatly valued (Isaiah 3:1; 33:16). Finding water was an important event; scarcity of water, a serious problem (Genesis 6:7; Deuteronomy 28:12; 1 Kings 17:1).

Water is also a picture for the Messianic age, good news, life, and grace (Psalm 23:2; Proverbs 25:25; Song of Solomon 4:15; Isaiah 30:25; 32:2; 35:6-7; John 4:7-15). Negatively, it is a picture of trouble or misfortune (Psalm 66:12; 69:1; Isaiah 8:7).

WATER OF SEPARATION. Water that was mixed with the ashes of a red heifer to remove impurity or sin (Numbers 19).

WAVE OFFERING. The rite of waving the sacrificial portion before the Lord was regularly performed in the peace offering, the guilt offering of lepers, and the meal offering of jealousy (Leviticus 7:30, 34; 9:21; 14:12; 21; Numbers 5:25). The sheaf of the first ripe grain as well as two loaves and two lambs at Pentecost were also waved before the Lord (Leviticus 23:10-11, 15, 20).

WEAVING. See *trade.*

WEDDING. See *marriage.*

WEEKS, FEAST OF. See *Pentecost 1.*

WEIGHT. The Hebrews used stones for weights and balances for scales (Leviticus 19:36; Deuteronomy 25:15; Proverbs 16:11). For the most part they followed the Babylonian system of weights where 60 shekels (.36 ounce) equaled 1 mina (about 1 1/12 pounds) and 60 minas equaled 1 talent (about 65 pounds). These were the regular weights and were called light shekels, minas, and standards.

There were also heavy shekels, minas, and talents which were exactly double the weight of the regular standards above.

WHALE. 1. Any large sea animal (Genesis 1:21; Ezekiel 32:2).

2. The Greek word used in Matthew 12:40 means any large fish or sea creature and is usually regarded as a sperm whale or shark. It is also translated as great fish (Jonah 1:17).

WHEAT. See *agriculture; food.*

WIDOW. Widows were protected under Mosaic law. They were to be treated with justice and special consideration (Exodus 22:22; Deuteronomy 14:29; 24:19-21; 27:19; Psalm 94:6; Ezekiel 22:7; Malachi 3:5). If a married man died without a son, his brother was obligated to marry the man's widow (Deuteronomy 25:5-6; Matthew 22:23-30). See also *levirate marriage.*

The New Testament church also cared for its widows (Acts 6:1-6; 1 Timothy 5:3-16). Older, pious widows who had neither children nor grandchildren to care for them were enrolled, probably for special service (1 Timothy 5:9-10).

WIFE. See *marriage.*

WILDERNESS. Either a desert or a wild, thinly populated, uncultivated region used for pasturage. One of the chief wildernesses the Bible refers to is the Wilderness of the Wandering, the place where the Children of Israel wandered in the Sinai Peninsula (Numbers 14:33; Deuteronomy 1:1; Joshua 5:6; Nehemiah 9:19; 21; Psalm 78:40, 52).

WILD OX. An animal, now extinct, that was known for its ferocity, strength, and speed (Numbers 23:22; 24:8; Deuteronomy 33:17; Job 39:9-10).

WILL. 1. Inclination or choice. God's will is that which He determines (Ephesians 1:11). It is revealed in His acts, His law, and especially in Christ (Matthew 6:10; Acts 22:14; Romans 2:18; 12:2; Colossians 1:9).

Humanity's fallen or natural will cannot will good (Romans 8:7). God's grace alone is able to incline a person's will to good (Philippians 2:13). See also *elect, election; predestination; sin, II.*

2. See *testament 1.*

WIND. The Hebrews recognized four winds (Ezekiel 37:9; Matthew 24:31). The wind that blew from the south was hot and dry; the wind from the north, cold (Job 37:22; Song of Solomon 4:16; Luke 12:55). The west wind brought rain (1 Kings 18:43-45; Psalm 148:8).

WINE, WINEPRESS, WINESKIN. See *vineyard.*

WINNOW, WINNOWING FORK (WIN-o, WIN-o-ing). See *agriculture.*

WINTER. In Israel the winter season proper (December—February) is short. Scriptural references to the winter season, however, often include fall and seasons of seedtime (Genesis 8:22; Psalm 74:17; Zechariah 14:8; Matthew 24:20). Although winters are usually mild, snow and hail occur in the higher regions.

WISDOM. Skill, intelligence, judgment, understanding (Exodus 31:6; Proverbs 10:1; 1 Kings 3:28; 5:12; Daniel 5:11). Wisdom is an attribute of God (Proverbs 3:19). It is the completeness and perfection of His knowledge (Job 10:4; 26:6; Proverbs 5:21; Isaiah 31:2). God's wisdom is seen in creation, especially His creation of man (Job 12; 38—39; Psalm 139:14). God's wisdom is far above that of people (Job 11:6-9; Isaiah 40:14, 28).

God gives wisdom to people (Proverbs 2:6). The fear of God is the beginning of wisdom (Proverbs 9:10). Since God's ultimate purposes in history are revealed in Christ, Jesus is Wisdom (1 Corinthians 1:30; Colossians 2:2-3).

By faith in Christ, this wisdom becomes one's own and is expressed in one's life (1 Corinthians 1:19-24; Ephesians 5:15). The Bible contrasts this wisdom to a worldly understanding (1 Corinthians 1:19-26; Matthew 11:25).

WISE MEN. See *Magi.*

WITCH, WITCHCRAFT. See *divination; magic.*

WOMAN. The helpmate of man. Together with man she forms a unity, created in the image of God, to rule over creation (Genesis 1:26-28; 2:18-23). See also *marriage.*

WORD. God created the heavens and the earth by His Word (Genesis 1). God's Word is His revelation to people (1 Kings 6:11; 13:20; Jeremiah 1:4, 11). By the Word, faith is created and the church is built

(John 14:26; Acts 4:29, 3l).

God's Word comes to people in various forms, for example, through speaking, writing, visions, and symbols (Jeremiah 1:11; John 3:14-15; 20:31; 2 Timothy 4:2). God's Word is dynamic, creative, and functional (Psalm 147:15-18; Isaiah 55:10-11; Matthew 8:24-27; Romans 1:16). Jesus Christ is the supreme revelation of God. He is the living Word (John 1:1-5; Revelation 19:13).

WORKS. 1. The works of God include creation, preservation, and redemption (Genesis 1; Job 37:14-16; Psalm 104:24; 107; John 5:20-36; 14:10-12).

2. Whether a person's works are good or bad depends on that person's relationship to God. Only a person who believes in Jesus Christ as Savior can do good works in God's eyes, since good works are a fruit of faith (John 6:28-29; Romans 6; 14:23; Galatians 2:20-21; Colossians 1:21-23). See also *faith; justification; sanctification.*

WORLD. 1. Universe (John 1:10).

2. The human race (John 3:16; 2 Corinthians 5:19).

3. The wicked; unregenerated; those who are opposed to God (John 15:18; 1 John 2:15). The devil is the prince of this world (John 12:31).

4. The earth (1 Samuel 2:8; Job 37:12; Isaiah 18:3).

5. The Roman Empire (Luke 2:1).

WORMWOOD. A bitter plant that grows in desert places (Proverbs 5:4; Jeremiah 9:15; Amos 5:7; 6:12; Revelation 8:11).

WORSHIP (WUR-ship, to bow down, kiss the hand to, revere, work, serve). The respect and reverence given to God or a god. The patriarchs worshiped God by building altars and sacrificing to Him (Genesis 12:7-8; 13:4). Mosaic law

established the place for worship and set the times and forms for it. The prophets condemn empty ceremonies and people who try to cover an ungodly life (Isaiah 1:11-17).

New Testament worship is centered in and around the Word of God. It involved reading the Old Testament and psalms, singing hymns and spiritual songs, teaching, praying, and celebrating the Lord's Supper (Luke 4:16-22; Acts 2:42; Romans 12:7-8; 1 Corinthians 11:23-24; 14:26; Ephesians 5:19).

WRATH. 1. Anger of people (Genesis 30:2; 1 Samuel 17:28;). It may be evil or a reaction to evil (1 Samuel 20:34; John 2:15; 2 Corinthians 12:20). Human wrath is described as a work of the flesh (Galatians 5:20).

2. The reaction of a righteous God to evil (Deuteronomy 9:7, 22; Isaiah 13:9; Romans 1:18; Ephesians 5:6; Revelation 14:10, 19).

WRITING. Probably invented by the Sumerians, who wrote in pictograms around 3,000 B.C. Their writing led to cuneiform, or wedge-shaped, letters written on clay. The Hebrews obtained their alphabet from the Phoenicians. Writing among the Hebrews was attributed to men of learning (Deuteronomy 17:18; 24:1, 3; Isaiah 29:11-12). Writing materials included clay, wax, wood, metal, and plaster (Deuteronomy 27:2-3; Joshua 8:32; Luke 1:63). Later vellum, parchment, and papyrus were used (2 Timothy 4:13; 2 John 12). A stylus was used to write on hard material; a reed pen, on parchment and papyrus (2 Corinthians 3:3; 2 John 12). Ink was made of lampblack or soot.

XERXES (ZURK-seez). See *Ahasu-erus*.

YEAR. See *time*.

YEAST. See *leaven*.

YOKE. A wooden bar or frame with thongs that went around the necks of two draft animals and another thong that fastened to a wagon or plow. The yoke was used to join the animals together so they could draw the wagon or plow (Numbers 19:2; Deuteronomy 21:3).

Figuratively, a yoke depicts subjection; the removal of a yoke, deliverance (Genesis 27:40; 1 Kings 12:4, 9-11; Isaiah 9:4; Jeremiah 2:20; Matthew 11:29-30). A yokefellow is one's co-worker at a difficult task (Philippians 4:3).

Z

ZACCHAEUS (za-KEE-uhs, pure). The chief tax collector of Jericho who climbed a sycamore tree to see Christ. Jesus told Zacchaeus to come down because He was going to his house that day. With joy, Zacchaeus came down. He became a follower of Christ (Luke 19:1-10).

ZACHARIAH (zak-ah-RIGH-ah). See *Zechariah 5.*

ZADOK (ZAY-dok, righteous). A descendant of Aaron's son Eleazor (1 Chronicles 24:3). Zadok was the son of Ahitub (2 Samuel 8:17). He was one of the young men, mighty in valour, who came to David at Hebron with the intention of making David king over Israel (1 Chronicles 12:28). Later, after David had become king, Zadok was high priest with Abiathar (2 Samuel 8:17). He supported David during Absalom's rebellion and remained faithful to David in his old age when Adonijah tried to take over the throne (2 Samuel 15: 24-29; 19:11; 1 Kings 1:7-8, 32, 45).

ZALMONAH (zal-MUN-AH, shady). A place southeast of Edom where Israel camped (Numbers 33:41-42).

ZALMUNNA (ZAL-mun-ah, shade denied). One of the two kings of Midian whom Gideon put to death (Judges 8:5-21; Psalm 83:11).

ZAPHENATH-PANEAH, ZAPHNATH-PAANEAH (ZAF-i-nath-pah-NEE-ah, ZAF-nath-pay-ah-NEE-a, the god speaks and he lives, or revealer of secrets). The name the pharaoh gave to Joseph (Genesis 41:45).

ZAREPHATH (ZAR-i-fath). A Phoenician town eight miles south of Sidon (1 Kings 17:9-10; Obadiah 20; Luke 4:26). When the brook Chereth dried up, Elijah went to Zarephath. There a widow gave him a home until the famine was over (1 Kings 17:8-24).

ZEALOTS (ZEL-uhtz). A Jewish party organized by Judas of Gamala in the time of Quirinius (A.D. 6) to resist Roman oppression. The apostle Simon, a member of this party, was referred to as the Zealot to distinguish him from Simon Peter (Luke 6:15; Acts 1:13). In Matthew 10:4 and Mark 3:18 Simon is referred to as the Cananaean, which is Aramaic for Zealot.

ZEBEDEE (ZEB-i-dee, Lord has endowed). A fisherman, the husband of Salome and the father of James and John (Matthew 4:21-22; 27:56; Mark 1:19-20; Luke 5:10; John 21:2).

ZEBIDAH (zi-BIGH-dah, given). Jehoiakim's mother (2 Kings 23:36).

ZEBOIIM (zi-BOI-im, gazelles). One of the five cities in the plain whose king was defeated by Chedorlaomer. God destroyed Zeboiim with Sodom and Gomorrah (Genesis 10:19; 14:2, 8; Deuteronomy 29:23; Hosea 11:8).

ZEBULUN (ZEB-yoo-luhn, dwelling). 1. The 10th son of Jacob and 6th son of Leah (Genesis 30:20; 35:23; Genesis 46:14). In his blessing Jacob describes Zebulun as dwelling by the sea (Genesis 49:13).

2. One of the 12 tribes of Israel that descended from Zebulun. After crossing over the Jordan into Canaan, Moses divided the tribes into two groups, one group to pronounce blessings and the other curses. Zebulun was one of the six tribes that stood on Mount Ebal to pronounce the curses (Deuteronomy 27:13).

The territory allotted to Zebulun was between the Sea of Galilee and the Mediterranean Sea. It included Nazareth (Joshua 19:10-16; Isaiah 9:1; Matthew 4:12-16).

ZECHARIAH (zek-ah-RIGH-ah, the Lord has remembered). The name of numerous men in the Bible, including the following: 1. The 14th king of Israel. He came to the throne in the 38th year of Uzziah, king of Judah, and reigned six months. He was the son of Jeroboam II. Shallum murdered Zechariah in order to become the king himself (2 Kings 14:29; 15:8,11).

2. A son of Jehoida, the high priest, and a priest like his father. He lived during the reign of King Joash of Judah. Zechariah was a reformer. On Joash's order Zechariah was killed in the court of the temple (2 Chronicles 24:20-22). He is probably the Zechariah referred to in Matthew 23:35 and Luke 11:51.

3. A prophet who advised King Uzziah (2 Chronicles 26:5).

4. A minor prophet; the son of Berechiah and grandson of Iddo (Zechariah 1:1). He was a contempory of Zerubbabel the governor and returned from the Babylonian captivity under his leadership. Zechariah also lived during the time of Jeshua the priest and Haggai the prophet. Along with Haggai he exhorted the leaders of the Jewish colony to resume work on the temple. It is likely that Zechariah was a priest as well as a prophet (Nehemiah 12:16).

5. The father of John the Baptizer. Zechariah was a priest of the division of Abijah (Luke 1:5). He and his wife, Elizabeth, who was related to Mary of Nazareth, were godly people who lived in the hill country of Judea.

One day while Zechariah was serving in the temple, an angel appeared to him and told him God had heard his prayer: he would have a son. And so, in their old age, Zechariah and Elizabeth became the parents of John the Baptizer, the forerunner of Christ (Luke 1:5-25; 39-80).

ZECHARIAH, BOOK OF. The 11th book of the Minor Prophets. The prophet Zechariah wrote this book in 520 B.C. after the Israelites' return to Jerusalem from the Babylonian exile. The book deals with the destiny of God's people.

Date: 519 to 518 B.C.

Audience: Judah

Outline: 1. Visions of the people of God under the new covenant (1—6). 2. The people's fasts shall become feasts (7—8). 3. God's kingdom rules over all (9—11). 4. Inherit the kingdom: Jews and Gentiles (12—14).

ZEDEKIAH (zed-i-KIGH-AH, righteousness of Lord). The son of Josiah and the last king of Judah. Because of Judah's wickedness, God allowed Nebuchadnezzar to come to Jerusalem and take Jehoiachin, Judah's king, to Babylon. Then Nebuchadnezzar placed Mattaniah, whom he renamed Zedekiah, on the throne as king. When Zedekiah rebelled a number of years later, Nebuchadnezzar seized him, put out his eyes, and took him to Babylon where he died (2 Kings 24:17-20; 25:1-21; 2 Chronicles 36:10-21; Jeremiah 21—39; Ezekiel 17:15-21).

ZEPHANIAH (zef-ah-NIGH-ah, the Lord hides). 1. The ninth minor prophet. Zephaniah was the son of Cushi and a descendant of Hezekiah. He prophesied during the time of Josiah, king of Judah (Zephaniah 1:1).

2. A priest, the son of Maaseiah. Zephaniah was one of those who carried messages between Zedekiah and Jeremiah (Jeremiah 21:1; 37:3). After Jerusalem was captured by the

Babylonians, Zephaniah was taken captive to Riblah, where he was put to death (Jeremiah 52:24-25).

ZEPHANIAH, BOOK OF. The ninth book of the Minor Prophets. It was written during the days of Josiah.

Date: About 625 B.C.

Audience: Judah

Outline: 1. God has fixed a day in which He will judge the world (1). 2. Fall of Philistia, Moab, Ammon, Assyria (2). 3. Sins of Jerusalem; admonitions (3:1-8). 4. God-fearing remnant remains untouched (3:9-13). 5. Restored daughter of Jerusalem (3:14-20).

ZERUBBABEL (zuh-RUB-ah-buhl, born in Babylon). The son of Shealtiel and the grandson of King Jehoiachin (Ezra 3:2, 8; 5:2; Nehemiah 12:1; Haggai 1:1, 12, 14).

When Cyrus allowed the Jewish people to return to their homeland, he made Zerubbabel the governor of the colony. Zerubbabel led the first colony of captives back to Jerusalem (Ezra 2; Nehemiah 7:7). With the support of Haggai and Zechariah, he supervised the rebuilding of the temple despite Samaritan opposition (Ezra 3—6; Haggai 1:12, 15; 2:2-4; Zechariah 4:6-10).

ZEUS (ZYOOS). The chief god of the Greeks corresponding to the Roman god Jupiter (Acts 14:12-13).

ZIKLAG (ZIK-lag). A city in southern Judah located between Beersheba and Gath (Joshua 15:31; 19:5). Achish, king of Gath, gave it to David and his men when they were fleeing from Saul (1 Samuel 27:6; 30:1-2: 2 Samuel 1:1; 4:10). Today it is probably Tell el-Khuweiefeh.

ZIMRI (ZIM-righ, mountain sheep). The fifth king of Israel. Zimri was a general under Elah, king of Israel. After murdering Elah, he set himself up as king in Terzah. Israel,

however, proclaimed Omri the new king. When Omri marched against Zimri and captured his capital, Zimri set fire to the palace and died in its blaze. Zimri's reign lasted only a week (1 Kings 16:9-20; 2 Kings 9:31).

ZIN (ZIN). A wilderness the Israelites crossed on their way to Canaan (Numbers 34:3; Joshua 15:1). Kadesh was on the boundary of Zin (Numbers 20:1). The Wilderness of Paran bordered it on the south (Numbers 13:26).

ZION (ZIGH-uhn). 1. One of the hills on which Jerusalem stood. It is first mentioned in the Old Testament as a Jebusite city. It was located on the southern spur of the eastern ridge of Jerusalem and received its water from Gihon Spring (Virgin Fountain) through an aqueduct. David captured the city, renamed it City of David, and made it his capital (Joshua 15:63; 2 Samuel 5:6-9; 1 Chronicles 11:5-8).

2. After the temple was built on Mount Moriah and the ark brought to it, the name Zion was extended to include Moriah (Isaiah 8:18; 18:7; 24:23; Joel 3:17; Micah 4:7).

3. David began an extension of the city, and the name Zion came to be used for the whole of Jerusalem (2 Samuel 5:9; 2 Kings 19:21; Psalm 48; 69:35; Isaiah 1:8).

4. Zion is a symbol of God's kingdom (Psalm 76:2; Isaiah 1:27; 2:3; 4:1-6; Joel 3:16; Zechariah 1:16-17; Romans 11:26).

5. Zion is the new heavenly Jerusalem (Hebrews 12:22-24; Revelation 14:1; 21—22).

ZIPPORAH (zi-PO-rah, sparrow) The daughter of Jethro, the priest of Midian. She became Moses' wife (Exodus 2:16-22; 4:25; 18:2-4).

ZOAR (zo-ur, little). One of the five cities of the plain on which Sodom and Gomorrah were located. When God's judgment was about to descend on the cities, Lot prayed for Zoar's safety, and it was spared destruction. Then Lot and his two daughters fled there, finding refuge in a cave where they stayed for awhile (Genesis 19:20-30). Zoar was originally called Bela (Genesis 14:2, 8).

ZOPHAR (ZO-fur, chirper). One of Job's three friends who came to counsel him in his affliction (Job 2:11; 11:1; 20:1; 42:9).

ZORAH (ZO-rah, hornet, scourge). A Canaanite city located at the highest point of the Shephelah about five miles northwest of Beth-shemesh. Manoah, Samson's father, came from Zorah, and Samson was buried near there (Joshua 15:33; 19:41; Judges 13:2; 16:31; 18:2, 8, 11; 2 Chronicles 11:10; Nehemiah 11:29).